EIGHTH ARMY
IN ITALY

By the same author:

Wall of Steel: The History of 9th (Londonderry) HAA Regiment, RA (SR), North-West Books, 1988

The Sons of Ulster: Ulstermen at War from the Somme to Korea, Appletree Press, 1992

Clear The Way! A History of the 38th (Irish) Brigade, 1941–47, Irish Academic Press, 1993

Irish Generals: Irish Generals in the British Army in the Second World War, Appletree Press, 1993

Only the Enemy in Front: The Recce Corps at War, 1940–46, Spellmount Publishers, 1994

Key to Victory: The Maiden City in the Second World War, Greystone Books, 1995

The Williamite War in Ireland, 1688–1691, Four Courts Press, 1998

A Noble Crusade: The History of Eighth Army, 1941–1945, Spellmount Publishers, 1999

Irish Men and Women in the Second World War, Four Courts Press, 1999

Irish Winners of the Victoria Cross (with David Truesdale), Four Courts Press, 2000

Irish Volunteers in the Second World War, Four Courts Press, 2001

The Sound of History: El Alamein 1942, Spellmount Publishers, 2002

The North Irish Horse: A Hundred Years of Service, Spellmount Publishers, 2002

Normandy 1944: The Road to Victory, Spellmount Publishers, 2004

Ireland's Generals in the Second World War, Four Courts Press, 2004

The Thin Green Line: A History of the Royal Ulster Constabulary GC, 1922–2001, Pen & Sword Books, 2004

None Bolder: The History of the 51st Highland Division in the Second World War, Spellmount Publishers, 2006

The British Reconnaissance Corps in World War II, Osprey Publishing, 2007

EIGHTH ARMY IN ITALY

The Long Hard Slog

by

Richard Doherty

Pen & Sword
MILITARY

First published in Great Britain in 2007 by
Pen & Sword Military
an imprint of
Pen & Sword Books Ltd
47 Church Street
Barnsley
South Yorkshire
S70 2AS

ISBN: 978-1-84415-637-5

A CIP catalogue record for this book is
available from the British Library.

Typeset in 10/12pt Sabon by
Concept, Huddersfield, West Yorkshire

Printed and bound in England by
CPI UK

Pen & Sword Books Ltd incorporates the Imprints of Pen & Sword
Aviation, Pen & Sword Maritime, Pen & Sword Military, Wharncliffe
Local History, Pen & Sword Select, Pen & Sword Military Classics
and Leo Cooper.

For a complete list of Pen & Sword titles please contact
PEN & SWORD BOOKS LIMITED
47 Church Street, Barnsley, South Yorkshire, S70 2AS, England
E-mail: enquiries@pen-and-sword.co.uk
Website: www.pen-and-sword.co.uk

Contents

To the memory of
Joe Radcliffe,
Royal Corps of Signals
1920–2005
and with thanks to
Lucia, Marina and Danilo

Maps

Acknowledgements

It has become a tradition for authors to include in their acknowledgements the comment that any errors are attributable solely to the author, thereby excusing from blame all those who have assisted. I do so willingly with this book since it would be invidious to try to blame any of my errors on those many individuals and organizations who have helped with the research and production of the book. Owing many debts of gratitude, I acknowledge them readily.

As always, I made considerable use of the facilities of the National Archives at Kew where the staff of the Reading Room, the Search Room and the Library provide an excellent service that is friendly, professional and capable of dealing with even the most obscure enquiries. At the Imperial War Museum, Lambeth, I used the Departments of Documents and Printed Books as well as the Photograph Archive. Once again the staff members of each department were always keen to help and demonstrated knowledge of their resources that showed the high level of their own commitment and professionalism. No one could ask for better cooperation than that to be found at Kew and Lambeth, and I am most grateful to all who assisted me at both institutions.

For much of the Italian campaign, Eighth Army included a very large proportion of Canadian soldiers and the National Archives of Canada hold an invaluable collection of photographs from Italy, some of which are reproduced in this book. Thanks are due to the Archives for their excellent service. Polish soldiers also played a major role in Eighth Army and I thank the Polish Museum and Sikorski Institute, especially Mr K. Barbarski, for their invaluable help. David Fletcher, Librarian of the Tank Museum at Bovington in Dorset, was patience personified when it came to dealing with my several enquiries about armoured warfare in Italy. The library of the Royal Irish Fusiliers Museum in Armagh was able to provide a long-term loan of important volumes and my thanks go to the curator, Amanda Moreno, while the Linenhall Library in Belfast tracked down several obscure titles that were also of great help in my research. Closer to home, the Central Library, Foyle Street, Londonderry provided a similar service. To each of them I offer my sincere thanks.

The reader who perseveres to the end of this book will realize that its gestation was lengthy with chapter notes indicating that information came my way over a period of some twenty years. I have always been interested in the Italian campaign and several of my earlier books have featured either the campaign or individuals who served in Italy. It has been a privilege for me to have known so many who served in Eighth Army in Italy, and although it would be impossible to name all of them special mention must be made of several individuals: Major General H.E.N. (Bala) Bredin CB, DSO** MC*, who commanded two battalions in Italy; Colonel Kendal Chavasse DSO*, who commanded 56th Reconnaissance Regiment for most of the campaign; Colonel John Horsfall DSO MC*, who also commanded two battalions; Lieutenant Colonel Desmond Woods MC*, who commanded a company for much of the campaign before serving with the *Gruppo Cremona*; Lieutenant Colonel Brian Clark MC GM, who was Adjutant of 1st Royal Irish Fusiliers for most of the campaign; Major John Duane MC, who was also a company commander; and Captain Alan Parsons MC, who served with a Gunner regiment as a Forward Observation Officer (FOO). Sadly, all have since died but each provided me with remarkable insights into the campaign.

I must also thank Mr Bobby Baxter BEM, Major Neville Chance, Major Geoffrey Cox, Major Sir Mervyn Davies, Mr George Doherty, Mr John Ledwidge, Mr Joe Robinson, Mr John Skellorn, Mr Len Trinder and Lieutenant General Sir James Wilson for their assistance. John Skellorn, who served in 16th/5th Lancers, was kind enough to lend me a copy of his Memoir of his wartime service. Lieutenant Colonel Val ffrench-Blake DSO, who commanded 17th/21st Lancers in the final months of the campaign, also allowed me access to a personal diary of the campaign which, coupled with his history of his own regiment (one of the best written regimental histories I have ever read), provided a wonderful picture of the role of an armoured regiment, especially in the final days of the campaign.

My fellow historian Ken Ford, who shares my keen interest in the war in Italy, was not only generous with both his time and notes but also did me the great service of putting me in touch with Colonel Val ffrench-Blake. Very warm thanks are due to Ken who, in addition, provided a number of photographs from his researches in the US Army's archives.

Roy McCullough, with the aid of Tim Webster, produced the maps included in the book and I thank both of them. The Pen and Sword team are responsible for a very professional production and the efforts of Brigadier Henry Wilson, Publishing Manager, and Bobby Gainher, my editor, are especially appreciated.

Quotations used in this book appear by kind permission of: Irish Academic Press Ltd, Dublin (*Clear The Way!* by Richard Doherty);

Greystone Press Ltd, Antrim (*Front of the Line* by Colin Gunner); A.M. Heath & Co Ltd (*The Monastery* and *Cassino: Portrait of Battle* (copyright © Fred Majdalany, 1957) by Fred Majdalany); Mr Michael Leventhal, Greenhill Books/Lionel Leventhal Ltd, London (2007 edition of *The Memoirs of Field Marshal Kesselring* with an introduction by James Holland); Carlton Publishing Group, London (*To Reason Why* by Denis Forman); Elsevier Ltd, Kidlington, Oxon (*The Fourth Division* by Hugh Williamson); The Queen's Printer, Ottawa, Canada (*The Canadians in Italy* by Lt Col G.W.L. Nicholson).

Crown copyright material is reproduced with the permission of the Controller of HMSO and Queen's Printer for Scotland (*Official History of the Second World War: The Mediterranean and Middle East*, Vol. V, Vol. VI, Pt I, by Molony et al, Cabinet Office *Official History of the Second World War: The Mediterranean and Middle East*, Vol. VI, Pt II, by General Sir William Jackson, Cabinet Office). Material from documents held in the National Archives, Kew, Richmond, Surrey, is reproduced with the permission of the National Archives.

In some instances, and in spite of the author's best endeavours, it has not been possible to trace the present copyright holders but the author and publishers would be happy to rectify this at the earliest possible opportunity.

A very special word of gratitude is due to the Radcliffe family. To Lucia, Marina and Danilo, thanks for all your kindness in Rome and for a friendship that spans many decades. This book is dedicated to the memory of Joe Radcliffe, a remarkable man, husband of Lucia, father of Marina and Danilo, one-time kindly neighbour to my family and veteran of the Italian campaign. That dedication is made with respect, admiration and love for Joe and his family who were the best neighbours anyone could ever ask for.

Finally, I thank my family – my wife Carol, children Joanne, James and Catríona, and grandson Ciarán – for their constant patience and understanding as yet another book confined me to my study, took me to London or Italy for research or had me requisitioning the dining-room table to study large-scale maps.

Richard Doherty
Co. Londonderry

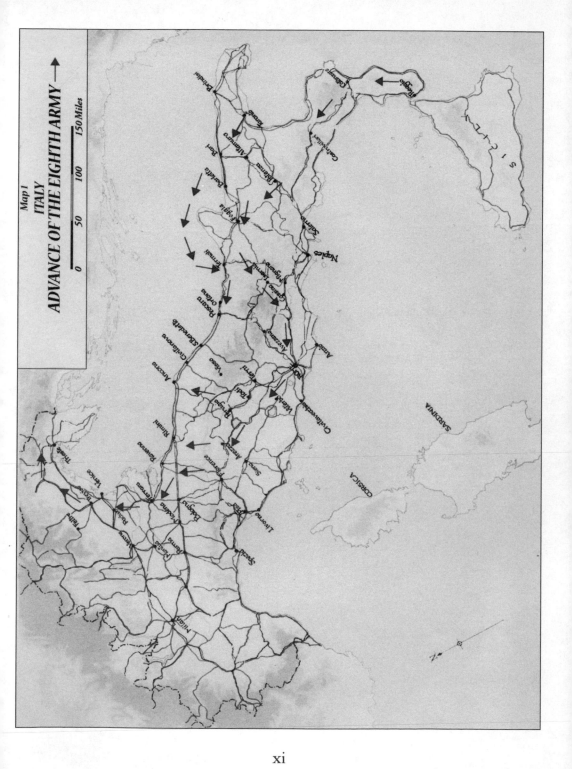

Map 1
ITALY
ADVANCE OF THE EIGHTH ARMY →

0   50   100   150 Miles

Chapter One

Into Calabria:
The Campaign Begins

Now sits Expectation in the air.

At 3.45am the order 'Fire' was given to Eighth Army's artillery. It was 3 September 1943, exactly four years since Britain had declared war on Germany. And on this September day, soldiers of Eighth Army's XIII Corps would cross the Straits of Messina to mainland Italy under cover of a bombardment that would unleash 400 tons of explosive – 29,000 rounds – on the Calabrian coast. Even higher above the troops in their assault craft flew night-fighters of the Allied air forces which were relieved by Spitfires as day broke, while bombers and fighter-bombers also provided direct support for the landings.[1] In all, the RAF flew some 651 sorties in support of the landings while the German air effort amounted to some attacks by fighter-bombers on the beaches but with no damage caused.[2] Naval gunfire from thirty-five vessels, from cruisers to landing-craft, added its powerful contribution.

Although the landings were almost unopposed, strong currents swept some craft off course to beach in the wrong places. Even so, Reggio di Calabria was occupied by 3 Canadian Brigade by 11.45am. The Canadians had made a dry landing, meeting no mines or demolitions and only 'very slight' hostile shelling.[3] They met their 'stiffest resistance of the day', not from Axis troops but from a puma that had escaped from its enclosure in Reggio's zoological gardens where brigade headquarters was established.[4] It seemed that the beast had taken a liking to the brigade commander, Brigadier M.H.S. Penhale. Elsewhere, Penhale's battalions advanced without meeting any resistance. General Simonds, GOC of 1st Canadian Division, ordered 1 Brigade to advance up the Aspromonte plateau towards Straorina, about five miles away in a direct line. The marching infantry soon realized that distances on maps were one thing but distances on the ground were another: by road they had to tramp some ten miles to reach Straorina which they did by 2.00am on 4 September.[5]

Elsewhere, 5th British Division pushed into the rugged Calabrian countryside. Fifteen Brigade struck out on Highway 18, the west coast road, or 'Monty's Highway', to Scilla on the 4th; 17 Brigade had already reached San Stefano, about four miles inland, while 13 Brigade had extended their beachhead and awaited further orders. Thirteen Brigade experienced their first opposition when a carrier patrol of Scottish Rifles met a German armoured car near Scilla – the armoured car drove off.[6] At Bagnara, the Special Raiding Squadron landed in the early morning of 4 September and, following a sharp skirmish, wrested the town from 3/15th Panzer Grenadier Regiment and held it until relieved later that morning by 15 Brigade; some Germans continued to resist with mortar fire until late afternoon.[7]

Although Eighth Army was invading Italy, the local population did not see them as invaders. Men of 2nd Royal Inniskilling Fusiliers were met by silence on landing until some Italians appeared with cries of 'Viva Inglesi', which must have amused this Irish battalion.[8] Unknown to Eighth Army's soldiers the Italian government had already concluded an armistice with the Allies which would not be made public for several more days. Italy was no longer an enemy nation.[9]

Before following Eighth Army on its travels through Calabria and beyond, it would be appropriate to consider the circumstances that brought Allied armies to Italy in the first place. Just why was Eighth Army fighting in the toe of Italy? The answer to that question takes us back to January 1943 and the Casablanca conference where Winston Churchill, President Roosevelt and their Combined Chiefs of Staff met to decide future strategy.

When that conference took place, the North African campaign was still underway in Tunisia. There was little doubt that fighting would be over in a matter of months leaving substantial Allied forces in North Africa; the purpose of the conference was to decide how to employ those forces. As early as autumn 1941 British plans had been made to invade Sicily, although these were abandoned. Then, in late November 1942, the British Chiefs of Staff prepared a similar outline plan. And so, at Casablanca, the British again proposed invading either Sicily or Sardinia after the Tunisian campaign.

Strategic arguments were advanced for this course of action: it would force the Germans to disperse their forces; it could force Italy out of the war; and, a long-cherished Churchillian dream, bring Turkey into the war alongside the Allies. The Americans, suspicious of British intentions, thought the proposals 'irrelevant to an integrated plan to win the war'.[10] They also saw them as being protective of British imperial interests which the United States had no desire to support, being almost as keen to see the end of Britain's Empire as that of the German Reich.

However, benefits could be gained from the British proposals: opening the Mediterranean would mean that convoys would no longer have to travel around the Cape; the tonnage thus made free would be available for the build-up in Britain of forces to liberate north-west Europe. Further-more, an operation against Sicily or Sardinia could be mounted using forces already in the Mediterranean, with no need to divert troops from the planned invasion of north-west Europe. Recognizing these factors, the Americans agreed to consider the options and chose Sicily rather than Sardinia as they felt that, both militarily and politically, it was the greater prize. But General Marshall, the US Army Chief of Staff, stated firmly that an American commitment to invade Sicily should not be seen as American agreement to further operations in the Mediterranean: it would be Sicily and only Sicily.[11]

The Sicily plans were agreed by Churchill and Roosevelt and, on 23 January 1943, the Combined Chiefs appointed General Dwight Eisen-hower, Allied Commander-in-Chief in North Africa, supreme commander for Operation HUSKY, the invasion of Sicily, which was to take place during the July moon.[12] Thus, on 10 July 1943, Allied forces landed in Sicily. Just under six weeks later, German forces were evacuated across the Straits of Messina to the mainland. And there, save for a possible invasion of Sardinia, should have ended the Mediterranean war, had Marshall had his way.

Winston Churchill, concerned that the Allies had no definitive plans to invade Italy following operations in Sicily, had pressed Roosevelt to commit to such a plan at the Trident conference in Washington in May.[13] Although no firm decision was made at Trident, subsequent events changed American attitudes. As Allied troops advanced through Sicily, Benito Mussolini's Fascist government fell on 25 July and, on 4 August, Italy's new government, under Marshal Pietro Badoglio, opened negotiations for an armistice. What now might the Allies do about Italy? In spite of Badoglio's peace feelers, Allied forces might not be welcome in Italy: their appearance might be met by tenacious defence. And the Germans might send strong reinforcements to keep their ally in the war. Even if Italy were to collapse the Germans might occupy the country, although Allied planners thought such a move unlikely. Could the Germans afford the troops needed, not only to occupy Italy but to replace Italian troops elsewhere? An Italian army had been included in the Axis order of battle on the Russian front,* while thirty Italian divisions were deployed in Yugoslavia, Greece, Albania and the Greek islands, with four more in southern France. Replacing those forces while maintaining the front against the Soviets ought to have been such a burden for the Germans that occupying Italy should have been out of the question.[14]

As more thought was given to invading Italy, the strategic advantages to be gained – apart from removing Italy from the Axis and the war – were

---

* This was Eighth Army.

considered. Italy could help contain German troops should Hitler send forces there; the substantial Italian fleet would no longer be a threat, thereby allowing Allied naval units to leave the Mediterranean; Allied bombers could operate from Italian airfields against southern Germany and the Rumanian oilfields; and it might be possible to attack the Balkans from Italy. Britain's Chiefs also believed that an invasion of Italy would assist the Russians by drawing off German strength from the Eastern Front. None of this necessitated a campaign from the toe of Italy to the Lombardy plain as, due to the terrain, such a campaign was not desirable. Instead, Allied strategic objectives could be met by a limited operation in southern Italy to give the Allies a good port, such as Naples, and the airfields on the Foggia plain. Thus Allied thinking concentrated on such limited objectives.[15]

Even from this brief outline, it is clear that the planners gave much thought to the nature of operations in Italy. Eisenhower and Admiral Cunningham favoured landings on the country's toe and heel to capture Naples, as well as seizing Sardinia and Corsica. Air Marshal Tedder, however, was unenthused about taking Sardinia and felt that his colleagues did not appreciate the possibilities arising from seizure of the Foggia airfields: aircraft operating from there against targets in Germany and the Balkans would not meet opposition such as faced those operating from Britain since it would be impossible for the Germans to replicate a similar defensive belt to meet raiders from Italy.[16]

At the end of May Churchill met with Marshall, Eisenhower, General Alexander, the Deputy Supreme Commander, Cunningham, Tedder and Montgomery, commander of Eighth Army, in Algiers. These discussions showed that Eisenhower might favour operations in Italy while both Alexander and Cunningham felt that an invasion of Italy should be undertaken if all went well in Sicily, a point that Marshall also emphasized. To Eisenhower now fell the task of planning for operations in Italy.[17]

Operations in Sardinia and Corsica were still being considered in addition to landings in the toe of Italy, all of which would use forces not committed to Sicily. Thus Italian operations would be carried out by the British V and X Corps, Fifth US Army would invade Sardinia and Free French forces Corsica. By 3 July the British Chiefs had reached the conclusion that 'the full exploitation of Husky [Sicily] would best be secured if offensive action be prosecuted on the mainland of Italy with all the means at our disposal towards the final elimination of Italy from the war.'[18]

As fighting progressed in Sicily, Eisenhower became a much stronger advocate of operations in Italy, reporting to the Combined Chiefs on 18 July that the war should be carried to the mainland, although he commented that this assumed that the Germans had not reinforced southern Italy substantially. Five days earlier, Churchill had asked the planners to prepare a plan for a landing on Italy's west coast to secure Naples and thence advance on Rome. Next day they produced Operation AVALANCHE. Although the American Chiefs opposed this at first, on 26 July the Combined Chiefs ordered Eisenhower to execute the plan as soon as possible. He had already allocated Fifth Army with the British X Corps for this operation, or for an alternative in the Gulf of Gioia (codenamed BUTTRESS, this never took place). However, on 1 August, he decided that, to secure the Straits of Messina, a lodgement in Calabria was necessary prior to AVALANCHE. This would be in the Reggio area and, as well as securing the straits, would act as a diversion and threaten forces defending Naples.[19]

On 16 August Eisenhower announced that Eighth Army would provide the landing force for Calabria. Thus Alexander, commanding 15 Army Group, told Montgomery, commander of Eighth Army, of his objectives: to secure the bridgehead; to enable Allied naval forces to operate through the Straits of Messina and, if the Germans withdrew from Calabria, 'to follow him up with such force as you can make available ... the greater extent to which you can engage enemy forces in the Southern tip of Italy, the more assistance will you be giving to AVALANCHE'.[20]

Eighth Army's operation, codenamed BAYTOWN, would take place between 1 and 4 September, while D-Day for AVALANCHE was 9 September. Many problems had still to be overcome, not least ensuring sufficient shipping, but it is an indicator of how well the Allies worked together, in spite of the inevitable differences, that these operations were executed on schedule. The shipping problem was never resolved satisfactorily, however, and plagued these and further Mediterranean operations since priority was given to building up forces in Britain for Operation OVERLORD.

Thus we return to those soldiers of Eighth Army in Calabria. Although two German formations, 26th Panzer and 29th Panzer Grenadier Divisions, had deployed to defend the eastern coastline of the Straits of Messina they had orders not to become involved heavily in fighting; the former division had left its tank regiment at Rome. When their artillery positions were shelled by Allied artillery from Sicily, and by aircraft, their commanders issued withdrawal orders, quitting their coastal positions two days before Eighth Army's arrival. As they withdrew, German engineers demolished bridges and corniches, blew craters in roads at junctions, cut down trees – Calabria is Italy's richest timber area – and planted mines and booby-traps to hinder Allied progress. So, although Calabrian hills were not defended as other hills in Italy would be later, the German soldier was showing his defensive skills. That he was not defending every hilltop and river line indicated that his commanders realized that doing so would offer both formations as hostages to fortune: a further landing along the east coast could cut them off. And so the divisions continued withdrawing to new battle lines.[21]

Faced with these demolitions, XIII Corps moved slowly as their engineers dealt with the damage the Germans had done on every road. The corps' leading elements took five days to travel a hundred miles north of Reggio. There, where Italy's toe and foot meet, Montgomery called a halt with his engineers almost completely out of stores and bridging equipment; these would have to be replenished before the advance resumed.[22] That halt was called on the 8th, the day Eisenhower broadcast the news of Italy's surrender, a political blunder that was most unusual for a man who was later to become President of the United States. Eisenhower's broadcast was picked up by the Germans and Hitler knew that his suspicions about the Italians, *sans* Mussolini, were justified. The Führer's plan for that eventuality, Operation ALARICH,* was implemented immediately. German forces in Italy received the message '*Ernte Einbringe*', 'bring in the harvest', and set about disarming Italian units. One Italian commander, General Gonzaga of 222nd Coastal Division, who refused to accept the German order, was shot dead in front of his troops.[23] Eisenhower had hoped to galvanize the Italian forces into active cooperation with the Allies but his broadcast led to their neutralization.

Let us now look at German strategy. There were two commanders in Italy with conflicting views on defending the peninsula: Field Marshals Albrecht Kesselring and Erwin Rommel. In May Hitler had decided that Rommel would assume command in Italy should the Germans take control of the country, a decision kept secret from the Commander-in-Chief, South (*Oberbefehlshaber Süd*, or *OB Süd*), Kesselring. Rommel's headquarters, controlling all German formations in northern Italy, was to be designated Army Group B; *OB Süd* would command those in southern Italy.[24] On 22 August, Tenth Army, under General Heinrich von Vietinghoff-Scheel, 'an old Prussian infantryman of the Guards, competent, sure of himself and adaptable',[25] was formed under *OB Süd* to command directly those formations in the south. Although neither Kesselring nor Rommel came from the traditional officer class and were thus more likely to be listened to by Hitler, they offered him markedly different advice. Rommel believed that Allied air superiority dictated a withdrawal into northern Italy, behind the line Pisa–Rimini, while Kesselring argued that Italy could be defended much farther south. Given Hitler's distaste for giving up any ground at all, it is no surprise that Kesselring's plans were accepted. Thereafter, Rommel took a back seat until his Army Group B Headquarters was transferred to France and he became responsible for defending against another Allied invasion.[26]

* Named for the Teutonic warlord whose Goths had captured Rome fourteen centuries before.

It was Kesselring who decided that Calabria would not be held. Foreseeing an Allied attack in the Naples area, he issued orders for the withdrawal of 26th Panzer and 29th Panzer Grenadier; these divisions were part of LXXVI Panzer Corps, under General der Panzertruppen Traugott Herr, which also disposed 1st *Fallschirmjäger* (Parachute) Division, and was responsible for Puglia as well as Calabria. (None was at full strength: 26th Panzer had but two companies of tanks while 29th Panzer Grenadier had only a few tanks; it was considered that heavy armoured units could not operate effectively in such rugged countryside. Some 1st Parachute Division units had also been detached for security duties around Rome.)[27] An Eighth Army Intelligence Summary, dated 2 September, had concluded that there was 'no evidence of any [German] intention to make a real stand even at the Catanzaro narrows'.[28] Kesselring had already identified a strong natural defensive line across Italy, from the mouth of the Garigliano river, on the Tyrrhenian coast, through the town of Cassino and along the Sangro river to the Adriatic coast. His strategy was to pull back to this line in a steady, fighting withdrawal, buying time for his engineers to fortify the line, which was codenamed the Gustav Line.

Von Vietinghoff's Tenth Army also disposed Lieutenant General Hans-Valentin Hube's XIV Panzer Corps, with 16th Panzer, 15th Panzer Grenadier and Hermann Göring Divisions, all held ready to meet the anticipated Allied landing near Naples. Hube was to have one division prepared to advance into Puglia if necessary and another available to meet a landing near Rome. Thus he could employ only a single division at Salerno, Major General Rudolf Sieckenius' 16th Panzer, the strongest German formation in Italy.[29] However, von Vietinghoff did not plan to engage the Allies on the beaches but to let them land and then wait and see if this was the real thing. Once he had deduced that he was not facing a feint he would reinforce Sieckenius.

As Montgomery stopped Eighth Army's advance, another force was sailing for Italy on Eisenhower's orders. This was not Fifth Army en route for Salerno but 1st British Airborne Division making its way by sea to Taranto. Although some historians consider this operation a waste of effort, it was intended to secure Taranto through which V Corps would be brought into Italy.[30] Codenamed Operation SLAPSTICK, which several thought appropriate, Major General G.F. Hopkinson's division was carried by ship from Bizerta.[31] (Since the number of ships allocated to the operation kept changing thereby upsetting staff calculations for loading, the operation also became known as BEDLAM.) The initial echelon of 1st Airborne* was transported in four ships of the Royal Navy's 12th Cruiser Squadron,

* This included Advanced Divisional HQ, 1 and 4 Parachute Brigade Groups and 9 Field Company, RE.[32]

the fast minelayer HMS *Abdiel* and the American cruiser USS *Boise*. There was some concern that the Germans might have taken over the coastal defence guns, and they were known to have mined the anchorages, but the operation was successful and the troops disembarked on 9 September. Port and city were soon in Allied hands, as was the airfield at Grottaglie, while patrols were pushing out northwards and eastwards. The new arrivals also saw the *Regia Marina*'s battleships *Andrea Doria* and *Caio Duilio* depart for Malta with an escort of two cruisers. Next day, Monopoli, on the Adriatic coast, was secured bloodlessly and the division's leading elements pushed on. On the 11th, opposition was encountered at Castellanata where, in a skirmish with German troops, the divisional commander was wounded. Hopkinson succumbed to his injuries and was succeeded by Major General E.E. Down. Bari and Brindisi fell that same day while, on the 12th, it became apparent that 1st Parachute Division, the principal opposition, had deployed rearguards from Altamura to Castellanata, Gioia del Colle and Ginosa. Although significant elements – most of two parachute regiments – of the division were in Calabria under command of 26th Panzer Division while one battalion was near Naples with the Hermann Göring Division, it was soon evident that the *Fallschirmjäger* were falling back on Foggia.[33]

While the Taranto operation was successful, German mines claimed victims. Swinging at anchor on 10 September, HMS *Abdiel* struck a mine, broke her back and sank within minutes with the loss of forty-eight naval personnel and 120 men of 6th Parachute Battalion; 120 soldiers and six naval personnel were injured.[34] But the build-up continued with the remainder of the airborne division soon in Taranto. Alexander signalled to Montgomery that port units and HQ V Corps would follow so that Taranto would be ready to receive 8th Indian Division by about 25 September and 2nd New Zealand shortly afterwards. He also told Eighth Army's commander that when V Corps had built up and he was within supporting distance that corps would come under his command.[35]

Alexander sent that signal to Montgomery on 10 September in response to one from his subordinate the previous day which noted that Eighth Army's divisions needed a rest but that 'intensive reconnaissance will be carried out to the line Crotone–Rossano–Spezzano–Belvedere', while main bodies would resume the advance on the 13th or 14th. That advance would be directed on the Spezzano–Belvedere neck. Alexander urged Montgomery to 'maintain pressure upon the Germans so that they cannot remove forces from your front and concentrate them against [Salerno]'. But Montgomery pleaded that his divisions were not yet up to even light scales of transport and that the build-up from Sicily was very slow.[36] Strangely, his HQ war diary recorded that 'ferry control worked so well on 3 September that 1,500 vehicles were ferried across'. This had, however, caused 'considerable congestion' on mainland beaches. In fact the ferrying programme had gone so well that the D+2 priorities were being shipped across the Straits of Messina before the end of D-Day.[37]

So, in spite of Alexander's exhortation, XIII Corps' advance did not resume immediately, although the official history suggests that 'after Alexander's message, Montgomery had no choice but to advance.'[38] That history goes on to describe how Montgomery 'continued concentrating' the corps in the Nicastro–Catanzaro area while pushing light forces as far northward as he could. This is hardly the advance that Alexander was urging. Not until the 13th did Eighth Army's commander report to Alexander that 'My forward move begins tomorrow.'[39] This was as Montgomery had originally suggested.

Montgomery's light forces included elements of both 1st Canadian and 5th British Divisions; they were supported by the Royal Navy which kept a monitor, destroyer and two gunboats off the coast to provide firepower.[40] On 11 September, RHQ 5th Reconnaissance Regiment (5 Recce), the 'eyes' of 5th Division, had arrived at Sambiase to learn that scout patrols, including sappers, were probing farther north while others were working into the mountains to contact the Canadians. At much the same time, 26th Panzer, although withdrawing northwards, was detaching a small force to Lagonegro to counter a rumoured landing at Sapri on the Gulf of Policastro.

Ordered to move to Amantea and then probe northwards, 5 Recce deployed two squadrons. Patrols made for Cosenza to see if the airfield there was still usable but all roads were impassable. This did not deter one enterprising officer of 1 Squadron, Lieutenant D.G. Cope, who found 'one very devious route open ... and got there first'.[41] Even so, Cope was upstaged by Major Harris of 2 Squadron who, finding every road blocked, discovered a single-track railway leading to Cosenza. Not only was the track undamaged but a working engine, complete with driver, was sitting at a small station. Engine and driver were pressed into service to take Harris' patrol into Cosenza. The nature of his arrival gained Harris publicity in the national press.[42]

Although Harris had found the railway from a map, these soon became scarce. As the regiment probed ahead it found that it had outstripped 5th Division's supplies.

> For a couple of days the only maps of the area in which it was operating in the Regiment's possession were two very aged motoring maps which Lieut Hugh Jarrett had borrowed from a friendly, retired Italian general.[43]

There were also problems with wireless communications due to the mountainous terrain and long distances involved. At times RHQ 5 Recce was over a hundred miles ahead of 5th Division HQ, while the regiment's leading patrols might be as far forward again.[44]

On 16 September a 5 Recce patrol met patrols from 36th US Division of Fifth Army at Vallo. The Salerno battle was all but over and on that day von Vietinghoff decided to withdraw while 5th Division reached Sapri and the Canadians were close to Spezzano. Patrols from each division met at Castrovillari and a Canadian patrol also met one from 1st Airborne some 40 miles south-west of Taranto. At the end of the day it 'could be said that the Allied armies were at least in touch ... from the Tyrrhenian coast to the Adriatic'.[45]

Notes

1. Molony, *The Mediterranean and Middle East*, vol. V, p. 238.
2. NA, Kew, WO169/8496, war diary Main HQ Eighth Army, Sep 1943.
3. Ibid.
4. Nicholson, *The Canadians in Italy*, p. 205.
5. Ibid.; Molony, op. cit., pp. 239–40.
6. Aris, *The Fifth British Division 1939 to 1945*, p. 144.
7. NA Kew, WO169/8520, war diary Eighth Army HQ GS I, Sep–Dec 1943.
8. Aris, op. cit., p. 144.
9. Molony, op. cit., pp. 274–5; Jackson, *The Battle for Italy*, pp. 92–4.
10. Molony, op. cit., p. 2.
11. Ibid.
12. Ibid., pp. 2–3.
13. Churchill, *The Second World War, Vol. VIII: The Hinge of Fate*, p. 356.
14. Molony, op. cit., p. 191.
15. Ibid., pp. 191–2.
16. Ibid., pp. 192–3.
17. Ibid., p. 193.
18. Quoted in ibid., p. 196.
19. Ibid., pp. 196–8; Graham and Bidwell, *Tug of War*, pp. 31–4. The latter also includes (pp. 28–9) a map illustrating the various options considered by Eisenhower.
20. Montgomery *Memoirs*, p. 192.
21. Molony, op. cit., pp. 239–40; Graham and Bidwell, op. cit., pp. 43–52.
22. Montgomery's signal to Alexander is quoted in Molony, p. 244, as is Alexander's reply. See also Montgomery, *Memoirs*, p. 196.
23. Graham and Bidwell, op. cit., p. 39; Jackson, op. cit., p. 111.
24. Molony, op. cit., pp. 208–9.
25. Von Senger, *Neither Fear Nor Hope*, p. 181.
26. Graham and Bidwell, op. cit., pp. 47–52.
27. Ibid.
28. NA, Kew, WO169/8520 op. cit., Intelligence Summary (IntSum) No. 544.
29. Graham and Bidwell, op. cit., p. 50.
30. Ibid., p. 98.
31. Molony, op. cit., p. 243.
32. Ibid., p. 242n.
33. Ibid., p. 243.
34. Ibid.

35. Alexander's signal to Montgomery, quoted in Molony, op. cit., pp. 244–5.
36. Molony, op. cit., p. 244.
37. NA, Kew, WO169/8496, op. cit.
38. Molony, op. cit., p. 245.
39. Ibid., p. 246.
40. NA, Kew, WO169/8496, op. cit.
41. Prince, *Wheeled Odyssey*, p. 38.
42. Ibid.
43. Ibid., p. 38.
44. Doherty, *Only The Enemy in Front*, p. 71.
45. Molony, op. cit., p. 246.

Chapter Two

To the Winter Line

In the painful field.

With the Germans withdrawing from Salerno and Fifth Army advancing towards Naples, Montgomery was 'ordered to transfer the operations of the Eighth Army to the east or Adriatic side of the main mountain range of the Apennines'.[1] This required major changes, not least switching the administrative axis, or logistical chain, of Eighth Army to south-eastern ports including Taranto, Brindisi and Bari. Meanwhile, the Canadians were pushing ahead, reaching Potenza on the night of 19/20 September. Although some resistance was met, 1st Parachute Division was deployed too thinly along the Potenza–Altamura line – with many men still detached elsewhere – to offer other than token resistance. Potenza fell, only the second town of any size that the Canadians had thus far seen in Italy; its sports stadium quickly became a divisional recreational centre.[2]

On 21 September, 5th Division reached Auletta. Lieutenant General Dempsey then ordered XIII Corps to halt on the line Altamura–Potenza–Auletta until 1 October and reorganize for the advance to Foggia; the Canadians were to make for Foggia on Highways 97 and 16. However, this plan became redundant when General Herr, fearful lest he be out-flanked, ordered his men back to positions west and north of Foggia. With the Foggia road now open, an ad hoc force of B Squadron 56 Recce, A Squadron The Royals, a 25-pounder troop of 17th Field Regiment, some troops from 1st Airborne Division and GHQ Liaison (Phantom) Regiment under Major Marcus Hartland-Mahon of 56 Recce was formed to seize and hold crossings of the Ofanto river before advancing to occupy Foggia.[3]

Both The Royals and 56 Recce met opposition while probing towards the Ofanto while a prisoner from a flak regiment claimed that a large force was deployed in Andrea. The advance continued and on the morning of 24 September the force began fording the Ofanto against heavy resistance. Mortar fire caused casualties in 56 Recce and a troop of Shermans from

12

3rd County of London Yeomanry (CLY) was placed under Hartland-Mahon's command. One Sherman was hit by anti-tank fire and another damaged accidentally. As the struggle continued under heavy shelling, Hartland-Mahon's force came under command of 4 Armoured Brigade to become A Force.[4]

Next day B Squadron and Battle HQ 56 Recce crossed the Ofanto unopposed and made for Foggia. Opposition about six miles from there was cleared by recce armoured cars and carriers with some CLY tanks. At 9.00am on the 27th, A Force reached Foggia and recce patrols moved out towards Lucera. These operations were 1st Airborne Division's swansong in Italy before withdrawal to the UK; it would next see action a year later at Arnhem. A Force's operations had taken place under command of V Corps, now part of Eighth Army, while Canadians of XIII Corps had also patrolled beyond Melfi to the Ofanto.[5]

Once again, Montgomery was stopping to reorganize his administrative base. In his *Memoirs* he criticized the Allies becoming 'involved in a major campaign lacking a predetermined master plan. We had not made in advance the administrative plans and arrangements necessary to sustain the impetus of our operations.'[6] This reflected argument that had taken place amongst the Allies and even within the British high command. It was still unclear whether operations would be restricted to southern Italy or expanded to include the entire country.

Hitler was concerned that the Allies intended to attack the Balkans from southern Italy and Eighth Army's recent operations would have strengthened that belief. He and his advisers were much more worried about such an invasion than any Allied advance through Italy since a Balkan operation would threaten Germany's Rumanian oil supplies, as well as chrome and bauxite imports, and encourage 'anti-Axis and partisan movements in the area, real or imagined'.[7] To counter such a move, Hitler ordered Kesselring to establish a line across Italy from Gaeta to Ortona – the narrowest part of the peninsula – and, if the Allies were preparing to invade the Balkans, launch a spoiling offensive.[8] (The Führer need not have worried: the Allies lacked the assault shipping needed to cross the Adriatic. Their plans were restricted to pushing northwards with Eighth Army seizing and securing the Foggia airfields.)

As we have noted, Eighth Army had been strengthened by the inclusion of V Corps. The arrival of 8th Indian Division, 78th Division,* 4 Armoured Brigade and 1 Special Service Brigade led to changes in the order of battle: 8th Indian joined 5th Division in V Corps, in which 1st Airborne remained until it left Italy; XIII Corps had 1st Canadian Division, 78th Division and 4 Armoured Brigade.[9] In addition to its three infantry brigades,

* Known as the Battleaxe Division from its divisional badge of a golden battleaxe on a black or dark-blue ground.

13

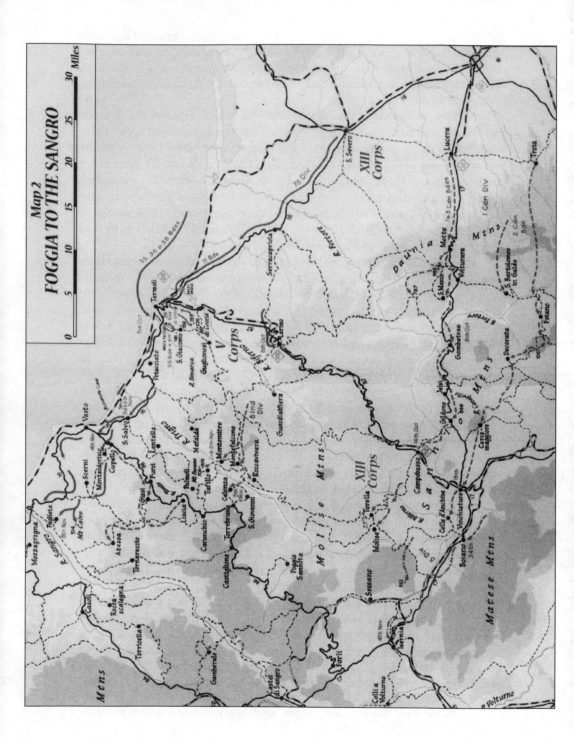

1st Canadian division also included 1 Canadian Armoured Brigade.*
Montgomery was regrouping Eighth Army for its next advance, to the
Termoli–Isernia line, along the Biferno river.

On 29 September Alexander issued instructions for the next phase of
Army Group operations, making clear that Allied strategy was now to
advance on and liberate Rome with its airfields, and establish a line from
San Benedetto on the east coast through Visso and Terni, and thence to
Civitavecchia on the west coast above Rome.[11] Alexander considered that
'a stabilised front south of Rome cannot be accepted, for the capital has a
significance far greater than its strategic location, and *sufficient depth*
[author's italics] must be gained before the Foggia airfields and the port of
Naples can be regarded as secure.'[12] Within this revised strategic plan,
Eighth Army was 'to continue [its] advance as quickly as possible to secure
the lateral road Pescara–Pópoli–Avezzano, in order to outflank Rome'.[13]
Such an objective proved much too optimistic in the mouth of an Italian
winter.

On 1 October XIII Corps began establishing itself on the line of the
Termoli–Vinchiaturo road, thereby securing the entire Foggia plain and
allowing the advance to Pescara to begin. The corps moved on a two-
divisional front with 78th Division using the main coast road, Highway
16, while the Canadians thrust into the mountains on Highway 17 towards
Vinchiaturo. This was also the day on which Allied troops entered Naples.
The new positions taken up by the Germans seemed to be aimed at denying
the Allies access to the main lateral from Termoli via Vinchiaturo to the
Capua area. Termoli, Vinchiaturo and Caserta all offered gaps to be
exploited. XIII Corps was to attempt the first exploitation at Termoli
where a seaborne operation would be harmonized with an overland attack.
V Corps would move up behind XIII Corps to protect the latter's left flank
as contact between Fifth and Eighth Armies would be difficult to maintain
in Italy's central spine.[14]

With some landing craft still at his disposal Montgomery had decided to
use these to support XIII Corps' operation by deploying 1 Special Service
Brigade (3 (Army) Commando, 40 (Royal Marine) Commando and the
Special Raiding Squadron) to seize and hold Termoli until the arrival of
78th Division, whose 36 and 38 (Irish) Brigades would follow by sea while
11 Brigade advanced overland through Serracapriola with 4 Armoured
Brigade and 56 Recce; the Special Service Brigade was under command
of 78th Division.[15] This was Operation DEVON. On 1 October, a day
before the commandos and raiders sailed from Bari, the landward advance

* Composed of: 11th Armoured Regiment (Ontario Regiment), 12th Armoured
Regiment (Three Rivers Regiment) and 14th Armoured Regiment (Calgary
Regiment).[10]

began. Air support had been planned but poor weather over the previous week had restricted flying, thereby reducing the support available to XIII Corps.[16]

Before considering the subsequent battle for Termoli, let us look at the experience of the marching force en route through Serracapriola to Termoli. This included 11 Brigade, 4 Armoured Brigade and 56 Recce with elements of 1st Kensingtons, 78th Division's support regiment, although only one regiment – 3 CLY – of 4 Armoured Brigade was present, and armoured cars of The Royals. In this advance Eighth Army's soldiers 'encountered more numerous and better executed demolitions than hitherto; while winter rains made rapid construction of high-level bridges essential'.[17] The first river obstacle was the Fortore where the Germans had destroyed the bridge, thus necessitating a detour. Unfortunately, this was over a route where a strong enemy force was present. Nonetheless, the leading troops, from 56 Recce, The Royals and 3 CLY, made the opposed crossing under heavy shellfire with supporting fire from the Kensingtons' Vickers MMGs. Lieutenant Roderick Court of 56 Recce was killed by an airburst but the crossing had been forced by 10.30am and the advance on Serracapriola continued over open country. Opposition was dealt with by artillery and the town was eventually taken, although many booby traps were left by the Germans; these killed several men.[18]

There was no clear road to Termoli as recce patrols on the 2nd proved. Sappers again built diversions, including some through Serracapriola where Luftwaffe aircraft bombed troop concentrations next morning. Every bridge along the road had been blown and, to make matters worse, it was raining heavily. The greatest obstacle en route was the Biferno which B Squadron and Battle HQ of 56 Recce reached on the 3rd 'by many and devious detours'.[19] No Germans were encountered, although many effective demolitions gave proof of their recent presence. Thanks to the heavy rain, the Biferno was impassable until sappers built a pontoon bridge. As the engineers laboured the Luftwaffe appeared again to bomb the area, but work continued and, an hour before midnight, RHQ and B Squadron 56 Recce crossed to harbour some two miles south of Termoli on a dark and very wet night. Next morning the squadron drove through Termoli to reconnoitre along the main road to Vasto. Having driven to within three miles of Petacciato, the recce men withdrew to Termoli, by which time the commandos had arrived.[20]

The Special Service Brigade had landed near Termoli before dawn on the 3rd, forced the withdrawal of a small German battlegroup – *Kampfgruppe* Rau, made up of about 400 flak personnel, sappers and some others with a few paras* – and captured the port before securing the town's approaches,

---

* A contemporary figure in an Intelligence Summary put the strength of *Kampfgruppe* Rau at 250 men.[21]

including the Biferno crossings. Although Major Rau had been warned repeatedly of the possibility of an Allied landing:

> he showed that he was in no way equal to the task which had been set him [and] his unit was completely surprised when British troops made the first landing ... and he and his troops were taken prisoner before they could fire a shot.[22]

On the night of 3/4 October, 36 Brigade disembarked at Termoli, took over the southern defences and prepared to move on to high ground in the morning; the commandos were relieved and withdrew to Termoli. Two battalions of 36 Brigade – 6th Royal West Kents and 8th Argylls – advanced to meet the enemy, while 56 Recce pushed patrols out along the coast road to Pescara. In spite of the weather and the Luftwaffe, which continued attacking, it looked as if all was going to plan. Intelligence reported that the only Germans nearby were paras with some artillery and a little armour. But a 56 Recce patrol then brought news that changed that relatively cosy picture. While probing towards Petacciato the patrol captured a German motorcyclist from 16th Panzer Division. Intelligence reports suggested that this formation was on the west coast, reforming and refitting after the Salerno battles, but the prisoner reported that the division had been travelling across Italy for the past two nights. This was confirmed when German tanks were encountered by 56 Recce; one patrol ran into a group of about fifty Germans with three tanks, while a second patrol clashed with a small German force and compelled them to withdraw. Before the morning was out some of those enemy tanks were advancing on Termoli.[23]

Kesselring himself had despatched 16th Panzer to Termoli.

> I happened to be at Tenth Army headquarters when the report [of the landings] came in, and immediately ordered the 16th Panzers to be rushed there with the mission of throwing the invaders back into the sea.[24]

Fortunately for the British troops at Termoli, Tenth Army's commander had not shared Kesselring's sense of urgency. Instead of moving as a division, 16th Panzer crossed the peninsula piecemeal and thus lacked concentration. The motorcyclist captured by 56 Recce was one of the leading soldiers from the first element of the division to arrive but the bulk of the formation was still travelling across Italy. Further delay was occasioned when Allied air attacks at Isernia disrupted the supply of fuel to the division as it travelled towards Termoli.[25]

When the German attack struck, 8th Argylls were making for the village of San Giacomo, some five miles from Termoli on the road to Guglionesi.

At about 10.00am B Company met German troops who were advancing on Termoli and took up defensive positions as enemy tanks and artillery opened fire. Their commanding officer, Lieutenant Colonel Scott-Elliott, deployed his anti-tank guns in a screen to cover his front but, while the Argylls stalled the enemy attack, the battalion suffered heavy losses from shelling and mortaring. However, artillery support aided their efforts to keep the Germans at bay.[26]

The West Kents had also run into the enemy. Having advanced about 1,000 yards they, too, were brought to a stop by infantry and mortar fire. There followed an attempt by the West Kents to resume their advance which led to a brisk firefight and a bayonet charge against enemy positions in a farm and wood, leaving the battalion with forty casualties. In between these two battalions of 36 Brigade was one from 11 Brigade: 2nd Lancashire Fusiliers. They, too, although due to hand over to 5th Buffs, were in action as their commanding officer, John MacKenzie, recounted:

> the furious firepower of the 16 Panzer Division was turned on to our positions. ... There was a shout 'Tanks in front!' – an armoured attack with infantry following. Companies were soon calling for their prearranged defensive fire tasks, which were quickly answered by our gunners. Medium guns were engaging enemy armour. The battle area had become alive as both sides became locked in battle.[27]

For Major General Evelegh, 78th Division's GOC, the German counter-attack presented a major problem – and he already had enough problems. Across the Biferno he had but four infantry battalions, with the two commandos – both under strength – and the Special Raiding Squadron (SRS), plus RHQ and a squadron of 56 Recce. He could not deploy immediately any of his other troops: from Serracapriola 5th Northamptons had advanced on Potocannone and San Martino to clear the divisional left flank and were still short of the Biferno; 1st East Surreys, with some Kensington machine guns and mortars, were at Larino trying to cut Highway 87; and the Irish Brigade was at sea en route to Termoli. Across the Biferno he had only one of his three field regiments – 138th – a handful of 17-pounder anti-tank guns and no tanks at all; the armoured cars of 56 Recce were no match for Panzer MkIVs. And, due to the sodden ground, those 17-pounders across the river could not be towed up to the infantry battalions who needed them.[28] Nor could Evelegh move anyone forward quickly: with the boat bridge across the river out of action his forces in and around Termoli were cut off. All now depended 'on the morale of virtually immobile and far too lightly supported infantrymen, face-to-face with tanks'.[29]

To provide right flank and rear protection to the Argylls, Lieutenant Colonel Kendal Chavasse, of 56 Recce, was given command of a force including his own RHQ, B Squadron, 3 Commando, an SRS troop and an anti-tank battery with orders to defend the high ground above the Simarca river, from the sea to west of the Valentino brickworks. With Chavasse's force in position, Brigadier Howlett, of 36 Brigade, ordered the Argylls to resume their attack on San Giacomo; he also requested urgent armour support.[30]

The engineers were working manfully to create a tank crossing by bulldozing a ford across the Biferno. In spite of heavy enemy shelling they succeeded and, next morning, six CLY Shermans crossed. But their passage turned the ford into a morass, making it impossible for others to follow. It was now the morning of 5 October, a wet, miserable day that found the Argylls in the open trying to stop both tanks and infantry but with few anti-tank guns and no armour. The CLY Shermans were now despatched to their aid but in spite of showing considerable dash the CLY lost four tanks to enemy fire and, with the surviving Argylls, were forced to withdraw to the brickworks.[31] There Brigadier Howlett and Colonel Scott-Elliott met to discuss the worsening situation. Shortly after Howlett departed that situation deteriorated even more when 16th Panzer tanks turned the Argylls' right flank. As the MkIVs drew closer, Scott-Elliott and two volunteers from 56 Recce manned an anti-tank gun in a determined effort to stop them, or at least slow their progress. As the brickworks was being shelled heavily, by both sides, the Argylls were ordered to move back, which they did in good order. It was then that Major John Anderson VC, the hero of Longstop Hill in Tunisia, was killed, one of five Argylls officers to lose their lives in the battle.[32] Another seven were wounded and 150 other ranks were killed or wounded. One of the Recce men manning an anti-tank gun was Trooper Alfred Ives, an old soldier – he was thirty-six – who single-handedly served a 6-pounder, taking on several panzers, before his weapon received a direct hit and he was killed.[33]

The Argylls were not alone in their suffering: the West Kents' line was broken by six tanks and the battalion withdrew in some confusion towards Larino. The MkIVs then turned against the Buffs who were also disorganized with their left flank in the air, but Brigadier Howlett steadied the battalion which held its ground. As the West Kents took up positions on the left flank they were down to eighty men.[34] Kendal Chavasse's force, protecting the Argylls' flank, was also imperilled. Three tanks were approaching the positions held by 3 Commando and the SRS troop while B Squadron was being shelled heavily. A farm on B Squadron's left flank was occupied by Germans and the squadron was out of contact with RHQ as its rear-link wireless vehicle had been destroyed. It seemed that the SRS had been overrun as tanks penetrated their position – in fact, they abandoned the position without permission – and Chavasse ordered the evacuation of all vehicles except the wireless recce cars; B Squadron was told to withdraw by the Argylls' CO. With only 3 Commando holding the line and the Germans trying to encircle his RHQ, Kendal Chavasse coolly informed his men that they now had 'an all round shoot'. The 56 Recce CO recounted the events of that evening:

> It was now getting dark, and we could hear the voices of enemy infantry, through the shelling. The order to withdraw came to me from Divisional HQ. I remember walking through the olive grove, with bullets whistling, to contact the CO of the Commando to tell him to withdraw. Then came the problem of getting our vehicles out. I got on to Division, over the air, and asked for as much *noise* as possible so that the enemy would not hear the engines starting up. I remember having to talk in a soft tone, as if I could hear their voices in the dark they could hear mine! I also remember the gunner saying to me that he had never been asked for 'noise' before! Anyway, they gave it, and plenty of it too, and we slipped away unnoticed to behind the firmer line that had been established behind us.[35]

That line had been formed by 2nd Lancashire Fusiliers and the withdrawal of Chavasse's men was complete by 2.45am on 6 October, by which time the Irish Brigade was landing at Termoli, the first troops having disembarked six hours earlier. Commenting on this operation, the brigade commander, Nelson Russell, said that they had originally thought that their voyage 'was to be a pleasant peacetime cruise – with fighting unlikely for a fortnight or so' but 'this did not go according to plan'. The small flotilla of seven landing craft came under shellfire while approaching the harbour while Russell had already received a message telling him to attend an Orders Group (O Group) 'down some unknown road near Termoli'. Closing on the harbour he felt that 'some grit had got into the works of our peacetime cruise' since burning German tanks could be seen and 'shells could be heard dropping in the town'.[36]

On disembarking, Russell found a commando officer waiting to take him to Colonel Durnford Slater, the Special Service Brigade commander. From him he learned that the 'grit' was 16th Panzer, which had counterattacked, that 36 Brigade had been hit hard and was now disorganized with their exact locations uncertain, and that the Germans were on the outskirts of Termoli.

> In fact there was no reason to suppose he wasn't actually in the town by now – and all that was between him and the sea were some very depleted Commandos, the Lancashire Fusiliers and perhaps – if still in existence – some of the Recce.*[37]

* Nelson Russell and Kendal Chavasse were both Irish Fusiliers which probably explains this mention of 56 Recce.

There was, however, some good news: tanks had crossed the Biferno – Russell was told that nine had crossed but that four had since been knocked out – but it was estimated that about twenty-five German tanks were also in the area. Suddenly it seemed that the Irish Brigade was disembarking directly into the front line. (Since the jetty could take only one vessel at a time the brigade was coming ashore at the rate of 300 men every ninety minutes.) But should the Germans enter the town the Irish battalions were battle-hardened with street-fighting experience from Sicily. However, Russell felt that there would be no immediate German attack since his experience was that they did not usually attack at night.[38] Of Russell's troops, one historian has written:

> The Irish had already shown a very soldierly competence in rapidly disembarking under heavy fire, and, in darkness and an unknown town, taking position on its perimeter; when it came to fighting they were brilliantly successful.[39]

From the meeting with Durnford Slater, Russell went to an O Group with General Evelegh and learned that between eighty and ninety tanks were expected across the Biferno by early morning; 214 (Staffordshire) Field Company had completed a Bailey bridge that afternoon.[40] Air support was also available with US aircraft assisting the Desert Air Force; 16th Panzer's efforts of the 5th had been blunted by air attacks.[41] An outline battle plan was then drawn up. Russell had already ordered his battalions – 6th Royal Inniskilling Fusiliers, 1st Royal Irish Fusiliers and 2nd London Irish Rifles* – to deploy in the Termoli perimeter. That would provide the start line from which, at 11.00am, they would advance, supported by a tank squadron, to take over San Giacomo ridge which was to be seized in an earlier attack – at 8.00am – by the Buffs and two armoured regiments.[42]

At 10.00am, Russell had a visit from Evelegh who had bad news: the tanks had been held up by an anti-tank obstacle. Since this would take hours to overcome, if at all, would it be possible for the Irish Brigade, with a single tank squadron, to take the ridge? Nelson Russell thought that it was. The attack was to be made by the two fusilier battalions with the Rifles providing a firm base; the tank squadron was Canadian, from the Three Rivers Regiment. At 11.30am the brigade advanced, Faughs on the right flank and Skins on the left. In spite of tough opposition, the Faughs were on their objective by 3.00pm and two hours later the Skins had secured theirs. The London Irish, who had been stepped up between the coast and the road by 3.00pm, then advanced to take the cemetery and a small hill about a mile from Termoli. By nightfall the battalion was

* The two fusilier regiments were known respectively as the Skins and the Faughs.

21

established firmly along the Simarca river. Major Bala Bredin, second-in-command of the Irish Fusiliers, thought the Canadian tankmen to be excellent, living up to their motto 'Have a Go, Joe'. In very quick time they had knocked out at least four enemy tanks in spite of being relatively raw, which Bredin considered an advantage as 'they hadn't got too careful'.[43]

The battle for Termoli was over and Eighth Army could continue its advance but ahead lay yet more rivers in flood as the rains, draining off the Apennines, rushed to the sea. It had been a close-run engagement. With *Kampfgruppe* Schultz, a para battlegroup, providing its right-flank guard, 16th Panzer had planned to capture the town on the 6th, with I and II Battalions of 79th Panzer Grenadier Regiment, supported by tanks and artillery. On the scale of the many battles to come, Termoli was not a major encounter, involving forces of less than divisional strength on either side. But it was critical at this time since German success would have had catastrophic effects for the Allies. That is one reason why a lengthy account of the battle has been given, but there is another: the need for accurate historical reporting. As Cyril Ray, 78th Division's first historian, wrote so aptly, this was a battle the outcome of which depended entirely 'on the morale of virtually immobile and far too lightly supported infantry-men, face-to-face with tanks'. It was won principally by those infantrymen with the support of some CLY and Three Rivers Regiment tanks, and it is sad to note that many historians have denigrated their achievements. This is especially true of those who write of light forces – commandos, Royal Marines, SAS* and SRS – many of whom state that 56 Recce was 'green', that its soldiers abandoned their anti-tank guns, that the opposition came from *26th* Panzer Division and that the river obstacle was the '*Bifurno*'. In fact, 56 Recce was far from green, having fought through the Tunisian and Sicilian campaigns. Only RHQ and B Squadron were involved in the battle while the regiment's anti-tank guns were never present; these were with HQ Squadron on the other side of the Biferno. However, as we have seen, some 56 Recce soldiers manned Argyll anti-tank guns and at least one of them, Trooper Ives, died while so doing. This hardly tallies with the comments made by some who have consistently failed to check their sources before writing about the battle, a failure emphasized by their references to 26th Panzer and the 'Bifurno'.

Finally, it is worth remembering that had von Vietinghoff shared Kesselring's sense of urgency the outcome might well have been a German victory.

I was therefore very surprised when, between 10 and 11pm the same day, Westphal reported that the Tenth Army commander was

---

* A small detachment of about twenty men from 2 SAS joined the Special Service Brigade before the German counter-attack.

still shilly-shallying while I was under the illusion that [16th Panzer] was racing to Termoli. As I did not share the commander's qualms I ordered my instructions to be carried out in double-quick time. The division arrived belatedly on 4 October and was thrown in piece-meal – Tenth Army headquarters bungled the whole thing and lost the chance of an assured success. ... The incident was a lesson ... which, however, we showed later we had taken to heart at the time of the Anzio landings.[44]

As a footnote to the battle, Kesselring arrived at 16th Panzer Division's headquarters near Palata on 7 October to investigate its defeat at Termoli. A month later Sieckenius was relieved and placed on the 'Reserve of Higher Officers'.[45]

With Termoli now secure, Eighth Army could resume its advance. Herr had ordered his corps to withdraw and 78th Division was able to advance to Larino, south of Termoli, and Petacciato, farther along the coast. Guglionesi was taken by the Buffs. As part of the original plan for the attack on Termoli, 1st East Surreys, of 11 Brigade, with 322 Battery, 132nd Field Regiment, and two platoons of 1st Kensingtons, were ordered to capture Larino, 15 miles away, on Highway 87, the lateral road. An attack by two companies, under Majors Andrew and Hill, at daybreak on 4 October, took the first ridge in front of the town before the Surreys came under heavy bombardment and were forced to dig in. No relief was available and Dempsey, XIII Corps' commander, ordered them to maintain their position but to make no further advance. He also told their commanding officer, Lieutenant Colonel H.B.L. Smith MC, that his men, by holding the Germans in Larino, were contributing vitally to the battle in Termoli, which was then in the balance. Thus:

> For four days the Battalion held on to its position under continuous artillery, mortar and machine-gun fire until the afternoon of October 8th when they entered Larino to be joyfully received by the Italians as the last of the Germans left on the other side of the town.[46]

It was then that Sergeant Bunting, who had been missing, believed killed, since the start of the battle, rejoined. His patrol had been engaged by German armoured cars and he was hidden by Italian villagers for four days, being moved from cellar to cellar during that time. His experience was an example of the attitude of the majority of Italians to the Germans and the British. The Surreys had also suffered many casualties – two stretcher-bearers, Lance Corporal S.C. Kemp and Private F.A.W. Ramsay, each received immediate awards of the Military Medal for tending and rescuing wounded under fire.[47]

23

While 78th Division had been engaged at Termoli, 1st Canadian Division advanced through the foothills of the Matese mountains towards Vinchiaturo against stubborn resistance that included the redoubtable paras. Brigadier H.D. Graham's 1 Brigade advanced from Motta to the upper reaches of the Fortore river, close to Gambetesa, between 2 and 6 October, with Gambetesa being captured by Penhale's 3 Brigade over the next two days, while 2 Brigade, under Brigadier B.M. Hoffmeister,* moved up on the left flank, using minor roads and travelling cross-country.[48]

The Canadians had reached Campobasso by 14 October and Vinchiaturo a day later. Their progress had been difficult. At the village of Motta Montecorvino they experienced their first major engagement on the Italian mainland, an action 'as intense as any that followed during the month'. Opposition came from soldiers of 1st Parachute Division who were well sited for defence. The village is perched on a hill on the first main ridge as Highway 17 ascends in twists and turns from the plain.

> Reconnaissance elements fanning out to either flank reported that for four or five miles on each side of the highway the ridge was defended by machine-gun posts and 88-millimetre guns. It was clear that an attack in force upon Motta would be necessary to dislodge the enemy from his advantageous position.[49]

At 8.00am on 1 October, A Squadron, Princess Louise's Dragoon Guards were the first to come under fire from Motta's defenders while negotiating the twisting road from the plain. It was soon clear that the Germans planned a vigorous defence. Meanwhile, B Squadron had moved quickly from Lucera to Alberona, another hill village about 6 miles south of Motta. The squadron leader, Major M.A.G. Stroud, had met up with Major Vladimir Peniakoff, 'Popski' and the founder of the eponymous Private Army, who had been able to describe German dispositions at Alberona. Stroud and Peniakoff decided to combine their commands with the result that a force of armoured cars and jeeps crawled up a narrow, corkscrewing track into the mountains to fall on Alberona from the rear. Taken completely by surprise the Germans were driven from the village. No attackers were injured but fifteen Germans, at least, lay dead. The bodies wore *Fallschirmjäger* uniforms, confirming that the ridge was being held by Major General Richard Heidrich's 1st Parachute Division; the dead were from 3rd Parachute Regiment.

---

* Strictly speaking, Hoffmeister was still a lieutenant colonel and was acting brigade commander since Brigadier Vokes was acting divisional commander in the absence of Major General Simonds who was ill. However, Hoffmeister was appointed to command 2 Brigade on 1 November.

The Canadian advance was spearheaded by a strong mobile force, commanded by Lieutenant Colonel Neroutsos of the Calgary Regiment, that included Princess Louise's Dragoon Guards with armoured cars, the Calgary Regiment with tanks, lorry-borne infantry of the Royal Canadian Regiment, 27 Canadian Anti-Tank Battery and 2nd Canadian Field Regiment; 66th Medium Regiment were in support. In turn, Neroutsos' force deployed a vanguard commanded by Lieutenant Colonel F.D. Adams of 4th Princess Louise's Dragoon Guards (4th Reconnaissance Regiment) which included his own regiment, a squadron of Calgaries and a company of Royal Canadians. The vanguard having run into the German defensive screen, the full power of the mobile force was called upon to clear Motta and a combined infantry and tank attack began at 4.00pm. But little artillery support was available since, other than 10 Battery, the field gunners had been delayed in traffic congestion between Foggia and Lucera.

The attack on Motta was led by A and B Squadrons, Calgaries, who pressed home their effort in the face of steady fire from 88s to fight their way into the town. But the infantry were unable to follow as machine-gun fire swept the slopes. Neroutsos therefore ordered his tanks back to a less dangerous position while Lieutenant Colonel D.C. Spry of the Royal Canadians prepared for a night assault. The first phase of that attack was complete by 9.00pm when C and D Companies secured some level ground north of the road and midway up the ridge. A Company sent a patrol into Motta which reported the edge of the town to be clear of enemy. However, when the remainder of the company followed, German machine guns opened up on them and a sharp firefight ensued. Spry decided to bring his men back down the slope and bombard the town before making a second infantry attack. With the remaining batteries of 2nd Field Regiment now arrived, all twenty-four 25-pounders fired a concentration into the town just before 3.00am. This storm of fire was followed by A and B Companies advancing through a heavy thunderstorm and, although there was some fire from the enemy, the far end of Motta was secured by first light. The German defenders were withdrawing westward along Highway 17 and the battle for Motta Montecorvino was over.[50]

As with Termoli this was not one of the major battles of the Italian campaign but it was important since it illustrated the tactics the Germans would use to such devastating effect in the weeks and months ahead. In succinct terms the British official historian describes these, and their effects, as 'the savage defence of a feature and then sudden withdrawal, delaying and vexing because on each occasion the attacker had to deploy most, or all, of his force'.[51] Such tactics were faced by the Canadians as they battled their way along the axis of Highway 17: small German forces fought ferociously on hilltops and in mountain villages such as Volturara, two miles on from the Sambuco ridge, where two nights' fighting cost Royal Canadian and Calgary Regiments some sixty-five casualties, while the Hastings and Prince Edward Regiment suffered thirteen. Although 48th Highlanders took Volturara against minimal opposition, heavy mortar and machine-gun fire from either side of the Catola valley, through which Highway 17 continued its westward meander, prevented movement along the main road. The Highlanders' A Company then forded the Catola river and cleared the south bank after a brisk encounter only to find that the main source of enemy fire came from San Marco, a village on a high ridge three miles north-west of Volturara, about a mile and a half from Highway 17; but no road linked the highway with San Marco.[52]

To clear San Marco, Brigadier Graham deployed the Royal Canadians while a company of 48th Highlanders moved to secure a road junction two miles north of the village. Another company of Highlanders was to create a diversion by making another crossing of the Catola while most of the divisional artillery, plus 66th Medium Regiment, supported the main attack. The operation was successful. C Company of the Highlanders and a troop of Calgary tanks attacked the road junction at 3.00pm on 4 October, wresting it from the enemy in a skirmish that left seven Canadians dead and three wounded; about sixty Germans were killed, wounded or captured. Spry's Royal Canadians moved against San Marco ridge but without their planned artillery support, due to problems in coordination, and his leading companies were pinned down by machine-gun fire. This deadlock was broken when Spry brought his dismounted carrier platoon forward with all its Bren guns, but the enemy still held the ridge as darkness fell. Although his own men were in close contact, Spry decided to call down concentrated fire by 2nd Field Regiment, which made the Germans believe that another attack was imminent. They considered this an appropriate time to leave San Marco and the Royal Canadians were able to occupy the village, descending to Highway 17 in the morning to march westward to the high ground dominating the Fortore crossing.[53]

And thus the Canadians continued on their bloody way to Vinchiaturo. Their main opposition had come at first from *Kampfgruppe* Heilmann, which included 3rd Parachute Regiment with a battalion of 1/67th Panzer Grenadier Regiment, later replaced by a battalion from 2/67th Panzer Grenadiers. As the advance continued both 4th Parachute Regiment and part of 29th Panzer Grenadier Division became involved in the delaying actions. Whatever the composition of the opposing forces one fact remained constant: the Germans would not yield ground easily. Behind the defensive screen 26th Panzer and 29th Panzer Grenadier Divisions, under pressure from Fifth Army, were pulling back across the axis of the Canadian advance, thus ensuring even greater tenacity from the Germans, as well as the advantage of additional soldiers as indicated by the appearance of men from 29th Panzer Grenadiers.[54] Such was the quality of the German defences that Montgomery signalled to Alexander on 5 October asking for assistance from Fifth Army.

Canadian threat against Campobasso and Vinchiaturo meeting stiff opposition. Suggest American diversion at Benevento be ordered to operate energetically northwards to Vinchiaturo as such a thrust would force the enemy to give ground in front of Canadians.[55]

But Mark Clark, Fifth Army's commander, was preoccupied with plans for an attack across the Volturno river a week later. All that he could do to help Montgomery was some patrol action. The Canadians were left to their own devices.

In spite of all the difficulties facing them, the Canadians succeeded and Campobasso was taken on 13/14 October with relative ease. The Germans had developed a respect for the Canadians as indicated by an entry in the war diary of 26th Panzer Division: 'Opposite the 29th Panzer Grenadier Division the First Canadian Infantry Division had appeared again, which explains the rapid advance of the enemy.'[56] This was praise indeed. Three days after Campobasso fell, Vinchiaturo was taken by a company of Seaforth Highlanders of Canada, supported by Saskatoon Light Infantry machine guns and mortars and a battery from 165th Field Regiment. However, it soon became clear that German reinforcements were arriving and, with a counter-attack in considerable strength likely, the Seaforth were withdrawn about 1,000 yards eastward to a hill. On the 18th another attack was launched, supported by a squadron from the Ontario Regiment who had relieved the Calgaries and were seeing their first action in Italy. During the afternoon the Germans withdrew from Vinchiaturo leaving thirty-five dead or captured; Seaforth losses over the two days were four dead and eleven wounded.[57]

While the Canadians fought their way into the mountains, Montgomery was adjusting Eighth Army's dispositions 'to maintain offensive strength and ensure efficient administration on his widening front'. The Adriatic sector, from the coast to Larino, was handed over to V Corps on 11 October and 5th Division was inserted to the Canadian right to strengthen XIII Corps which became responsible for the sector from Larino to the Matese mountains. V Corps now included 78th Division, 8th Indian Division, 4 Armoured Brigade and 1st Army Group Royal Artillery (AGRA), while XIII Corps included the Canadians, 5th Division and 6th AGRA.[58]

Meanwhile the Germans continued building their defensive line across Italy. Kesselring's engineers, under General Bessel, had been busy with concrete and steel to strengthen the natural barrier already identified.

It was to follow the general line Garigliano–Mignano–course of the Volturno–Maiella massif–Sangro, being strongest below the Cassino valley, in the Garigliano, at the southern spurs of the Maiella range and on the Adriatic plain. It was not to be a single line but a system of

27

positions organized in depth which would allow possible enemy penetrations to be sealed off.[59]

This was the Gustav Line. Coinciding with part of it was the Bernhardt Line, which used the Garigliano valley, forward of Gaeta on the western flank, included the formidable Monte Camino then, via Mignano and Venafro, carried on to link with the Gustav Line near Alfredena in the Maiella mountains.[60]

After the Termoli clash 78th Division paused to reorganize, with the Irish Brigade holding San Giacomo ridge and along the Simarca. Replenishment of ammunition, fuel, equipment and other stores took place as the division waited for its next bound forward. There were still some small-scale operations: the Royal West Kents took Montecilfone, following some hard fighting by A Squadron 56 Recce, and the Recce also took Montenero. The Irish Brigade, patrolling actively forward, quickly dominated the area up to Petacciato. Brigadier Russell considered that his brigade should take Petacciato ridge so that the division might have a better idea of the next major river, the Trigno. Russell put this idea to Evelegh who approved, on condition that only one battalion deployed. The task was assigned to the London Irish for an attack on the night of 19/20 October, with support from a squadron of 44th Royal Tank Regiment and fire from 17th Field Regiment.[61]

After a five-mile approach march, the attack was made on a two-company front with the tank squadron in support and the Faughs' battle patrol on the right flank to ensure that a German machine-gun post did not harass the attackers. So swift was the Rifles' advance that F Company's leading platoon was in Petacciato five minutes after the artillery bombardment had ceased. Most defenders were still in cover or just emerging, including the crews of several 75mm guns. G Company entered the village at the far end and F's other platoons, although delayed by enfilading machine-gun fire, were there before dawn, having been joined by E Company. By daybreak Petacciato was in the Rifles' hands with the battalion having suffered no casualties. The Germans had lost some dead and nineteen prisoners were taken as well as much equipment. Divisional HQ then approved the move of the Irish Fusiliers on to Petacciato ridge to the left of the village; the Inniskillings remained at San Giacomo. Petacciato ridge would provide the jumping-off point for the next advance, to the Trigno. This, too, would be carried out by the Irish Brigade.[62]

The line of the Trigno was covered by positions manned by 16th Panzer Division, now much weakened* and soon to come under new command, with elements from 26th Panzer and 1st Parachute Divisions. It was not a

---

* Its fighting strength on 4 November was 4,598 men with 6 MkIV tanks, 5 command tanks and 9 assault, or self-propelled, guns.[63]

line the Germans intended to hold but they would use it to delay Eighth Army's advance. However, Montgomery was showing typical reluctance to move forward unless assured that his base was firm and supply lines intact. Even though additional port facilities had become available, the development of the supply and administration sinews of the Army had not matched the pace of operational planning, and so Montgomery noted that 'major operations awaited the administrative adjustments which were being made in the rear areas'. He also commented that this 'was now to have serious consequences'. In fact, every effort was being made to ensure that supply lines were working to best effect and that full allocations of ammunition, fuel and equipment were ready for the fighting troops. Additional vehicles were arriving to bring divisions up to full transport scales, most having had to make do with light scales thus far.[64]

Montgomery was not ready to move again in strength until 21 October although there had been some operations, as we have noted, that had cleared the area to the Trigno for V Corps. By Trafalgar Day, however, Montgomery was ready to renew the offensive and preparations began to cross the Trigno. A patrol of London Irish, under Major Desmond Woods MC, discovered an intact bridge and brought this information back to 78th Division. The assault on the Trigno was assigned to 1st Royal Irish Fusiliers but, as the Faughs approached the bridge in the early hours of 23 October, they were deafened by a mighty explosion and, in the day's early light, saw that a gap of about 200 feet had been blown in it. They would have to get their feet wet.[65]

Undeterred by the prospect of wet feet, the Faughs waded across the ankle-deep water. Other than some shellfire and mines, there was little sign of the enemy. Closer to the coast 2nd Lancashire Fusiliers also waded across to establish a second bridgehead, from which they probed towards San Salvo but returned to the bridgehead following clashes with German troops. San Salvo was to be 78th Division's next objective with the task, planned for the night of 27/28 October, assigned to the Irish. Torrential rain prompted Brigadier Russell to seek a postponement but this was refused and the attack went ahead, led by the Irish Fusiliers and London Irish. Advancing over sodden ground the infantry found that several enemy machine-gun posts had been overshot by the artillery and these caused many casualties. There was also intense mortar and shellfire. Soon the Faughs were pinned down with both leading company commanders and every platoon commander in one company dead. As their commanding officer, Beauchamp Butler, rallied his soldiers to renew the advance he, too, was killed, hit in the head by a machine-gun bullet. The London Irish had also stalled and taken heavy casualties with one platoon all but wiped out. A withdrawal to the bridgehead was ordered.[66]

A new plan was cast with 36 Brigade, to which was added 6th Inniskillings, supported by tanks of 46th Royal Tanks, of 23 Armoured

Brigade, and an artillery programme including not only the divisional artillery but three additional field regiments and three medium regiments. D-Day was set for 3 November with 36 Brigade directed on San Salvo and the Buonanotte canal north of the town. On the coast, some four miles distant, 11 Brigade would attack San Salvo railway station. The Royal Navy was to contribute two destroyers and some light craft to simulate a landing while bombarding Vasto and other targets. This was intended to engage coastal defence guns and distract 3/2nd Panzer Regiment from the main effort. Further diversion was provided by six Bofors guns of 49th Light Anti-Aircraft (LAA) Regiment and the Kensingtons. To the left of the real attack, the Bofors would fire tracer on fixed lines while the Kensingtons would create much noise with mortars and machine guns, thereby making the Germans believe that an attack was coming from that sector.[67]

Such diligent planning deserved to be successful and so it proved. The attack by 36 Brigade, led by 5th Buffs and 6th Inniskillings with two tank squadrons, struck at the junction of two German battalions. Allied aircraft strafed enemy positions and, with German communications disrupted, San Salvo and the Buonanotte canal were in 36 Brigade's hands by noon. At the railway station 11 Brigade met tough opposition and then a counter-attack that was beaten back by artillery and 46th Royal Tanks. By last light the Germans, abandoning their positions, were drawing back towards Vasto. But this was to be a fighting retreat since the German commander wished to keep Eighth Army from Vasto as long as possible. A rearguard group stopped the West Kents' advance beyond San Salvo but the Argylls then forced that group to withdraw after a very confused encounter. By first light on 4 November it was obvious that the Germans were in retreat and Evelegh ordered his division to follow them up. Thus, by 9 November, the Battleaxe Division was deployed along the Sangro from Paglieta to Monte Calvo. To the left of 78th Division, V Corps' front was extended by 8th Indian Division, which had 19 Brigade south-west of Atessa, 17 Brigade, which had moved up on 78th's left flank, at Gissi and 21 Brigade covering the left flank between Castiglione and Torrebruna.[68]

Eighth Indian Division had been deployed about ten miles upstream on the Trigno, on 78th's left flank as the latter prepared for its renewed attack on San Salvo. On the night of 1/2 November the Indians crossed the Trigno under an umbrella of fire provided by their own divisional artillery, an additional field regiment and a medium regiment. The divisional objective was to cut the lateral road from Vasto to Isernia, and 19 Brigade struck for the hills at Tufillo and Monte Farano while 21 Brigade made for Celenza and Torrebruna. Tufillo was held by 3rd Parachute Regiment whose soldiers were not prepared to yield any ground as 19 Brigade attacked their positions on the 2nd. The day ended in stalemate following several attempts by the Frontier Force Rifles to get into Tufillo via a wooded spur, and three counter-attacks by the defenders. To the left 5th Essex were also stalled.[69]

Brigadier Dobree, commanding 19 Brigade, sent 3/8th Punjabis to support the Frontier Force Rifles in the small hours of the next morning. The Punjabis suffered from fierce mortar fire and Dobree then opted for a night attack on 3/4 November which led to a series of vicious small-scale battles. Still the Germans held fast. As Indian pressure continued the paras began thinning out, following their corps commander's orders, and 19 Brigade was able to occupy Monte Farano and Tufillo on the 5th. In stark contrast to their comrades' experience, 21 Brigade met no serious opposition on the advance to Celenza.[70]

While 78th and 8th Indian Divisions had been pushing forward, XIII Corps had been involved in diversionary operations, having been ordered by Montgomery to draw German attention inland as V Corps prepared for operations on the right flank. XIII Corps was to perform this diversionary task by attacking on the axis Vinchiaturo–Isernia. Weather conditions and demolitions slowed the operations of both 1st Canadian and 5th British Divisions but, by 24 October, the Canadian 2 Brigade had cleared Colle d'Anchise and Boiano, while 1 Brigade went on to clear the high ground twixt Molise and Torella. This had been achieved by the 27th before, next day, 5th Division passed through 2 Brigade en route to Isernia. Montgomery wanted Isernia to deprive Tenth German Army of a principal front-line communications centre; its possession would also open the way to Eighth and Fifth Army troops linking up once the latter had cleared the Volturno valley.[71]

Yet again the Canadians faced tough opposition with the Loyal Edmontons* attacking Colle d'Anchise on the 23rd. Their assault had eschewed the obvious approach in favour of scaling a 700-foot escarpment to their objective. Heavy fog helped mask their approach and the battalion ignored enemy fire so as to gain surprise.

By daybreak A Company had reached the top of Point 681, an eminence at the eastern end of the single straggling street which is Colle d'Anchise. Caught unawares, the garrison – members of the 1st Battalion, 67th Panzer Grenadier Regiment – tumbled out of their billets to engage the attackers in bitter hand-to-hand fighting. Soon all the Edmonton rifle companies were involved in the struggle, which continued throughout the morning without producing a definite decision. At one point an NCO, Sgt R.B. Whiteside, of A Company,

---

* Less than two weeks earlier, the Edmonton Regiment received royal authority to adopt the prefix 'Loyal'; it was affiliated to the Loyal Regiment (North Lancashire), known as the Loyals.[72]

31

single-handed and armed only with a rifle, successfully engaged two German machine-gun posts, inflicting an estimated eleven casualties. He was awarded the DCM.[73]

That German soldiers taken so off guard could rally in such fashion was an indicator of the professionalism of the German army. That Canadian citizen soldiers could take the fight to them as they had, and continue in such robust manner, was an indicator of the determination of the Allied armies. And the Edmontons were fighting without armoured support as the tanks of A Squadron of the Ontarios had met considerable problems getting forward, by the obvious route, and had no radio contact with the infantry. In mid-morning seven Ontario tanks were ambushed about 800 yards south of the village by German tanks. Three Shermans were knocked out while the remainder either threw tracks or bogged down. German tanks and infantry reinforcements now pressed on the Edmontons, whose D Company was pushed out of the western end of the village. The Canadians had nothing but PIATs with which to engage the tanks but ammunition for those was soon in short supply as a mule column could not reach the village. Although the Germans reported retaking three-quarters of the village, they then began to withdraw in accordance with LXXVI Panzer Corps' plan to pull back from the Colle d'Anchise–Spinete area. During the night the Germans melted away to the Lüttwitz position, the Cantalupo–Torella lateral, allowing the Edmontons to consolidate. The battalion had suffered thirty casualties but German losses exceeded a hundred.[74] The struggle for Colle d'Anchise had emphasized the need for better infantry/armour cooperation which was to lead to new training methods that would show dividends in the battles of 1944.

To the Edmontons' right, Princess Patricia's Canadian Light Infantry attacked Spinete with support from South African Air Force light bombers and artillery. Unlike the Edmontons, the Patricias met little resistance, the Germans having begun to quit Spinete and, in the early evening, the battalion entered the village without a single casualty.[75]

The way was now open for 1 Brigade to strike against 29th Panzer Grenadier Division on the Torella–Molise feature but the brigade had first to secure two villages – Castropignano and Roccaspromonte – which stand about a mile apart 'on the edge of the almost sheer rampart which formed the left bank of the Biferno opposite Oratino'. Plans were made for what looked to be a very difficult operation involving 48th Highlanders, Royal Canadians and the Hastings and Prince Edwards. But, once again, the Germans chose not to stand at Roccaspromonte, into which A Company, Royal Canadians were guided by Italian civilians while B Company entered Castropignano where a single machine gun was the only opposition. But the Canadians could not expect this experience to be repeated at every obstacle: the Torella road was critical to 29th Panzer Grenadier Division, being its main axis of withdrawal, while Highway 17 through Isernia fulfilled a similar function for 26th Panzer. Until these two formations were safely away, rearguards could be expected to provide doughty resistance.[76]

Point 761 provided the first example of such resistance. A German position there overlooked the junction with Highway 17 of the road from Spinete and Roccaspromonte and it was there that C Company, Royal Canadians met their first serious resistance. As the Canadians ascended the slopes, German troops fired parachute flares by the light of which machine gunners opened fire. The company commander was killed and the company forced to withdraw. Artillery fire was then brought to bear on Point 761 which was finally reported clear at noon the following day. This allowed the attack on Torella to proceed and, on the morning of the 25th, forty-seven Allied aircraft bombed the village in advance of 48th Highlanders advancing from Point 761. When that advance was brought to a halt by mortar and heavy shellfire Brigadier Graham decided to deploy tanks across the treeless ground between his men and their objective. With great difficulty some tanks crossed the Biferno that afternoon, carrying dismantled guns and gun detachments of a battery of airlanding light artillery to give the Highlanders close support.

The advance resumed early on the 26th with the tanks supporting the infantry. Enemy fire was intense and the Germans did not appear intimidated by the Shermans; the Canadian historian noted that they 'provoked a considerable increase in the fire sweeping the bare ridges in front of Torella'. Progress remained slow and not until dusk could the Highlanders close on their objectives, following a pounding of the enemy positions by all seventy-two guns of the divisional artillery. Some twenty or more casualties had been suffered by the Highlanders but no more were to be sustained since, yet again, the enemy melted away: 29th Panzer Grenadier Division's commander had ordered a withdrawal that evening and Canadian patrols found Torella clear next morning.[77]

By the 28th the Canadians had advanced 28 miles in three weeks and now formed a firm base for the next phase of XIII Corps' advance as the first elements of 5th Division passed through 2 Canadian Brigade en route to Isernia. On 30 October two battalions of 13 Brigade, 2nd Inniskillings and 2nd Wiltshires, attacked objectives some 5 miles beyond Boiano; the Scottish Rifles then moved up to cover the rear of the other battalions.

A base was now secure for the capture of the important communications centre of Isernia, once an old walled Samnite city commanding a pass into the basin of the Apennines. This was designed to create the general impression that the main effort was going to be inland on the left of V Corps.[78]

On the night of 29/30 October the attack began with 13 Brigade's leading battalions moving off in pouring rain to trudge over steep, wooded slopes towards San Massimo and Cantalupo, both of which were taken on the 30th. Next day a patrol set out for Roccamondolfi, a village perched on a mountaintop, and fought their way into it against spirited opposition. With the patrol was the brigade gunner OP party from 91st Field Regiment and machine gunners of B Company, 7th Cheshires. As 5th Division pushed forward, and upwards, it was supported by nearly a hundred guns of XIII Corps which pounded 26th Panzer Division's positions. When a German despatch rider was captured near Cantalupo by the Wiltshires on 1 November, one of his captors referred to him as 'one of those bastards that bombed Coventry'. He was surprised to hear the German riposte, in flawless English, 'I happen to live in Hamburg.'[79]

Also advancing was 17 Brigade who found the enemy equally tenacious in defence of rocky outcrops. Whenever one of these was captured the German artillery would turn its attention on it and, with the ground precluding digging in, the soldiers built sangars as some of the 'old sweats' had done on India's North-West Frontier. Macchiagodena was taken by 2nd Northamptons on 31 October, with 6th Seaforth taking more ground to the north. The Seaforth fought their way into Castelpetroso on 1 November but were then driven off Point 1146 by heavy mortar fire. On the 2nd the divisional artillery fired a concentration on the area and 2nd Royal Scots Fusiliers took Point 1146 and the Northamptons Point 1385. Neither unit suffered heavily as, once again, the Germans had slipped away. Patrols from 5th Division then made their way towards the road junctions around Isernia.[80] Of this period the divisional historian wrote:

During this hilltop fighting the magnificently energetic and enter-prising patrolling of all battalions brought back some very valuable information; this was handsomely acknowledged by Div HQ. The going could not have been worse, nor indeed the weather. Main-tenance of companies on these rocky outposts had to be almost entirely by mules, which suffered heavy casualties from shellfire and mortaring. Wireless was the only possible form of communication and it worked well despite the difficulties of battery maintenance. This mule maintenance had to continue until 13 Inf Bde had cleared a passable road at a lower level.[81]

Since Isernia was the last key town held by the Germans in southern Italy, it was seen as a special prize by the Allies. Both leading brigades of 5th Division vied to be first into the town, as did the Americans of Fifth Army. With the mountains in front of the town now in British hands, Isernia was untenable and 13 Brigade planned an attack by the Wiltshires to deal with any Germans who might still be there. But, during the night of 4/5 November, the Wiltshires were upstaged. The Inniskillings had infiltrated the enemy outposts before Isernia and reckoned that they could also take the town. Their commanding officer, Lieutenant Colonel Joseph O'Brien-Twohig, organized a special night patrol that included a pioneer armed with a pot of paint, a stencil and a brush. Under Lieutenant Long, this patrol found Isernia deserted by the Germans and the pioneer set to work. His stencil was of the castle of Inniskilling, the battalion badge, which he painted on every available surface. At dawn a Wiltshire patrol arrived to find that they were not the first into Isernia. Then, at 8 o'clock, an American patrol from Fifth Army, confident that they were ahead of everyone, entered the town, to be greeted by laughing Inniskillings and other troops of 13 Brigade.[82]

Both Inniskillings and Wiltshires patrolled actively from Isernia. They also liaised with American patrols to their left and when an Inniskillings' patrol forced the Germans out of Vincenzo village the latter were driven into the not-so-welcoming arms of a Fifth Army patrol approaching from the other side. The Inniskillings also amazed the Americans by placing outside their battalion HQ a full-length mirror emblazoned with the legend 'Do you look like a victorious British soldier now?' Good for morale, the mirror became something of a legend in 5th Division and farther afield.[83]

For the time being, Isernia was to be the limit of 5th Division's advance since there had been so many and such severe demolitions in and around the town that the divisional sappers were employed fully.

Theirs had been a superhuman task so far and they were not then to know that this was to be their last big effort on the central axis – the bridging of the River Vandra under the able leadership of Lieut-Colonel K.H. Osborne, the Commander of the Divisional Royal Engineers well to the fore as usual. Since landing in Italy the Sappers had undertaken a full and successful programme which included the development of beaches, many road diversions, two dozen odd Bailey bridges erected, repair of railway bridges, lifted thousands of mines, most of this in appalling weather conditions and some of it under fire.[84]

Elsewhere, 17 Brigade had moved up through the mountains on the divisional right flank until relieved by 15 Brigade who moved to Pesche by lorry but, because of demolitions, had to take to their feet as they made for Rionero, a village overlooking the upper Sangro. Germans from the newly-arrived 305th Division were pushed out of Forli on 9 November but retained positions on Monte Greco, dominating the Barrea–Castèl di Sangro road. In appalling weather conditions, operations continued in XIII Corps' area but Eighth Army's main efforts were focussed on the right flank and V Corps.[85]

On that right flank Eighth Army was about to assault the winter, or Bernhardt, line, about which soldiers had heard so much, often from prisoners. The British Chiefs of Staff still believed that Rome could be taken by Christmas without an amphibious operation but that, if such an operation proved necessary, Italy's capital might not fall until January. This attitude prompted the official historian to comment that 'It seems doubtful whether anyone in high places fully understood what a winter campaign in Italy implied.'[86]

Notes

1. Montgomery, *Memoirs*, op. cit., p. 196.
2. Molony, *The Mediterranean and Middle East*, vol. V, op. cit., pp. 246–52 for details of Eighth Army's administration; Nicholson, *The Canadians in Italy*, op. cit., pp. 224–9.
3. Aris, *The Fifth British Division 1939-1945*, op. cit., p. 153; Molony, op. cit., pp. 344–5; Doherty, *Only The Enemy in Front (OTE)*, op. cit., p. 76.
4. Doherty, op. cit., p. 76.
5. Ibid., pp. 76–7.
6. Montgomery, op. cit., p. 199.
7. Graham and Bidwell, *Tug of War*, op. cit., p. 104; Molony, op. cit., pp. 377–8.
8. Graham and Bidwell, op. cit., p. 104; Kesselring, *Memoirs*, p. 187. Kesselring attributes the decision to himself rather than Hitler.
9. Molony, op. cit., p. 346.
10. Nicholson, op. cit., p. 687.
11. Molony, op. cit., p. 380.
12. Ibid.
13. Montgomery, *El Alamein to the Sangro*, p. 169.
14. NA, Kew, WO169/8520, war diary Eighth Army HQ GS I, Sep–Dec 1943.
15. NA, Kew, CAB106/409, p. 36.
16. Molony, op. cit., p. 434.
17. *Engineers in the Italian Campaign*, p. 13.
18. Doherty, op. cit., p. 77; Commonwealth War Graves Commission (CWGC) Debt of Honour Register www.cwgc.org
19. NA, Kew, WO169/8836, war diary 56 Recce, Jul–Dec 1943.
20. Ibid.; Doherty, op. cit., pp. 77–8.
21. NA, Kew, WO169/8520, op. cit.
22. Vietinghoff, quoted in NA, Kew, CAB44/133, Cabinet Office war histories draft chapters, Section IV, Chapter M: 'Advance to Termoli and the advance to the line of the river Volturno, 17 Sep – 11 Oct 1943', by Major F. Jones, p. 185.
23. NA, Kew, WO169/8881, war diary 11 Bde, Jul–Dec 1943 (Bde Narrative: The Battle of Termoli); WO169/8928, war diary 36 Bde, Jul–Dec 1943; WO169/8836, war diary 56 Recce, Jul–Dec 1943; Ray, *Algiers to Austria*, pp. 86–7; Ford, *Battleaxe Division*, pp. 85–92; Doherty, op. cit., pp. 78–9.
24. Kesselring, op. cit., p. 188.

25. Molony, op. cit., p. 435.
26. NA, Kew, WO169/10174, war diary 8 A & SH, 1943; Ford, op. cit., pp. 93–4; Ray, op. cit., pp. 88– 9.
27. McKenzie, *CO 2LF 78 Division*, quoted in Ford, op. cit., p. 90; NA, Kew, WO169/10242, war diary 6 RWK, Jul–Dec 1943; WO169/10251, war diary, 2 Lancs Fus, Jul–Dec 1943.
28. Ray, op. cit., pp. 89–91; Ford, op. cit., p. 92.
29. Ray, op. cit., p. 88.
30. NA, Kew, WO169/8836, war diary 11 Bde, op. cit.; Chavasse, 'Some Memories', pp. 74–5; Molony, op. cit., p. 435.
31. Molony, op. cit., pp. 435–6; NA, Kew, WO169/8836, war diary 11 Bde, op. cit.
32. NA, Kew, WO169/8836, war diary 11 Bde, op. cit.; Ray, op. cit., pp. 88–9; Doherty, *A Noble Crusade*, pp. 164–5.
33. www.cwgc.org op. cit. Alfred Ives was from Armagh in Northern Ireland and had previously served in the Royal Ulster Rifles.
34. Ray, op. cit., p. 89; Ford, op. cit., pp. 94–5; NA, Kew, WO169/10242, war diary 6 RWK, op. cit.
35. Chavasse, op. cit., pp. 74–5.
36. Russell, *Account of the Service of the Irish Brigade*; NA, Kew, WO169/8929, war diary 38 (Irish) Bde, Jul–Dec 1943 (Appx. No. 3: The part played by the Irish Bde in the Battle at Termoli).
37. Russell, op. cit.
38. Ibid.
39. Linklater, *The Campaign in Italy*, p. 99.
40. Russell, op. cit.
41. Molony, op. cit., p. 436, provides figures for sorties flown.
42. Russell, op. cit.
43. Ibid.; Bredin, interview with author, 1989.
44. Kesselring, op. cit., p. 188.
45. Nicholson, op. cit., p. 255.
46. Squire and Hill, *The Surreys in Italy*, pp. 14–15.
47. Ray, op. cit., pp. 91–2; Squire and Hill, op. cit., p. 15.
48. Nicholson, op. cit., p. 235; Molony, op. cit., pp. 436–7.
49. Nicholson, op. cit., pp. 236–7.
50. Ibid., pp. 235–8.
51. Molony, op. cit., p. 437.
52. Nicholson, op. cit., pp. 238–9.
53. Ibid., p. 239.
54. Ibid., pp. 240–1.
55. Quoted in ibid, p. 241.
56. Nicholson, op. cit., p. 247.
57. Ibid., pp. 256–7.
58. Molony, op. cit., p. 454.
59. NA, Kew, CAB44/135, Cabinet Office war histories draft chapters, Section IV, Chapter N: 'Italy operations winter 1943-1944; part I, introduction and summary', by Major F. Jones, p. 1.
60. Doherty, *Clear The Way! (CTW)*, pp. 96–7.
61. NA, Kew, WO169/8826, war diary 78th Division GS, Jul–Dec 1943; Ray, op. cit., p. 94; Russell, op. cit.
62. Russell, op. cit.; Doherty, *CTW*, op. cit., p. 91; NA, Kew, WO169 8929, war diary, 38 (Ir) Bde, op. cit.; WO169/8861, war diary, 4 Armd Bde, Jul–Dec 1943.

63. Molony, op. cit., p. 457n.
64. Montgomery, *El Alamein to the River Sangro*, op. cit., p. 171; Molony, op. cit., pp. 424–7.
65. Woods, 'A personal account of his service with 2nd London Irish Rifles in Italy'; Doherty, *CTW*, op. cit., pp. 92–3; NA, Kew, WO169/8929, war diary, 38 (Irish) Bde, op. cit.
66. Doherty, *CTW*, op. cit., pp. 93–4; WO169/10235, war diary, 1 RIrF, Jul–Dec 1943.
67. Doherty, *CTW*, op. cit., p. 96; *A Noble Crusade*, pp. 167–8; Ray, op. cit., pp. 95–7; NA, Kew, WO169/8927, war diary, 36 Bde, Jul–Dec 1943.
68. NA, Kew, WO169/8881, war diary, 11 Bde, op. cit.; WO169/8906, war diary, 23 Armd Bde, Jul–Dec 1943; WO169/8927, war diary, 36 Bde, op. cit.; WO169/10234, war diary, 6 Innisks, Jul–Dec 1943; WO169/10186, war diary, 5 Buffs, Jul–Dec 1943.
69. Molony, op. cit., pp. 458–9; NA, Kew, WO169/10209, war diary, 5 Essex, Jul–Dec 1943.
70. Molony, op. cit., pp. 459–60.
71. Ibid., p. 458; Nicholson, op. cit., pp. 258–62; Aris, *The Fifth British Division*, p. 157.
72. Nicholson, op. cit., p. 246n.
73. Ibid., pp. 259–60.
74. Ibid., p. 260.
75. Ibid., p. 261.
76. Ibid., pp. 261–2.
77. Ibid., p. 262.
78. Aris, op. cit., p. 157.
79. Ibid., pp. 157–8.
80. Ibid., p. 158.
81. Aris, p. 159.
82. Ibid.; Fox, *The Royal Inniskilling Fusiliers in the Second World War*, p. 87.
83. Aris, p. 159.
84. Ibid, p. 160.
85. Ibid.
86. Molony, op. cit., p. 473.

Chapter Three

Mountains and Floods

Let each man do his best.

Alexander had devised a three-phase strategy with Eighth Army opening army group operations. At first Eighth Army would get astride the Pescara–Pópoli road – Highway 5, the Via Valeria of Roman times – before advancing through Avezzano, thereby threatening the lines of communication of the German formations facing Fifth Army. Phase Two would see Fifth Army attack through the Liri and Sacco valleys to Frosinone, the best route for an armoured advance to Rome. Then a seaborne landing would be made south of Rome, directed on the Alban Hills. Alexander's strategy was dictated by the state of Fifth Army, now exhausted and facing mountainous, muddy country and a foe that matched it division for division. The combined strength of both Allied armies was needed to drive the enemy from his positions. By striking first and threatening enemy lines of communication, Eighth Army would assist Fifth Army's attack and give its commander time to reorganize.[1]

The German defences facing Eighth Army were about nine miles in depth. East of Italy's spine was the Bernhardt Line with, north-west of the Sangro, the advanced Sangro Line, through which Eighth Army would have to punch to reach the Pescara–Pópoli road in the Pescara valley. To that road from the Sangro the crow need fly only 22 miles. But soldiers can seldom take the same route as their avian friends and especially not with German soldiers in their way. Conditions along the way were already bad: with winter setting in, low ground was either flooded or muddy, while the higher ground was receiving its first layer of snow. Roads and tracks had suffered from the weather and would suffer even more from Kesselring's engineers if the defenders were forced to withdraw. And those defenders were now in strong, well-sited positions, determined to make Eighth Army pay for every piece of ground in the coin of warfare: soldiers' blood.[2]

The Allies had already pierced the Viktor Line (from the Volturno estuary to Termoli), the Barbara Line (from Mondragone in the west to the vicinity of San Salvo) and Eighth Army now faced the advanced Sangro

Line. Many enemy prisoners had boasted that the Allied armies would be smashed on the Winter Line. As if the existence of that line was not enough the Germans were forming an additional army, Fourteenth, in northern Italy under General Eberhard von Mackensen, to come into being on 21 November.[3] Faced with the known quality of enemy positions, Montgomery was concerned about Eighth Army's overall strength since many formations remained in Africa. Reaching the Pescara–Pópoli road was not going to be possible with four infantry divisions; Montgomery considered that he needed at least one more. Furthermore '[m]y troops were getting very tired and my formations had suffered considerable casualties since the landings at Reggio. In particular the officer situation in the infantry had become acute.'[4] Some reinforcements arrived as Eighth Army prepared to assault the Sangro defences. General Sir Bernard Freyberg's 2nd New Zealand Division had begun landing in Italy during October and was now ready to resume its place in the line of battle. The division had been restructured to deploy an integral armoured brigade, 4 New Zealand Armoured Brigade, with two infantry brigades. This order of battle had been adopted by Freyberg to ensure that his division would always have its own armour. Following heavy losses in July 1942, the original 4 Brigade had been taken out of the line and the division reinforced as necessary by brigades from other formations. It had also had 9 Armoured Brigade under command during Operations LIGHTFOOT and SUPERCHARGE, the final El Alamein battles. However, as Eighth Army prepared to attack along the Sangro, the New Zealand Division was reinforced by 19 Brigade from 8th Indian Division, providing it with three infantry and one armoured brigades.[5]

For the Sangro operation, Eighth Army deployed 690 guns, the majority from twenty-two field regiments, each with twenty-four 25-pounders, and the balance from seven medium regiments. In 4 Armoured Brigade and the Three Rivers Regiment, Montgomery could also deploy 186 Shermans with another thirty-seven tanks in workshops under repair or maintenance;[6] the tanks of 4 NZ Armoured Brigade would reinforce that number.* In the initial phase, Montgomery hoped to convince the Germans that his main effort would come from XIII Corps and be directed towards Avezzano. However, V Corps would be making the real effort before which a jumping-off line on the north bank of the Sangro would be seized. The deception plan required XIII Corps to advance towards the upper Sangro before V Corps' attack began. In addition, XIII Corps was to make:

---

* At this time an armoured brigade deployed the same number of tanks as an armoured division, about 160, as the latter included one armoured brigade and an infantry brigade. However, the armoured brigade lacked the substantial element of other arms, such as artillery and engineers, that were integral to a division.[7]

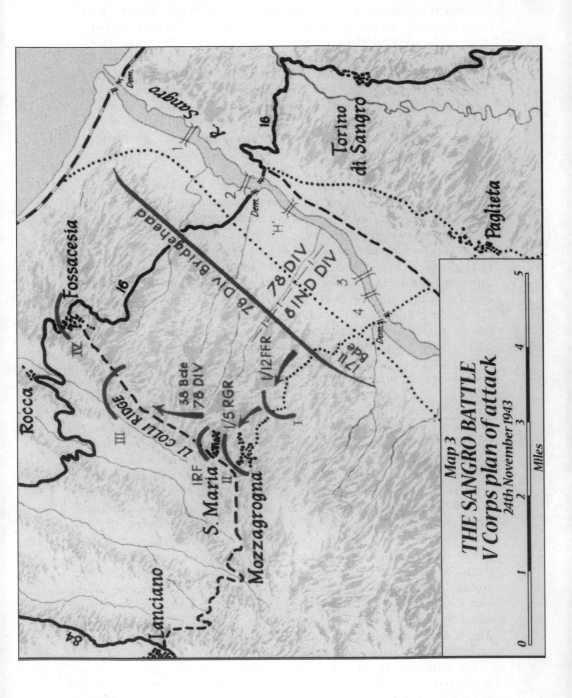

Map 3
THE SANGRO BATTLE
V Corps plan of attack
24th November 1943

Miles
0 1 2 3 4 5

ostentatious troop movements, and to plant bogus dumps in its maintenance area to simulate far-reaching administrative support. A wireless deception scheme was contrived to make the enemy think that Army Tactical Headquarters and 8th Indian Division would arrive in [XIII Corps'] sector. Operations by 19 Indian Infantry Brigade were to screen 8th Indian Division's actual eastward side-step to Paglieta and the New Zealand Division's arrival near Scerni. Wireless silence, patrolling of unimportant ground, dummies and camouflage all played their parts. A naval demonstration towards Pescara was arranged to foment the enemy's known fears for his sea flank.[8]

Montgomery held his first planning conference on 14 November. Although he hoped that D-Day would be the night of the 19th/20th this depended on two dry days immediately beforehand. Nonetheless, XIII Corps was pushing towards Castèl di Sangro and Alfedena along the axis of Highway 17 by the 18th. The roads had suffered the very professional attentions of German engineers and, off-road, conditions were appalling, continuous rain creating thick, glutinous mud. From a base at Carovilli, 3 Canadian Brigade advanced to Capracotta and San Pietro whence patrols probed across the Sangro. On 24 November the brigade launched an attack on Castèl di Sangro but a change in Montgomery's plans led to cancellation. A similar attack, by 5th Division on Alfedena, was also abandoned after the division reached Monte Civitalta, overlooking Alfedena, and began its attack on the 22nd. In addition to its fighting responsibilities, XIII Corps had assumed another duty: the Germans had implemented a scorched-earth policy that left many civilians homeless; by the end of November, about 4,000 were seeking shelter and food with an additional 500 refugees arriving daily. Both the corps' medical and transport services were strained dealing with this humanitarian emergency.[9]

As part of the preliminaries to the main assault, 8th Indian Division, less 19 Brigade, side-stepped to Paglieta between 14 and 18 November, while the New Zealanders had their first action in Italy on the 17th when 19th Armoured Battalion and 3/8th Punjabis of 19 Indian Brigade captured Perano from elements of 64th Panzer Grenadier Regiment. On the following day, 19 Brigade took Archi and prepared to seize the high ground between the Sangro and Aventino rivers prior to a crossing by 2nd New Zealand Division. During the night of 22/23 November, the Punjabis and 1/5th Essex waded the swollen Sangro to attack San Angelo and Altino. Many casualties died of exposure as they could not be evacuated back across the Sangro for medical attention.[10]

The Battleaxe Division had also been involved in these preliminary operations as patrols from the division crossed the Sangro almost every night. With the Germans appearing most unusually quiescent, 78th Division dominated the area between the river and the escarpment on the German side. But then nature took a hand and, from the 15th, the spates on the Sangro became an ally of the Germans. 'No patrol when crossing the river knew when it would be able to return and the always deepening, greasy mud in the approaches to the river bedevilled the preparation of fords.'[11]

And so the stage was set for Eighth Army's main thrust. The weather refused to comply with Montgomery's plan, however, and rain poured down on the 16th, frustrating those engineers who had been constructing fords and their approaches along the Sangro. This work was undone as torrents of water from the mountains rushed to the Adriatic. It thus became necessary to build bridges and D-Day was set, hopefully, for 24 November, although Montgomery now revised his plan, limiting his advance to Lanciano and announcing a pause for two or three days to allow the Sangro valley to be reorganized thoroughly for movement.[12]

Four bridges were to be built, two for wheeled vehicles and tracked carriers, one to take all types of wheeled vehicles and, in an emergency, tanks, and the fourth to carry tanks. Two bridges, No. 1 and H, the tank bridge, were completed during the night of 21/22 November, but work on No. 3 was delayed because traffic congestion held up vehicles carrying bridging equipment. Then the weather intervened again with heavy rain in the upper reaches of the Sangro on the 22nd, although the weather was fine in V Corps' area. That night the river was in flood and the CCRE* of V Corps described the results:

> Old Man Sangro, deciding that our task was not meeting with sufficient opposition, rose in all his wrath and came down in spate. Where the water gap was 100–150 feet it suddenly became 1,000 and [the bridges] were to be seen at daylight splendidly forlorn in the middle of a vast span of swiftly flowing water.[13]

How the engineers must have felt. The CCRE's comments are a masterly example of the capacity of British officers to understate problems. Such was the flooding that no further bridging work could be undertaken until the 26th. Two DUKW companies of RASC – 156 and 385 Companies – ferried supplies to the bridgehead and brought back wounded; some DUKWs made the dangerous return sea passage from Vasto. Then, on 24 November, General Allfrey, the corps commander, issued final orders for what was now going to be a slower, limited operation.[14]

The Germans had not fallen for Montgomery's deception plan. They considered that the main effort would be in V Corps' area, against 65th Infantry Division, and that XIII Corps' operations were diversionary. Thus the drawing off of reserves that Montgomery had hoped for never

* Corps Commander, Royal Engineers.

happened. Furthermore, the additional time provided by the weather allowed a strengthening of the defences, with new minefields laid on the plain, creating more headaches for the sappers who would have to clear passages.

Allfrey's plan provided for 8th Indian Division to secure the left flank by capturing high ground near Mozzagrogna before taking Mozzagrogna itself and Santa Maria; this would require a brigade. With this achieved, 78th Division, with tanks of 4 Armoured Brigade, would pass through, wheel right on Li Colli ridge and roll up the German lines from there to the sea before swinging left to follow the coast road for possible exploitation to the Moro river. The Indians were to attack on the 26th with their operations to be complete by the 28th and 78th Division going into action on the 29th or 30th.[15]

Having lost their mastery of the plain across the Sangro, 78th Division, supported by 4 Armoured Brigade, was now to create a bridgehead. In this they were successful although the first attempt by companies from 36 Brigade was repulsed; by 22 November 11 Brigade and 36 Brigade were ensconced about Fossacésia; six battalions and tanks of 3 CLY and 50th Royal Tanks were on the escarpment; the infantry included 2nd King's Royal Rifle Corps, 4 Armoured Brigade's motor battalion.[16]

By 26 November the bridges, one the longest on V Corps' front, were back in use. Early on the 27th, 1/12th Frontier Force Rifles of 17 Indian Brigade secured a jumping-off place below Mozzagrogna while the Irish Brigade crossed the river. In the evening, Mozzagrogna was captured by 1/5th Royal Gurkha Rifles, supported by more than 200 guns and some men of 1st Royal Fusiliers.[17] A fierce battle raged with fighting from street to street as Gurkhas hunted down Germans with grenades, bullets, bayonets and kukris. Montgomery's HQ had assessed 65th Infantry Division as being of low quality[18] but its soldiers, although shaken by the bombardment and with communications destroyed, fought tenaciously. They also had the support of a company of tanks and a reconnaissance squadron of 26th Panzer Division which arrived on the morning of the 28th. On this dry morning the panzer troops launched a determined counter-attack and 17 Brigade's commander decided to withdraw his troops to meet it.

The German armour consisted of no more than five MkIV tanks, five flame-throwers, the first German use of these weapons in Italy, and six Italian SPGs. Brigadier Wyndham's decision to withdraw gave the hard-earned ground back to the enemy and 1/12th Frontier Force had to retake it that night.[19] There was another negative aspect to this withdrawal: it eroded confidence in 8th Indian Division for some time at HQ V Corps. Both Nelson Russell and John Currie, of the Irish and 4 Armoured Brigades, proposed a joint plan of attack in which their formations would take Li Colli ridge and Santa Maria to secure the base for the main 78th

Divisional attack. Russell commented that when his men and those of 4 Armoured 'took a place we knew we had it'. He felt that the Indians had not yet found their feet but had every confidence in his and Currie's brigades which had been practising tactics together and whose companies and squadrons knew and trusted each other.[20]

The Russell/Currie plan was accepted and, at 6.30am on 29 November, B and D Companies of 6th Inniskillings, with two squadrons of 44th Royal Tanks, attacked Li Colli ridge. Defensive fire was heavy and the tanks were stopped by mines but the Inniskillings infiltrated from strongpoint to strongpoint. When the Shermans rejoined them the advance accelerated and the ridge was in 78th Division's possession by 3.00pm. Two hours later, Santa Maria had also fallen. The operation had been an excellent example of infantry and armour working together, although this was still not the norm in Eighth Army. Among the casualties of the battle had been Brigadier 'Swifty' Howlett, 36 Brigade's popular commander, who was killed while visiting his forward troops.[21]

Freyberg's New Zealanders had also been busy with 5 and 6 Brigades controlling the high ground north of the Sangro and attacking towards Castèl Frentano. Their efforts drew the usual counter-attacks but air strikes and artillery fire stopped these. Eighth Army had bitten into the enemy positions and prepared the way for the next phase of operations. This saw 17 Indian Brigade, on the night of 29/30 November, seize high ground north-west of Mozzagrogna which dominated the road to Santa Maria and Fossacésia, thereby opening that road for tanks. By midday of the 30th, 3 CLY, 44th Royal Tanks and 2nd London Irish were in Fossacésia from where tanks and Irish Fusiliers pushed to the sea. Next day Rocca fell to the Irish Brigade while New Zealanders were poised before Castèl Frentano.[22]

Such was the chunk that Eighth Army had now bitten out of the German defences that LXXVI Panzer Corps' commander, Herr, considered the tactical situation such that retreat was in order. Even though reinforcements were coming up, Herr issued withdrawal orders; his troops were to hold Eighth Army on the line San Vito–Lanciano–Castèl Frentano while stronger defensive locations were made ready on the line of the Ortona–Guardiagrele road through Orsogna and Melone. San Vito was taken by two Irish Fusilier companies on 1 December. Although counter-attacked and forced to withdraw they stayed close to the town which fell eventually to 6th Inniskillings supported by tanks of 3 CLY.[23]

Herr's new line was beyond yet another river, the Moro. Eighth Army had to plan to force that obstacle but, meanwhile, 8th Indian Division was to hold Li Colli ridge and secure Lanciano. The latter task was completed on 3 December as the Irish Brigade probed towards Ortona. With the

Inniskillings securing the flank, the Faughs and London Irish advanced to the Feltrino and then to the Moro. Having dealt with several counter-attacks, the leading elements of the Irish Brigade were reconnoitring the Moro's banks on the night of 4/5 December. But the brigade was not to take part in operations across the river as Montgomery had decided to rest 78th Division which would be relieved by 1st Canadian Division. With XIII Corps now in a holding role that required only a single division, the Canadians could be brought across to relieve the Battleaxe Division which went into XIII Corps' reserve. Later, when Montgomery ordered HQ XIII Corps and 5th Division to move to the coastal sector, 78th Division assumed control of the mountain sector under Army command.[24]

Alongside the Canadians in the next phase of operations were Indians and New Zealanders, underlining the cosmopolitan nature of Eighth Army. Freyberg's men had Orsogna as their objective while the Canadians closed on Ortona and the Indians on Villa Grande. But Montgomery's pause to permit reorganization in the Sangro valley proved to have been a major error since this had also granted the Germans time for reorganization and concentration. Herr's men were able to dig in along the line Melone–Orsogna–Arielli–Villa Grande–Ortona to meet Eighth Army's next attack. Montgomery would have done much better to have maintained pressure on his foe, thus keeping him off balance. Instead he had allowed an enemy who excelled in the defensive battle an opportunity to prepare for yet another such encounter.[25] By now Montgomery had seen sufficient evidence of the defensive skills of the German soldier, not to mention his tenacity, to have persuaded him that it was never a good idea to give such men time to prepare a defensive position; but it would seem that he had never absorbed that lesson.

On the left flank, 2nd New Zealand Division was already advancing on Orsogna. That advance continued but the New Zealanders were rebuffed by defenders who appreciated the strategic and tactical importance of Orsogna, which perches on a ridge 1,300-feet high and forms the western bastion of a line created by nature from that ridge, and Pascuccio and Sfasciata ridges. The three features stretch for more than four miles, guarding a stretch of road from Orsogna to Ortona which became the focus of a struggle between New Zealanders and Germans since it was one of the only two practicable approaches close to Orsogna; the other was Brecciarola ridge, 'steep, narrow-crested, and dotted with olive-trees, vine-yards, and farm buildings'. Orsogna's importance lay in that it could be

the starting-point of an attempt to roll up the German line by a stroke eastwards down the road to Ortona. It would form moreover a necessary guard for the right flank of any force which might advance northwards aiming at Chieti via Guardiagrele and S. Martino.[26]

Freyberg was determined that his division would take Orsogna but to do so he needed to take the ridges and the road. However, without Orsogna no attacker could be secure upon those ridges. In turn the capture of Orsogna would have made untenable the new German line behind the Moro.[27] The situation was complicated by 2nd New Zealand Division's unique orbat of two infantry and an armoured brigade.* However, Freyberg could count on his own divisional artillery supported by 6th AGRA's two medium and two field regiments. Strong air support was also available.

Napoleon's maxim that a good general also needed to be lucky was now to be proved true. A gap had occurred near Colle Chiamato between 26th Panzer and 65th Divisions and, on 2 December, 6 New Zealand Brigade found it and entered Castèl Frentano; 24th NZ Battalion reached Brecciarola ridge while 25th Battalion reached Colle Chiamato where a machine-gun battle developed. The New Zealanders, not realizing that the enemy defence was almost non-existent, halted. As Germans rushed to close the gap, Freyberg recognized the opportunity to push through the enemy lines. Holding 5 Brigade at Castèl Frentano, he deployed 6 Brigade against Orsogna while 4 Armoured Brigade was told to dash straight for San Stefano via Guardiagrele. His brigade commanders gave the task of taking Orsogna to 25th Battalion – it was to attack at dawn on the 3rd – with 22nd Motor Battalion to clear a route for the Shermans of 4 NZ Armoured Brigade.

New Zealand luck seemed to run out as the attacks went forward. At Orsogna 25th Battalion took advantage of cloud and mist to pass two companies along Brecciarola ridge and into the eastern edge of the town. There one company assumed defensive positions while the second charged into the main street. Although surprised, the Germans reacted with speed and fury. An armoured car deployed to meet the New Zealanders but was soon joined by other AFVs and infantry. However, this should not have presented a severe problem to the attackers who had a gunner FOO to call down accurate fire on the enemy's positions. Sadly, the FOO's jeep with its wireless sets was hit by an enemy shell and destroyed; no fire support could be called on. The German counter-attack was so fierce that the battalion, having sustained eighty-three casualties, was forced to withdraw before their brigade could reinforce their efforts. Meanwhile, at Melone, three miles south-west, 22nd Motor Battalion's advance had also been brought to a stop. The outcome prompted the New Zealand official historian to comment:

* The concept of a 'mixed' division, with two infantry and one armoured brigades, had been tried and found wanting in the British Army which had sent 4th Division to Tunisia with such an orbat, but this had been reconfigured as an infantry division in December 1943 after eighteen months as a 'mixed' formation.[28]

No one can predict the outcome of a hypothetical attack, but if 25th Battalion (or 24th Battalion) had struck twelve or even seven hours earlier, it seems probable that they could have carried the town and established themselves on its western perimeter. Thence, with artillery support, they would have had excellent command over the counter-attack, and might have proved as difficult to evict as the Germans did once they had taken full possession.[29]

All was not lost: Freyberg planned a fresh assault next afternoon with his division reinforced by 2 Parachute Brigade* and an airborne artillery regiment. Massive air support was laid on for the attack, which was timed to allow the infantry to consolidate on their objectives before dark and deny the enemy sufficient time for effective counter-attacks. With the paras guarding the divisional flank, 5 Brigade was to deploy 23rd and 28th (Maori) Battalions against objectives on Sfasciata ridge and on Pascuccio respectively, while 24th Battalion from 6 Brigade, supported by 18th Armoured Battalion, was to attack Orsogna from Brecciarola ridge. The other New Zealand battalions were assigned holding roles.[31]

Air support for this operation included thirteen fighter-bomber squadrons attacking over a two-and-a-half-hour period but so low was the cloud that only a few strikes were made late in the day. Artillery support was not affected, however, and the attacking battalions advanced under an umbrella of steel. Both 23rd and 28th Battalions took their objectives although the Maoris had some sharp fighting while counter-attacks, with tank support, continued past midnight. Brigadier Kippenberger decided to withdraw the Maoris when he realized that their position on Pascuccio, in 'a kind of a saucer', would be untenable in daylight. But Orsogna again proved too tough a nut, although 24th Battalion entered the village. With the tanks held up by mines, demolitions and anti-tank gunfire, Freyberg ordered both tanks and infantry to fall back. Casualties totalled 160 men and two tanks but his division now had a firm lodgement on Sfasciata.[32]

Not until a week later did the New Zealanders try to crack the German line again, this time with the additional aim of assisting V Corps' operations. The objective on this occasion was to 'by pass Orsogna and sweep down to Melone, where a renewed attempt to penetrate would be made by part of 4 NZ Armoured Brigade. If all this succeeded, Orsogna – isolated – might fall.'[33] In heavy fighting on 15 December the New Zealanders had some initial success although casualties were high; but the defenders also suffered heavily. An attack on Orsogna by two armoured units was stopped when anti-tank fire knocked out twenty-five tanks. Overnight, a strong counter-attack by infantry and tanks was beaten off

* Since 17 November this had been redesignated 2 Independent Parachute Brigade Group.[30]

48

and a fresh assault made with Shermans of 20th Armoured supporting the Maoris. This attack met strong resistance and stalled. Stalemate now prevailed. Although Freyberg considered attacking from his right flank, resistance was still such that any forward movement could be made only at a price that the New Zealanders could not afford. It could all have been so different had the initial attack at Colle Chiamato been pressed on. Such was the strength of opposition at Orsogna that it was dubbed the 'Stalingrad of the Abruzzi'.[34] The New Zealanders were also discovering the primary disadvantage of the 'mixed' division: it left an attacking division with insufficient infantry.

What of their Commonwealth cousins? Having relieved 78th Division, the Canadians were deployed with 1 Brigade at San Vito, close to the coast, 2 Brigade near San Apollinare and 3 Brigade waiting to cross the swollen Sangro. Opposition in the coastal sector was provided by 90th Panzer Grenadier Division, which had just relieved 65th Infantry Division. On 4 December Allfrey told Major General Vokes, the new Canadian commander,* that his men should cross the Moro as soon as possible since a rapid advance was imperative. With an equal sense of urgency, Vokes set his objective as the junction of Highway 16 with the Ortona–Orsogna road, subsequently dubbed 'Cider Cross-Roads', some four miles ahead. Thus did it appear on the map but those miles were almost doubled by a road route that crossed four 500-foot-high ridges.

On the night of 5/6 December, without artillery to alert the defenders, 1st Canadian Division, less 3 Brigade, made its crossings; the Moro was fordable everywhere. The Germans were taken by surprise at Villa Rogatti where Princess Patricia's crossed. Meanwhile the Seaforth of Canada led the main crossing at San Leonardo; a five-hour battle saw two companies ensconced in the town. To the right of the Seaforth, the Hastings and Prince Edward Regiment, the Hasty Ps, also won a small bridgehead. Then came the inevitable counter-attacks. Mounted with considerable fury, these eventually forced both Patricias and Seaforth to return to their starting points but the Hasty Ps tenaciously held their ground.

Undismayed, Vokes quickly ordered a fresh attack. On the 8th, 1 Brigade crossed at San Leonardo while 2 Brigade, with tanks from 1 Armoured Brigade, passed through to race for the final objective. It was far from a straightforward battle. Following lengthy air and artillery bombardment – some 45,000 rounds were fired on 8 and 9 December – a company of Royal Canadians stepped off just as the Germans attacked the Canadian bridgehead. A two-hour battle ensued but the other Royal Canadian companies could still advance and, by 10.00pm – the attack had started

* Christopher Vokes succeeded Guy Simonds who took command of 5th Armoured Division on 1 November.

at 4.30pm – were halfway to San Leonardo when they too were hit by a counter-attack. But the German effort was broken when Colonel Spry called down defensive fire almost on top of his own men. As the Germans drew off, the Canadians reorganized to continue their advance.

On the left flank, 48th Highlanders seized La Torre spur as a start line from which a Seaforth company could take over the battle for San Leonardo. Supported by a squadron of Calgary tanks, the Seaforth went into action. Throughout the 9th the battle continued with both regiments being committed completely and, by 6.00pm, San Leonardo was in Canadian hands. The Calgaries had lost twenty-seven of their fifty-one tanks but the Germans were broken and in retreat, harassed by artillery fire. Elsewhere along the front 21 Indian Brigade, which had taken over Rogatti on the 8th, also advanced to create a small bridgehead. It was there that 69 Field Company, Bengal Sappers and Miners, built the 'Impossible Bridge', the name given to a Bailey that had to be built backwards. With space on their own bank so restricted that assembly and launching was impossible, the engineers chose to manhandle their equipment to the enemy bank, assemble the bridge there and place it over the river. Their actions showed both great courage and initiative and the incident is typical of how Eighth Army's sappers took the seemingly impossible in their stride.[35]

Vokes may have been determined to move quickly but the Germans, equally determined that he should not, held the advantage of well-sited defensive positions with the Canadians advancing across the grain of the country. In spite of Allfrey's exhortation, the Canadian push towards Ortona was destined to be another slow and bloody affair that brought pain and suffering to infantry and tankmen. The morning of 10 December saw the Edmonton Regiment, with a Calgary squadron, reach the position known as the 'Gully'. Here a ridge and a ravine crossed Highway 16 and the defence was in the hands of paratroopers. As his soldiers and their supporting tanks approached the Gully that morning the Edmonton CO signalled that 'We are now proceeding on final objective.' He was much too optimistic: the Germans had other ideas. Mortar bombs and machine-gun bullets met the advancing Canadians. The advance ground to a halt.[36]

More than a week was to pass before the Gully and Cider Cross-Roads fell to the Canadians. During the intervening days Vokes made eight attacks, each delivered in what had become the signature of his division: small assaults on a narrow front with strong artillery and armour support. The Canadian front was just over a mile in length and Vokes seems still to have hoped for an early breakthrough that would allow him to make straight for his main objective. But there was no quick blow smashing the enemy's defensive crust. Each attack was made by one or two battalions, with tanks in support, but movement was hampered by rain-soaked ground and each attack failed because

The enemy's fire, much of it cross-fire, was very heavy and his counter-attacks were frequent, determined and well-timed. The Canadian infantry often 'lost' their artillery support because of the ordinary mischances of battle and because the artillery was firing at a disadvantage. This was because the succession of attacks was so quick that often two or three fire plans were being prepared at once, largely from not altogether accurate maps. The resulting fire plans were often faulty, and frequent calls for heavy Defensive Fire to meet counter-attacks sent them further astray.[37]

It was not until the eighth attack, made by three battalions on 19 December, that success was gained although the first weaknesses in the enemy defences began to show on the 13th. From the high vantage point gifted by hindsight the historian may make such an assessment. Soldiers slogging forward in the mud of that winter day might not have seen any weakness at all. Making a frontal attack towards Cider Cross-Roads were the men of the Carleton and York Regiment with the Patricias and West Nova Scotias on the flanks. All three battalions were repulsed. So where was the chink in the German armour? It had been uncovered, as the battle was being fought, by two reconnaissance patrols. One, consisting of B Squadron, Ontarios, with a platoon of West Novas, found a track from San Leonardo to the Ortona road. It was this same track, a mile or so west of Casa Berardi, that the second patrol, four tanks from C Squadron, Ontarios with A Company, Seaforth, discovered. Both groups identified weaknesses in the German right flank as well as eliminating some enemy detachments and they pushed forward almost as far as Casa Berardi.

Since the main battle was still underway, Vokes was unable to exploit this discovery but he took the first chance to do so and, next day, ordered the Royal 22^e Regiment – the Van Doos – with C Squadron, Ontarios, to advance along the track. At the same time the Patricias made a frontal attack to try 'to cross the Gully and cut the lateral road, while the Hastings maintained pressure along the coast'. By now, of course, the Germans were paying much more attention to their right flank but the Canadians were undeterred and attacked with such spirit that a lodgement was gained at Casa Berardi. Even a counter-attack as the Royal 22^e prepared to move off was no deterrent; 48th Highlanders had a company in cover waiting for just such a move and put paid quickly to the attackers, of whom nine were killed, thirty-one captured and the remainder fled.[38]

The lodgement was achieved by Captain Paul Triquet's C Company of the Van Doos and the Ontario tanks, but such was the German reaction that Triquet had only two sergeants and fifteen men still standing by the time he entered Casa Berardi, while only four Shermans remained battle-worthy from the Ontario squadron. Such a small force stood little chance against determined German counter-attacks. But, in spite of all they threw at the Canadians, the Germans failed to dislodge Paul Triquet and his men. The Canadian captain inspired his surviving soldiers with General Pétain's stirring order to the 1916 defenders of Verdun: 'Ils ne passeront pas.' And, as they did not pass at Verdun, so did the Germans fail to dislodge the determined Van Doos and their Ontario comrades.[39] Such was Triquet's courage and leadership that he was subsequently awarded the Victoria Cross, the citation for which noted that:

> During the attack on Casa Berardi, Italy, when all the other officers and half the men of his company had been killed or wounded, Captain Triquet dashed forward and, with the remaining men, broke through the enemy resistance. He then forced his way on with his small force ... into a position on the outskirts of Casa Berardi. They held out against attacks from overwhelming numbers until the remainder of the battalion relieved them next day. Throughout the action Captain Triquet's utter disregard for danger and his cheerful encouragement were an inspiration to his men.[40]

Triquet's was Eighth Army's first Victoria Cross of the Italian campaign and the first of three earned by Canadians in Italy. Major Smith of the Ontarios, who had commanded the tanks supporting the Royal 22^e and, earlier, the Seaforth, received the Military Cross.[41]

The lodgement made by Triquet's men was consolidated when Lieutenant Colonel Bernatchez, his commanding officer, brought up a larger force to ensure that Casa Berardi remained in Canadian hands. It proved a valuable gain as the new tenants prevented the enemy from restoring his flank and thus assisted Vokes' efforts to move forward. Another tank squadron moved up to Casa Berardi while the Carleton and York Regiment made yet another abortive attack on 15 December. The Germans were still determined to hold on. They were, however, concerned that the two defending divisions now lacked any immediate reserves after the fighting of 13 and 14 December. Following the rebuff of the 15th, Vokes mounted no operations on the two days that followed but then, on the 18th, sent his men forward in a shrewdly planned three-phase operation from west of Casa Berardi. Allied aircraft supported 48th Highlanders, Royal Canadians and Hastings as they struck the German positions with tanks of the Three Rivers Regiment alongside. This time Vokes met with success. In an 'admirably executed' attack the Canadians forced the Germans to give ground, although not without a bitter fight. Eventually the enemy began withdrawing and the Canadians were at last able to take Cider Cross-Roads.[42]

As New Zealanders pounded the enemy on the left and Canadians on the right, both 5th Division and 8th Indian Division advanced in between.

52

The Indians, also across the Moro, captured Villa Caldari on 14 December to be followed, two days later, by Villa Jubatti. Poggofiorito was taken by 5th Division on the same day, 16 December. Both divisions had had to fight for every yard. Fifth Division's historian described some of the ground over which they fought:

> Huge craters and the twisted wreckage of guns, tanks and trucks with gnarled tree stumps alone pierced this eerie wilderness; a veritable abomination of desolation. ... Movement during daylight was not encouraged and only permitted if absolutely necessary operationally.[43]

This slugging advance continued as the Indians closed on Villa Grande three days before Christmas. Nineteen Brigade reached the village on 22 December but it took six days of fighting to wrest it from the Germans with 1/5th Essex and 3/8th Punjab locked in close combat with the defending paras. In truth, Villa Grande was taken house by house. The Indian battalions would charge forward to seize one or two houses and then prepare for the inevitable counter-attack. At other times the Germans would make the attacks and the Indians the counter-attacks. This was attritional warfare of the worst sort: the Essex suffered 285 casualties and had to be withdrawn to reform. Major General Russell, the divisional GOC, was starting to push elements of 21 Brigade into the battle on the morning of 28 December when it was realized that the paras were pulling back. They were not admitting defeat but, with 90th Panzer Grenadiers, were withdrawing on orders to the line of the Tesoro river from Torre Mucchia on the coast to a point west of Villa Grande. However, from near Crecchio to Orsogna the existing line was still manned.[44]

While 8th Indian Division took on the paras in Villa Grande, the Canadians were engaged in a similar struggle at Ortona. But this was on a much larger scale and represented 'the first example in the Mediterranean war of a large pitched battle in a town'. Ortona had neither strategic nor tactical significance and Kesselring accused the British of attributing to it an importance that all but equalled that of Rome. His own dispositions suggest that he also attributed significance to Ortona that it did not have: its defence was assigned to a force built on 2nd/3rd, 3rd/3rd and 2nd/4th Parachute Regiments.[45] Perhaps this was simply part of Lemelsen's promise that the British would be 'made to fight for every house and every tree',[46] but equally it may have been a result of the shortening of LXXVI Panzer Corps' front.

Ortona was fought for street by street and house by house in actions that were more often the work of sections or platoons rather than companies or battalions. First into the town on 21 December were the Edmontons, supported by some Three Rivers' tanks, making their incursion on a

53

500-yard front along the axis of the central streets. But this was too much for a single battalion and so Brigadier Hoffmeister of 2 Brigade deployed a company of Seaforth. On the 23rd the entire Seaforth battalion was committed. German defensive measures were, as ever, scientific with demolitions aimed to funnel the Canadians into a killing ground in the Piazza Municipale. But the Edmonton commander chose not to advance by the route desired by the Germans. He allowed the tanks to use that approach, having ensured that it was clear of mines, while his companies made parallel approaches.

> The German paratroopers, fresh, well trained and equipped and thoroughly imbued with Nazism, fought like disciplined demons. Each sturdy Italian house that they elected to defend became a strong-point, from every floor of which they opposed the Canadian advance with fire from a variety of weapons. They left other buildings booby-trapped or planted with delayed charges; and if these faced houses which they were holding, they demolished the front walls in order to expose the interiors to their own fire from across the street. Every obstructing pile of rubble was covered by machine guns sited in a second storey,* and the litter of shattered stone and broken brick usually concealed a liberal sowing of anti-tank and anti-personnel mines.[47]

The Three Rivers' Shermans proved invaluable with tank and infantry commanders devising tactics on the hoof as the tanks switched from being mobile pillboxes, providing covering machine-gun fire for the infantry, to being assault guns with their 75mm shells 'smashing gaping holes in the walls of enemy-held buildings', to bringing forward ammunition and evacuating wounded. All the while they faced the constant threat of 'German anti-tank guns sited to cover the obvious approaches and often concealed close behind the barricades so as to catch the attacking tank's exposed underside as it climbed over the rubble'.[48]

Further invaluable support was provided by the 6-pounder anti-tank guns of the infantry battalions and the 6- and 17-pounders of 90 Anti-Tank Battery. These weapons proved much more suitable than field artillery for fighting in a built-up area and provided devastating support as well as very accurate fire against buildings concealing snipers. As the battle progressed the infantry devised a method of moving from house to house without appearing outdoors. This was an improved version of the 'mouse-holing' already taught in battle schools which involved breaking through a dividing wall with a pick or crowbar. Now the pioneers used 'Beehive'

* In North American parlance; this equates to the British first storey.

demolition charges to achieve the same result much faster. While infantry sheltered in a ground floor, pioneers set charges against the wall in the top storey and when the explosive blew the infantry section charged through the gap to clear the enemy from the neighbouring house.[49] Thus did the Canadians clear entire rows of houses forcing the paras to pull back ever more.

On 28 December the Canadians emerged victorious at the northern end of Ortona and with 'an enhanced reputation, and a technique of street fighting which was to be closely studied by training staffs in all the Allied armies'. They had, however, paid a heavy price with 650 casualties.[50]

As the Germans withdrew from Ortona the struggle continued elsewhere. Santa Nicola and Santa Tomassa were taken by 1 Brigade on 31 December before 3 Brigade took over to push forward to Torre Mucchia which was reached on 4 January 1944. On 23 December 5th Division took Arielli in an attack co-ordinated with a New Zealander thrust against the Fontegrande plateau. The latter attack aimed to isolate Orsogna but the German garrison there still held out. An attack on Christmas Eve had also been rebuffed and by the afternoon of Christmas Day it was clear to Freyberg that there could be no further advance for the time being. He commented that it was now more a question of being able to hold what the Division had rather than making any further gains.[51]

The new year of 1944 saw Eighth Army only 14 miles forward from its positions of 28 November. Pescara was still eight miles away and Rome seemed farther away than ever since the average daily rate of advance was down to half a mile; from Termoli to San Vito it had been just over twice that. Herr's LXXVI Panzer Corps was toughening its resistance and the weather was weighing in on the side of the Germans. Ahead of the Allies lay country no better than that they had already fought over; in other words, British superiority in armour would provide no advantage and the struggle would still fall on the shoulders of the poor bloody infantry. And those infantrymen were being worn down: of the 6,453 casualties in Eighth Army during December most were in the infantry. Since the Sangro the three divisions most involved had suffered almost 7,000 casualties: 8th Indian had 3,400, 1st Canadian had 2,339 and 2nd New Zealand 1,200.[52]

All these factors combined to persuade Montgomery to stop offensive operations. It was probably his last decision as army commander as, on 30 December, he handed over to Sir Oliver Leese and prepared to leave for Britain to command the land forces for Operation OVERLORD, the invasion of north-west Europe. He bade farewell to Eighth Army by addressing the officers and men of Army HQ, as well as corps and divisional commanders, in the cinema at Vasto where he read his farewell message to his soldiers. In that message he commented:

It is difficult to express to you adequately what this parting means to me. I am leaving officers and men who have been my comrades during months of hard and victorious fighting, and whose courage and devotion to duty always filled me with admiration. . . .

In all the battles we have fought together we have not had one single failure; we have been successful in everything we have undertaken.

I know that this has been due to the devotion to duty and whole-hearted co-operation of every officer and man, rather than to anything I may have been able to do myself.

But the result has been a mutual confidence between you and me, and mutual confidence between a Commander and his troops is a pearl of very great price. . . .

You have made this Army what it is. YOU have made its name a household word all over the world. YOU must uphold its good name and its traditions.[53]

Writing to Lord Louis Mountbatten less than a week earlier, Montgomery commented that 'spectacular results' had been achieved in Italy and that Eighth Army had fought over 700 miles of country from 3 September to 3 December. That Rome had not fallen before the weather broke he attributed to a lack of grip at 15 Army Group which had resulted in both armies becoming bogged down.[54] But he failed to lay any blame on himself – that would, of course, have been most uncharacteristic – and chose to forget the occasions on which he had failed to take the initiative. Remember that Montgomery was privy to ULTRA information which gave him an excellent insight into German intentions and dispositions; after the war he claimed that he kept a picture of Rommel in his caravan so that he might read his adversary's mind but ULTRA was doing that for him. The seaborne right hook at Termoli had been an exception to the rule that saw Montgomery wait until he was certain that his administrative base was firm and everything was 'tee-ed up' before making any move. Had he been prepared to take more risks before and immediately after Termoli, Eighth Army might well have been much closer to Rome at the end of November. That Termoli came close to being a German victory must have preyed on his mind and, in spite of his fine words on relinquishing command, he seems never to have had that level of confidence in Eighth Army that would have allowed him to use it with greater vigour. Since the appearance of 16th Panzer at Termoli had been without warning he must also have had some doubts about the accuracy and completeness of his intelligence; this would have exacerbated his caution. And yet, in early November, he had been writing about unleashing the New Zealanders in a right hook towards Rome, following which he would be exhausted, require some leave and 'probably write a book "Alamein to Rome" '.*[55]

As Eighth Army faced a new year with a new commander how was it positioned? It had broken into the Winter Line but was unable to follow through with an advance to Pescara. Although the Canadian advance continued it met 'strong enemy resistance ... in the form of mortaring, machine-gun fire and minefields'.[56] Alexander noted that the mountainous terrain of the Molise region 'offered few chances of a decisive success to an army attacking ... across the grain of the country. The further north we pushed our advance the more numerous and close together were the river lines'.[57] Hitler had also ordered the reinforcement of the Italian theatre and, unusually for him, permitted giving up ground as a tactic. As a result:

> The impetus of the Allied attacks had been blunted and held at the point where the coastal strip between the impassable Maiella [mountains] and the sea is narrowest. To make the positions even stronger, Kesselring exchanged the battered 65th Division for the 334th, which was at Genoa. With this, and with the help of the prevailing bad weather, the northern flank was saved till spring.[58]

Many Allied soldiers had thought of Italy as a country of permanent sunshine but were now learning the truth of the peninsula's climate. Heavy snowfalls added to their misery and soldiers suffered from exposure and frostbite; some even succumbed to hypothermia. On New Year's Day, 21 Indian Brigade recorded ten casualties, including two men who died from exposure; one company in each battalion was 'withdrawn to thaw out'.[59] In 17 Indian Brigade there were seventeen casualties from exposure but no fatalities. Units of 78th Division were cut off in the mountains: 56 Recce and 6th Inniskillings were resupplied by air and Kendal Chavasse noted that he visited his squadrons on skis but that 'I usually ended on my bottom when skiing downhill.' On the night of 31 December he noted that he woke at 3.00am 'to find 2 feet of snow on my bed'.[60] But he believed that he enjoyed comparative luxury when he considered what others were enduring. In 5th Division it was noted that the Moro had risen from ankle-depth to eight feet,[61] while

> those units ... scattered in the high ground to the left flank were seriously hindered in their movement. Supply routes were closed and some transport was buried under the drifts. On 3rd January these troops had to be put on half rations, and some of these rations were

* The book was written but was called *El Alamein to the River Sangro*.

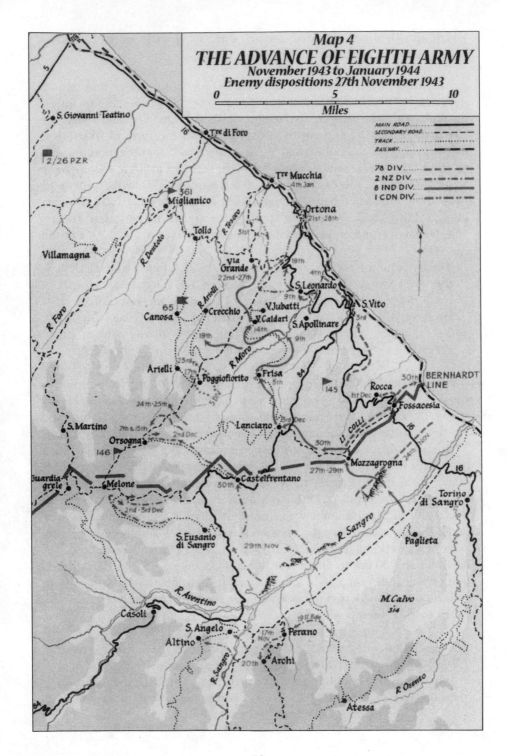

Map 4
THE ADVANCE OF EIGHTH ARMY
November 1943 to January 1944
Enemy dispositions 27th November 1943

0   5   10

Miles

MAIN ROAD
SECONDARY ROAD
TRACK
RAILWAY

78 DIV
2 NZ DIV
8 IND DIV
I CDN DIV

N

2/26 PZR

S. Giovanni Teatino

16

Tre di Foro

Tre Mucchia
4th Jan

361

Miglianico

Tollo

R. Tesoro

31st

Ortona
21st - 28th

Villamagna

R. Dentolo

R. Foro

Via
Grande
22nd - 27th

19th

4th

S. Leonardo
9th

S. Vito
3rd

65

R. Arielli

Canosa

Crecchio

V. Jubatti
14th

V. Caldari

S. Apollinare
9th

19th

R. Moro

Arielli

25th

17th

Poggiofiorito

Frisa
5th

145
1st Dec

Rocca

30th

BERNHARDT
LINE

Fossacesia

S. DIV

24th - 25th

S. Martino

7th & 15th

2nd Dec

Lanciano

3rd Dec

30th

LI COLLI

16

Orsogna

146

30th

Mozzagrogna
27th - 29th

24th Nov

16

Guardia
grele

Melone

2nd - 3rd Dec

Castelfrentano
50th

R. Sangro

Torino
di Sangro

S. Eusanio
di Sangro

29th Nov

Paglieta

R. Aventino

Casoli

M. Calvo
3i4

S. Angelo

Altino

17th
Nov

19 II Edge

Perano

R. Sangro

20th

Archi

R. Osento

Atessa

58

successfully dropped from aircraft the next day. The dominating high ground of Mount Maiella looked more magnificent than ever, particularly with the red winter sun on its snowbound slopes.[62]

The New Zealanders reported that at least six stretcher-bearers were needed to carry a casualty in either snow or driving rain. And it was the latter that presented the main problem on the lower ground; sleet and rain created a quagmire of slush and mud through which both men and vehicles struggled.[63]

The weather might have stopped major operations but Eighth Army's soldiers soon learned that it did not deter the Germans from patrolling or raiding on a small scale. Two attacks were made against 56 Recce's positions in the mountains. On the first occasion local civilians warned of the approaching Germans and the attack was subjected to heavy artillery fire, which forced an enemy withdrawal while, on the second, a small patrol on skis was seen off with a fusillade of grenades and mortar bombs.[64] More success attended German efforts on 19 January when they attacked a company of 2nd London Irish just after stand-to, capturing most of a platoon, wounding fifteen men and killing five. The company commander, Major Mervyn Davies, organized a swift counter-attack that, in the face of enemy machine-gun fire, pushed the Germans out of the area and rescued the captured platoon commander and four of his men. One German was captured and six killed.[65]

Such enemy activity ensured that a high state of alert was maintained, although one war diary noted that an American unit on 78th Division's left flank 'reported the loss of a perfectly good sentry not far away' while 'strangely coloured parachutes' were reported to be falling near the Sangro. There were, however, no parachuting nuns. But there was at least one tragic incident when, on 4 January, a patrol of unidentified soldiers was seen 'acting suspiciously' in 1st Royal Irish Fusiliers' sector. The patrol was fired on, one man was killed, and another wounded, before it was discovered that the intruders were from the Belgian Troop of No. 10 Commando, an inter-Allied unit with personnel from several occupied countries as well as Britain.[66]

The tragic culmination of that patrol draws attention to the main form of activity on Eighth Army's front: patrolling. To dominate no man's land and ensure up-to-date intelligence on enemy activity and dispositions, many patrols were carried out. Such infantry patrols were 'primarily the antennae of an army, feeling forward to flash signals, sometimes of danger, sometimes of opportunity to the brain; but they serve purposes other than short range reconnaissance'.[67] While some were relatively uneventful – a state of affairs that could not be predicted – others produced considerable excitement. On one such occasion the battle patrol of 1st East Surreys linked up with a patrol from the battalion's D Company to carry out a three-day operation deep into enemy-held territory, raiding one German post and visiting two half-destroyed villages. Local civilians sheltering in the remains of their homes provided valuable information on enemy activity. A German soldier, on a private looting expedition, was also captured. When the patrols returned Lieutenant Woodhouse MC, the battle patrol commander, was able to make his report to the army commander as Leese was visiting the Surreys' HQ.[68]

While some officers seemed to be cut out for the role of leading such patrols, others were not. Colin Gunner, of 1st Royal Irish Fusiliers, hated the experience, although he never 'pulled the old trick of getting out of sight and holing up for the night before coming back with a pack of lies'. Nonetheless, he

> hated the cold and the dark; above all I hated the loneliness. The men hated it too, as they knew too well that anyone hurt during these visits to no man's land was nearly always left behind in the fracas to die or, if lucky, to be picked up later. To myself also I admitted that whereas an attack was infinitely more dangerous, there was a feeling of all being together and of someone, in our case the major, giving orders: too much imagination or the mentality of a born follower I suppose. The use of patrols will be argued for as long as they are sent out but they call for a peculiar brand of courage which I for one did not have.[69]

Such patrolling was an essential element of British military doctrine: it allowed domination of no man's land, as already noted, and ensured that troops did not become defensively minded but maintained an attitude of aggressiveness in their soldiering.

Colin Gunner would not have been happy in the company of Lionel Wigram of the Royal West Kents. The former chief instructor of the GHQ Battle School at Barnard Castle in Yorkshire, the forerunner of the modern School of Infantry, Wigram commanded a group known as Wigforce, drawn from the battalions of 36 Brigade* and Italian partisan units. Major Wigram's command 'was a truly offensive force' and was much stronger than the usual battle patrols or raiding parties.[71] Wigforce raided deep into German-held territory where some were shocked to see the degree to which Italian civilians suffered under the Germans. One officer, Denis Forman, later wrote of how German foraging parties, usually an NCO and four men, would not only take food but also destroy property. The party

---

* These were 5th Buffs, 6th Royal West Kents and 8th Argyll and Sutherland Highlanders.[70]

would approach a hamlet or a farm, open fire, drive out the inhabitants, loot every article of value, kill all the animals and set the buildings on fire. This exercise was carried out with varying degrees of savagery.

Sometimes the men would be shot as they ran away, sometimes the women captured and raped. There were plenty of eyewitness accounts of these occurrences and, even allowing for the inevitable degree of exaggeration, it was clear that in our area alone several dozen men had been shot, some by putting a rifle in their mouths and discharging it so that it scattered their brains over the walls and roof of the room where the atrocity was committed.[72]

One of the worst atrocities occurred in Sant'Agata, a mountain village, where a German patrol rounded up everyone they could find, locked them in a farmhouse room and then set the building ablaze. Those who attempted to escape were shot. At least forty villagers were murdered.[73]

In early February Wigforce raided Pizzoferrato, surprising the Germans, but Wigram was killed in the first burst of enemy fire and a confused battle ensued with many more raiders being killed. Pinned in the village, many Wigforce survivors were still there when German reinforcements appeared half an hour later. Those remaining were killed or captured: five British soldiers and eleven Italian partisans were killed while twenty-one of the former were wounded and captured. The group had set out with forty British soldiers and a hundred Italian partisans.[74]

But events elsewhere were exerting influence on Eighth Army. With its advance on Rome stalled, Fifth Army was to take over the running for the Eternal City while Eighth Army held the enemy 'in a tight grip around Ortona and Orsogna'. To strengthen Fifth Army, 'the practically intact 5 Div was to be transferred ... in conditions of the utmost secrecy'.[75] And so the 'Cook's Tour' division was off on its travels once more, moving across country by convoy on roads that were collapsing under the volume of traffic using them. The last element of the division to quit the line, 15 Brigade, was relieved by 2 Parachute Brigade on 3 January. Other formations were moving even farther: 7th Armoured Division, which had been with Fifth Army, and 1st Airborne Division were sent back to Britain, as were 50th (Northumbrian) and 51st (Highland) Divisions, neither of which had been committed to Italy* but, as Eighth Army formations,

---

* Although 51st Division's artillery had supported Eighth Army's crossing of the Straits of Messina and one battalion had even crossed into Italy.

might have been. And 1st Division, newly arrived in Italy, was assigned to Fifth Army from 1 January.[76]

Montgomery had taken some of his commanders to Britain with him, including the Canadian Guy Simonds;* he had also wanted Leese but was not allowed to have him as the latter was to succeed him as army commander rather than Montgomery's nominee, Sir Richard O'Connor, recently escaped from a PoW camp. This removal of commanders and HQ staff did Eighth Army no good and Montgomery even intended to inflict another wound by taking Freyberg's division with him for OVERLORD. In this case he was overruled by the CIGS, Brooke. However, Eighth Army was to be reinforced with the arrival of 5th Canadian Armoured Division which, with 1st Canadian Division and 1st Army Group Royal Canadian Artillery (1st Canadian AGRA), would form I Canadian Corps; the necessary corps troops also arrived. Alexander was surprised at the arrival of the Canadian armour since he had not been consulted and believed that he already had sufficient armour for the conditions in which his command was operating. His signal to Brooke asking that he be consulted before any such decisions were made in future was unusually tetchy; but such changes would affect his order of battle and hence his plans. By the end of January, I Canadian Corps, under Lieutenant General Harry Crerar, was included in the army order of battle while the New Zealanders passed to army group command.[77]

February brought another corps to Eighth Army with the arrival at Vasto on the 11th of Lieutenant General Wladyslaw Anders, commander of II Polish Corps. Not only did Anders command a Polish corps but he was also regarded as an army commander, his corps being the Polish army in exile, and an Allied C-in-C, in much the same way as Freyberg. His story, and that of his corps, is remarkable. During the German invasion in 1939 Anders had been wounded and, when the Soviet Army invaded from the east, was transported to the Soviet Union to be held captive in Moscow's Lubyanka prison. Following an agreement between General Sikorski, leader of the exiled Polish government, and Stalin, Anders was released to command a Polish army to be formed in Russia to fight the Germans who had by then invaded the USSR. Anders later suggested to Stalin that this army should move to the Middle East to train and, surprisingly, the latter agreed. Accordingly, over 100,000 Poles, including families, crossed into Persia and thence Iraq where they were joined by the Carpathian Brigade, a Polish formation that had served in North Africa.[78] By the time II Polish Corps joined Eighth Army in 1944 it was well trained, with good discipline and extremely high morale. Of it one writer has commented:

* Simonds was promoted to command II Canadian Corps on 30 January 1944.

There was a deep seriousness in its attitude to war, derived largely from a knowledge of what the Germans were doing in their own country. Harold Macmillan wrote of the Polish Second Corps: 'It was more than a military formation. It was a crusade.'[79]

Another new arrival for Eighth Army was 4th Indian Division, veterans of the desert war. One effect of all these comings and goings was to leave 78th Division as the only major British formation in the army's order of battle. Across the line, Eighth Army now deployed I Canadian Corps on the right – with 1st Canadian and 8th Indian Divisions – and XIII Corps on the left with 78th British and 4th Indian Divisions, part of 5th Canadian Armoured Division, 3rd Carpathian Division and HQ 5th Canadian Armoured. The army front was static and would remain so until the bulk of Eighth Army moved to the Liri valley in the spring. There was, however, a Canadian attempt to wrest from the enemy some high ground north of Ortona preparatory to an attack by part of XIII Corps against Orsogna, Guardiagrele and San Martino; V Corps was also to prepare to continue the advance to Pescara. But this plan came to naught: although 78th Division commenced Operation FORCEFUL on 16 January with a sixty-minute artillery concentration the infantry of 11 Brigade were unable to follow up due to deep snow following an overnight fall.[80]

And so Eighth Army waited while Fifth Army tried to push through to Rome. On the Adriatic coast, Leese was required to maintain pressure on LXXVI Panzer Corps to prevent it deploying support to the divisions facing Fifth Army. However, Leese was not convinced that minor operations by Eighth Army would hold LXXVI Panzer Corps in place. Believing that the Germans would not be concerned by anything less than a major thrust along the coast, he suggested to Alexander that he should intervene with such a thrust in mid-February, by which time his new formations would have found their feet. Agreeing in principle, Alexander advised Leese that he should be ready to make a major effort at short notice from 26 January. Since he felt that Eighth Army could best support Fifth Army operations by attacking in force in mid-February, to coincide with the latter's operations, Leese disagreed with Alexander. However, Alexander had already decided to reinforce Fifth Army at Eighth Army's expense and, on 30 January, Leese was ordered to send 4th Indian Division to Fifth Army with 78th Division to be ready to follow eight days later.[81]

Early in January, 90th Panzer Grenadier Division quit the German line opposite Eighth Army while 26th Panzer was transferred to Avezzano towards the end of the month. Eighth Army still had the task of holding LXXVI Panzer Corps, to which end 1 Canadian Brigade was detailed to seize part of the Villa Grande–Tollo road on 30 January. Once again, however, resistance was stout and the attack was called off. Eighth Army now passed to defensive tasks only.[82]

Notes

1. Molony, *The Mediterranean and Middle East*, op. cit., pp. 473–4.
2. Ibid., pp. 476–80; Kesselring, *Memoirs*, op. cit., pp. 186–9.
3. Molony, op. cit., p. 477.
4. Montgomery, *El Alamein to the Sangro*, p. 175.
5. Molony, op. cit., p. 482n; Doherty, *A Noble Crusade*, op. cit., p. 173.
6. Molony, op. cit., p. 483n.
7. Joslen, *Orders of Battle, Second World War*, p. 141.
8. Molony, op. cit., p. 485.
9. NA, Kew, WO169/8521, Main HQ Eighth Army, 1943; WO169/8619, war diary A/Q Br XIII Corps, 1943; Montgomery, op. cit., pp. 178–9; Molony, op. cit., pp. 486–7; Nicholson, *The Canadians in Italy*, op. cit., pp. 282–7; Aris, *The Fifth British Division*, op. cit., pp. 162–3.
10. Molony, op. cit., p. 486.
11. Molony, op. cit., p. 485; Ray, *Algiers to Austria*, op. cit., pp. 98–9.
12. Molony, op. cit., p. 487.
13. Ibid., p. 488.
14. Ibid.
15. Ibid., pp. 488–90.
16. Ray, op. cit., pp. 100–1; NA, Kew, WO169/8826, war diary, 78 Div, Jul–Dec 1943; WO169/8861, war diary, 4 Armd Bde, Jul–Dec 1943.
17. Molony, op. cit., p. 489.
18. Montgomery, op. cit., p. 152.
19. Molony, op. cit., p. 489.
20. Russell, *Account of the Service of the Irish Brigade*, op. cit.
21. Ibid.; NA, Kew, WO169/8861, war diary, 4 Armd Bde, op. cit.; WO169/8929, war diary, 38 (Irish) Bde, op. cit.; WO169/9373, war diary, 44 RTR, 1943; WO169/10234 , war diary, 6 Innisks, op. cit.; Ray, op. cit., pp. 101–3.
22. Molony, op. cit., pp. 489–90; Russell, op. cit.
23. Molony, op. cit., pp. 490–1; Doherty, *CTW*, op. cit., pp. 100–4.
24. Molony, op. cit., p. 494; Doherty, *CTW*, op. cit., pp. 104–6.
25. Molony, op. cit., pp. 494–5.
26. Ibid., p. 495.
27. Phillips, *The Sangro to Cassino*, vol. I, *Italy: The History of New Zealand in the Second World War*, p. 98.
28. Joslen, op cit, p. 45.
29. Phillips, op. cit., p. 93.
30. Joslen, op. cit., p. 409.
31. Molony, op. cit., pp. 497–9.
32. Ibid., pp. 498–9; Kippenberger, *Infantry Brigadier*, pp. 329–32.
33. Molony, op. cit., p. 499.
34. Phillips, op. cit., p. 96.
35. Nicholson, op. cit., pp. 291–303; Molony, op. cit., pp. 500–2.
36. Nicholson, op. cit., p. 304; Molony, op. cit., pp. 503–4.
37. Molony, op. cit., p. 504.
38. Nicholson, op. cit., pp. 310–11.
39. Ibid., p. 312.
40. *London Gazette,* 6 Mar 1944.
41. Nicholson, op. cit., p. 314.
42. Molony, op. cit., p. 505; Nicholson, op. cit., pp. 315–20.
43. Aris, op. cit., p. 167.

44. Molony, op. cit., pp. 505–6; NA, Kew, WO169/10209, war diary, 5 Essex, op. cit.
45. Molony, op. cit., pp. 506– 7.
46. Ibid., p. 503.
47. Nicholson, op. cit., p. 326.
48. Ibid.
49. Ibid., p. 327.
50. Ibid., p. 324.
51. Ibid., pp. 336–7; Aris, op. cit., pp. 169–70.
52. Molony, op. cit., p. 507.
53. Montgomery, op. cit., pp. 195–6.
54. Brooks, *Montgomery and The Eighth Army*, p. 348.
55. Ibid., p. 328.
56. NA, Kew, WO170/140, Main HQ Eighth Army, Jan 1944.
57. *London Gazette*, 6 Jun 1950.
58. NA, Kew, CAB44/135, p. 17.
59. NA, Kew, WO170/140, op. cit.
60. Chavasse, 'Some Memories', pp. 75–6.
61. NA, Kew, WO170/140, op. cit.
62. Aris, op. cit., p. 171.
63. Kippenberger, op. cit., p. 338.
64. Doherty, *OTE*, op. cit., pp. 120–1; NA, Kew, WO169/8836, war diary, 56 Recce, 1943, op. cit.; WO170/506, war diary, 56 Recce, Jan–Jun 1944.
65. Doherty, *CTW*, op. cit., p. 111; Woods, 'A Personal Account of his service with 2nd London Irish Rifles in Italy', op. cit.
66. Russell, *Account of the Service of the Irish Brigade*, op. cit.; NA, Kew, WO170/605, war diary, 38 (Irish) Bde, Jan–Mar 1944; Doherty, *CTW*, op. cit., p. 110.
67. Phillips, *The Sangro to Cassino*, p. 54.
68. Ray, op. cit., p. 98; Ford, *Battleaxe Division*, op. cit., p. 141.
69. Gunner, *Front of The Line*, p. 121.
70. Joslen, op. cit., p. 284.
71. Ford, op. cit., p. 141.
72. Forman, *To Reason Why*, p. 157.
73. Ibid., pp. 167–8; Ford, op. cit., p. 141.
74. Ford, op. cit., pp. 141–2; Forman, op. cit., pp. 183–6.
75. Aris, op. cit., p. 172.
76. Molony, op. cit., pp. 594–6.
77. Ibid., p. 590 & pp. 594–6.
78. Ibid, pp. 591–2; Anders, *An Army in Exile*, pp. 47–149, provides the background to the birth of the Corps and its arrival in Italy.
79. Howarth, *My God, Soldiers*, p. 108.
80. NA, Kew, WO170/140, op. cit.
81. Ibid.
82. Ibid.

Chapter Four

Prelude to Cassino

Of our labours thou shalt reap the gain.

With Eighth Army at a standstill and operational emphasis switching to Fifth Army, we should look at how the latter had progressed. Pushing hard against the German positions on the other side of Italy's spine, Mark Clark's men had sustained many casualties during December. Some gains had been made but fighting about the Mignano Gap had been fierce with advances measured in yards rather than miles. In mid-December the French Expeditionary Corps' 2nd Moroccan Division had taken Pantale and the northern slopes of Monte Casale, while 45th (US) Division, catching the Germans during a handover, seized Monte Cavallo. With the general aim of reaching the Liri valley, through which runs Highway 6, the old Via Casilina, the main Naples–Rome road, Fifth Army pushed forward towards the Gustav Line in January. Monte Trócchio was taken on the 15th by 34th (Red Bull) Division, the Germans having abandoned it lest its garrison be isolated from the main positions of the Gustav Line which was anchored on Monte Cassino.[1] It would be several months before Allied troops captured the latter which, to many, epitomizes the Italian campaign.

An effort was made to outflank the Gustav Line by landing VI (US) Corps at Anzio on 22 January 1944 in Operation SHINGLE to coincide with a renewed direct assault. Twelve days earlier Clark had issued orders for a fresh offensive with three primary aims: pinning the Germans to the Gustav Line so that they could not reinforce at Anzio; drawing German reserves into the Gustav Line; and breaking through the line to advance rapidly through the Liri valley to join VI Corps at Anzio. Clark's plan proved much too ambitious: Major General Lucas, commanding VI Corps, failed to seize the initiative at Anzio by spending too much time preparing to meet a counter-attack. Naturally, such an attack came, heralding the beginning of a siege of the beachhead that would last until May. Nor was the attack on the Gustav Line any more successful with 36th (US) Division repulsed with severe loss in its attempts to cross the Rapido river. Although X British Corps had more success with 5th and 56th Divisions forming bridgeheads across the Garigliano river both divisions suffered heavily and there were insufficient reinforcements available to restore them to full strength. The third of X Corps' divisions, 46th, was repulsed in its attempt to cross the river. Collectively, 5th, 46th and 56th Divisions required 4,686 new personnel during January. They received only 219. And the manpower situation was to worsen. Elsewhere on Fifth Army's front the French Expeditionary Corps gained all its objectives; Juin's Algerian, Moroccan and Tunisian soldiers excelled in mountain fighting and also had an unsettling effect on enemy morale due to their bloodthirsty, and, seemingly, fearless, approach to battle.[2]

Allied attention now turned to Monte Cassino, topped by its Benedictine monastery, established by Saint Benedict in AD 529. The mountain, 1,700 feet high, looks down on the town of Cassino and on Highway 6, which passes through the town.* Also overlooking the town was a smaller feature known as Castle Hill, from the ruined castle that stood on it; this is 300 feet high. Monte Cassino itself is overlooked by Monte Cáiro, some miles away, which was also in German hands. Any movement in the valley could be seen by observers on these heights who could call down artillery, mortar or machine-gun fire on the intruders.

On 1 February Clark launched a fresh assault, using mainly US troops of II Corps, supported by Juin's men, aimed at breaking through the critical Cassino position. Its failure led to the second battle of Cassino in which the New Zealand Corps played the leading role. This formation owed its title to being commanded by Bernard Freyberg, GOC of 2nd New Zealand Division; as well as Freyberg's division it included 4th Indian and 78th British Divisions.[3] The second battle began on 15 February: 4th Indian attacked the mountain while the New Zealanders concentrated on the town. Having taken the mountain the Indians were to swing into Cassino town from the west. It never came to that: fierce defensive fire from the mountain brought the attackers to a standstill and although the New Zealanders gained a lodgement in Cassino their stay was short as the Germans ensured their departure after only a few hours. But the battle was not called off at that point – it raged until the 18th and Freyberg commented that the destruction wrought in the town reminded him of the Great War.[4]

The New Zealand Corps included three formations from Eighth Army which had been transferred, first, to army group command,[†] and

* A modern *autostrada* or motorway now bypasses Cassino completely but Highway 6 still follows its old route.
[†] Alexander's command became Allied Armies in Italy (AAI) on 11 January 1944 and then Allied Central Mediterranean Force a week later. On 10 March it reverted to the Allied Armies in Italy title and to the original title 15 Army Group in 1945, by which time army groups were using ordinal rather than cardinal designations, making it 15th Army Group.

then, to Fifth Army command. Thus Eighth Army had no part in either of the first two battles of Cassino but would play a major role in the final battle. When Eighth Army soldiers came to fight at Cassino their battleground would have been dictated to some extent by the preparations for the second battle. Major General 'Gertie' Tuker, GOC of 4th Indian, believed that the Germans were using the monastery as a defensive position. This was not true, but Tuker's belief was shared by General Ira Eaker, commanding the Allied air forces. Eaker flew over the mountain and, convincing himself that the monastery was occupied by the Germans, agreed with Tuker's demand to bomb the monastery; Freyberg supported Tuker. Strategic bombers pounded the monastery to ruins into which moved German soldiers of 90th Panzer Grenadier Division, their defensive positions created for them by their enemy.[5]

Yet another assault was planned on Cassino and once again it fell to the New Zealanders. Weather conditions forced its postponement until 15 March by which time 90th Panzer Grenadiers had been relieved by Major General Richard Heidrich's 1st Parachute Division. Following heavy bombing and an artillery bombardment of nearly 200,000 rounds the attack was made but the Germans were as determined as ever while renewed heavy rain made the going difficult. Even so, the attackers took much of the town and Castle Hill, while Gurkhas of 5 Indian Brigade captured Hangman's Hill.*[7] When the attack was called off, no one could have been more relieved than the men of 78th Division, then awaiting their turn to enter the fray. Alexander planned to use the gains of the third assault in the major offensive he was already planning, the fourth and final battle of Cassino.†

Plans for that final battle began crystallizing at a conference between Alexander and his army commanders on 21 March. Also present was Freyberg who reported on his corps' situation. Alexander told his commanders that there were two immediate options: Freyberg's Corps' attack could be reinforced, in the hope of capturing the monastery within days; alternatively, the operation should be abandoned. It was decided to abandon operations and prepare for a fresh assault, this time by Eighth

* According to one historian, so called because there was a large wooden scaffold on its summit from which flew a Nazi flag with its swastika.[6] In fact, it was the support structure for the cable cars that operated from Cassino station to the mountain.
† Just to confuse matters, when battle honours were awarded in the 1950s the committee charged with defining honours chose to identify only two battles which were dubbed Cassino I and Cassino II. The former was said to have lasted from 20 January to 17 March and the latter from 11 to 16 May. Logic is defied by this decision. The official history, however, uses the more precise breakdown into four battles which are described here.

Army which would sidestep across from the Adriatic sector, leaving V Corps, under army group command, holding that sector. That Alexander had already been planning for this is indicated by the fact that Eighth Army HQ had begun moving from Vasto to Venafro on 11 March; it was complete at the latter location two days later. Freyberg's corps was disbanded on 26 March with XIII Corps assuming responsibility for the Cassino sector; 78th Division then moved into positions gained by the New Zealand Corps.[8]

Further reorganization saw all British and Commonwealth divisions, except 1st and 5th British Divisions at Anzio, pass to Eighth Army command.[9] Eighth Army retained II Polish Corps and received some reinforcement with the arrival of 6th (South African) Armoured Division, although this formation initially remained under army group command; as 1st South African Division, it had served earlier in the infantry role with Eighth Army. Also due to join Eighth Army from Fifth Army was the British 6th Armoured Division, once part of First Army in Tunisia, but a proposal to transfer 2nd Division from India to Italy did not go ahead. Two additional armoured brigades, 7 and 9, a tank brigade, 25, and an infantry brigade were also planned for Eighth Army's order of battle as well as an Italian Brigade Group, *1° Raggruppamento Motorizzato*. Alexander obtained a delay in the transfer of some major formations – including the French Expeditionary Corps – out of his command for Operation ANVIL, the invasion of southern France, due to coincide with OVERLORD. (In the event, ANVIL was delayed until August by which time it had been renamed DRAGOON.) Thus Alexander was confident that he would enjoy the superiority in manpower needed to smash the Gustav Line.[10]

AAI's next assault on the Gustav Line, codenamed DIADEM, was to be delivered along a 20-mile front, from the coast to the mountains around Cassino. On the left flank, Fifth Army was to attack through the Aurunci mountains while VI Corps was to break out of Anzio at a time considered appropriate by Alexander and strike northwards to cut off the German retreat. The main effort was to fall on Eighth Army with Oliver Leese's command committed to cracking open the Gustav Line so that his armour might burst through into the Liri valley and advance on the axis of Highway 6 to the area east of Rome. By timing the operation for mid-May it was hoped that the ground would have been dried out by the spring sunshine so that the harder earth would provide better going for the tanks. Once the armour had achieved its aim, Eighth Army was to 'pursue the enemy on the general axis Terni–Perugia' and 'thereafter advance on Ancona and Florence, the main objective at that stage to be decided later'.[11] This showed optimism of an immense degree, especially when one reflects on the previous months. In 'Allied Armies in Italy Operational Instruction No. 5', issued on 5 May 1944, the strategic intention of DIADEM was defined more succinctly.

> To destroy the right wing of the German Tenth Army; to drive what remains of it and the German Fourteenth Army* north of Rome; and to pursue the enemy to the Rimini–Pisa line inflicting the maximum losses to him in the process.[12]

Thus the aim was not to seize any geographical objectives, such as Rome, but to destroy both German armies in the field, thereby forcing the Germans to deploy more reinforcements to Italy if they wished to continue the fight there.

Eighth Army began preparing for the final battle: its part was codenamed Operation HONKER. To prevent the Germans detecting the preparations for DIADEM an elaborate deception plan, Operation DUNTON, was executed. This was the work of Alexander's Chief of Staff, Lieutenant General A.F. 'John' Harding, a man of exceptional talent as both a fighting soldier and a staff officer. Harding knew that the Germans expected another attack on the Gustav Line but could not know the 'when' and the 'where' of that attack, nor the strength with which it would be delivered, nor the troops who would deploy. Harding's aim was to keep the Germans guessing as long as possible.[13]

Among measures included in DUNTON was a scheme to convince Kesselring that there might be further amphibious operations; these were a particular worry to the Germans who had little or no experience in such operations. And so the American 36th Division was sent to the Naples–Salerno area to carry out amphibious exercises. The Americans also masqueraded as Canadians to give the impression that I Canadian Corps was in that sector; Canadian maple leaf signs marked roads, buildings and vehicles in the area; the Canadians had moved back to the front in unmarked transport and had deployed behind XIII Corps on the Gari river. To increase further German apprehensions about a seaborne landing, Allied reconnaissance aircraft paid special attention to the beaches around Civitavecchia; seaborne beach reconnaissances were also made and nearby radar stations were bombed. The impression was given that the landings would take place on 15 May; the hope was that the opening of DIADEM, scheduled for 11 May, would be interpreted as a prelude to those landings.[14]

Harding also planned to deceive the Germans about the whereabouts and strength of the French Expeditionary Corps. Following its withdrawal from north of Cassino, Kesselring's staff lost track of Juin's force, thereby presenting a considerable headache to their chief who wrote that 'The role of the French Expeditionary Corps with its composition and direction of possible thrust remained an important and dangerous unknown factor till

---

* Commanded by von Mackensen.

the fourth day of the offensive.'[15] The movement of II Polish Corps into the Cassino sector was also camouflaged by the simple step of having British signallers in Anders' corps so that enemy monitoring would pick up signals in English rather than Polish. This, too, was completely successful.[16] And, of course, since the Allies enjoyed complete air superiority, the Luftwaffe was unable to provide much intelligence from its occasional reconnaissance flights. Although they could see a build-up taking place and knew that much of Eighth Army had moved from the Adriatic sector, the Germans had no accurate up-to-date information. Contrast that with the Allies who, by D-Day for DIADEM, knew the locations of almost every German artillery piece and mortar.[17]

Although Kesselring's memoirs suggest that he was not duped by Harding's scheme, the evidence indicates otherwise. Reserves were held back to deal with a range of threats, including the seaborne landing at Civitavecchia against which both the Hermann Göring and 92nd Infantry Divisions were deployed. Likewise, 26th Panzer and 29th Panzer Grenadier Divisions were ready to meet further landings at Anzio while 90th Panzer Grenadier Division prepared to meet an Allied airborne assault in the Liri valley near Frosinone.[18] None of these mobile formations would be available immediately to meet the real threat.

The Allied Armies were well catered for by their administrative systems with good logistical arrangements for supplying front-line troops by both road and rail; mule transport was used in some sectors on the Cassino front and even the most seemingly isolated positions did not go short. A good communications system had been established and there were 'comfortably large' supplies of fuel, both petrol and diesel, even though a typical division consumed 49,000 gallons of fuel daily.[19] There were, however, two problems facing British commanders: ammunition for field and medium artillery, and reinforcements, especially for the infantry.

There was nothing that Alexander and his commanders could do about the first: British industry simply could not keep pace with the demand for 25-pounder and medium artillery ammunition, a problem aggravated in Italy by the high expenditure of such munitions. On 21 March Alexander was compelled to restrict 25-pounder ammunition to fifteen rounds per gun per day, while medium ammunition was rationed to ten rounds per gun daily; exceptions were either to repel attacks or support operations that Alexander ordered or approved.[20] It was fortunate for infantry and artillery morale that only Alexander, his higher commanders and staff officers appreciated the true extent of the ammunition famine.

The shortage of reinforcements was also outside Alexander's control. Britain was coming close to the limits of its available manpower – not only the armed forces but also crucial industries such as agriculture, coal and munitions needed personnel – and the level of casualties in Italy had been much higher than expected. In early 1944 Alexander learned that 13,250 infantry reinforcements were being sent to the Mediterranean but no more could be expected until September. Local arrangements would have to be made to replace battle casualties.[21]

The Mediterranean Allied Air Forces* were playing their part in the build-up to DIADEM with some two thirds of their operations being in preparation for the assault, the remainder on targets outside Italy. From 1 April to 12 May, 60,345 air sorties were flown, an average of 1,472 per day, some 20 per cent greater than the rate during March. These figures exclude anti-shipping strikes or raids on ports.[22]

Soldiers on the ground were aware that something big was being prepared. Meanwhile, however, their war went on as normal. Some held positions very close to the enemy while others were much farther from the German positions. For those at the front, Alexander described the cheek-by-jowl closeness of the adversaries when he wrote that 'The Germans were at most 150 yards away; at least in the next-door room.'[23] The British 4th Division, which had served with First Army in Tunisia, joined Eighth Army from Fifth Army on 26 March. Under the latter's command its soldiers had already experienced the peculiar form of static warfare that was the lot of those facing the Gustav Line in the mountains. Relief from that routine was followed by a spell of rest and maintenance before the division relieved 3rd Algerian Division in the mountains north of Cassino. During the divisional commander's reconnaissance of the sector, on 26 March, Brigadier Ivan Smith, the Commander Royal Artillery (CRA), was killed by shellfire.[24]

Fourth Division's new sector had an eight-mile front 'across the wild and mountainous country of the Upper Rapido'. North and north-west of Vallerotonda was deployed Prestonforce, including 4 Recce, under Lieutenant Colonel Preston, the Somersets and a detachment of No. 2 Support Group. Prestonforce's task was to cover the mountain village of Valvori and the Ancina. North and north-west of Sant'Elia, 12 Brigade blocked the Secco valley and the road from Belmonte, while 10 Brigade guarded the heights covering Colle Belvedere and the southern part of the road wending upward from Cáira to Terelle. Everywhere, however, divisional positions were overlooked by German positions. Frequent and accurate enemy shelling and mortaring caused many casualties while the Germans were more aggressive than the division had found along the Garigliano, 'possibly because here it was their turn to hold the dominating positions'.[25] Wooded and scrub-covered ground, laced with deep gullies,

* Including Mediterranean Allied Strategic Air Forces, Mediterranean Allied Tactical Air Forces (the Desert Air Force and US XIIth Tactical Air Command) Mediterranean Allied Coastal Air Forces and Allied Mediterranean Photo-Reconnaissance Wing.

provided cover for enemy patrols operating by night; these would often pass without a shot being fired by either side, the Germans because they had no desire to provoke a firefight, the British because they had not seen the foe.

> The infantry had orders to fire only at Germans within twenty-five yards; but ambushes were organized to wait for unwary enemy patrols. Often the Germans would shout a few words in English, to gain time in a surprise encounter. Sometimes they would carry out a full-scale raid: during the day they would bring down prolonged harassing fire on a company position, perhaps make some sort of demonstration, and then after dark put in the raiding party, covered by a box barrage, on one of the more isolated platoons.[26]

Since the Germans could observe all that happened on the lower ground, resupplying and relieving front-line units caused problems. But those problems were overcome. Food, fresh supplies of ammunition and other necessities were brought up to forward positions under cover of darkness with mules carrying the loads uphill to where they were needed; the normal nightly resupply of a battalion needed about fifty mules.

> A mule could carry 160 lb, thus making it necessary to sort out the food carefully to avoid overloading. It was essential to put the more valuable items, such as rum, tea, sugar and milk on separate mules in case one did not complete the journey. Mail was put in metal boxes to keep it dry. Water was carried in cans. Loads were tied together with metal rings on them in order that they could easily be fixed to the saddle, and were placed side by side with a space in between. Thus when all the tying up was completed there would be a double row of loads. At 1800 hours ... the mules would be led up the centre of these two rows and the loads hooked on to each side of them. The loads were placed in position on the order 'load' given by CSM Mann. The Sergeant-Major's muleing abilities were excellent. His experiences in the earlier battles for Tunisia proved invaluable.[27]

Even before the supplies were loaded onto mules, they had already survived a hazardous journey. Everything needed in the line was transported by road from field maintenance centres, or supply dumps, in the rear and all was assembled in an area hidden from the German artillery observers on the heights. When it was dark enough in the evening a military policeman would give the order to 'move' and everybody rushed off. And 'rushed' is an entirely appropriate verb, especially on that stretch of road dubbed the 'mad mile'. In spite of the condition of the road surface no driver took it easy; along the roadside were posted notices such as 'Shell Trap – No Halting' urging the unwary to greater speed. From their lofty advantage the German gunners had registered* every yard of road and the principal salvation of those who travelled that route was the smokescreen, codenamed Cigarette, that prevented the enemy seeing where exactly their targets were. And the final trek by mules to the forward positions was also along registered tracks. Many were killed by enemy mortar bombs or fell to their deaths from those twisting tracks. They could not be buried as the ground was rocky and thus, as the days grew warmer, the stench of death and decomposing flesh was added to the horrors of Cassino. Although attempts were made to ameliorate the smell by treating the corpses with lime, the stench persisted. Another smell was that of human waste: the average man produces 2.5 pounds of solid and liquid waste daily and that has to go somewhere. In normal circumstances, latrines are dug and a strict sanitary routine imposed but that proved impossible where digging could not be done and improvisation became the order of the day.[28]

That hard, rocky ground, 'like the mountains of the moon', also made it impossible for soldiers to dig in, the infantryman's best form of protection. Instead, adopting a practice from the North-West Frontier of India, they built protective shelters from rocks, known as sangars. As Colin Gunner noted

> Sangar life engulfed us now. No digging down six feet into the sandy soil of Capua – laborious piling of rock with a pathetic little roof took place on these adamantine slopes. . . . These were no Pathans or Afridis facing us here. This enemy dealt not in the single brain-splashing shot of the rifle, but in generalised and wholesale death. No need to view Dead Mule Corner for proof. By day and night the stench was eloquent testimony to their efficiency. . . . We were many times better off than the battalion directly facing the Monastery, where throwing the contents of his lavatory tin out of the back of his sangar earned for many a man a hail of mortar bombs. Just try sharing a rock hole about the size of two coffins with three others, then, in a prone position, lower your costume and fill a small tin held in the hand. The stink of excrement competed with the death smell on every position. Bowels will not wait for nightfall. Down below in [Cassino] matters were similar and here we heard of stretcher bearers of both sides meeting for a friendly chat, but I never did get confirmation of that German Major who asked a stretcher party if they had any Players cigarettes.[29]

* In other words, they had recorded the range, bearing, elevation and other data needed to drop a shell at any point along the road.

Gunner's battalion, 1st Royal Irish Fusiliers, was in the valley from Cáira village up to Monte Cáiro, a position lacking the protection of reverse slopes. Battalion HQ was in the most heavily shelled part of the line, apart from Cáira village where Irish Brigade HQ was located. Pat Scott, the Brigade's new commander, was recovering from a broken ankle and needed a stick to move about; he very soon banned the Irish Fusiliers' mortars, positioned above his HQ, from firing anything other than defensive tasks as there was already quite enough hot metal descending around him without retaliatory fire on the Faughs' mortars adding to it. It was believed that Cáira was the most heavily shelled place in Italy. Scott's other two battalions were not quite as exposed as the Faughs but were still in unpleasant positions: 2nd London Irish were on Monte Castellone, a 2,300-foot-high feature with excellent observation of the enemy positions. It also drew considerable fire from his heavy artillery, some of which sailed over the Rifles' heads to land near Brigade HQ at Cáira, although most such rounds failed to explode.[30]

But the most 'extraordinary position' held by the Irish Brigade was that of the Inniskillings whose right-hand company could look down on the monastery. The Inniskillings covered one of the few tracks that led into the German positions and the enemy were very active in the area. Troops of 3rd Algerian Division had held these positions before the Irish Brigade and had suffered considerably from German night raids and patrolling. This was partly the fault of the French themselves who seemed not to believe in patrolling. However, the Inniskillings' commanding officer, Lieutenant Colonel Bala Bredin, was not inclined to allow the Germans a free run of no man's land. An Ulster Rifleman with an MC from Palestine, where he had commanded Wingate's Special Night Squads in Wingate's absence, Bredin had seen service in France in 1940. Later appointed as brigade major of an airborne brigade he had been posted to North Africa and, when the campaign there ended, found life in his brigade so dull that he transferred himself to the Irish Brigade, assuming the position of second-in-command of the Irish Fusiliers as they were embarking for Termoli; he threw away his red beret and donned a Faughs' sidecap on the quayside. Later he was appointed to command the Skins, as the Inniskillings were known.[31]

Even if the British Army did not believe in dominating no man's land as a matter of military principle, Bredin would not have tolerated German activity in that area. He ensured that the Germans soon learned that the Skins controlled the in-between ground. As night fell, patrols from either side would slip into no man's land and begin the race for cover, including knocked-out tanks, from which to spring ambushes. More than forty years later Bredin said, 'The Skins always won and we soon established our superiority over the Germans.'[32]

75

One of the greatest dangers of those mountain positions came from flying rock splinters as well as shell splinters. In normal ground an exploding round will send much of its energy into the soil thus reducing the amount of metallic debris that flies about. This was not the case when a shell burst on or against rock: not only was all its energy unleashed to fling debris to the four winds but it also added splinters from the rock. These fragments flew both farther and less predictably than with shells bursting on normal ground; splinters could wound or kill at more than a hundred yards. Many more soldiers needed treatment for head wounds than hitherto since shells bursting overhead would rain splinters into the sangars where overhead protection was either non-existent or flimsy. Eye wounds became more common with many losing their sight; so numerous were such injuries that 92nd General Hospital was turned over largely to ophthalmic cases, while 65th General Hospital treated head and facial wounds as well as neurosurgical cases.[33]

Arguably the most vulnerable positions held by any battalion of 78th Division were those occupied by the West Kents on Castle Hill. The Germans in the monastery could look straight down into the courtyard of the ruined medieval castle and those paratroopers still in Cassino town were at the most about a hundred yards away on the south and east sides. So why hold the castle at all? The reason became clear to the West Kents when they took possession: Castle Hill dominated a valley leading from the town to Monte Cassino and since this was the most obvious route for an approach to the monastery it meant that Eighth Army would want to hold the hill in spite of the possible costs.[34]

All that remained of the castle itself was the central courtyard, part of a strong stone tower and the ruins of a curtain wall, about ten feet in height.* To reach the castle the West Kents had to climb vertical rocks.

> At first it was held by two complete companies, but this was later considered to be unnecessary. It was more economical to hold the vulnerable spot with just two platoons, each of which was relieved after forty-eight hours. It was further decided to rotate this onerous task so that the two platoons were taken from each company, and each battalion in [36 Brigade], in turn. Everyone was to have the 'honour' of holding the castle.[35]

Although it is now fifty years since it was first published, the best book on the battles for Cassino remains Fred Majdalany's *Cassino: Portrait of a Battle*. Majdalany, who commanded a company of 2nd Lancashire Fusiliers in 11 Brigade, wrote movingly of one of the sights that faced those who fought at Cassino:

* The castle has since been restored.

One of the most touching sights on these corpse-littered mountains was a Gurkha cemetery. The graves seemed too short for a man, and the boots at the end of each one, too small. (There was always a steel helmet at one end of the grave, boots at the other.) The rows of little boots always gave the impression that this was a burial ground of children.[36]

As with the other Battleaxe Division battalions, the Lancashire Fusiliers deployed into positions around Cassino, and as with the other battalions they were happy when their turn for relief came. That relief, at the end of April, was carried out under cover of darkness with Polish troops moving in to take their places; the Lancashire Fusiliers

marched back ... in the way of the Infantry, their feet scarcely leaving the ground, their bodies rocking mechanically from side to side as if that was the only way they could lift their legs. You could see that it required the last ounce of their mental and physical energy to move their legs at all. Yet they looked as if they could keep on moving like that for ever.

Their clothes were torn and ragged. They carried their weapons every conceivable way they could be carried. Every few minutes they would change shoulders or change positions. The heavier burdens, like the Brens and the mortars, were passed along from one to another. Every man took his turn.

Their bearded faces were black with honourable dirt, and their eyes stared to their front and appeared to see nothing. No one sang or whistled, and hardly anyone spoke unless it was to utter a curse when his rifle slipped off his shoulder.[37]

Handing over to the Poles created a communication problem with few able to converse in a common language. Captain Brian Clark, the Irish Fusiliers' adjutant, noted the irony that he was able to hand over to his Polish counterpart in a language they both understood: German.[38] Units of 4th Division were deployed in Cassino town, described by their historian as

like another world. The conditions in which the garrison had to live were so bad that troops were allowed to stay there for only eight days, and the foremost positions were so bad that they could be occupied without relief for only half that time. The place could be reached only at night, and even then the approach had to be covered by a heavy smoke screen, known as Cigarette.[39]

Here we meet another battalion of the Royal West Kents, the regular 1st Battalion in 12 Brigade. With the other two battalions of 12 Brigade, the West Kents took over from 1 Guards Brigade, the Kentish men relieving

3rd Grenadiers in the more open southern sector. Thus the West Kents had positions that were spaced more widely than those of their fellows; their left company occupied the ruins of three large houses known as Mary, Helen and Jane, facing the lateral strip of Highway 6, on which were the Hotel des Roses and the Baron's Palace, and separated from the enemy by the Rapido. However, Battalion HQ was in less salubrious surroundings, sharing the crypt of the church with the HQ of 6th Black Watch. This

completely subterranean room would have been anything but spacious for one of them. The only subdivisions of the available space was into cubicles with low vaulted ceilings. All the members of the headquarters, from commanding officers to orderlies, worked, ate and slept there; the wireless sets on battalion, brigade and artillery frequencies were continuously, and noisily, working; the wounded were brought in for treatment, and waited there until night-fall, when they could be evacuated; whatever cooking was possible, including the essential brew-ups, went on in all odd corners at odd hours of the day and night; and the sanitary system – buckets carried out and emptied at night – was unavoidably more public than in normal conditions.[40]

But the crypt did have some advantages: there was so much rubble atop it that it withstood even the heaviest, 210mm, enemy artillery shells. And the ventilation was good, although light was entirely artificial.[41]

Elsewhere in the town A Squadron 4 Recce took over the area of Cassino station at the beginning of May. Overhead they could watch bombers attacking the mountain and were close enough to see the bombs tumble out of the aircraft and plunge down to impact. Bob Pite commented that 'We gloried then. Now, I don't want to see it again.' There was a constant drip of casualties in 4 Recce as in every other unit in the area; A Squadron suffered one man killed and eight wounded when the station was mortared on 4 May while C Squadron lost five dead and fifteen wounded, one of whom later died, from German shelling.

The outstanding [memory] was ... a defensive position in Cassino Station, through one window the Baron's Castle, from the next – not window but dug-out under the wall – the monastery with the road zigzagging right in front of us up to the top and the 'hill' to the right. At night, and we [No. 2 Troop] stayed three whole days living under the floor with just enough room to sit up, the fireflies. I'll never forget the sight of them, little red sparks glowing and hovering everywhere.

I got my closest shave ... here. We were stretching our legs and moving about the passageway above ground one midday. Someone pushed his camera through a hole in the wall and took a photograph of the Baron's Castle. A minute later there was a sharp ping behind me, and there was a bullet with the tracer just dying, resting amongst the tickets of the ticket board inches from my backside. .... Nobody took any more snaps, I can tell you.[42]

Casualties from shelling and mortaring were many. Stretcher-bearers risked their lives to assist the wounded as did one of 78th Division's chaplains. Father Dan Kelleher, of the Irish Brigade,

> was at Battalion HQ in the Cáira area when heavy shelling was reported in Cáira village causing several casualties to one of the platoons. The Rev. Kelleher immediately raced to the village, which was under very heavy shelling. He found the wounded men and assisted the stretcher bearers in their work, carrying wounded in his arms, at great personal risk, to the shelter of a ruined building.
> He comforted the badly wounded ... and assisted the overworked stretcher bearers in applying bandages to their wounds.[43]

Dan Kelleher was later awarded the Military Cross.

As final preparations were being made for Operation DIADEM, the attacking formations were rehearsing their roles with infantry and armoured units training together to create balanced and effective battlegroups. Since the forthcoming battle would begin with river crossings, those units that would carry out such crossings trained in the use of assault boats. There were also exercises in street fighting but the main emphasis was on infantry/armour cooperation which, for 78th Division, meant joint training with 26 Armoured Brigade, of 6th Armoured Division, whose 16th/5th Lancers would support the Irish Brigade. This pairing was appropriate as the 5th Lancers had once been the Royal Irish Lancers and the amalgamated regiment's NCOs wore an Irish harp on their chevrons. The other two regiments of 26 Armoured Brigade were assigned to support 4th Division, with 17th/21st Lancers assaulting with 10 and 28 Brigades, while 2nd Lothians and Border Horse would operate with 12 Brigade, the divisional reserve. Each battalion had a squadron of tanks assigned and the intensive training led to the establishment of an excellent rapport that helped to break down the suspicion and mistrust that the infantry had hitherto felt towards the tankmen.[44] Of course, there was also an element of socializing in the training programme that prompted one Irish Fusiliers officer to comment: 'The bigger the blind, the better the battle.'[45]

While each division was out of the line, its soldiers were granted six days' leave, which could be spent at rest camps at Maiori, Ravello or Amalfi. Some took day trips to Capri or to view the ruins of Pompeii – made even more interesting since Vesuvius had erupted in March – or to 'the squalid, cheerful, captivating bustle of Naples'. The San Carlo Opera House had been reopened and many soldiers were to be found in its audiences, captivated by the beauty of music. But there was another side to Naples and

> Many a stolid soldier, wandering around the streets ... felt a pang of pity as he saw the hard face of hunger mirrored in the patient eyes of some ancient Italian crone, or saw the need rather than the impudence in the unselfconscious pose of a begging child little bigger than a baby.[46]

The respite was short, however, since less than 50 miles away the monastery-cum-fortress on Monte Cassino continued to deny Highway 6 to the Allied Armies and the day of reckoning for the defenders was close. No written operational order was issued for Eighth Army,[47] whose order of battle on the eve of DIADEM was:[48]

Corps	Divisions/Brigades
X Corps (Lt Gen R.J. McCreery)	2nd New Zealand Division (Lt Gen Sir Bernard Freyberg VC) 24 Guards Brigade (Brig A.F.L. Clive) 2 Parachute Brigade (Brig C.H.V. Pritchard) 12 South African Motorized Brigade (Brig R.J. Palmer) 1 (Italian) Motorized Brigade Group (Brig Gen Vicenzo di Pino)*
XIII Corps (Lt Gen S.C. Kirkman)	6th Armoured Division (Maj Gen V. Evelegh) 4th Division (Maj Gen A.D. Ward) 78th Division (Maj Gen C.F. Keightley) 8th Indian Division (Maj Gen D. Russell) 1 Canadian Armoured Brigade (Brig W.C. Murphy)
I Canadian Corps (Lt Gen E.L.M. Burns)	5th Canadian Armoured Division (Maj Gen B.M. Hoffmeister) 1st Canadian Division (Maj Gen C. Vokes) 25 Tank Brigade† (Brig J.N. Tetley)
II Polish Corps‡ (Lt Gen W. Anders)	3rd Carpathian Division (Maj Gen Duch) 5th Kresowa Division (Maj Gen Sulik) 2 Polish Armoured Brigade (Maj Gen Rakowski)
V Corps (Lt Gen C.W. Allfrey)	4th Indian Division (Maj Gen A.W.W. Holworthy) 10th Indian Division (Maj Gen D. Reid) 23 Armoured Brigade (Brig R.A. Hermon)
Army Reserve	6th South African Armoured Division (Maj Gen W.H. Evered Poole)

* The group included 67th Infantry Regiment, 51st Bersaglieri Battalion, 11th Artillery Regiment, 5th Anti-Tank Regiment and an Engineer battalion, and had shown considerable élan while under Fifth Army Command.
† A tank brigade was so-called to distinguish it from an armoured brigade. Its role was to support the infantry with I-, or Infantry, tanks, by now Churchills, whereas the armoured brigades operated faster-moving cruiser tanks, although in Italy they were usually equipped with Shermans.
‡ II Polish Corps divisions each disposed only two infantry brigades.

Sidney Kirkman's XIII Corps was to provide the main striking force but before the corps could begin its push through the Liri valley it had first to cross the Gari. This river was about 60 feet wide, six or more feet deep, and flowed at about eight miles per hour between steep, soft banks with flood banks from three to seven feet high. On the Gari's west bank were sited typical German defensive positions including strong points and pillboxes, all connected by trenches, and protected by mines and wire. But these defences lacked strength in depth with no prepared positions for reserves in the rear. In fact the next prepared defensive positions were in the Hitler Line, between Aquino and Pontecorvo, about eight miles behind, and there was a lack of mobile reserves, due to fear of Allied seaborne or airborne operations.[49]

To cross the Gari, XIII Corps relied on its engineers to build bridges, although the assaulting infantry would cross in folding boats. The initial assault was assigned to two divisions, 4th British, operating from north of Monte Trócchio, and 8th Indian, from south of Trócchio and against the 'Horseshoe'. Held in reserve at this stage, 78th Division was 'to be ready to operate on the south flank of 8th Indian Division, or to pass through it or through 4th Division'.[50] This would also be the time for 6th Armoured Division to begin its advance to reinforce and expand the bridgehead with 78th Division and then break out to crack open the Gustav Line south of Cassino. With the line broken I Canadian Corps would take over and exploit towards Valmontone through the Liri valley.[51]

Once XIII Corps' attack was underway the Poles would begin their operations which were to:

I 1. Isolate the area Monastery Hill–Cassino from the north and north-west and dominate Highway 6 until a junction is effected with XIII Corps;
   2. Attack and capture Monastery Hill.

II Gain contact with the Adolf Hitler Line North of Highway 6 and develop operations with a view to turning it from the North.[52]

General Richard McCreery's X Corps was deployed to protect Eighth Army's right, or northern, flank with a minimum of troops. Freyberg's New Zealanders, who had already suffered heavily in the earlier battles, constituted the largest formation in X Corps and helped create the illusion that the corps might attack towards Atina; the Germans always expected aggression from the New Zealanders. In addition, McCreery was to be prepared to release formations to the main battle.[53]

Careful husbanding of ammunition had allowed the artillery to build up substantial stockpiles. Eighth Army had almost 2,000 guns, excluding anti-tank and anti-aircraft weapons, and for the beginning of the offensive each heavy gun in XIII Corps had 200 rounds available while 350 rounds were available per medium gun and 600 per 25-pounder; II Polish Corps had no heavy guns but had 700 rounds for each medium and 1,090 for each 25-pounder. As ever the artillery would play an important role in the offensive with 300 guns deployed in the Polish sector and 700 in XIII Corps'; the opening bombardment was made with 1,100 guns on Eighth Army's front. Leese was placing his trust in the artillery playing a battle-winning role.[54]

Before examining the battle, a glance at German dispositions and thinking would be worthwhile. They had created very strong defences in the Liri valley but, in keeping with their doctrine of defence in depth, these were not confined to the Gustav Line but also included the Hitler Line. That line, renamed the Senger Line by the Germans in January (the Allies retained the earlier title), lay some miles west of the Gustav Line and ran southwards from Monte Cáiro to Piedimonte, Aquino, Pontecorvo, Monte Faggeto, Fondi and thence to the coast at Terracina. It had two subsidiary lines, the Dora, which branched off near Santa Oliva towards Esperia and then around the lower slopes of Monte Fammera to Gaeta, while the other, named Orange and intended to deny the Ausonia valley to an attack from Minturno, struck out from near San Apollinare through Vallemaio and Corena to Monte la Civita. The Dora Line could fulfil two roles: as an outwork of the Hitler or a layback of the Gustav. As if these were not enough there was yet another line, the C Line, north of Avezzano through Valmontone to Velletri, to be met along the road to Rome.[55]

Defending against Eighth and Fifth Armies was Tenth German Army under von Vietinghoff which disposed XIV Panzer (von Senger und Etterlin) and LI Mountain Corps (Feuerstein), as well as *Korpsgruppe* Hauck, under Major General Friedrich-Wilhelm Hauck, of two infantry divisions, and an Army Group Reserve, of one infantry division, under Major General Ernst-Günther Baade. In all, Tenth Army, holding a line from coast to coast, deployed nine divisions while Fourteenth Army, under von Mackensen, included six divisions and was deployed against VI Corps at Anzio. In army group reserve Kesselring held 26th Panzer, 29th and 90th Panzer Grenadier Divisions, while in northern Italy was *Armeegruppe* von Zangen of four divisions and a number of independent units. By the end of April the Germans were certain that an attack was coming and were agreed generally that XIV Panzer Corps might be attacked simultaneously at several points. To ease the pressure on that corps, LI Mountain Corps was ordered, on 24 April, to take under command the divisions in the centre of Tenth Army's line: 44th Infantry, 5th Mountain and 114th Jäger, to which were added 1st Parachute Division on 7 May. This re-organization was to take effect from 10 May. D-Day for DIADEM was 11 May and thus it may be seen that the Germans were caught on the hop.[56] Senger wrote that the attack 'was a complete surprise'. He and von Vietinghoff had been 'superfluously ordered to meet Hitler to receive our decorations' after which they went on leave.[57]

My deputy, an experienced but not so young general, had been rash enough to send my Chief of Staff on leave as well, and without his expertise to fall back on, the general was not up to his task in this major battle.[58]

Senger was confident that no attack would be made before his return in late May.[59]

As usual, the smokescreen was laid on the evening of 11 May. Not to have done so would have seemed strange and alerted the Germans to a change of Allied routine and the possibility of an attack. The day had been cloudy, 'with a little rain, but the night was clear'.[60] So it was that everything seemed normal on what was one of the quietest evenings for a long time on the Cassino front. Normality ended at 11.00pm as the ground was shaken by the roar of Allied guns, over 1,600 of which crashed out their thunder along the front. For forty minutes the artillery pounded the known positions of every German artillery unit along the front. Then their attention switched to the first objectives of the assaulting Allied infantry.[61] With the night sky lit up for miles around, and the earth quivering, there could be no doubt that a major operation was underway: Operation DIADEM had begun.

Notes

1. Molony, *The Mediterranean and Middle East*, vol. V, op. cit., pp. 598–602.
2. Ibid.
3. Ibid., p. 697.
4. Ibid., pp. 714–22.
5. Ibid., pp. 708–9; Blumenson, *Mark Clark*, p. 186.
6. Parkinson, *Always a Fusilier*, p. 178.
7. Molony, op. cit., pp. 785–8.
8. NA, Kew, WO170/146, war diary, Main HQ, Eighth Army, Feb 1944; WO170/151, war diary, Main HQ Eighth Army, Mar 1944; Molony, op. cit., p. 802; Ray, *Algiers to Austria*, op. cit., p. 116.
9. Army Inst No. 1419, in NA, Kew, WO170/151, war diary Main HQ Eighth Army, Mar 1944, op. cit.
10. Molony, *The Mediterranean and Middle East*, vol. VI, pt 1, pp. 12–16; NA, Kew, WO170/151, war diary, Main HQ Eighth Army, Mar 1944, op. cit.; WO170/156, war diary, Main HQ Eighth Army, Apr 1944.
11. Molony, op. cit., p. 58.
12. Ibid., p. 57.
13. Carver, *Harding of Petherton*, pp. 134–5.
14. Ibid.; Doherty, *A Noble Crusade*, op. cit., pp. 199–200; Kesselring, *Memoirs*, p. 200.
15. Kesselring, op. cit., p. 199.
16. Ellis, *Cassino: The Hollow Victory*, p. 276.
17. Scott, *An Account of the Service of the Irish Brigade*.
18. Molony, op. cit., pp. 68–75 detail the German order of battle prior to the Allied attack.

19. Ibid., pp. 26–7.
20. Ibid., pp. 29–31.
21. Ibid., pp. 30–1.
22. Ibid., Table II, following p. 53.
23. Alexander, *Memoirs*, p. 244.
24. Williamson, *The Fourth Division*, p. 108; www.cwgc.org Brig Ivan Victor Russell Smith was aged forty-seven.
25. Williamson, op. cit., pp. 109–11.
26. Ibid., p. 110.
27. *Northants History*, quoted in Ford, *Battleaxe Division*, p. 151.
28. Scott, *An Account of the Service of The Irish Brigade*, op. cit.; Norman Bass, Transport Officer 1 RIrF, interview with author 1992.
29. Gunner, *Front of The Line*, op. cit., p. 81.
30. Scott, op. cit.
31. Bredin, interview with author, Feb 1989.
32. Ibid.
33. Majdalany, *Cassino*, p. 207.
34. Williamson, op. cit., p. 120; Ford, op. cit., p. 149; Ray, op. cit., p. 117.
35. Ford, op. cit., pp. 149–50.
36. Majdalany, op. cit., p. 200.
37. Majdalany, *The Monastery*, pp. 75–6.
38. Clark, interview with author, Aug 1990.
39. Williamson, op. cit., p. 116.
40. Ibid., p. 118.
41. Ibid.
42. Pite, letter to author, 1992.
43. *The Faugh A Ballagh Gazette*, No. 159, p. 227.
44. Ray, op. cit., pp. 122–3; Doherty, *CTW*, op. cit., p. 126; Ford, *Mailed Fist*, pp. 131–2.
45. The comment was attributed to John Horsfall by Brian Clark during an interview with the author, 1990.
46. Ray, op. cit., p. 123.
47. NA, Kew, CAB106/418, 'Campaign in Central Italy, 26 Mar–10 Aug 1944', p. 11.
48. Molony, op. cit., pp. 14–15.
49. Ibid., p. 76.
50. Ibid., pp. 78–9.
51. Ibid., pp. 60–1; Nicholson, *The Canadians in Italy*, op. cit., p. 400.
52. Molony, op. cit., p. 59.
53. Ibid., p. 61.
54. Ibid., p. 32n.
55. Ibid., pp. 56–7.
56. Ibid., pp. 47–53.
57. Von Senger, *Neither Fear Nor Hope*, p. 244.
58. Ibid.
59. Ibid.
60. NA, Kew, CAB106/418, 'Campaign in Central Italy, 26 Mar–10 Aug 1944', p. 12.
61. Ibid.; WO170/929, war diary, 17 Fd Regt, 1944; Molony, op. cit., p. 99; Williamson, op. cit., pp. 11–12; Doherty, *A Noble Crusade*, op. cit., p. 200.

Chapter Five

Operation HONKER:
The Battle for Monte Cassino

He'll remember with advantages what feats he did that day.

Eighth Army's artillery bombardment was followed by XIII Corps' attack. This was scheduled for 11.45pm with II Polish Corps attacking at 1.00am on the 12th. General Alexander had noted that 'there is no doubt that the Germans intend to fight for every yard and that the next few days will see some extremely bitter and severe fighting.' His prediction proved very accurate. For the leading formations of XIII Corps, 4th British and 8th Indian Divisions, their experience was as bloody and confused as had been that of the infantry in the opening hours of the Battle of El Alamein. This time they were trying to cross not a dusty desert but a fast-flowing river under cover of darkness and in small folding boats. Mist added to their difficulties, making it almost impossible to cross in the assault boats. Those small groups that did cross the Gari were cut off and wiped out, thus preventing the sappers bridging the river. In spite of all the punishment they had taken, German machine gunners were manning their weapons and firing on fixed lines at the obvious bridging points while artillery and mortars bombarded pre-arranged targets. Anyone approaching the river-banks on Eighth Army's side, especially the bridging points, was caught in their fire.[1]

Two assaults were planned by 4th Division: 10 Brigade on the right, and 28 Brigade on the left. Brigadier Shoosmith, 10 Brigade's commander, had selected two crossing points, Rhine and Orinoco, the first where the Ascensione stream enters the Gari and the second about 600 yards downstream. Brigadier Montagu-Douglas Scott, of 28 Brigade, had also chosen two crossing points: X, 550 yards below Orinoco, and Y, some 250 yards beyond X. Both groups were reinforced strongly; 17th/21st Lancers provided armour support, one squadron with 28 Brigade and the other two

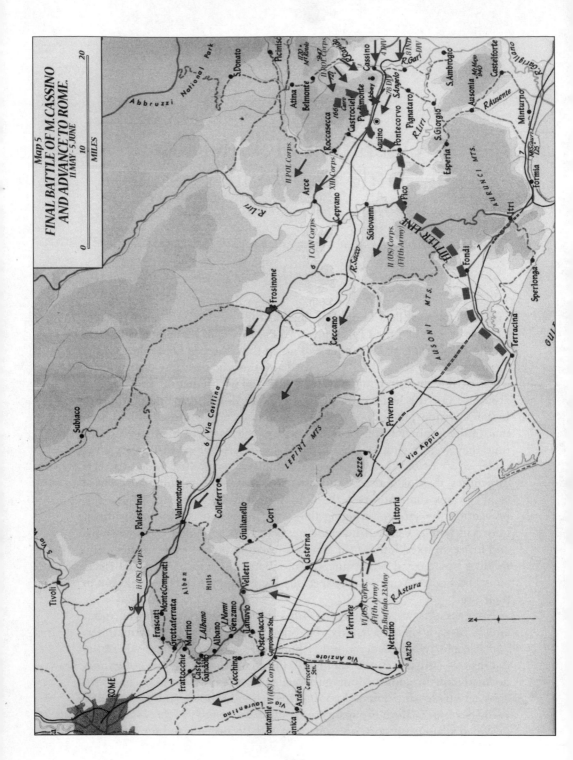

Map 5
FINAL BATTLE OF M.CASSINO
AND ADVANCE TO ROME.
11 MAY – 5 JUNE

with 10 Brigade. Of assault boats the former brigade had thirty and the latter forty-two.[2]

Having crossed the river both assault groups 'were to advance as quickly as possible to a depth of some three thousand yards beyond the river'. Once there the GOC, Major General Dudley Ward, who had assumed command on 20 April, planned to push 12 Brigade forward, preferably through 10 Brigade, after which, with 12 and 28 Brigades in forward positions, 10 Brigade could wheel right to seize Cassino. This advance was to take the form of four 'bounds' to successive reporting lines: Brown, 1,000 yards beyond and parallel to the Gari; Blue, another 1,000 to 1,500 yards farther on; Red, a bulge some 2,000 yards in depth beyond Blue; and Green, about another 1,500 yards forward. Brown Line would allow the crossing points to be covered against counter-attacks; Blue, along the first high ground beyond the Gari, would shield those crossings from observers in the Liri valley; while Green extended to the right in a deep salient towards the rear of Monte Cassino and the point where XIII Corps and II Polish Corps were to link.[3]

The advance of 10 Brigade was led by 1/6th East Surreys whose entry into the river was met by a storm of machine-gun and mortar fire, in spite of which A and D Companies secured footholds on the Gari's western bank. Forming up was difficult since platoons were mixed up, troops having crossed in an order other than that planned. River mist combined with the smoke of battle and the dust raised by artillery and mortars to produce a thick fog that created more confusion. At this stage the troops were to be guided forward by Bofors guns firing tracer but, with the tracer invisible in the fog, both companies blundered into a minefield, suffering many casualties.

Nonetheless, A and D Companies pressed ahead, although they had fallen behind the artillery curtain. B Company then crossed without loss and moved forward, but no more than 200 yards from the riverbank. C Company also followed. A and D were forced to stop at Point 36 by intense machine-gun fire and were joined by C. Battalion HQ also crossed but remained close to the bank where it was forced three times to move by mortars and machine guns. B Company, moving once again, joined elements of 2nd Bedfords just before dawn while C and D Companies took Point 36 in a bayonet charge, capturing twenty-four prisoners and thirteen machine guns. B Company later joined them, having been repulsed from Point 63, and the entire battalion consolidated there. Under constant enemy fire, the Surreys held their position throughout that day and night.[4]

Other elements of the brigade had also crossed and advanced. The Bedfords had all four companies across but found their compasses erratic. Two companies wandered into minefields but maintained their advance and by dawn were on or near 'Queen Street', the road from Cassino to Sant'Angelo, where they were told to dig in while the brigade tightened its hold on its bridgehead. For this they were joined by 2nd Duke of Cornwall's LI, 10 Brigade's third battalion. Fortunately for 10 Brigade thick fog shrouded the valley until well into the morning of 12 May, preventing the Germans from observing clearly the crossing places and the troops already over the Gari. Smoke bombs thickened and sustained the fog but when it lifted the ferrying and bridging operations had to stop. Ward 'ordered only minor advances and consolidation until each Brigade had four [anti-tank] guns on the west bank'.[5] Bad as 10 Brigade's situation was, 28 Brigade faced even more difficult circumstances, having been pinned to the riverbank. Both assaulting battalions, 2nd King's (Liverpool) and 2nd Somerset LI, had been mauled badly by the defenders. Reaching the crossing points half an hour late, the King's lost the benefit of the counter-battery programme which was drawing to a close. As their boats were launched enemy fire came down on them, destroying many. Even so, three companies crossed but, having already lost many men, these were disorganized. When B Company tried to advance they ran into a minefield while D Company was down to one officer with ten men and C Company took heavy losses crossing a minefield under heavy fire.[6]

Further confusion followed in 28 Brigade as the Somersets prepared to follow the King's. They became so badly disorganized that one company even withdrew, believing erroneously that there had been an order to that effect. The net effect was that 28 Brigade's attack had failed in a manner that raised questions about the leadership in Brigade HQ and in the King's and Somersets, both regular battalions of whom much more was expected. On 14 May the brigade was withdrawn for reorganization and did not rejoin 4th Division until the 20th. During that time its third battalion, 2/4th Hampshires, a TA unit, was attached to 12 Brigade.[7] The brigade commander, who had assumed command only on 12 April, remained in post until the end of July.[8]

What of 8th Indian Division? They also suffered crossing the Gari with many boats swept away by the current before they could reach the western bank. Those soldiers who did reach that bank also found thick fog blotting out the tracers intended to guide them forward. However, the fog was not a completely negative element since it concealed the attackers from enemy observers. Divisional objectives for the opening twenty-four-hour phase of HONKER included the establishment of a bridgehead which had now been achieved. Having pushed that bridgehead out to a depth of some 2,000 yards, 8th Indian Division was then to mop up in Sant'Angelo village before consolidating on the ridge beyond the village. At that stage either 78th Division or I Canadian Corps would pass through the Indians en route for the Hitler Line.[9]

Not surprisingly, the advance fell behind schedule. The plan had been for an advance of a hundred yards every six minutes but, although the artillery maintained this programme, the infantry could not keep pace. The historian of the Royal Fusiliers, the 1st Battalion of which served in 17 Indian Brigade, wrote of how

by 0400 the Commanding Officer [1st Royal Fusiliers] signalled the leading companies to halt and later to reorganize on the river bank. ... The Commanding Officer went boldly forward into the mist to locate the line of advance and, encountering wire, made the complete circuit of an enemy strongpoint. But no attack could be launched in such conditions [and the fusiliers] proceeded to dig in and wait for the mist to clear. It cleared all right the following morning and the sun came out at 09.00 hours. But with it came ... enemy fire ... and the slightest movement brought down fire.[10]

The soldiers of 17 Brigade's other assaulting battalion, 1/12th Frontier Force Regiment, suffered similar difficulties. Added to those was a touch of farce when, prior to the crossing, the battalion beachmaster could not even find the river; the adjutant, none too pleased at this, informed his fellow officer quite curtly where he might find the Gari. When 1/12th Frontier Force tried extending the bridgehead they attacked left of Sant'Angelo but met mines and wire that forced a rethink. As they tried working their way around they came under heavy fire, the platoons spread out and the leading companies lost contact with each other. Flares fired in an effort to re-establish contact were invisible in the mist but when some soldiers started shouting regimental war cries the problem was soon resolved and contact re-established.[11]

Both Fusiliers and Frontiersmen then made flanking attacks on the village but were brought to a standstill by enemy fire. The third battalion of 17 Brigade, 1/5th Gurkha Rifles, was brought forward for a frontal attack. An excess of optimism led to a decision to attack with a single company which might have worked had not two platoons lost their bearings crossing the Gari and moving to the start line. When it was launched, the attack was made by only a single platoon, which had already suffered casualties. Not surprisingly, it was beaten off.[12]

The principal objective for 19 Brigade was Pignataro, with 3/8th Punjabis leading the attack. Although most of the boats had been lost, the Punjabis got almost all their men across by improvising a shuttle service with the remaining boats. But this took longer than had been planned originally and the battalion did not move off until the following morning. A Company then ran into a minefield where many men were lost either to mines or small-arms fire. Of those who had stepped off from the start line only fifteen were still standing and when the company reached the road running parallel to the river only nine men remained; a company had been reduced to a section. Undaunted by their predicament the nine *jawans* tried to advance but were forced to take cover after a few yards. In their new position they were subjected to several counter-attacks in the course of the day, each of which they fought off. On the morning of 13 May only three men were able to fight and were eventually forced to surrender when their ammunition ran out.[13]

This outstanding example of courage from Indian soldiers was not unusual. Their battalion had already gained Eighth Army's first Victoria Cross of the Cassino battle when nineteen-year-old Sepoy Kamal Ram from Karauli State silenced three machine-gun posts that had stopped his company's advance. Fire was directed on the Punjabis from four posts on their front and to the flanks. 'Movement meant death, until the shining heroism of young Kamal Ram saved the day.'[14]

> The capture of the position was essential and Sepoy Kamal Ram volunteered to get round the rear of the right post and silence it. He attacked the first two posts single-handed, killing or taking prisoner the occupants and together with a havildar he then went on and completed the destruction of a third. His outstanding bravery undoubtedly saved a difficult situation at a critical period of the battle.[15]

Kamal Ram had never been in action before that eventful day on which he became the youngest soldier to earn the Victoria Cross during the Second World War.[16]

Elsewhere, the Punjabis' B Company met no significant opposition and were closing on Point 63 by noon. Seizing that point was assigned to D Company which moved up to within yards of the objective before making a line-abreast charge. Such raw courage proved pointless in the face of machine-gun fire and barbed wire. The attack ground to a halt with the officer leading it amongst the dead. Also dead were all the soldiers of the platoon which had nearly reached the German positions. D Company made a further attack that took the ridge but by then only thirty of its soldiers remained. The company had been reduced to platoon strength.

To the Punjabis' right 1st Argyll and Sutherland Highlanders were thwarted in their endeavours almost before they began. The Argylls' chosen crossing point had also been selected by German gunners for a defensive fire task and, with but five platoons over the river, the battalion found all its boats destroyed by shellfire. Those who had crossed proved doughty soldiers, digging in and holding their ground.[17]

Since both assaulting divisions were so far behind schedule, and the bridge-head remained shallow, the follow-up divisions, 78th and 6th Armoured, could not be brought forward. But the sappers had worked wonders on 8th Indian Division's front. In spite of their difficulties, including machine-gun and mortar fire, they had two bridges over the Gari which were in use by 9.15am on 12 May, although one, Plymouth, was damaged by enemy fire, restricting its use to light vehicles. Nonetheless, Shermans of the Calgary Regiment still crossed by Plymouth.* However, the second bridge, Oxford, remained intact and over it passed the Ontario Regiment's tanks. By dusk five squadrons were in the bridgehead and the Canadian Shermans had helped the Indians to push forward, clear part of Sant'Angelo and press on towards Panaccioni.[19]

There was no bridge in 4th Division's area until the 13th although three, Amazon, Congo and Blackwater, had been planned. Amazon was the first to be completed, Ward having ordered its building during the night of 12/13 May. The division's three sapper field companies, with a field squadron from 6th Armoured in reserve, began the task under constant fire. By 5.30am on the 13th the bridge was ready for use at a cost of eighty-three casualties amongst the engineers. With all the bulldozers out of action, Amazon was actually pushed into place by a Sherman of 17th/21st Lancers and the tank commander, Lieutenant Wayne, crossed the bridge to reconnoitre the exit.[20] The rest of C Squadron 17th/21st Lancers then crossed and, by 8.00am, two battalions of 12 Brigade – 2nd Royal Fusiliers and 6th Black Watch – had followed. Tanks of 2nd Lothians and Border Horse also crossed the river to support a 12 Brigade attack directed westwards to the Cassino–Sant'Angelo road, or Queen Street. Brigadier Heber-Percy deployed two battalions on a 600-yard front with the Fusiliers directed on Point 31 and the Black Watch on Point 33.[21]

The battalions of 12 Brigade with their Lothians' tanks advanced steadily against determined opposition. On the right the Fusiliers reached Point 41, some 1,500 yards west of the Gari, by noon while the Black Watch, now 1,000 yards to the south-west, were at Massa de Vivo, Point 69. En route the tanks and artillery had assisted in destroying several posts held by troops of 115th Panzer Grenadier Regiment. During the afternoon 2nd Duke of Cornwall's LI, of 10 Brigade, and 1st Royal West Kents, of 12 Brigade, took up the running, supported by 17th/21st Lancers. Once again success met their efforts with the DCLI and Lancers making a quick run to Point 63 and discovering that positions held by troops of the Parachute Machine-Gun Battalion could be approached from behind –

* Plymouth was the first bridge ever carried on a tank, an idea conceived in the HQ A Mess of 8th Indian Division by its GOC, Russell, his CRE, GSOI and the CO of a Canadian armoured regiment. The carrying tank was shunted into the river by another tank and the crew of the first jumped out. German prisoners expressed considerable interest in this 'secret weapon'.[18]

these had been sited to cover Cassino town. The unexpected appearance of infantry and tanks to their rear caused consternation amongst the paras and about 100 prisoners were taken while survivors took to their heels. The Royal West Kents also had a good run, pushing along the Piopetto stream for about a mile on its northern bank; one company crossed and occupied Casa Petracone until night came.[22]

But the greatest success of all came from 2/4th Hampshires who, it will be remembered, were on loan from 28 Brigade which was being reorganized. Supported by the Lothians, the Hampshires advanced along the Piopetto to Point 33 on the Cassino–Sant'Angelo road before wheeling south which allowed them to roll up, one by one, the German posts facing the Gari. At one point Captain Richard Wakeford, accompanied by his orderly and armed only with a revolver, tackled an enemy post, killing several Germans and taking twenty prisoners. This was to be the first element in his earning Eighth Army's second Victoria Cross at Cassino; the second element would follow next day. Deciding that this was his battalion's day, Lieutenant Colonel Fowler-Esson led his men 'unswervingly onwards until he reached Points 50 and 46'. These were a half mile north of Sant'Angelo and within 8th Indian Division's boundary.[23]

The infantry and supporting tanks of 4th Division had worked together exceptionally well, demonstrating the value of the joint training carried out prior to DIADEM. The great defect of the British Army earlier in the war seemed to have been eliminated as tank and infantry units got to know each other on a squadron/company basis. The fruits of that training were to be seen on a day in which five infantry battalions and two tank regiments crossed the Gari to enlarge the bridgehead to the depth of about a mile. All the infantry anti-tank guns were now over as well as two troops from 14th Anti-Tank Regiment, while the sappers were able to work on Blackwater and Congo bridges.[24]

Both divisions continued moving forward on the 14th with 8th Indian clearing the Liri Appendix and probing towards the Cassino–Pignataro road. The two brigades of 4th Division were also making steady progress and Captain Richard Wakeford was again in action.

When attacking a hill feature his company came under heavy fire, but although wounded in the face and both arms, Captain Wakeford pressed home the attack. He was wounded again, but reached the objective and consolidated the position.[25]

Wakeford had displayed not only outstanding courage but also inspiring leadership. Soldiers will always follow the example of such a man whose personal bravery will boost that of the men under his command. Both this and the previous day's incident earned Richard Wakeford the Victoria Cross. None of his soldiers would have doubted that he deserved it.

While 10 Brigade made its way northward in the direction of Highway 6 some German defenders were showing less than the usual dedication to their tasks. At Platform Knoll, a strongpoint just north of Sant'Angelo, the local garrison surrendered as soon as they saw the village fall to Gurkhas and Canadian tanks. Whether this was anything to do with the reputation of the little soldiers from Nepal or not, the men of 1st Royal Fusiliers were spared the problems of mounting an attack; they were about to form up to assault the knoll. There were some other incidents of a similar nature but most German opposition was still determined with a group of mountain warfare students demonstrating German aptitude for defence when attacked by 6/13th Frontier Force. They

> fought fanatically as the Pathans swarmed in amongst them. After the position had been overrun little groups which had fled in the face of the onslaught returned to dig in and to die in last stands. Prisoners emerged with their hands above their heads, holding grenades which they hurled as their captors went forward to secure them.[26]

A 12 Brigade attack towards the Cassino–Pignataro road was led by 6th Black Watch supported by Lothians' tanks but the ground was shrouded in heavy mist which prompted the CO of the Black Watch, Lieutenant Colonel Madden, to form his battalion into a hollow square around the tanks before advancing. It allowed infantry and armour to maintain contact and the attackers were able to take a strongpoint from which a German anti-tank gun team had been unable to engage the Shermans because the mist had hidden them. However, mist always clears and when this particular one burned away the highlanders were ahead of their flanking battalions and offering a choice target for counter-attacks. As always the Germans seized the opportunity and launched a series of counter-attacks which were repulsed. The Black Watch held out until that evening when they were relieved by 1st West Kents with tank support.[27]

Eighth Army's tanks were meeting difficulties other than enemy guns. Mist created problems for them in the early part of the day but the ground had not yet dried out completely and was not as firm as it would become in a few more weeks. As a result some tanks were bogging in soft ground, reducing the pace of the advance or leaving groups of infantry with reduced or no support. The terrain also favoured the defender as anti-tank guns could be concealed in folds in the ground, in sunken lanes or behind walls or hedges, allowing them to engage tanks at very close range. Their fire was devastating as one regiment, 17th/21st Lancers, learned: in six days of action they had fifty-seven men killed or wounded. For them it truly had been a case of 'death or glory'.*[28]

By now XIII Corps had achieved much of what it had set out to do: it had taken and secured the bridgehead over the Gari between Cassino and the Liri. Its orders now required it to isolate Cassino from the west, cut Highway 6 and link up with II Polish Corps. It was time to feed 78th Division into the bridgehead to assist in cutting Highway 6. But before joining the Battleaxe Division we should step back to the early hours of 12 May as General Anders' Poles moved off in their element of Operation HONKER.

The very name of Eighth Army's operation had inspired the Poles, many of whom believed that it had been chosen specially for them as an allusion to the call of wild geese; they regarded themselves as 'wild geese', far from their native land. In this they shared the imagery of the Irish 'wild geese', those soldiers in exile who had served the armies of France and Spain over many generations. But the choice of codename had been unintentional. Nonetheless, it was to that same Polish spirit that Anders appealed in his special order of the day prior to HONKER. Commenting that the time for battle, and with it 'revenge and retribution' on Poland's traditional foe, had arrived he went on to say:

> Shoulder to shoulder with us will fight British, American, Canadian and New Zealand divisions, together with French, Italian and Indian troops. The task assigned to us will cover with glory the name of the Polish soldier all over the world. At this moment the thoughts and hearts of our whole nation will be with us. Trusting in the Justice of Divine Providence we go forward with the sacred slogan in our hearts: God, Honour, Country. [29]

Probably more than any others engaged in the battle the Poles considered this a personal struggle. They were determined to avenge not just the injustice currently being meted out to Poland by Germany, but also centuries of similar injustice. Geography has fated Poland to lie between

---

* The regiment's cap badge was the skull and crossbones with a scroll reading 'Or Glory', giving them the nickname 'Death or Glory Boys', although the regiment called themselves the 'Tots' (a reference to the German *Totenkopf Hussaren*, who also used the skull and crossbones). It is probably the most gruesome badge in the British Army but it is certainly the most recognizable. Within the regiment the badge is known as 'The Motto'. The author was given an example (actually a Great War brass economy issue) some fifty years ago by his late father who had received it from a Great War veteran during his own army service which began in the 1920s. The Motto is still worn by the Queen's Royal Lancers, the successor regiment to the 17th/21st and the 16th/5th Lancers.

two great neighbours, Germany and Russia, and to be fought over by both – and others. Nor has Poland traditionally taken kindly to either great neighbour, thus ensuring that both always considered the Poles to be nuisances.

Leese had intended originally that XIII Corps and II Polish Corps should go into action at the same time but then, reconsidering, delayed the Poles' H-Hour to 1.00am on 12 May. When they did cross their start lines the Poles met a hurricane of artillery and mortar fire. As they closed on their objectives, machine-gun and small-arms fire was added but, in spite of all that fury from the defenders, 1 Carpathian Rifle Brigade seized and held Point 593. The Carpathians then set out to attack Point 569. Meanwhile 5 Vilno Infantry Brigade had climbed Phantom Ridge to engage the defenders in close-quarter combat that raged throughout the morning and into the afternoon. Elements of the brigade had moved on to tackle the next objective but the 'main mass' continued fighting in the rocky and overgrown terrain of Phantom Ridge.

The Poles were having considerable difficulties and it was clear to Anders that taking some objectives had been much easier than holding them. In the rugged terrain it was not easy for attacking troops to consolidate and the preferred option of deploying fresh troops for that purpose could not be exercised due to congested approach roads and tracks. Anders therefore ordered his attacking brigades to withdraw to their start lines where they would be relieved by other formations that would continue the attacks.

> Our detachments accordingly withdrew in the evening of May 12, but some remained in their positions until May 13. One lesson learned was that our artillery fire, intense though it was, was unable effectively to silence the enemy batteries or to destroy the enemy infantry in their battle stations, which, as we now know, were mostly laid on the opposite hill slopes, in places inaccessible to our supporting fire.[30]

During the afternoon of the 12th Leese arrived at Anders' HQ. The latter was pleased to learn that the army commander considered that the Poles had already made a valuable contribution to the overall battle. Not only had they kept the Germans on Monte Cassino tied up, but they had also drawn on themselves German artillery fire from other sectors and prevented the deployment of enemy reserves, especially in XIII Corps' area. Thus II Polish Corps had been 'of great assistance' to XIII Corps in their crossing of the Gari and subsequent establishment of a bridgehead. Leese, however, suggested that Anders' plan for a fresh attack should not be implemented immediately but should depend on XIII Corps' progress in the Liri valley. Leese did not want the Poles fighting an isolated battle.[31]

The Poles now set about reconnoitring the enemy positions, bombarding them with artillery fire, making local attacks and patrolling aggressively. On 16 May, as XIII Corps penetrated farther into the Liri valley, Leese ordered II Polish Corps and XIII Corps to coordinate operations to keep the greatest possible pressure on the enemy and prevent him from making 'free use of his reserves or his artillery'.[32] D-Day for the new Polish attack was set for the 17th with 7.00am as H-Hour. By the time the Poles went back on the offensive their actions and those of XIII Corps were interlinked and 78th Division was fighting towards Highway 6.[33]

The move of 78th Division into the bridgehead was complicated by the shortage of bridges and, since the assaulting divisions were using the existing bridges, the Battleaxe Division had to join queues, thus falling behind schedule. During the afternoon of the 14th the Irish Brigade entered the bridgehead to find the Germans still on parts of their start line, codenamed Grafton. Eviction duties would have to be undertaken to dispossess enemy rearguards before the attack proper could begin. But even as they moved into the bridgehead the Irishmen were left in no doubt of the quality of the enemy they faced and the strength of his defences.[34] One young Irish Fusiliers officer recalled being led to what had been the German trenches covering this part of the Gustav Line. These had 'been very well dug and camouflaged, all the spoil removed and until you were right on top of them they were practically invisible – also safe from anything but a direct hit, they were so deep'.[35] It was a chastening sight.

The task of clearing the Germans from Grafton was assigned to the Inniskillings. Since they were to have the line clear by dawn, their CO, the redoubtable Bala Bredin, ordered his battalion to move off at 3.00am on the 15th. Bredin's two leading companies were on their objectives by 4.00am, having met no opposition, but that situation changed for the worse at 4.45am when withering machine-gun fire stopped the advance. As dawn broke the leading companies were still about 70 yards from the enemy positions and German tanks were entering the fray while the Inniskillings' supporting tanks were still waiting to cross the Gari. Fortunately, the weather came to the Inniskillings' aid as a morning mist formed to leave the German tankmen almost blind. The panzers blundered about seeking targets but without causing any real harm although one tank almost ran over an Inniskilling platoon commander.[36]

Because of the congestion on the original bridges, 78th Division's sappers had begun work on another bridge spanning the little Piopetto stream, a tributary of the Gari. This was in operation before the mist lifted, allowing a squadron of 16th/5th Lancers to cross at 8.00am. Inniskilling guides led the Shermans forward through marshy ground to the leading troops. As the Shermans engaged the panzers an artillery bombardment was brought down on the enemy positions and the Inniskillings were soon fighting the defenders. Ten minutes after noon, Bredin reported that all his objectives had been taken with severe loss to the Germans. Inniskilling dead numbered eleven and fewer than sixty were wounded. The baton now passed to 2nd London Irish Rifles to execute the second phase of the advance.[37]

Eleven Brigade had also crossed the Gari to move up on the Irish Brigade's right flank with 5th Northamptons meeting opposition from artillery, mortars and machine guns; they, too, awaited the arrival of tanks. As with the Inniskillings, the Northamptons were also making for a start line but found many enemy troops in the vicinity. Two soldiers, Lance Corporal Allkin and Private McGill knocked out a German self-propelled gun (SPG) with a PIAT,* the British spring-operated answer to the bazooka and *panzerfaust*. Lieutenant Hillian earned an immediate Military Cross by launching a one-man attack on a German patrol that he spotted approaching his platoon. Firing a Bren from the hip, Hillian charged the Germans, killing or wounding five and forcing the others to retreat.[38]

The London Irish attack was to begin at 3.00pm with 2nd Lancashire Fusiliers, of 11 Brigade, advancing on their right. With the tanks now present, the COs of both Rifles and Lancers held an O Group to refine their plans but enemy shellfire fell on the immediate area with one round landing amidst the little gathering. John Loveday, CO of the Lancers, and Ion Goff, CO of the Rifles, were both wounded fatally. Several others received severe wounds including a Rifles company commander. Major John Horsfall took command of the Rifles and the brigade commander, Pat Scott, was soon on the spot, but the attack was delayed. Initially, the postponement was until 7.30pm but then came an order from the GOC, Keightley, to put H-Hour off until 9.00am next day to allow 2nd Lancashire Fusiliers to make ready; they reached their start line only at nightfall.[39]

In spite of these delays the next phase of 78th Division's attack was successful with three companies of London Irish reaching their objectives, although suffering heavy bombardment from enemy artillery, while two companies of Lancashire Fusiliers also took their objectives. But these attacks are memorable for the fact that the LFs earned Eighth Army's third Cassino VC while the London Irish also had a VC-worthy exploit to recall.

Fusilier Francis Jefferson was a runner with C Company of the Lancs who, with support from 16th/5th Lancers, were advancing against determined opposition. A German counter-attack, employing tanks, was launched and a deadlock soon developed with opposing armour on either side of a rise in the ground; a sunken lane prevented any outflanking movement. Seeing German tanks advance on his company's partially dug trenches Fusilier Jefferson grabbed a PIAT and raced forward under heavy

* Projector, Infantry, Anti-Tank.

fire to a position behind a hedge. However, he could not see properly from there and so came out into the open to face the tanks.

> standing up under a hail of bullets, [he] fired at the leading tank ... twenty yards away. It burst into flames and all the crew were killed. [He] then reloaded the PIAT and proceeded towards the second tank, which withdrew before he could get within range. By this time our own tanks had arrived and the enemy counter-attack was smashed with heavy casualties.[40]

Jefferson's action had saved the day by breaking up that counter-attack. This was the turning point of the action. The LFs resumed their advance and took their objectives although C Company had almost half its number killed or wounded.[41]

By nightfall 2nd London Irish were on Colle Monache ridge beyond the battalion objective and had repelled a counter-attack. Their earlier advance had been delayed on the way to Sinagoga by an enemy anti-tank gun which knocked out several 16th/5th Lancers' tanks. The advance had already suffered heavily from shelling which had claimed as victims two platoon commanders of H Company. Seeing the gun that was delaying the Shermans, Corporal Jimmy Barnes led the survivors of his platoon, no more than a section strong, in an attack on the gun position but

> one by one the men were cut down by machine-gun fire on their left flank until Corporal Barnes remained alone. He went on by himself and then he fell dead, cut by a machine gun, but by then the crew of the 88 had baled out and the tanks were able to get forward once again.[42]

As his last conscious act, Jimmy Barnes had lobbed a grenade at the gun, killing at least one of its crew. His company commander, Major Desmond Woods MC, recommended that he be awarded a posthumous VC but no award was ever made. Major Woods received a Bar to his MC for his own gallantry and leadership. H Company took Sinagoga with only Woods, a sergeant, a few corporals and a handful of riflemen still standing.[43]

So why was Francis Jefferson awarded the VC while James Barnes was not? It would be difficult, no, impossible, to differentiate between their courage. Jefferson used a weapon that was unpopular and perceived as ineffective to turn around the dangerous situation in which his company found itself. Jimmy Barnes used his initiative – both his platoon commander and sergeant had become casualties – to do likewise for his company, and paid with his life for his courage. Brian Clark, then adjutant of the Irish Fusiliers, suggested to the author that there was a morale motive in awarding the VC to Jefferson, simply because he had used the unloved PIAT, and that there was an unofficial rationing system for the VC which meant that only one would be awarded to 78th Division, irrespective of the number of gallant acts performed by its men. That one VC was awarded to each assaulting division of XIII Corps would support Clark's argument.[44]

The turn of the Irish Fusiliers came on the 17th when the battalion attacked with two companies supported by 16th/5th Lancers. This attack also met strong opposition from artillery, mortars and machine guns, and C Company lost its commander, Major Laurie Franklyn-Vaile, killed, as was the squadron leader of the Lancers, Robert Gill. Even so the Faughs took their objectives and by nightfall had pushed a patrol out to disrupt German traffic on Highway 6.[45]

And now the Poles return to the picture. With both 4th and 78th Divisions menacing Highway 6, the Poles renewed their attack on Monte Cassino. On the night of the 16th the northern sector of Phantom Ridge had been taken by the 16th Battalion of 5th Kresowa Division while, by sunrise, the 15th Battalion had also secured the southern sector. Then, at 7.00am on the 17th, the Corps launched its fresh attack, its divisions strengthened by extemporized infantry battalions made up of men from the 'Anti-Tank Regiment, MT drivers, workshop personnel and so forth'. Colle Sant'Angelo and Monte Calvario – Point 593 – were taken in bitter fighting. A counter-attack was beaten back and the Poles clung tenaciously to what they already held. Snake's Head ridge was scaled by the Carpathians using ropes and it too was taken from the Germans.[46] But the enemy was still fighting grimly and repulsed for a time a 4th Division attack on Cassino town.[47]

XIII Corps had pierced the Gustav Line and the Poles were about to do likewise. Two British divisions now dominated Highway 6 and, in Fifth Army's sector, Juin's French Expeditionary Corps had thrust through the Aurunci mountains. As the Germans pulled back before the French attack the line in that sector crumbled. Now, with XIII Corps menacing the road to Rome and II Polish Corps pushing into the mountains, neither Cassino town nor the monastery retained strategic or tactical value. Kesselring ordered Heidrich's paras to withdraw and, towards midnight, they began slipping out of their positions to make for the Hitler Line.[48] That night patrols from 3rd Carpathian Division reported that Monastery Hill appeared abandoned, a report verified when a patrol from 12th Podolski Lancers, under Lieutenant Gurbiel, reached the monastery ruins and found it, and the mountaintop, clear of Germans, save for some wounded, two medical orderlies and a junior officer. A regimental 'pennant hastily cobbled together from parts of a Red Cross flag and a blue handkerchief' was hoisted on an equally makeshift flagpole atop the ruins on that morning of 18 May.[49] The world could see that the Poles had taken Monte Cassino. One of the most brutal battles of the war was all but over. It was finished later when Polish units cleared up Colle Sant'Angelo and Villa Santa Lucia. Today the poignant memorial atop Point 593 recalls the courage and sacrifice of the Polish soldiers who, twice, took that eminence. The inscription, in four languages, reminds us that

> For our freedom and yours
> We soldiers of Poland
> Gave
> Our soul to God
> Our Life to the soil of Italy
> Our hearts to Poland

However, the real success of Operation HONKER was not to be measured in ground taken but in the destruction of German forces. Such destruction demanded that the retreating Germans be pursued vigorously to prevent any further strengthening of the defences of the Hitler and C Lines. Engineer battalions from both 305th and 334th Infantry Divisions were already deploying to improve the anti-tank defences of Pontecorvo while, on the 17th, the Germans had mounted a vicious rearguard action at Piumarola where a mistaken report that the Lothians and Border Horse had captured and passed beyond the town led to initial confusion. The truth was that the Lothians had been stopped short of Piumarola by some of Heidrich's men, forming *Kampfgruppe* Schultz, with anti-tank guns, SPGs and a Mark IV tank.[50]

Once again the Irish Brigade was called upon. Bredin's Inniskillings, with a squadron of 16th/5th Lancers, were to persuade Schultz and his men to quit Piumarola. It turned out to be the hardest fighting of that day, 'an afternoon and evening of confused fighting with the tanks cramped in a sunken lane and the infantrymen playing a lethal game of hide-and-seek in the houses and the rubble-strewn streets'.[51] Among the casualties was the Inniskillings' CO. Early in the battle Bala Bredin was wounded in both legs by a burst of machine-gun fire but refused to leave his men.* His answer to his lack of mobility was to have himself strapped to the bonnet of a jeep from where he continued coordinating the actions of his Skins and their supporting Lancers. But he was losing blood and eventually passed out. Only then did he leave the battlefield for treatment. With the support of two companies of London Irish the attack succeeded and the gratifying

---

* There was an interesting afternote to Bredin's wounding. Many years later, when he was Colonel of the Royal Irish Rangers, he visited one of his battalions in Berlin. They were exercising with German police who would have formed part of the Berlin Brigade in the event of war and the latter were using an updated version of the wartime MG42 machine gun. On being shown one of these weapons by a German police officer, Major General Bredin confided that he knew the weapon very well, as did both his legs.

sight of over a hundred paras, hands high in surrender, marked the end of the battle and the final abandonment of the Gustav Line.[52]

Next came the Hitler Line. In some respects this was even more impressive than the main Gustav Line with 20-feet-deep steel shelters, concrete emplacements for anti-tank guns or machine guns with 360-degree fields of fire and mobile steel cylindrical cells, dubbed 'crabs' that

> could be inserted in pits above which their steel domes rose to a height of only 30 inches; and the turrets of new Panther tanks, eighteen in all, mounting 75mm guns with all-round traverse, which also made barely visible intrusions above their concrete emplacements. All were sited and camouflaged with great skill, and since installation they had received an extra layer of covering from the great sproutings of spring.[53]

The Battleaxe Division, reinforced with units from 6th Armoured Division, was to make Eighth Army's first attack on the Hitler Line. First Derbyshire Yeomanry, 6th Armoured's reconnaissance unit, and 10th Rifle Brigade made the first probe on 18 May with a troop of Derbys entering Aquino; the regiment employed a mix of American tanks, light Stuarts, or Honeys in British parlance, and Shermans. However, the Green Jackets were held up and the Derbys were withdrawn. Next day 5th Buffs and 8th Argylls of 36 Brigade, with two Ontario squadrons, attacked under cover of fog which helped as the attackers approached Aquino. However, the fog dispersed and the high-domed Shermans made excellent targets for anti-tank gunners. Every tank was hit and thirteen were lost. Their tank support eliminated, the infantry were at the mercy of machine gunners and, after midday, the attack was abandoned. Both battalions lost their COs: Lieutenant Colonel Geoffrey de Baillou Monk MC, of the Buffs, was killed and Lieutenant Colonel J. Taylor MC, of the Argylls, was wounded. It was not a good time to be a CO in 78th Division. However, the battalions had not suffered excessively, with fewer than seventy casualties altogether.[54]

The Hitler Line battle was to be associated with the Canadians who had remained out of the battle in the opening days. Leese had decided to commit them on the night of 15/16 May, passing them through 8th Indian towards Pontecorvo, due west along the Liri valley.[55] With XIII Corps wheeling northward to envelop the Cassino position there should be no major traffic problems from the Canadian deployment. Presumably Leese had unhappy memories of the chaos created by Montgomery's deployment of two corps in the opening hours of Operation LIGHTFOOT at El Alamein in October 1942.

I Canadian Corps was now commanded by Lieutenant General E.L.M. Burns who had been GOC 5th Canadian Armoured Division until Harry

101

Crerar had been sent back to Britain as commander-designate of First Canadian Army. Because elements of the Indians were still on his axis, Burns chose to lead with 1st Canadian Infantry Division, as its GOC, Vokes, was the more experienced of his divisional commanders.[56] As Vokes' leading brigade pushed forward to Pignataro, it ran smack into the leading elements of 90th Panzer Grenadier Division which Kesselring had just committed, exactly as Alexander had hoped he would. But the timing could hardly have been worse for the Canadians: the first regiment of 90th Panzer Grenadiers had deployed south of the Liri to meet the French and the second came into action north of the river just as the Canadians passed through the Indians.[57]

Supporting the Canadian infantry were Churchills of 25 Tank Brigade; 1 Canadian Armoured Brigade was still supporting 8th Indian Division. This, the first occasion on which the Churchill I (infantry) tanks saw action in Italy, proved a chastening experience. The countryside in which they were operating was one of vineyards, cornfields and coppices offering first-rate cover for enemy infantry armed with *panzerfausten*, the German shoulder-launched anti-tank weapons. With the tanks probing gingerly forward, the infantry were also suffering losses, especially as Leese, unimpressed by Canadian progress, had made his feelings known to Burns who, in turn, had passed them on to his subordinates. In spite of this goading the Canadians did not close on the Hitler Line, five miles forward from Pignataro, until 19 May. Early next day, Leese issued orders for the assault on the line.[58]

The Canadians were to make the main assault on the night of 21/22 May as XIII Corps maintained pressure against Aquino while being ready to exploit any opportunity to advance. Anders' Poles were engaged at Piedimonte where the switch to the Hitler Line from the Gustav was at its shortest. On the 20th, the Polish commander had launched a battlegroup, formed from the two battalions that had suffered least in the struggle for the mountains, against Piedimonte, but the attackers had become locked against a redoubt manned by Heidrich's paratroopers who remained as determined as ever. In an effort to outflank the paras, 8th Indian Division came back into the battle on the Polish left, astride Highway 6.[59] If Leese had been trying to avoid doing a Montgomery, he had now outdone the latter with three corps deployed on a front of just over six miles. Logically, the entire operation should have been entrusted to a single corps but this was coalition warfare and national sensibilities had to be considered. As Gregory Blaxland commented:

> Leese would himself have replied that the commander of an international army is clothed in the straitjacket of national pride, and just as the Poles had to fight as a corps on their own, so did the 1st Canadian Infantry and 5th Canadian Armoured Divisions.[60]

102

The Canadian plan, Operation CHESTERFIELD, brought further criticism from Leese since it imposed additional pressure on Eighth Army's already heavily loaded wireless network. Traffic congestion, which was hardly surprising, also delayed deploying artillery in support of the Canadian attack. Eventually, the assault was postponed with H-Hour set at 6.00am on the 23rd. Before that, however, Vokes, presuming that the rapid French advance to the left might make the German grip less tight, attacked Pontecorvo. The sole result was to prove that the Germans still held a firm grip and were determined not to be hustled out. Between Pontecorvo and Piedimonte was arguably the strongest sector of the Hitler Line; those six miles were held by two experienced formations under two of the best German commanders: Baade of 90th Panzer Grenadiers and Heidrich of 1st Parachute.[61]

Intense artillery fire preceded the Canadian attack: over 800 guns fired 1,000 rounds per hour over eighty-four hours; this rate of fire increased to 810 rounds each minute as the attack began.[62] Under this storm the Canadians moved off at 6 o'clock on the morning of the 23rd, just thirty minutes before General Lucian Truscott's VI Corps began its breakout from Anzio, Operation BUFFALO. Three battalions from 2 and 3 Brigades led the assault between Pontecorvo and Aquino: on the left the Carleton and York of 3 Brigade had 51st Royal Tanks in support, while in the centre and right the North Irish Horse supported the Seaforth of Canada and the Princess Patricias, both of 2 Brigade.[63]

The storm of artillery did not eliminate German resistance. On the right flank the Patricias' A and C Companies led the attack.

Immediately, the enemy opened a devastating defensive fire from concealed pill-boxes and from Aquino on the flank. Col Ware received a report that A Company had reached the wire. Then nothing more was heard. All attempts to communicate by liaison officers and runner failed and supporting arms could not get forward through the intense enemy fire. The North Irish Horse attempting to help the Regiment forward were restricted in their movement by the Forme D'Aquino on the right and by deep laid mines which had defied detection. They were caught in a trap of concealed self-propelled guns and twenty-five of their tanks were destroyed that day.[64]

The advancing Patricias suffered heavily. Companies and platoons were broken up and the attack became one of small groups dashing from cover to cover. Major W. de N. Watson, A Company commander, saw his entire company HQ go down but carried on alone, hoping to find his platoons on their objective. Twice wounded en route, Watson made it to the objective but of his company he found none. To avoid capture he hid in a shell hole

103

where, next morning, he was discovered by another officer, suffering from arm and head wounds 'and a tremendous appetite'.[65]

In the centre the Seaforth reached their objective but the leading companies had been wiped out and the defences had also taken a heavy toll of their supporting tanks. The deeds of one anti-tank team of the Seaforth came to the attention of the corps commander who wrote that the men 'stalked a tank in the Hitler Line, through trees and undergrowth. When in range, the leader removed his spectacles, wiped them carefully, then aimed and destroyed the tank.'[66] Burns noted that the man was recommended for the DCM but does not indicate whether he received the medal. Meanwhile, eleven North Irish Horse tanks had used a different axis of advance and breached the Hitler Line, reaching the Phase II line of CHESTERFIELD, the road from Pontecorvo to Highway 6, but with no infantry support had to withdraw.[67]

Moving up in support of the Patricias, the Edmontons met what was described as murderous machine-gun, mortar and artillery fire, and although the battalion reached the enemy wire, penetrating it at two points, the assaulting companies had lost contact with Battalion HQ. With the attack at a standstill, the battalion was later withdrawn. Success, however, did crown the efforts of the Carletons who had reconnoitred the terrain the previous day, identifying routes through minefields and barbed wire. The fruits of that reconnaissance were plucked in the attack with the infantry using the routes uncovered by the recce patrols. Following close behind the curtain of shellfire, the Carletons were able to advance on to their objectives. Their supporting tanks, from 51st Royal Tanks (Leeds Rifles), sustained many losses from both the fixed defences and SPGs. Around 10.00am, the tanks and infantry met on the Pontecorvo–Aquino road and 3 Brigade's supporting battalion, the West Nova Scotias, moved up ready to launch the next phase of the advance.[68]

Vokes delayed launching the West Novas in the hope of having some positive news from 2 Brigade but, with none forthcoming, chose to allow 3 Brigade to go ahead alone. The Royal 22ᵉ deployed forward as brigade reserve while tanks from the Three Rivers Regiment arrived to support the West Novas. Tanks and infantry set off at 4.40pm. This was a speedy advance which had the good fortune to catch the German reserves off balance. Preparing to counter-attack, the latter were smote by a heavy artillery bombardment and the few local counter-attacks that they were able subsequently to make proved no deterrent to the West Novas who reached the Phase II line by 6.15pm. Now the Van Doos were brought forward to expand the gap in the German defences. They seized objectives in front of the Seaforth and, by 9.15pm, had consolidated on high ground not a mile north of the West Novas.[69]

By now the Germans were beginning to fall back. The Hitler Line had been breached and its hours were numbered when 1 Brigade forced and then expanded a bridgehead near Pontecorvo on the left flank. With both 48th Highlanders and the Hastings pressing hard, the Germans were falling back there by early evening. Next day, the 24th, the Royal Canadians entered Pontecorvo; they were almost unopposed.[70]

The Hitler Line was finished from the evening of the 23rd, a day on which 2 Brigade had sustained the highest day's casualties for any brigade in the Italian campaign. That same day Eighth Army's gunners set another record: the CRA of 1st Canadian Division, Brigadier Ziegler, called for a 'William Target', bringing all the army's artillery into operation and, just over thirty minutes later, more than 600 guns fired together to drop 3,500 shells on German positions in two minutes.[71]

Now came the opportunity for 5th Canadian Armoured Division to deploy operationally in their true role for the first time. As Pontecorvo fell to the Royal Canadians on the morning of 24 May, tanks advanced through the Royal 22ᵉ's bridgehead at 8.00am. In the following hours Canadian Shermans clashed with German armour, including some of the new Mark Vs, or Panthers; four Shermans were disabled as were three Panthers. Midday saw the leading Canadian tanks at Mancici, north-west of Aquino, with others over the Melfa river, forming a new bridgehead. Initially, the Canadians had the advantage as they had taken the Germans off balance, but in the course of the afternoon resistance stiffened and seventeen Shermans of Lord Strathcona's Horse were lost.[72]

XIII Corps' front remained static until the 25th when troops from 78th Division found that, overnight, the Germans had abandoned Aquino. They had done likewise at Piedimonte as the Poles discovered while probing the defences that morning. In two weeks' fighting Anders' soldiers had suffered 3,784 casualties, including 860 killed, at the hands of Heidrich's paratroopers; among the Polish dead was Colonel Kurek, commander of 5 Vilno Brigade, killed at Sant'Angelo while directing the attack.[73] Eighth Indian Division, with the New Zealand armour in support, pursued the Germans along the sides of the Liri valley while New Zealand infantry probed into the mountains north of Cassino before setting off around Monte Cáiro to pursue the enemy.[74] The Battleaxe Division committed infantry to the pursuit as well; with them were tanks of 9 Armoured Brigade which had last seen action at El Alamein where they had suffered horrendously along the Trigh el Rahman. (The brigade, with its 850 vehicles, had crossed Italy on 18 and 19 May and then waited five days at Triflisco.[75]) Although the Warwickshire Yeomanry had initially been assigned to 8th Indian Division, this was changed and the regiment supported 11 Brigade with A Squadron operating with the Northamptons, B with the Lancashire Fusiliers and C with the East Surreys.[76]

Also committed to the pursuit was 6th Armoured Division with 26 Armoured Brigade ordered to break out through the Canadian sector but, as this exacerbated congestion in the Liri valley, it was not until late afternoon that the Derbyshire Yeomanry reached the Melfa. Some tanks crossed but, with no infantry support and stiffening opposition from German infantry and anti-tank guns, the crews were later told to leave their tanks and recross the river; they did so but brought twenty-one prisoners with them.[77] Before the Derbys arrived the Canadians had already experienced the hardening of German opposition as several fierce counter-attacks threatened to force them out of their bridgehead.[78] That the Germans did not succeed in their intentions was due largely to the initiative, courage and leadership of a young Canadian officer, Major John Keefer Mahony of the motorized Westminster Regiment who, with his company, had established the first bridgehead over the Melfa.

> For five hours the company maintained its position in the face of enemy fire and attack until the leading companies and supporting weapons were able to reinforce them. Early in the action Major Mahony was wounded in the head and twice in the leg, but he refused medical aid and continued to direct the defence of the bridgehead. The enemy saw that this officer was the soul of the defence and consequently made him their particular target.[79]

Mahony saved the bridgehead for which he received the Victoria Cross. He may also have distracted the Germans enough to have assisted an assault crossing of the Melfa by 11 Canadian Lorried Infantry Brigade which was then able to advance a thousand yards beyond the river and further disrupt the German defences. That night saw another German withdrawal that was followed up next day by a Canadian advance.

Another factor in the German decision to withdraw was the speed of the French advance through the Aurunci mountains. General Juin criticized Eighth Army for failing to keep pace with his own corps. While this is true it does not reflect the terrain over which Juin's and Leese's men were fighting. The former were advancing over mountains where the defences were weakest and the German commitment of troops had not been the strongest. In contrast Eighth Army faced the toughest German divisions and with five divisions deployed, including armour, depended heavily on roads and bridges. Demolition of the latter inevitably slowed the rate of advance although the sappers were adept at swift replacement, even under fire. In spite of the attention of enemy artillery, 577 Field Company, Royal Engineers bridged the Melfa in twenty-four hours. The same company, under Major Donald Booth, later excelled themselves at Arce by erecting a bridge in a record five hours.[80]

As Eighth Army's advance continued, the Canadians and 78th Division found themselves in close company again and when the Irish Brigade met the Canadians some five miles from Ceprano, the Irish Regiment of Canada was relieved by 1st Royal Irish Fusiliers, an event remembered for the Canadian soldier who was heard to shout directions: 'Canadian Irish this way, English Irish that way.' No offence was taken by the Irish Fusiliers, however, and the story became the stuff of regimental legend.[81] But there were still many actions being fought. Giving up ground at their own pace the Germans continued to make the Allies fight for their gains. Fighting for hills alongside Highway 6, the soldiers of 1 Guards Brigade, the infantry of 6th Armoured Division, took many casualties. Dogged resistance also met 17 Indian Brigade as they attacked yet more mountains; 1/5th Gurkhas had a tough battle with paratroopers before taking Rocca d'Arce on 29 May, the morning that 3rd Grenadier Guards found that the enemy had slipped away from Monte Grande, thereby allowing 3rd Welsh Guards to motor into Arce on Lothians' tanks.[82]

Since the breaking of the Hitler Line XIII Corps had advanced 11 miles, less than two miles in each of the six intervening days. Although the Canadian Corps had stepped up the pace they still lagged behind the French. On 30 May Canadians were pushing along the difficult Sacco valley,* filled with 'wooded ridges, sunken, twisted lanes, gullies, brooks, and riverlets', not to mention German demolitions and booby traps, while XIII Corps had 78th Division making for Frosinone and 8th Indian following up the retreating Germans in a north-westerly direction through the mountains.[83] It was on the 30th that the Buffs, of 36 Brigade, took Ripi from the Germans, while the Canadians, en route to Frosinone, cut Highway 6. The deed was done by a single Sherman whose commander, Corporal J.B. Matthews, raced along the road from Arnara, knocked out an SPG and two tanks of 26th Panzer and held his ground so that it could be consolidated. Matthews' dash was an excellent example of the way in which the actions of a small group, or even one man, can influence the course of a battle; it was recognized with the award of the DCM.[84] On 31 May the Edmontons took Frosinone from 26th Panzer infantry and armour while the Maoris entered Sora that afternoon to link up with the New Zealand Armoured Brigade. The latter had been supporting 8th Indian while Freyberg's infantry had deployed to try to cut Highway 82 at Sora, about a dozen miles north-east of Frosinone, in an effort to block the retreat of Feuerstein's Mountain Corps.[85]

The Indians had had an especially tough time in the mountains but proved adept at such fighting:

The jagged terrain was ideally suited to delaying tactics, by gun, mine and demolition, and 8th Indian had a long, gruelling, and daunting task in an advance towards Terni, for ever trying to maul

* The Sacco is a tributary of the Liri into which it flows near Ceprano.

nightly shifting rearguards of skilled Para or Mountain troops; they persevered and had occasional successes which sustained their enthusiasm.[86]

The New Zealand tanks had had an interesting time, to say the least, supporting the Indians in such country. On arrival at Sora they reverted to their own division while 1 Canadian Armoured took over the support of 8th Indian Division.[87]

As June dawned the Canadians could look ahead at a stretch of country that was more than suitable for tanks. The going was much better as the ground had dried out considerably and 25 Tank Brigade's Churchills advanced with Canadian infantry on Ferentino. On the 2nd the Royal Canadians entered Anagni to find it already occupied by jubilant Italian partisans and, next day, the first junction was effected with Truscott's VI Corps from Anzio when soldiers from 1 Canadian Brigade met a motorcycle-borne US Army sergeant. This NCO had travelled down Highway 6 but had had a much easier journey than 6th South African Armoured Division which spent the same day travelling that route in the opposite direction while seeking to escape congestion and pass through the Canadians to continue the advance and thereby make its own entry into the war.[88]

The reader might ask: but what of the C Line? In truth this line (the Allies called it the Caesar Line but this was an invention from the imagination of an intelligence officer) proved of little substance and Fourteenth Army's failure to hold the Alban hills ensured that it could not be held for long. Mackensen's dispositions also threatened the survival of both German armies.[89]

Truscott's Operation BUFFALO had been successful, threatening the Germans with the destruction of their armies in the field. This, of course, had been the Allied strategic objective and with VI Corps' planned advance along the Anzio–Valmontone axis there was every prospect of the Germans being caught in a pincer and suffering a crushing defeat. But the opportunity to land a decisive killing blow was lost when Clark allowed himself to be seduced by the glory of entering Rome as a hero and the liberator of the first European capital to fall to the Allies. He ignored Alexander's orders and switched VI Corps from its planned axis to a new one that would take it to Rome, which passed into Allied hands on 4 June.[90] Clark's decision meant that many of Kesselring's troops who might otherwise have been captured were able to escape north of Rome where, very soon, the German armies would recover their equilibrium and the Allies would once again have to battle against a stout German defensive line. On 5 June Clark entered Rome with a praetorian guard of soldiers, photographers and newspapermen. He noted that he was the first conqueror to enter Rome from the south since Belisarius in AD 536.[91] His use of the word 'conqueror' allows an interesting glimpse into Clark's mind: the man, after all, was supposed to be a liberator and Italy was now one of the Allies. Such was his concentration on taking Rome, and being seen to do so, that, as he later told an American journalist, he was prepared for his soldiers to open fire on any Eighth Army troops or units that approached the city.[92] At least some of the latter could testify that their routes were blocked by armed Americans with an attitude to non-Americans that would be familiar to anyone passing through a major US international airport today.

Fifth Army's failure to cut off Tenth Army around Valmontone compounded the problem created by Eighth Army's slow rate of advance through the Liri valley. This had allowed the Germans to choose their own rate of withdrawal and it was a situation caused, in part at least, by deploying three distinct corps in the operations through the Liri valley. Alexander's use of I Canadian, II Polish and XIII British Corps gave the impression of someone trying to pour the proverbial quart into a pint pot, but Alexander had to consider the sensitivities of the different nationalities under his command, as did Leese who drew up the plans for HONKER; the Canadians had direct recourse to their own government and the Poles were, in effect, a national army. Given a homogeneous army, Alexander and Leese would have been able to exercise much firmer control and even have allowed the French Expeditionary Corps to swing in from the west to sever Highway 6 ahead of Eighth Army, thereby causing the Germans to lose part of their cohesion. But the offensive had prompted the Germans to feed reinforcements into the Italian theatre and Hitler and OKW* remained convinced that large Allied forces remained in reserve in North Africa. This latter belief had convinced Hitler's Operations and Intelligence staffs to move formations from Croatia, Hungary and the Eastern Front to Italy.

But the fact remained that the opportunity to remove a large part of Kesselring's order of battle had been lost. That failure would lead to another winter of struggle in the mountains of Italy and increase the casualty toll of Eighth Army which, between 11 May and the fall of Rome on 4 June, had suffered 13,756 casualties.[93]

---

* *OberKommando der Wehrmacht*, or high command of the German forces; the *Wehrmacht* included the army (*Heer*), navy (*Kriegsmarine*) and air force (*Luftwaffe*), but not the SS.

Notes

1. NA, Kew, CAB106/418, *Campaign in Central Italy, 26 Mar–10 Aug 1944*, p. 12; Molony, *The Mediterranean and Middle East,* vol. VI, pt 1, p. 105; Williamson, *The Fourth Division*, pp. 124–5.
2. Molony, op. cit., pp. 105–7; Williamson, op. cit., p. 125; NA, Kew, WO170/ 407, war diary, 4 Div HQ G Br, Jan–Jun 1944.
3. Williamson, op. cit., p. 125; NA, Kew, WO170/407, war diary, 4 Div HQ G Br, op. cit.
4. Williamson, op. cit., pp. 130–1; Squire & Hill, *The Surreys in Italy*, op. cit., p. 36.
5. NA, Kew, WO170/407, war diary, 4 Div HQ G Br, op. cit.
6. Williamson, op. cit., pp. 132–3; NA, Kew, WO170/1358, war diary, 2 Beds & Herts, Jan–Jul 1944.
7. NA, Kew, WO170/596, war diary 28 Bde, Jan–Aug 1944; Williamson, op. cit., pp. 134–5.
8. Joslen, *Orders of Battle*, op. cit., p. 448.
9. Molony, op. cit., pp. 107–9.
10. Parkinson, *Always a Fusilier*, op. cit. pp. 186–7.
11. Doherty, *A Noble Crusade*, op. cit., p. 208.
12. Ibid.
13. Ibid.
14. Anon, *The Tiger Triumphs*, p. 72.
15. *London Gazette*, 27 Jul 1944.
16. Doherty, op. cit., p. 209.
17. Molony, op. cit., p. 108; NA, Kew, WO170/1356, war diary, 1 A & SH, Feb–Dec 1944.
18. Pal, *The Campaign in Italy*, p. 166.
19. Nicholson, *The Canadians in Italy*, op. cit., p. 405.
20. ffrench-Blake, *The 17th/21st Lancers 1759–1993*, p. 102.
21. Ibid.; Williamson, op. cit., pp. 139–40; NA, Kew, WO170/558, war diary 12 Bde, Jan–Jun 1944.
22. Williamson, op. cit., pp. 139–41; NA, Kew, WO170/558, war diary 12 Bde, op. cit.
23. Molony, op. cit., pp. 117–18; Williamson, op. cit., pp. 141–2.
24. Molony, op. cit., pp. 116–17.
25. *London Gazette*, 13 Jul 1944.
26. *The Tiger Triumphs*, op. cit., p. 78.
27. Williamson, op. cit., pp. 145–8; NA, Kew, WO170/1366, war diary, 6 BW, Mar–Dec 1944.
28. NA, Kew, WO170/829, war diary, 17/21 L, 1944.
29. Anders, *An Army in Exile*, op. cit., p. 174.
30. Ibid., p. 177.
31. Ibid.; Molony, op. cit., p. 111; Ryder, *Oliver Leese*, pp. 166–7.
32. Anders, op. cit., p. 177.
33. Molony, op. cit., pp. 129–31.
34. Scott, *Account of the Service of the Irish Brigade*; NA, Kew, WO170/606, war diary, 38 (Ir) Bde, Apr–Jun 1944.
35. Trousdell, notes to author.
36. Scott, op. cit.; Doherty, *CTW*, op. cit., pp. 133–4; Ray, *Algiers to Austria*, op. cit., pp. 126–7.
37. Scott, op. cit., Doherty, op. cit., pp. 135–6.

38. Ray, op. cit., p. 128.
39. Scott, op. cit.; Doherty, op. cit., pp. 136–7; Horsfall, *Fling Our Banner to the Wind*, p. 49.
40. *London Gazette*, 13 Jul 1944; Ray, op. cit., pp. 129–30.
41. Ray, op. cit., p. 130.
42. Woods, 'A personal account of his service with 2nd London Irish Rifles in Italy', op. cit.
43. Ibid.; Horsfall, op. cit., p. 59.
44. Clark, interview with author, Aug 1990.
45. Scott, op. cit.; Doherty, op. cit., pp. 140–2; NA, Kew, WO170/1406, war diary, 1 RIrF, 1944.
46. Anders, op. cit., pp. 177–8; Molony, op. cit., pp. 131–4.
47. Williamson, op. cit., p. 151.
48. Kesselring, *Memoirs*, op. cit., pp. 200–2.
49. Piekalkiewicz, *Cassino*, p. 180.
50. Ray, op. cit., pp. 131–2.
51. Ibid., p. 132.
52. Ibid.; Scott, op. cit.
53. Blaxland, *Alexander's Generals*, p. 103.
54. Ray, op. cit., p. 134; www.cwgc.org
55. Nicholson, op. cit., pp. 400–1.
56. Ibid., pp. 411–13.
57. Molony, op. cit., pp. 188–9; Nicholson, op. cit., pp. 413–14.
58. Nicholson, op. cit., p. 411.
59. Molony, op. cit., pp. 180–1; Blaxland, op. cit., pp. 106–8.
60. Blaxland op. cit., p. 106.
61. Doherty, *A Noble Crusade*, op. cit., p. 216; Molony, op. cit., p. 189; Blaxland, op. cit., p. 119.
62. Nicholson, op. cit., pp. 417–18.
63. Blaxland, op. cit., p. 119.
64. Williams, *Princess Patricia's Canadian Light Infantry*, p. 56.
65. Ibid., pp. 56–7.
66. Burns, *General Mud*, pp. 152–3.
67. Nicholson, op. cit., p. 419.
68. Ibid., pp. 419–20.
69. Ibid., pp. 420–1.
70. Ibid., pp. 422–5.
71. Molony, op. cit., p. 193; Mead, *Gunners at War*, p. 90.
72. Nicholson, op. cit., pp. 428–31.
73. Anders, op. cit., p. 181; Blaxland, op. cit., p. 106.
74. Molony, op. cit., pp. 200–1 & 241–2; Blaxland, op. cit., pp. 121–2.
75. Platt, *The Royal Wiltshire Yeomanry*, p. 161; NA, Kew, WO170/838, war diary, Warwickshire Yeo, 1944.
76. Ibid.
77. Molony, op. cit., p. 200; Blaxland, op. cit., p. 122.
78. Nicholson, op. cit., p. 431; Molony, op. cit., p. 199.
79. *London Gazette*, 13 Jul 1944.
80. Doherty, op. cit., p. 220.
81. Scott, op. cit.; Doherty, *CTW*, op. cit., p. 148.
82. Blaxland, op. cit., p. 124.
83. Ibid., pp. 124–5.
84. Ibid., p. 127; Nicholson, op. cit., p. 445.

85. Blaxland, op. cit., p. 127.
86. Ibid., p. 125.
87. Ibid., p. 127.
88. Ibid.
89. Molony, op. cit., p. 227.
90. Molony, op. cit., pp. 287–9.
91. Blaxland, op. cit., p. 135.
92. Whiting, *The Long March on Rome*, p. 141; Blaxland, op. cit., p. 135 includes a story of a British staff officer who was refused entry to Rome by an American military policeman who pointed his firearm at him.
93. Doherty, *A Noble Crusade*, op. cit., p. 223; Molony cites British, Canadian, New Zealand, Indian and Polish losses at 16,064 (p. 284n) but this figure includes British troops in Fifth Army and under AAI command.

Chapter Six

Pursuit to the Gothic Line

Let slip the dogs of war.

It is easy for the historian to define a new phase in the Italian campaign following the liberation of Rome. Although many who experienced the campaign have also done so, no sharp demarcation line separates events before 4 June 1944 from those that followed. There remained a determined and tough opponent, capable of making best use of the terrain to defend his positions and of improving on what nature had provided through his engineers' skill. (Montgomery had once considered that Eighth Army might be in Rome by Christmas 1943; Avezzano, scheduled by him to fall in November, was finally taken by the New Zealanders on 10 June.[1]) Eighth Army, and Fifth, would fight in Italy for another eleven months, but the liberation of Rome was followed by a brief period when its soldiers felt that the end was near and anything was possible. That period coincided with the days when the Allied armies were moving faster than they ever had hitherto in Italy. Little compares with a speedy advance for giving a soldier a sense of confidence and the same rule, writ large, applies to armies. So it was with Eighth Army in those heady June days.

As the German tide receded beyond the Eternal City, soldiers of both armies at last felt that they were winning, a feeling reinforced by news of the Normandy landings on 6 June. Alexander sensed this high level of morale when he suggested to General Wilson, Supreme Commander Mediterranean, that his armies should now strike towards the Gothic Line with Fifth Army pushing towards Pisa and Eighth towards Florence. Both cities, along the Arno river, could be in Allied hands by mid-July, thereby allowing an attack on the Gothic Line (Rommel's Pisa–Rimini line) by mid-August. Alexander's proposal that the main effort against the Gothic Line should be made in the mountainous centre indicates that he had learned from Juin's advance through the Aurunci mountains. Having broken the Gothic Line, which he thought would present no great obstacle, the Allies would debouch on to the Lombardy plain towards the Po valley, whence they might wheel left into France or strike into Austria via the

Ljubljana gap. This was a highly optimistic plan, even without the French or Austrian ventures, but Alexander believed that his forces could complete it with one proviso: no reduction in ground or air strength.[2]

Unfortunately such reductions were already underway. Alexander had had to fight to retain all those troops he considered necessary for DIADEM as the plan for invading France had envisaged two discrete operations: OVERLORD in Normandy and ANVIL on the Mediterranean coast. However, Alexander's need to deploy in DIADEM formations intended for ANVIL played a part in the postponement of the latter. It had not been cancelled since the Americans remained enthusiastic about it and the prospect of Mediterranean ports as part of the US forces' logistical chain in Europe. So, while Churchill and the British Chiefs believed that ANVIL had been scrapped, the American Joint Chiefs resurrected it with a new name, DRAGOON, with D-Day set as 15 August. To DRAGOON were assigned Lucian Truscott's VI Corps – and, in Truscott, the best American commander in the Mediterranean – as well as Juin's French Expeditionary Corps in a reborn Seventh US Army under General Alexander M. Patch. These formations would leave Allied Armies in Italy just when Alexander most wanted them, although the French would be available for a time. With the Americans not to be dissuaded, planning had to take account of the impending departure of the French with their particular mountain fighting skills.[3]

While the liberation of Rome was a milestone in the campaign, fighting continued, albeit of a more fluid nature, as the Germans were pursued north of Rome. It was now possible to make much more use of the armoured formations which, in turn, each received an additional infantry brigade. Sixth British Armoured Division, with 1 Guards Brigade as its infantry, now included the newly-formed 61 Brigade, a Green Jacket formation including 2nd, 7th and 10th Battalions of the Rifle Brigade, while 6th South African Armoured Division received 24 Guards Brigade – 5th Grenadier, 3rd Coldstream and 1st Scots Guards – to add to 12 Motorized Brigade.[4]

But it will be remembered that there was a manpower shortage in Britain's land forces that was beginning to bite in the Mediterranean with the huge manpower requirements of Second Army in France. Eighth Army had now to seek replacements for battle casualties and other losses from within the Mediterranean area. The prime means of doing so was by retraining soldiers as infantrymen from their original, but now redundant, roles. Not only soldiers were thus re-roled: RAF personnel, including aircrew, as well as some naval personnel found themselves despatched for infantry training. Many soldiers sent for retraining were Royal Artillery gunners from anti-aircraft regiments assigned to the Mediterranean theatre, the need for which was much reduced as the Luftwaffe was a greatly diminished force. Kesselring noted that 'air support had practically ceased,

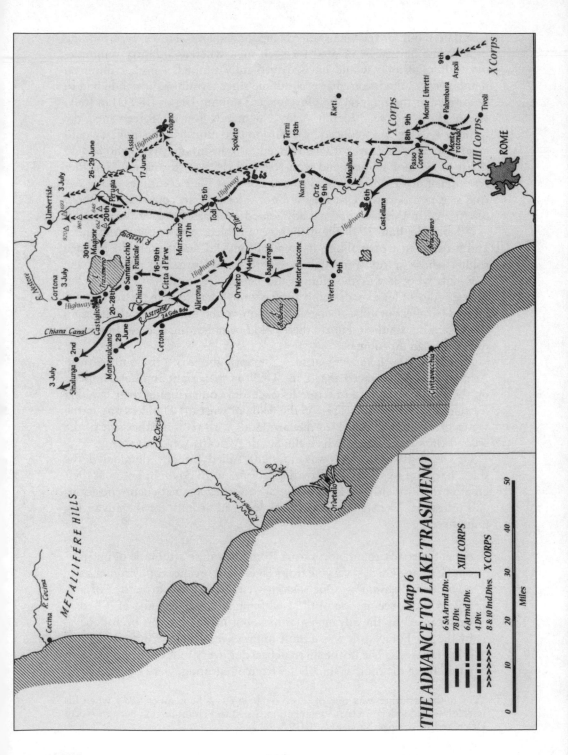

Map 6
THE ADVANCE TO LAKE TRASIMENO

R. Cecina
Cecina
R. Cecina

METALLIFERE HILLS

R. Ombrone

R. Orcia

R. Orcia

Sinalunga
3 July

2nd
3 July

Montepulciano
29 June

Cortona
3 July

Castiglione
20–28th

Chiana Canal

Highway

Trasimeno
L. Trasimeno

Cetona

Chiusi

24 Gds Bde

Astrone

Cortona

Umbertide

30th

Magione
965

920
907 656 648

Lago Trasimeno

Perugia
20th

26–29 June
3 July

Assisi
Highway
17 June

Foligno

Santafucchio

Panicale

16–19th

Citta d'Pieve

Allerona

Marsciano
17th

Todi
15th

R. Tiber

R. Tiber

Highway
3 bis

Spoleto

Terni
13th

Rieti

Narni

Orte
9th

Magliano

Passo
Corese

Castellana

Highway
6th

Monte
rotondo

Monte Libretti

Palombara

Arsoli
9th

X Corps

XIII Corps

Tivoli

ROME

X Corps

8th 9th

7

14th

Highway

Orvieto

Bagnoregio

Montefiascone

Viterbo
9th

Bolsena
L. Bolsena

Bracciano
L. Bracciano

Orbetello

Civitavecchia

	6 SA Armd Div.			
	78 Div.	] XIII CORPS		
	6 Armd Div.			
	4 Div.			
	8 & 10 Ind.Divs.	X CORPS		

Miles
0   10   20   30   40   50

[with] even our air reconnaissance being inadequate'. However, a training programme had to be created for such men whereas infantry reinforcements from Britain would have arrived fully trained. Another drain on manpower resulted from that programme since a training battalion had to be formed at the Infantry Reinforcement Training Depot (IRTD) in Italy. In an effort to meet Eighth Army's demands for reinforcements, the training syllabus was reduced by a third to two months. This policy would create morale problems with men forced into the infantry role who had no desire to be foot soldiers and who resented the transformation.[5] Further resentment arose when those men saw some of their comrades in the AA role sent home to the UK; they did not take time to consider that those repatriated in this way had already served overseas for over four years.*

Whereas in June 1944 the manpower problem was one for Alexander and his staff to worry about, its implications did not trouble the average soldier whose spirits were high as Eighth Army surged in pursuit of the Germans who, it was thought, 'could be hustled to defeat'. That belief spurred Alexander to order both army commanders to take 'extreme risks' in their parallel pursuits.[7] Geography favoured the pursuers: with the main rivers running south and north there could be no strong defence line south of the Tuscan Apennines.

Spearheading Alexander's armies, the Springboks of 6th South African Armoured Division raced ahead, the Tiber on their right and Lake Bolsena on their left, at the rate of ten miles each day, outstripping their flanking formations. 'Wild poppies, as on the fields of wartime Flanders and in the wadis of Cyrenaica, sprinkled the farmlands with red on either side of the second-class roads along which the South Africans were advancing.'[8]

Of the Luftwaffe there was no sign. Allied aircraft dominated the skies, harrying Kesselring's retreating troops. With daylight hours at their greatest the airmen were able to fly more sorties against enemy positions and transport. The signs of their work were all around for the advancing units to see.

> on all the roads going North from Rome was mile after mile of burnt out German vehicles, varying from Tigers and seventy ton Ferdinands down to volkswagens. One seldom went more than a quarter of a mile without seeing one of these edifying spectacles. Some of it had been caused by the advancing armies, but most of it had been done by the Air Force[s]. It was a most impressive, visible tribute to their excellent work. The Boche slit trenches, dug every four or five hundred yards along the road as funk holes from air strafing, were a tribute to

* The author's father was one of those repatriated in September 1944 when his unit, 9th (Londonderry) HAA Regiment, returned to Britain having been in North Africa and Italy since November 1939.[6]

1. Artillery of Eighth Army comes ashore at Reggio on 3 September 1943. As an M7 Priest self-propelled howitzer comes off the ramp of an LCT there is an almost casual atmosphere on the beachhead where no opposition has been met. *(IWM: NA 6205)*

2. *Viva Inglesi!* Italian citizens cheer the arrival of British soldiers in Gallico Marina.

(IWM: NA 6368)

Communications are vital to an army. Signallers of the Royal Corps of Signals work on lines over the rooftops of an Italian town.

(Author's collection)

4. While supporting the advance of the West Nova Scotia Regiment, 'Adjunct' of A Squadron, 14th Armoured Regiment (The Calgary Regiment), fires on Potenza. The Regiment's tanks bore names beginning with their Squadron letter. *(Alexander M. Stirton/National Archives of Canada/PA144103)*

5. With Taranto in British hands, reinforcements arriving through the port included 8th Indian Division. The divisional reconnaissance regiment was 6th (Duke of Connaught's) Lancers (Watson's Horse) whose equipment included this India Pattern Mk II armoured carrier, based on a Canadian Ford 4x4 chassis. This patrol is observing the Trigno river where the regiment gained its first battle honour in Italy. *(IWM: NA 8532)*

6. Also in the reconnaissance role was the New Zealand Divisional Cavalry Regiment which was equipped with American Staghound armoured cars. At almost 14 tons these cars were often too cumbersome for rural roads in Italy. *(IWM: NA 9270)*

7. The Maiella mountains provide an imposing backdrop to this Stuart tank of HQ Squadron 44th Royal Tank Regiment of 4 Armoured Brigade. The brigade saw considerable action in the early days of the campaign but was withdrawn in late January 1944 to take part in Operation OVERLORD. *(IWM: NA 9160)*

8. A mortar team from 3 Canadian Brigade engaged in a bombardment of enemy positions along the Sangro on 1 December 1943 cover their ears as they fire their weapon.
(Frederick G. Whitcomb/NA of Canada/PA153182)

9. The first Victoria Cross of the campaign was earned by Captain Paul Triquet of the Royal 22^e Regiment, the *Van Doos*, at Casa Berardi in December 1943 as 1st Canadian Division pushed towards Ortona. Triquet survived to receive his VC. (*Photographer not known/NA of Canada/PA157376*)

10. There are few individuals whose homes and family names have become battle honours but Signor Guido Berardi is one such. His 200-year-old house (*casa*) was held by the Germans and became the scene of a desperate encounter between German and Canadian troops, including tanks on both sides. Signor Berardi stands in front of a hole blasted in the wall of his home.

(*C.E. Nye/NA of Canada/PA135864*)

11. Lieutenant General Sir Oliver Leese succeeded General Montgomery as Army commander in January 1944 and soon set about making himself known in his army. In this photograph, Leese (left) is talking to Major General Christopher Vokes, GOC 1st Canadian Division (centre) and Brigadier Tyler (back to camera). (*IWM: NA 10988*)

12. Gunners of 17th Field
    Regiment, Royal
    Canadian Artillery, firing
    their 25-pounder at
    enemy positions near
    Castel Frentano in
    February 1944.
    *(A.M. Stirton/NA of
    Canada/PA193901)*

13. The Allied efforts to liberate Rome before the end of 1943 came to naught against the
    German defences of the Gustav Line. Eighth Army was moved across the peninsula to bring
    the weight of two armies to bear on the line between the Apennines and the Tyrrhenian Sea.
    The most notorious part of the Gustav Line was in the area of Cassino. This US official
    photograph shows Cassino town and Monte Cassino with the famous Benedictine monastery,
    not yet destroyed, and the height of Monte Cairo in the background.

    (US official, via Ken Ford)

MONASTERY   MT. CAIRO   CASSINO

TO ROME   TO NAPLES

14. Cassino town suffered heavily from Allied bombing and shelling. This photograph was taken from Monte Trocchio, captured by Fifth (US) Army in January 1944, as Allied bombers struck at the town on 15 March 1944. *(US official, via Ken Ford)*

15. The bombing of the town and monastery left little intact as in this view of Cassino with Castle Hill in the left background. Today a restored castle overlooks the town but even before the bombing only the central keep was standing. *(US official, via Ken Ford)*

16. Well-camouflaged Shermans of 1 Canadian Armoured Brigade prepare to move forward in support of 8th Indian Division in Operation HONKER, Eighth Army's attack on the Gustav Line, on 11 May 1944. *(A.M. Stirton/NA of Canada/PA139891)*

17. The battle for Rome. Major General B.M. Hoffmeister, GOC 5th Canadian Armoured Division, briefs his officers prior to the assault on the Hitler Line. The plan was for the division to advance down the Liri valley, through the Hitler Line and thence to Rome. *(Strathy Smith/NA of Canada/ PA189922)*

FOR OUR FREEDOM AND YOURS

WE SOLDIERS OF POLAND

GAVE

OUR SOUL TO GOD

OUR LIFE TO THE SOIL OF ITALY

OUR HEARTS TO POLAND

18. On 18 May soldiers of II Polish Corps finally took Monastery Hill. They had suffered greatly in their assaults on the German defensive positions and after the war a Polish memorial was constructed on Point 593. The memorial bears this poignant inscription on all four faces, in Polish, Latin, Italian and English. *(Author's photo)*

19. The Polish cemetery seen from the rebuilt Benedictine Monastery atop Monte Cassino. *(Author's photo)*

20. Among the German defences of the Liri valley was this PAK (anti-tank) gun. After the battle it sits knocked out as a silent testimony to the fury of the defences and the courage of the Allied troops who broke into the valley. *(A.M. Stirton/NA of Canada/PA139891)*

21. On the Melfa river, in the Hitler Line battle, troops of the Westminster Regiment of 5 Canadian Armoured Brigade fought a bitter battle with the Germans during which Lance Corporal J.A. Thrasher knocked out this self-propelled 88mm gun with a PIAT. The 88 had been engaging tanks of Lord Strathcona's Horse east of the Melfa.

(Strathy Smith/NA of Canada/ PA169121)

22. A hero of the final battle for Cassino is decorated. HM King George VI pins the Victoria Cross ribbon on the shirt of Sepoy Kamal Ram VC of 3/8th Punjab Regiment. Kamal Ram earned his VC at Sant'Angelo on 12 May when he knocked out three enemy machine-gun posts on his first day in action. He was the youngest man to earn the VC in the Second World War.

(Author's collection)

23. Italian forces were now part of Allied Armies in Italy. General Taddeo Orlando, the Minister for War in Marshal Badoglio's government, decorates Corporal Piettot Waldo with the Croix de Guerre. At this stage the men of the Italian Corps of Liberation are wearing Italian uniforms but these will be exchanged for British uniforms later in the campaign. *(IWM: NA14616)*

24. The Allies were faced with another major defensive line north of Rome, the Gothic Line, through which they battled in the summer and autumn of 1944. Here an M10 Achilles self-propelled anti-tank gun of 93rd (Argyll & Sutherland Hldrs) Anti-Tank Regiment (note the Tam o'Shanter on the gunner to the right) passes a column of infantry from 5th Sherwood Foresters of 139 Brigade, 46th Division, on the road to Petriano in late August 1944.
(IWM: NA18091)

25. In September 1944 Rimini fell to Eighth Army. The first soldiers of the army to enter the city were these men of 1 Greek Mountain Brigade. In spite of its designation the Greek Brigade had been assigned to the coastal area of operations. *(IWM: NA18781)*

26. Eighth Army's advance was one of river crossing after river crossing. Soldiers of 2/3 Gurkha Rifles cross the Ronco on 1 November 1944 using a lifeline to help them keep their footing in the strong current. *(IWM: NA19843)*

27. During the cold winter of 1944/45 the New Zealand division experienced heavy snowfalls and snow-camouflage clothing was issued. These men are part of a patrol that has closed up to the Geman lines without being detected. *(IWM: NA21370)*

28. Italian soldiers of 21st Infantry Regiment, Gruppo di Combattimento Cremona, in the line near Lake Comacchio. British battledress and equipment is worn although regimental distinctions may be seen on the collars. These men of 12th Mortar Platoon are firing British 3-inch mortars.
(IWM: NA21936)

29. Eighth Army troops in the Senio Line during the final winter of the war experienced conditions akin to those of the Western Front in the Great War. Trench raids were always a possibility and this determined-looking soldier of 78th Division appears ready to meet any German attack.
(Author's collection)

30. Aerial OPs were an established feature of operations in Italy and it was from a light aircraft such as one of these Austers that General McCreery, Eighth Army's new commander, identified the possibilities of the Argenta Gap for the army's final offensive in Italy.

(A.M. Stirton/NA of Canada/PA 137419)

31. McCreery identified Commachio and the flooded land beside it not as a barrier but as something to be exploited. That exploitation was carried out using Buffaloes, nicknamed Fantails in Italy, to carry troops across the water. These amphibious vehicles gave Eighth Army the advantage of surprise as they carried men of 56th (London) Division into action.

(Author's collection)

32. Italian partisans had played a significant role in Allied operations, tying down many German troops who might otherwise have been in the line against the two Allied armies. Following the liberation of Ravenna, Sir Richard McCreery, commanding Eighth Army, decorated the partisan leader Major Buloff with the Medaglia d'Oro. The ceremony was held in the Piazza Garibaldi in the shadow of Garibaldi's statue. The soldier to the right is Italian as may be seen from the tricolour flash on the sleeve of his British battledress. *(IWM: NA22058)*

33. During operations near Bastia a Sherman tank of the 10th Hussars supporting 167 Brigade was deployed in an attack on a factory. The tank crew found hilarious the plight of a warrant officer of the Royal Fusiliers who fell into a shell hole filled with treacle. Moments later their tank also plunged into a treacle-filled bomb crater. This was the result: a Sherman that was going nowhere. *(IWM: NA24123)*

34. Asked about the dispositions of his corps General Graf von Schwerin, of LXXVI Panzer Corps, told his captors that they could be found 'south of the Po'. This is some of the detritus of what had been his formation. *(Author's collection)*

35. *Viva i Liberatori!* Eighth Army troops liberated Venice on 30 April with Italian troops in the van. Soldiers of Gruppo di Combattimento Cremona are cheered by Venetians as they drive into the city.
(Polish Institute/ Sikorski Museum)

36. War brings death and destruction but it can also bring love. Joe Radcliffe of the Royal Signals was one of many Eighth Army soldiers to meet and marry an Italian girl. On 6 October 1946, Joe and Lucia Bederchi were married in St Patrick's Church on Rome's Via Boncompagni. Their first child, Marina, was born in Rome in August 1947 but the family returned to live in Northern Ireland and then in England. When he retired from the Ministry of Defence, Joe and Lucia went back to Rome where he died on 24 February 2005.
(Lucia and Marina Radcliffe)

the air activity that must have gone on for a longish period along those roads to Rome.[9]

These wrecks represented symbols of a defeated army, the sight of which caused Eighth Army's tail to be high. Those with memories of France in 1940 could visualize the hammering that Kesselring's men were taking day after day and it was easy to assume that their aggressive spirit had been beaten out of them. Then, at Bagnoregio on the morning of 11 June, 24 Guards Brigade received a reality check. On that wet and misty morning, 5th Grenadiers reported that enemy troops held in strength the line of a ravine near the village. The defenders, from the recently arrived 356th Division, were deployed in a well-chosen blocking position. Their division was among reinforcements that Kesselring was feeding into the battle to slow the Allied advance. During the afternoon the mist cleared to show that Bagnoregio, a village of stoutly built houses along a ridge, was a formidable obstacle but, before tackling the village, the ravine had to be cleared. It took the Grenadiers all that night and much of the following day to evict the soldiers of 356th Division, thereby allowing an attack on Bagnoregio itself. That attack again involved the Grenadiers who, with the Royal Natal Carabineers, put in a two-pronged assault that forced the enemy out early on 13 June.[10] Then the two units

> met inside this apparently impregnable village ... having forced the enemy into retreat. The steadiness and discipline of the Guards blended surprisingly well with the stealth and informality of the Afrikaners – or Springboks as they preferred to be called – forming a firm fellowship.[11]

The Springboks went on to take Orvieto next day, having advanced 75 miles in the ten days since the liberation of Rome. However, their daily rate of advance was now down by a quarter and the check at Bagnoregio had been a sharp reminder that Kesselring retained his skills and that his soldiers had regained their balance. Mackensen had resigned as commander of Fourteenth Army – he would have been sacked anyway – and General Joachim Lemelsen had succeeded him. The Allies were to find their advance met by many more checks, often of a minor nature but slowing the advance all the same.[12]

Kesselring was seeking to delay the Allied armies on the roads around Lake Trasimene as his armies fell back to the Gothic Line, the last major defensive line before the Po valley. Checks would be imposed on both Fifth and Eighth Armies by the Albert Line, which began near Orvieto and ran via the Tiber and Lake Trasimene to Gubbio, where once Italy's patron, Saint Francis of Assisi, had tamed a wolf that had been terrorizing the citizenry. Gubbio now had grey-green wolves in the form of Kesselring's soldiery. Once through the Albert Line, Clark and Leese's men would meet the Arno Line, from Bibbiena to Pisa, and then the Arezzo Line. Both Arno and Arezzo Lines were designed for rearguard actions; the latter was well suited for this, especially at gaps in the Tuscan mountains south of Arezzo.[13] Reflecting on the pummelling that the Germans had taken it is a tribute to their professionalism that they were able so quickly to mount a cohesive defence.

Leese's two armoured divisions were operating on opposite sides of the Tiber with 6th British now part of Richard McCreery's X Corps which was pushing towards Perugia, a historic hill city some ten miles east of Lake Trasimene. Also in X Corps was 8th Indian Division which had taken Terni on 14 June and fought a series of actions against enemy rearguards with the divisional sappers overcoming many demolitions en route.[14]

As it drove towards Perugia 6th Armoured Division was confronted with the deep gorge through which flows the Nera river. At Narni, about 50 miles south of Perugia, this gorge had to be bridged. Once again the Royal Engineers came into their own, erecting in twenty-four hours a Bailey bridge capable of bearing Shermans. This 180-foot construction was one of 856 Baileys built by Allied engineers in that summer's advance, which also included a 400-foot Bailey across the Tiber codenamed, appropriately, 'Romulus'.[15] In their efforts the sappers were assisted by the 'Sheldrake Pioneers', divisional light AA gunners, whose primary role had all but disappeared, and anti-tank gunners who were also underemployed, who provided labour parties for many engineering tasks.[16] The importance of the engineers is illustrated by two verses quoted in the 17th/21st Lancers' history:

> The Guards, with battle's chronic thirst,
> Stood waiting for the Sixty-First.
> The Sixty-First, with swords aglow,
> Stood waiting for the Guards to go.
>
> An awkward pause, and then the twain
> Agreed 'twas Armour's turn again.
> The Armour, harboured 'neath a ridge,
> Cried, 'Hi-de, Holdfasts! build that bridge.'*[17]

Little opposition was met at Narni, the Germans having withdrawn after blowing the bridges, which happy situation continued after 6th Armoured crossed the gorge when the Guards took the direct route to Perugia, while 26 Armoured wheeled left to swing around the city. Closing

---

* Holdfast was the contemporary radio callsign for the Engineers, while Sheldrake was the Gunner callsign. The reference to Sixty-First is to 61 Brigade who, as riflemen, referred to swords rather than bayonets.

on Perugia the country becomes much closer and hillier which presented problems for the advancing troops especially when it began to rain on Waterloo Day, 18 June.

In spite of brilliant summer weather with stifling heat and billowing dust for two thirds of the time, sudden storms and longer periods of rain occurred which were so heavy that they turned Sapper built diversions into impassable quagmires and prevented the supply vehicles from reaching the forward troops with essential fuel, ammunition and food.[18]

German shells also came down on 6th Armoured's units but did not deter 61 Brigade in its attack that night in which 10th Rifle Brigade took Lacugnano, west of the city. Next night 7th Rifle Brigade attacked through pouring rain and darkness to seize Monte Malbo, north-west of Perugia. Meanwhile 1 Guards Brigade was meeting stiff opposition along the main road to Perugia. Every bound forward was followed by a counter-attack which was very wearing with the guardsmen having to contest every yard of road. The Grenadiers, in the van, took many casualties, among them Lieutenant Lord Lascelles, nephew of the King. Lascelles had strayed into the enemy lines, was wounded and taken prisoner. While 3rd Grenadiers fought along the main road, 2nd Coldstream took the railway below Perugia in a flanking attack early on the 20th. As the sun rose over the horizon the Grenadiers discovered that, yet again, the Germans had slipped away under cover of darkness, leaving open the road to Perugia. When 12th Royal Lancers, General McCreery's own regiment, entered the neighbouring city of Assisi, home of Saint Francis, Italian partisans had already taken possession.[19]

The Guards went on to clear the heights north-east of Perugia thus allowing 1st King's Dragoon Guards to move forward, but any further advance on Trasimene's eastern shore was blocked by 15th Panzer Grenadier Division which had just deployed. Leese therefore moved 6th Armoured Division back to XIII Corps on the other shore, relieving the division on 27 June with 10th Indian which had arrived from the Adriatic sector. Just before their departure from X Corps, 8th Indian Division had advanced beyond Assisi and Perugia and had a hard fight on 18/19 June when two battalions, 1st Royal Fusiliers and 1/5th Gurkhas, took 300 casualties while capturing Ripa ridge, but inflicted such damage on the German 44th Division (*Hoch und Deutschmeister*) that they were unable to withstand a 'rare and brilliant dash' by 3rd King's Own Hussars on 23 June. That dash took the Hussars in their Shermans over four miles of mountainous terrain to seize Biccione village and with it 200 Germans and eleven guns. This was a fine achievement by Russell's men who had fought long and hard since 11 May.[20]

119

Leese's HQ had switched 3rd Hussars to 8th Indian Division from 78th in one of several such temporary attachments that demonstrate the competence of his staff in assessing the tactical situation and the need to move units quickly to where they might best serve the overall design. While 3rd Hussars raced for Ripa the other two regiments of its parent 9 Armoured Brigade, Royal Wiltshire Yeomanry and Warwickshire Yeomanry, remained with the Battleaxe Division which was covering XIII Corps' right flank, having returned to operations on 8 June. The division had then moved to Orvieto, already taken by the Springboks, passing quickly through towns and villages liberated by either South Africans or Americans. The sole check to their progress, and then only minor, was at Pianicciale where there was a brief skirmish.[21] But the most spectacular aspect of the divisional advance was the race by Chavasseforce from Orvieto to Lake Trasimene.

Chavasseforce was a battlegroup commanded by Kendal Chavasse, CO of 56 Recce, which included his own regiment, A Squadron Warwickshire Yeomanry, a company of Irish Fusiliers, later augmented to the entire battalion, two anti-tank troops, a field battery and a detachment of Royal Engineers.

From Orvieto to Lake Trasimene [Chavasseforce] captured or destroyed twenty-six enemy guns of more than 26mm, fifty-five machine guns and almost forty vehicles. A total of [120] prisoners [was] taken while a further [145] Germans lay dead on the route. In one sharp, savage encounter a Faugh company, supported by mortars, defeated a small German force leaving twenty-five of the Germans dead. One of the vehicles captured ... was found to be a German 'NAAFI' truck loaded with French brandy and sweets. ... The run ended with the capture of Castello di Montalara, taken by D Company on June 21st.[22]

In a subsequent letter to the Warwickshire CO, Kendal Chavasse commented on the excellent support provided by A Squadron writing that 'We have had tank support before, but never has it worked so well. They did really brilliantly.' The Warwicks felt that the advance might have been faster had 'even one bulldozer and a platoon of REs ... been under command' to clear obstructions and demolitions.[23]

Alexander's pursuit of the enemy was, thus far, going as planned but there were already signs that the Germans were preparing to hold their latest defensive positions. Although the main portion of 78th Division was midway twixt Rome and Florence it was about to be delayed by the enemy. Eleven Brigade crossed the Paglia river on 15 June, the day before 5th Northamptons, supported by the Wiltshire Yeomanry, divisional artillery and 1st Kensingtons' 4.2-inch mortars, attacked Monte Gabbione, some ten miles from Lake Trasimene's southern shore. Against stiff opposition the Northamptons pressed home their attack which the divisional historian described as 'one of the best actions ever fought by the battalion'.[24]

The attack showed considerable skill on the part of the Northamptons' officers, especially the junior officers. When the leading company – A – met heavy rifle fire the company commander left one platoon behind to provide fire support while the other two were directed on the school and a large building to its right. Both objectives were taken although the victors were subjected to several hours of fierce fire from nearby buildings. C Company also fought its way into the town and S Company's commander directed fire from Wiltshire Shermans on to buildings still occupied by the enemy. Unusually, there were no counter-attacks. The Germans pulled out during the night leaving the Northamptons in possession.[25]

During the afternoon of the 17th, the East Surreys, under command of 9 Armoured Brigade, ran into a strong group of paratroopers at Città della Pieve, a hillside town some 2,000 feet up on Highway 71. Heidrich's men were covering the withdrawal of 334th Division's battlegroups to their left and were not prepared to concede ground. Meanwhile Lieutenant Len Manson's platoon of Irish Fusiliers, operating as lorry-borne troops with 9 Armoured, had taken the nearby town of Monteleone, also on Highway 71, before making for Città della Pieve. About a mile before there they met paras who were determined that the Faughs would not pass, but two men, Corporal Patton and Fusilier Bell MM, had different ideas and, using infiltration tactics, prised the Germans from their positions; thirty paras were captured and several more killed or wounded. Manson then raced for Città with his platoon and a troop of Shermans, and reached the centre of the town where they began consolidating. Taken completely off balance the Germans withdrew.[26]

But Città della Pieve was soon back in German hands. It was not regained through counter-attack but rather through the actions of a British officer. This was Lieutenant Colonel James Dunnill DSO, CO of 1st Royal Irish Fusiliers, who, inexplicably, ordered Manson and his men to withdraw, allowing the Germans to return and create new and better defensive positions. Two senior Irish Fusiliers' officers told the author that Dunnill ought not to have been in command of a battalion at all. Brian Clark, then the Adjutant, was convinced that Dunnill had already lost his nerve when he assumed command after the death of his predecessor, while John Horsfall, who succeeded Dunnill as CO and confirmed Clark's belief, considered Dunnill to have been in this state even earlier.[27]

Dunnill's inexplicable order meant that a brigade-strength attack had to be mounted to seize Città. However, 36 Brigade by-passed the town and, by nightfall on 18 June, were north of it. Then 78th Division had a stroke of good fortune, which was bad fortune for many German paras. A wireless message ordering the paras to withdraw was intercepted and, with the time of withdrawal known, the divisional artillery drew up a fire plan to bombard all exit routes from the town two minutes after the withdrawal time. The artillery was astonishingly successful and, next morning, exit roads from Città della Pieve were strewn with para corpses. Those who survived, however, engaged the advancing troops with what Major General Charles Keightley, GOC of 78th Division, described as 'the deadliest sniping I have seen in the war'. Keightley almost became a victim of that sniping when a bullet shattered his field glasses. Finally, 5th Buffs and 6th West Kents advanced to clear the high ground beyond, putting Città della Pieve firmly in 78th Division's hands.[28]

But the delay along Highway 71 lost 78th Division three days in its advance on Trasimene. In the view of John Horsfall, Città della Pieve was the key to the Albert Line and had Dunnill not ordered Len Manson's platoon out of it when he did then '78th Division would have piled into the enemy at Trasimene three days earlier – before they were ready – and probably rolled the whole lot up in the process.'[29] In other words, Eighth Army would have 'bounced' the Albert Line and Alexander's classical pursuit might have succeeded, proving Clausewitz's axiom that the fruits of victory are to be found in the pursuit.

The Battleaxe Division had nosed ahead of the Springboks who were moving up to their left. Advancing over difficult countryside the South Africans were delayed by soft ground, following heavy rain, and then met with stout resistance at Chiusi which turned out to be the western anchor of the German defensive line, which was farther south than anticipated. Holding the line at Chiusi was the Hermann Göring Panzer Division. Elsewhere, 78th Division was also running up against enemy defences: at Vaiano, 8th Argylls were rebuffed by fierce counter-attacks on 20 June while, next day, 5th Buffs also failed to take that objective. XIII Corps' commander, Kirkman, concluded that a corps attack was necessary to break the German line and brought forward 4th Division to strengthen the assault.[30]

Fourth Division was deployed south of Vaiano with 28 Brigade relieving 36 Brigade on the night of 22/23 June. Kirkman ordered the advance to continue with 78th Division moving along Highway 71, the South Africans by the Chiusi–Sinalunga road, which runs north on the western bank of the Chiana canal, and 4th Division relieving 78th Division of all its eastern sector should the battle still be underway when the Battleaxe Division was due to withdraw at the end of June. For the time being, however, 78th Division was probing at the defences about Sanfatúcchio, held by 334th Infantry Division. Any British gains were counter-attacked while heavy defensive fire from artillery and *nebelwerfern*,* was on call.[31]

* Multi-barrelled mortars.

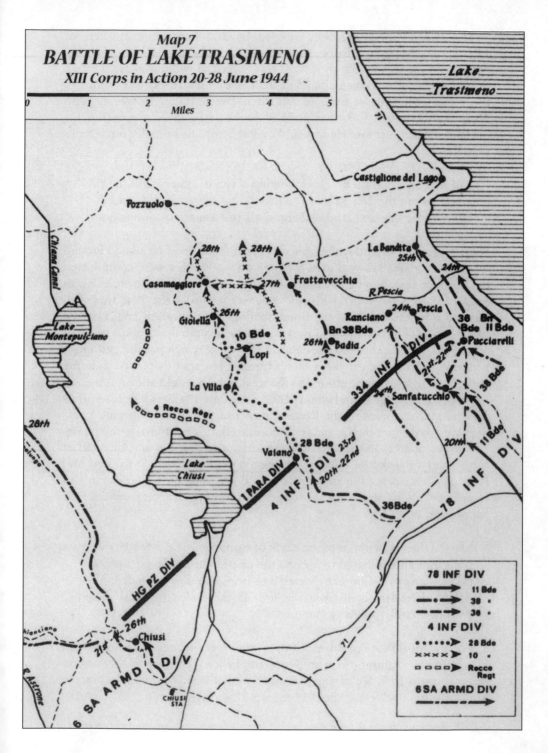

Map 7
BATTLE OF LAKE TRASIMENO
XIII Corps in Action 20-28 June 1944

0 1 2 3 4 5
Miles

Lake Trasimeno

Castiglione del Lago

Pozzuolo

La Bandita
25th

28th   28th
24th
Casamaggiore   27th   Frattavecchia
R. Pescia
Ranclano   24th   Pescia
Gioiella   26th   Bn 38 Bde   36   Bn
Bde   11 Bde
10 Bde   26th   Badia   Pucciarelli
Lopi
La Villa   334 INF   I DIV   36 Bde
Sanfatucchio
4 Recce Regt   24th
20th   11 Bde
28th   DIV

Lake Montepulciano

Chiana Canal

28 Bde   23rd
Valano   DIV   20th-22nd   78 INF DIV
1 PARA DIV   4 INF
Lake Chiusi   36 Bde
78 INF

HG PZ DIV

26th
21st   Chiusi

CHIUSI STA
71
R. Astrone
6 SA ARMD DIV

78 INF DIV
———————▶ 11 Bde
—·—·—·—▶ 38 "
– – – – –▶ 36 "
4 INF DIV
••••••▶ 28 Bde
×××××▶ 10 "
▢▢▢▢▢▶ Recce Regt
6 SA ARMD DIV
– – – – –▶

123

The attack on Sanfatúcchio was led by 2nd Lancashire Fusiliers of 11 Brigade who, shortly before midnight on 20 June, sent a strong fighting patrol into the village. But the patrol was forced to withdraw and the task of taking the village was assigned to the London Irish who, with tanks of the Ontario Regiment, were to launch a fresh attack. However, John Horsfall, the Rifles' CO, was amazed to hear the GOC's proposal for outflanking the position. He was told by Pat Scott, his brigade commander that Keightley

> had had an inspiration. The following day, or rather night, he pro-
> posed to sail the 2nd Rifles in 'ducks'* down the ten-mile length of
> Lake Trasimene and land us behind all this vexatious opposition.[32]

Scott persuaded Keightley that this was really not a good idea and Horsfall was able to make his own plan for the attack. Matters were complicated by the fact that some Lancashire Fusiliers were pinned down close to Sanfatúcchio – the official history suggests, erroneously, that they had secured a foothold[33] – and the usual artillery concentration could not be used for fear of hitting them. However, smoke was put down and a troop of 17th Field Regiment did 'some delicate shooting' which proved extremely accurate. Rather than make a direct attack, Horsfall employed flanking tactics, using folds in the ground to the west, which would allow his men to approach the village from behind. The Lancashire Fusiliers lent support as did the machine guns of the Kensingtons and 6-pounder anti-tank guns, deployed to distract the Germans on Pucciarelli ridge in the opening phase.

Two companies led and most enemy machine-gun fire was directed at the Canadian tanks. In spite of an enemy who appeared 'possessed and fighting like maniacs' the attack made good progress, the Ontarios worked their way on to the ridge and by mid-morning E Company and its supporting tanks had

> blasted their way into the first block of buildings. The defenders were
> tenacious and prepared to fight to the death. Before the position was
> taken many of E Company's men had been killed or wounded: most
> of the defenders died from the fire of the tanks; of those taken
> prisoner hardly one was uninjured.[34]

Enemy resistance ceased at 1.00pm and the advance continued with H Company fighting forward to San Felice cemetery. Once again opposition to Irish Rifles and Canadian tanks was considerable but the attackers had achieved their objectives by early evening. A German

* DUKWs, amphibious 2.5-ton 6-wheeled lorries developed for the US forces.

124

counter-attack was broken up by artillery and mortar fire and, with a successful attack by 6th Inniskillings on Pucciarelli village, the ridge was almost entirely in Irish Brigade hands. There were, however, some Germans still on the ridge and the morning brought further counter-attack which saw the Kensingtons involved in close-quarter battle. Two enemy strongpoints along the ridge were eliminated during a day of fierce fighting that saw excellent cooperation between all arms. By 6.00pm the Irish Brigade had advanced to take Casa Montemara. Then the Germans put in a counter-attack that was defeated by the doughtiness of F Company, London Irish, and exceptionally effective artillery support. Captain Alan Parsons, the FOO with the company, brought fire from individual guns down all around the farm in shooting that John Horsfall described as 'masterly', since the opposing troops were so close together that Parsons' job demanded the greatest skill and fine judgement. Parsons was wounded next day during a further counter-attack on Casa Montemara.[35]

On the 24th the Irish Brigade captured Pescia and Ranciano villages while 28 Brigade, of 4th Division, attacked towards Vaiano which fell a day later. Pushing on from Vaiano, 28 Brigade took La Villa and the ridge running east from that village. The Somersets advanced to Poggia and then towards Badia. Resistance continued to be tough and, while the Hampshires were attacking La Villa ridge, the Germans shelled and mortared Vaiano. Among the casualties were 4th Division's GOC, Dudley Ward, and 28 Brigade's commander, Brigadier Montagu-Douglas Scott, both of whom were wounded slightly. In the meantime their soldiers continued advancing and, on the 26th, the Somersets found Badia empty before meeting up with the Lancashire Fusiliers of 78th Division.[36] On that same day 36 Brigade lost their commander, Brigadier John Gwynne James DSO, killed by shellfire while visiting one of his battalions.[37] Porto was also found clear of enemy by 4 Recce who sent a patrol out towards Gioiella. That afternoon 2nd King's, with a squadron of Canadian tanks from the redoubtable Three Rivers Regiment passed through 2/4th Hampshires round Lopi to attack Gioiella.

The Germans opened fire on their advance with machine guns, inflicting casualties, and the fighting became fierce. In a series of checks and advances the battalion pushed on towards a hill five hundred yards south of the town. Here the Germans fought back so stubbornly that the leading companies could move no farther; a fresh fire-plan had to be made, and a new attack mounted. After another hour and a half of hot fighting, the tanks got into the town, with the infantry a little way behind; and after still more fighting the town was taken, and positions in it were consolidated by eleven o'clock that night.[38]

With Gioiella taken, Ward passed 10 Brigade through 28 Brigade in the direction of Casamaggiore. The brigade advance was led by 2nd Duke of Cornwall's LI with a Three Rivers' squadron which moved through the Hampshires at Lopi before encountering stiff opposition in the difficult country beyond. It took two and a half hours to push forward some 400 yards, as far as the valley floor beyond Lopi, but the attackers then seized the ridge east of Gioiella before gaining a foothold on the next ridge, a thousand yards east of Casamaggiore. Here they held a cemetery with two companies and some Shermans while a standing patrol covered the ground between the main positions and Casamaggiore. As the divisional historian commented: 'every yard over which the division had advanced since breaking through the Trasimene positions had been fought for.' There seemed no prospect of the Germans yielding any ground and the 28th proved another day of hard fighting. But, with support from 2nd Lancashire Fusiliers on their right, 10 Brigade's DCLI and 2nd Bedfords cleared the ridge, 1/6th East Surreys took Casamaggiore and the Lancashire Fusiliers entered nearby Frattavecchia.[39]

Similar tough fighting had faced the South Africans. To the west 11 Armoured Brigade's Imperial Light Horse had been thwarted by the Hermann Göring Division in their first attempt to enter Chiusi. A new plan was made and a night attack was launched on 21/22 June with 1st Capetown Highlanders advancing towards the town from the railway station with an armoured regiment to each flank; this allowed a company of Highlanders to enter the town.* Once there the Highlanders were counter-attacked with much ferocity and, isolated, were overrun during the morning of the 22nd. But the division had been successful in blocking the western road from Chiusi to Chianciano while, farther west, 24 Guards Brigade's advance was hampered by poor tracks made almost impassable by heavy rain. By 23 June the Guards were two miles south of the Astrone river but about to enter Sarteano on the extreme western flank of Eighth Army. In spite of all the difficulties they faced the guardsmen persevered in their advance: they were, after all, the elite of Britain's army and the monarch's personal troops.[41]

By the evening of 28 June the Albert Line was broken. The Germans had fought hard to hold the attackers while the next line, the Arezzo, was occupied. Here one must reflect on John Horsfall's analysis of James Dunnill's failure to reinforce success at Città della Pieve, the key to the Albert Line. Dunnill had thrown away that key.

*

* The South African history notes that 'Chiusi and Stazione di Chiusi were two quite different places, and the latter was a spot hidden beneath the shading on the map where the two grids met, to make confusion worse.'[40]

Its part in the breaking of the Albert Line concluded, 78th Division moved forward again to reach Cortona where, on 4 July, it was relieved by 6th Armoured Division and withdrawn to Egypt for rest and training. The Battleaxe Division would not return to Italy until the autumn. Now 16th/5th Lancers' battlegroup took up the running, moving along the Chiana valley on Highway 71; the group included C Battery 12th Royal Horse Artillery, 111 Anti-Tank Battery, 8 Field Squadron and 10th Rifle Brigade. Eighth Army was directed on the Arezzo Line to seize Arezzo, a communications centre with access to the Arno valley, a score of miles north of Lake Trasimene. Five miles before Arezzo, 16th/5th Lancers ran into 15th Panzer Grenadier Division. The Green Jackets were stopped by counter-attacks while 26 Armoured Brigade was blocked in the valley. Initially, the full strength of the German defences, from LXXVI Panzer Corps, was not appreciated although the entire 6th Armoured Division was coming under artillery fire directed from OPs on Monte Lignano. Fourth Division, in the centre of XIII Corps' advance, was checked in the hills about Civitello di Chiana, while the South Africans, moving in twin columns through Rapolano and Palazzuolo, were also brought to a stop on the north side of Highway 73.[42]

XIII Corps' leading brigades continued probing forward expecting the German line to crumble without a major attack. Evelegh, GOC 6th Armoured, considered that progress could be made if Monte Lignano was cleared. This task was given to 10th Rifle Brigade which attacked on the night of 5/6 July but lacked the strength to take the heights. Eventually all of 61 Brigade was committed but still the Germans held on and the Green Jackets consolidated along the lower slopes on the night of 7/8 July. Attempts by 4th Division to take Civitella di Chiana met with some success but consolidation was impossible and the enemy continued holding Civitella. Spread over a front of more than ten miles, the two South African infantry brigades were also at a standstill. It seemed that a full corps operation was needed to evict the Germans.[43]

Kirkman realized that he needed more infantry but the only fresh infantry available were Freyberg's New Zealanders.* Leese was anxious to keep the latter for the Gothic Line assault but eventually, on 7 July, agreed to place them under Kirkman; it would take several days before they could arrive. In the meantime XIII Corps' eastern flank had to be protected until X Corps came up alongside and McCreery was ordered to release part of 9 Armoured Brigade for this task. Once Kirkman had his force strengthened the battle for Arezzo began. Considerable air support

---

* The freshest infantry were in 4th Indian Division but this formation had just been committed to X Corps' advance along the Tiber valley, east of Arezzo, and 8th Indian Division was already on its way back to refit and rest.

was provided while artillery firepower included 6th AGRA, with four field, five medium and one heavy regiments, as well as divisional artillery and two HAA regiments from 12 AA Brigade.[44]

Arezzo fell at last on 16 July. Sixth Armoured Division had begun its attack at 1.00am on the 15th with 1 Guards Brigade, all three battalions deployed in depth, advancing through a thunderstorm along Monte Lignano's lower slopes. Simultaneously, 6 NZ Brigade attacked the panzer grenadiers on the crest, forcing them out of their positions. But the Germans continued fighting hard for the reverse slopes of Lignano and only conceded ground with great reluctance. This struggle continued throughout the day. Having taken their objectives in the early morning, 3rd Grenadiers passed the baton to 2nd Coldstream who continued the advance, fighting off counter-attacks in the process. Opposition north of Monte Lignano held the New Zealanders. Then during the night a heavy bombardment was put down by the German artillery. By now this was recognized as the signature tune for a withdrawal and, true to form, the defenders pulled out under cover of darkness.[45] Next morning 16th/5th Lancers entered Arezzo at 9.15am to be greeted by large numbers of partisans.[46] Meanwhile 26 Armoured Brigade was able to push on with 17th/21st Lancers, the Lothians and 10th Rifle Brigade making good progress along the westbound and north-westbound roads from Arezzo. The Lothians quickly reached Quarata where they overran enemy anti-tank guns and captured the bridge over the Arno at Ponte a Buriano before the Germans could demolish it. That evening the Scottish tankmen were advancing north-west by the Pratomagno massif.[47]

On the west side of the Arno valley, 16th/5th Lancers and 10th Rifle Brigade pushed along Highway 60 towards Montevarchi, but were brought to a halt when the Germans blew the bridge over the Chiana canal as the Green Jackets approached. John Skellorn, of the 16th/5th Lancers, recalled that his regiment 'worked its way laboriously along the narrow Arno valley towards Florence. The work was mainly done by the infantry. We plodded along behind, enjoying the tomatoes, peaches, and local wine.'[48]

However, XIII Corps was moving again and Leese expressed himself well pleased with Kirkman's success, describing his plan as 'first rate'; 'It was an excellent battle, well planned and well executed.'[49] As the advance continued, 6th Armoured Division worked along the Arno valley with 1 Guards Brigade securing the foothills of the massif and winkling out German defenders, while 61 Brigade, across the valley, pushed back paras. On the left of 6th Armoured, Dudley Ward's 4th Division, with Three Rivers' Shermans, advanced by fighting bounds from village to village; San Leolino was followed by Pergine and Castiglione Alberti, while Canadian tanks played a major part in persuading the Germans to quit La Querce. Sappers built bridges, notably at Levine which they described as a 'monster task' and the gunners provided constant support. On the approach to Montevarchi, 'an attractive town which stretches for more than a mile along Route Sixty-nine, with many pleasant villas and flowering gardens', South African sappers bridged a stream that ran into the Arno, the Germans having demolished the existing bridge. When the new span of Bailey was complete, the sappers dubbed it 'Twazabuga Bridge'.[50]

In the Chianti the Sherman crews of 11 South African Armoured Brigade treated their tanks as if they were Churchills, climbing rocky hills and negotiating dense scrub that ought to have defied the American tanks and unnerved their crews. Instead, it was the soldiers of 356th Division who were unnerved by the presence of tanks where no tanks had been expected. The infantry of 24 Guards Brigade also appreciated the tank-men's support and, on 20 July, 1st Scots Guards attacked and captured Monte San Michele, the dominating height of the Chianti hills.[51] From its top they could look down on Florence, only 15 miles away.*

Kirkman could now broaden the corps frontage to 30 miles with five divisions in the line, taking over part of Fifth Army's front that had been the responsibility of the French Expeditionary Corps in its last operation in Italy before departing for southern France. On his left flank, Kirkman now deployed 2nd New Zealand and 8th Indian Divisions, replacing respectively 2nd and 4th Moroccan Divisions. Eighth Indian Division had 1 Canadian Armoured Brigade under command, thus adding to the international aspect of XIII Corps.[53]

As XIII Corps advanced along the Arno valley, General Anders' II Polish Corps had been making for Ancona on the Adriatic coast. The only decent port on that coastline north of Bari, Ancona was a valuable prize. On 13 June the Poles had relieved 4th Indian Division and, with General Umberto Utili's Italian Corps of Liberation (*Corpo Italiano di Liberazione*)† under command, began advancing. By 5 July the Poles and Italians were but five miles from Ancona, having severely buffeted 278th Division. At this point Anders stopped and so deployed his divisions as to make the Germans believe that 3rd Carpathian would continue the attack along the coast road. But the real attack was to come from 5th Kresowa Division sweeping inland on the left flank to come out on the coast north of Ancona. This sweep was supported by all Anders' armour, with the addition of 7th Hussars, and met with complete success. Taken off balance the Germans

---

* Gregory Blaxland puts the height of Monte San Michele at 892 metres.[52] Modern maps of Italy show its height as 893 metres but it is unlikely to have grown in the intervening sixty years.
† The Corps included 4th Bersaglieri and 68th Infantry Regiments, each with two battalions, 185th Parachute Battalion, the Piedmont Alpini Battalion and 11th Artillery Regiment.[54]

began evacuating Ancona on 18 July but over 2,500 men were trapped and captured. Just five days later a British convoy docked there with supplies for Eighth Army. On the other side of Italy the port of Livorno was captured by Fifth Army on 19 July, thereby completing most of the preliminaries for the attack on the Gothic Line. All that was needed now was for XIII Corps to take Florence.[55]

With Ancona secure, II Polish Corps continued along the coast. At the same time, McCreery's X Corps was working to widen Eighth Army's approach to the Gothic Line. Both 4th and 10th Indian Divisions, supported by 9 Armoured Brigade, struck out eastward from Arezzo on this task. The Indians had gained another Victoria Cross on 10 July as 10th Division advanced on Città di Castello in the Tiber valley. During an engagement with 114th Jäger Division, a rifle section of 3/5th Mahratta Light Infantry, commanded by Naik* Yeshwant Ghadge, came under heavy machine-gun fire at close range.[56] All the soldiers of the section, save its commander, were killed or wounded but

> Without hesitation Naik Yeshwant Ghadge rushed the machine-gun position, first throwing a grenade which knocked out the machine gun and then he shot two of the gun crew. Finally, having no time to change his magazine, he clubbed to death the two remaining members of the crew. He fell mortally wounded, shot by an enemy sniper.[57]

The Indians captured Città di Castello on 22 July following a flanking attack into the mountains to the west by 1st Durham LI and 2/4th Gurkhas. As the infantry advanced, 3rd Hussars pushed forward, forded the Soara river, which flows into the Tiber on its eastern bank, and created turmoil in the German defences. Fourth Indian Division's sappers had constructed a remarkable cross-country track 'which defied rather than circumvented obstacles' to assist the divisional advance from Monte Civitella and Monte Pagliaiola to Alpe di Poti. But the track, known as 'Jacob's Ladder', became redundant with the fall of Arezzo and the opening of Highway 73 towards Alpe di Poti.[58]

The division's successful attack was led by 1/2nd Gurkhas and Royal Wiltshire Yeomanry tanks, while sappers played their part in clearing roadblocks.

> In this operation a Madrassi bulldozer driver, Sapper Benglase, distinguished himself. He completed three diversions on the scene

* Corporal.

130

of road blows and proceeded to construct a fourth under heavy shell, mortar and spandau* fire. He continued at work until severely wounded.[59]

Monte di Alpe was taken by 1/2nd Gurkhas on the night of 17/18 July. Intense resistance had been expected but the mountaintop was not held in strength, although 2nd Royal Sikhs, advancing on Point 966 on the eastern side of the mountain, came under heavy fire and did not reach their objective until noon, nine hours after the Gurkhas had gained theirs. The division was soon preparing for the next phase of its advance. On the evening of 24 July 3/12th Frontier Force Rifles attacked Campriano, a village in the uplands north of Arezzo, under the gaze of their King-Emperor. Travelling under the pseudonym General Collingwood, King George VI was in Italy to visit his troops from across the Commonwealth and Empire. He asked to inspect the 'Jacob's Ladder' track and made a formal inspection of Eighth Army in which representative detachments of every division paraded before him. The King also decorated many of his soldiers and dubbed Generals McCreery and Harding with the accolade of knighthood.[60]

The New Zealanders had attacked towards Florence on the 22nd, their advance assisted by the Springboks who forced 356th Division off the Chianti ridge next day. By 27 July, Freyberg's men, having taken San Casciano, were closing on Florence. On the night of 1/2 August the New Zealand Division struck for Florence but the attack achieved only partial success and had to be followed by a renewed effort next night. Intended to dislodge the Germans from the Pian dei Cerri hills that dominate the approach to the city this led to a day of small-scale but brutal skirmishes with German defensive groups that included infantry, tanks and 88s. With the New Zealanders continuing their battles, 6th South African Armoured Division sent the Imperial Light Horse/Kimberley Regiment forward to make Eighth Army's entry into Florence. The South Africans probed into the city on the morning of 4 August and were shelled heavily, although Florence had been declared an open city and the Germans ought to have evacuated it. General Jodl, Chief of Operations at OKW, had described Florence as the jewel of Europe while Kesselring had ordered that the Arno would not be defended within the city limits. However, the commander of I Parachute Corps, General Schlemm, thought otherwise and defied Kesselring by organizing resistance along the river within the city.[61]

By the time the South African infantry pushed into Florence as far as the riverline they found that there were no bridges intact, save for

* Allied soldiers usually, but incorrectly, referred to the German MG34 and MG42 machine guns by this name.

the Ponte Vecchio. Schlemm's defiance of Kesselring's orders had even included blocking either end of the Ponte Vecchio by demolitions, a pointless exercise since the bridge was impassable to tanks and vehicles anyway.

Having reached Florence, both New Zealanders and South Africans were relieved by 1st Canadian and 1st British Infantry Divisions. The latter has not thus far appeared in this account although it had already fought in Italy. Although the Spearhead Division had served with VI Corps at Anzio this was its first time with Eighth Army, and its first time in action since the Anzio breakout. On 8 August the Canadians handed over their front to 17 Indian Brigade and a stand-off across the Arno continued for another three days until, on the 11th, it was found that Schlemm's soldiers had slipped away. Three platoons of Buffs from 18 Brigade, of 1st Division, then crossed the Arno to occupy the city centre leading to a further act of defiance from Schlemm when shells fell on some buildings occupied by the Buffs.[62]

Now Alexander could prepare for Operation OLIVE, the attack on the Gothic Line.* His options were limited by terrain and the fact that both German flanks rested on the sea. Decisive results were achievable only by concentrating force at a selected point while maintaining sufficient flexibility to shift the weight of attack elsewhere should circumstances demand or allow it. Of course, he had to be able to make that shift faster than his opponent or forfeit the advantage. There could be no major manoeuvres.

Alexander now had less manpower than he had hoped for with the withdrawal of the US and French forces constituting Seventh Army, which landed in southern France on 15 August. He had tried to obtain more troops, cajoling his superiors in an effort so to do. At one time he thought that 52nd (Lowland) Division which had trained in mountain warfare – probably as part of the deception plan to convince the Germans that the Allies planned to invade Norway – would be sent out from the UK to join Eighth Army, but this formation was not released and went to north-west Europe in September. Likewise 6th Indian Division was not released from Persia–Iraq Command and, with 78th Division resting in Egypt, although available to Alexander, Eighth Army could have benefited from the arrival of either, or preferably both, formations. Fifth Army was strengthened by 92nd Infantry Division and the Brazilian Expeditionary Force, of divisional strength and US-equipped, but only single brigades of either formation had

* Hitler had ordered that the line be renamed Green Line on 16 June but the Allies continued to use the title Gothic, as shall this narrative.[63]

arrived by late July. From the Middle East Alexander obtained 3 Greek Mountain Brigade, 66 Brigade, recently formed from two battalions from Gibraltar's garrison and a third that had been due to disband,* while 43 Gurkha Lorried Infantry Brigade was also made available for Allied Armies in Italy. In the case of the last-named the C-in-C India warned that he doubted his ability to keep the brigade supplied with reinforcements as there was a shortage of Gurkhali-speaking British officers.[65]

In the longer term Alexander intended strengthening his forces with three British-equipped Italian divisions, the deployment in Italy of a Jewish Brigade, which was not yet in being but had been proposed, and the raising of two additional brigades for II Polish Corps. Manpower for the latter would be found from prisoners taken from the German armies in France, many of whom were Poles forced to fight for Germany. Anders had been promised 11,000 such men by General Sosnkowski, the Polish C-in-C. In addition, the Canadians would produce another infantry brigade for 5th Armoured Division so that it would conform with the new structure adopted by other armoured divisions.

With the Germans in well-prepared positions, Alexander's staff had to devise a plan that would make them misjudge the impact point of the main attack. Thus Alexander intended that Eighth Army would force the centre of the Gothic Line through Lemelsen's Tenth Army and then pin von Vietinghoff's Fourteenth Army between the Adriatic and the Po. In readiness for such an attack, formations were already deploying. But Leese disagreed, arguing that Eighth Army's main effort should be on the Adriatic sector where best use could be made of its manpower and of the 1,000 guns available for the attack. In his thinking he was supported by Kirkman who pointed out that the coastal sector offered the best opportunity for armoured operations. By now, Eighth Army deployed only two armoured divisions as XIII Corps, including 6th British and 6th South African, had been transferred to Fifth Army on 10 August, much to Leese's displeasure. Now in Leese's order of battle was 1st Armoured Division, returned to Eighth Army for the first time since North Africa; it was the only Alamein veteran division to rejoin the Army in Italy. Even so, Leese had only half the armour he expected in a country where he felt he could make good use of armour.[66]

In addition, 'Leese, for emotional and personal reasons, had resolved never to fight shoulder to shoulder with Clark again if he could avoid it, and Kirkman now supplied him with a persuasive tactical argument.'[67]

---

* The brigade came into being on 20 July; 2nd Royal Scots joined on 5 August, followed by 1st Hertfordshires the next day, while 11th Lancashire Fusiliers did not arrive until the 28th.[64]

Topography had also to be considered:

In the region of the upper Tiber, the Apennines ... turn north-west to join the Maritime Alps in Liguria, and thereby isolate central Italy from the Po Valley. In the west the narrow coastal plain north of Pisa does not give access to the Po Valley, the mountains still bar the way. In the east, however, there is direct access to the north along the coastal belt south-east of Rimini. This is the easiest route to Northern Italy but nonetheless it has disadvantages: the Apennine foothills extend in difficult ridges to within not many miles of the coast, there [is] a series of water obstacles at right angles to movement north-west, there is only one first-class road for an access ... the route gives access only to the most extreme north-east corner of the Po Valley, the Romagna, itself dissected by another series of parallel water obstacles, and, finally, this eastern approach is separated from Western Central Italy by the central Apennines across which lateral communications are long, few and difficult.[68]

Rather than dismissing Leese's concerns, Alexander met him to discuss the plan for OLIVE. The meeting, also attended by Harding, was held at Orvieto airfield on 4 August and Leese's view prevailed. However, while Clark accepted the revised plan, he had no wish to see a reduced role for Fifth Army and argued for a major role. It was Alexander's agreement to this that led to XIII Corps' transfer to Fifth Army. In turn, that deprived Leese of a reserve for Eighth Army. With the departure of the French and Truscott's corps, Fifth Army had been reduced to an armoured division and four infantry divisions.[69]

Alexander stressed that the purpose of the offensive was to destroy enemy forces on the ground so that they could offer no further resistance. In his Order of the Day to Eighth Army, Leese wrote:

You have won great victories. To advance 220 miles from Cassino to Florence in three months is a notable achievement in the Eighth Army's history. To each one of you in the Eighth Army and in the Desert Air Force, my grateful thanks.

Now we begin the last lap. Swiftly and secretly, once again, we have moved right across Italy an Army of immense strength and striking power – to break the Gothic Line.

Victory in the coming battles means the beginning of the end for the German Armies in Italy.

Let every man do his utmost, and again success will be ours. Good luck to you all.[70]

At corps and divisional levels similar messages were issued. Keightley of V Corps emphasized that the smashing of the Gothic Line was to be followed by the destruction of all enemy forces in the valley of the Po.

Once again deception tactics were used to fool the Germans about the timing of OLIVE and the location of major attacks. Originally the operation was scheduled to coincide with DRAGOON on 15 August but was delayed for ten days. A measure of the success of the deception programme was shown by the absence, on leave, of von Vietinghoff and Heidrich when the attack opened. There had also been an attempt to confuse the Germans about the location of I Canadian Corps. This was not successful, in part because the original plan had called for the apparent presence of the Canadians in the Adriatic sector and their actual presence in the centre, whereas the plan as executed required them to be on the Adriatic. Moving the Canadian and V Corps from the Foligno area across the Apennines to the Adriatic sector was a massive undertaking requiring the erection of sixteen Bailey bridges and, since secrecy was vital, all movement had to be made under cover of darkness with vehicles and personnel hidden during the day. It took ten nights but was completed without the Germans learning of it.[71]

As its soldiers waited for H-Hour, Eighth Army was stronger than at any time in its history, even with the loan of XIII Corps to Fifth Army. Across its front it disposed four corps – I Canadian, II Polish, V and X – totalling eleven divisions. V Corps was much the strongest, almost an army in itself, and included 1st Armoured, 4th British, 4th Indian, 46th and 56th (London) Divisions with the Italian Corps of Liberation;* 43 Gurkha Brigade was assigned to 1st Armoured Division while 46th Division had 25 Tank Brigade under command and 56th Division had 7 Armoured Brigade. Just before midnight on 25 August the assaulting brigades of 5th Kresowa, 1st Canadian and 46th Divisions crossed the undefended Metauro river. Only as the leading troops began crossing did Eighth Army's artillery open fire along the seven-mile front. About eight miles off to the left, 8th Indian Division advanced into mountainous terrain to provide left-flank protection.[73]

The ten-day delay in D-Day for OLIVE gave Alexander an opportunity to estimate the effect, if any, that DRAGOON might have on his operations. With Seventh Army advancing rapidly up the Rhône valley, it seemed that an Allied breakthrough in the Apennines would compel the Germans to evacuate north-western Italy to avoid their forces there being cut off. In turn that would lead to a shorter German line, from the Swiss border to the

* The Corps disposed 21,000 men, of whom 7,000 were parachute-trained soldiers of Nembo Division, and was armed and equipped entirely with Italian materiel.[72]

Adriatic coast, and Fifth Army, with its left flank free, could wheel right to push across the Po to Mantua and Verona while Eighth Army could make for Venice. The latter would provide a port to shorten Eighth Army's stretched lines of supply. All this seemed possible as the armies waited for D-Day, but it would be many months before these advances became reality.

Notes

1. Jackson, *The Mediterranean and Middle East,* vol. VI, pt II, p. 17.
2. Ibid., pp. 52–3; Blaxland, *Alexander's Generals,* op. cit., p. 142.
3. Molony, *The Mediterranean and Middle East,* vol. VI, pt I, see Ch VI (pp. 295–338) which covers the ANVIL debate.
4. Ford, *Mailed Fist,* op. cit., p. 156; Anon, *The History of 61 Infantry Brigade,* p. 14; Joslen, *Orders of Battle,* op. cit., pp. 17, 269 & 297.
5. Kesselring, op. cit., p. 208; Molony, op. cit., vol. VI, pt I, p. 448.
6. Doherty, *Wall of Steel,* p. 168.
7. Blaxland, op. cit., p. 143.
8. Orpen, *Victory in Italy,* p. 78.
9. Scott, *Account of the Service of the Irish Brigade.*
10. Blaxland, op. cit., p. 144; NA, Kew, WO170/586, war diary, 24 Gds Bde, Jun–Dec 1944; WO170/1350, war diary, 5 Gren Gds, 1944.
11. Blaxland, op. cit., p. 144.
12. Blaxland, op. cit., pp. 144–5; Molony, op. cit., p. 270.
13. Jackson, *The Battle for Italy,* p. 260; Doherty, *A Noble Crusade,* op. cit., p. 227.
14. Jackson, *The Mediterranean and Middle East,* op. cit., pp. 28–9.
15. Anon, *Engineers in the Italian Campaign,* pp. 35–7.
16. ffrench-Blake, *A History of the 17th/21st Lancers,* op. cit., p. 186.
17. Ibid., p. 187.
18. Jackson, op. cit., p. 25.
19. Ibid., pp. 28–9; Blaxland, op. cit., pp. 146–8; Anon, *The History of 61 Infantry Brigade,* pp. 31–2; NA, Kew, WO170/514, war diary, 1 Gds Bde, Jan–Jun 1944.
20. Blaxland, op. cit., p. 148.
21. Ibid., pp. 148–9; Jackson, op. cit., pp. 26–7; NA, Kew, WO170/ 838, war diary, Warwickshire Yeomanry, 1944.
22. Doherty, *CTW,* op. cit., p. 163.
23. NA, Kew, WO170/838, war diary, Warwickshire Yeomanry 1944 op. cit.
24. Ray, *Algiers to Austria,* op. cit., p. 144.
25. Ibid., pp. 144–5; NA, Kew, WO170/1446, war diary, 5 Northants 1944.
26. Ray, op. cit., p. 145; Doherty, *CTW,* op. cit., p. 162; Horsfall, *Fling Our Banner to the Wind,* op. cit., p. 137.
27. Doherty, op. cit., p. 162; Horsfall and Clark, interviews with author, 1990 & 1991.
28. Doherty, op. cit., pp. 162–3; Ray, op. cit., p. 145; Scott, *Account of the Service of the Irish Brigade,* op. cit.; NA, Kew, WO170/602, war diary 36 Bde, Jan–Jun 1944.
29. Horsfall, op. cit., p. 137.
30. Orpen, op. cit., p. 87; Ray, op. cit., p. 146.
31. Jackson, op. cit., p. 42.

32. Horsfall, op. cit., p. 143.
33. Jackson, op. cit., p. 43.
34. Horsfall, op. cit., p. 151; Doherty, op. cit., p. 167.
35. Horsfall, op. cit., pp. 152–68; Doherty, op. cit., pp. 167–74; Ray, op. cit., pp. 147–8.
36. Doherty, op. cit., pp. 174–5; Williamson, *The Fourth Division*, op. cit. pp. 165–7.
37. Ray, op. cit., p. 150; www.cwgc.org
38. Williamson, op. cit., p. 168.
39. Ibid., pp. 168–71.
40. Orpen, op. cit., p. 88.
41. Ibid.; Blaxland, op. cit., p. 149.
42. Ray, op. cit., p. 152; Ford, op. cit., p. 166; Williamson, op. cit., p. 177.
43. Ford, op. cit., pp. 166–7; Anon, *The History of 61 Infantry Brigade*, op. cit., pp. 46–7.
44. Jackson, *The Mediterranean and Middle East*, vol. VI, pt II, pp. 76–8.
45. Ibid., pp. 78–9; Doherty, *A Noble Crusade*, op. cit., p. 236; Blaxland, op. cit., pp. 152–3.
46. Skellorn, op. cit., p. 17.
47. Doherty, op. cit., p. 236; Blaxland, op. cit., p. 153; Anon, *The History of 61 Infantry Brigade*, op. cit., pp. 47–8.
48. Skellorn, op. cit., p. 18; Anon, *The History of 61 Infantry Brigade*, op. cit., p. 48.
49. Jackson, op. cit., p. 79.
50. Ford, op. cit., pp. 169–70; Anon, *The History of 61 Infantry Brigade*, op. cit., pp. 49–53; Williamson, op. cit., p. 188; Blaxland, op. cit., pp. 154–5.
51. Blaxland, op. cit., p. 155.
52. Ibid.
53. Doherty, op. cit., p. 237.
54. Jackson, op. cit., p. 15; Rosignoli, *The Allied Forces in Italy*, p. 110.
55. Jackson, op. cit., pp. 81–3; Blaxland, op. cit., p. 154.
56. Jackson, op. cit., pp. 80–1; Blaxland, op. cit., pp. 155–6; Doherty, op. cit., p. 237.
57. *London Gazette*, 2 Nov 1944.
58. Stevens, *Fourth Indian Division*, p. 331.
59. Ibid., p. 332.
60. Ibid, pp. 332–5; Jackson, op. cit., p. 91n; Doherty, op. cit., p. 238.
61. Jackson, op. cit., pp. 89–94; Blaxland, op. cit., pp. 157–8; Doherty, op. cit., pp. 237–8.
62. Blaxland, op. cit., pp. 158–9.
63. Nicholson, op. cit., p. 460n.
64. Joslen, op. cit., p. 298.
65. Jackson, op. cit., p. 55.
66. Ibid., pp. 55–6.
67. Bidwell and Graham, op. cit., p. 348.
68. NA, Kew, CAB44/145, p. 7.
69. Jackson, op. cit., pp. 119–26; Blaxland, op. cit., pp. 161–3.
70. NA, Kew, WO170/1386, war diary 1/4th Essex, 1944, App J-4.
71. Jackson, op. cit., pp. 126–32; Nicholson, op. cit., pp. 497–8; Doherty, op. cit., p. 240.
72. Badoglio, *Italy in the Second World War*, p. 178.
73. Doherty, op. cit., p. 240.

Chapter Seven

Forcing the Gothic Line

The greater therefore should our courage be.

By dawn on 26 August the assaulting brigades had advanced about two miles against minimal opposition. This led to speculation at Leese's HQ that Kesselring, anticipating the offensive, had pulled his armies back to a stronger line along the Foglia river, some 11 miles to the rear. However, it was soon discovered that the withdrawal was only local and 4th Parachute Regiment had suffered many casualties from British artillery while pulling back. And from German prisoners came the pleasing information that both Tenth Army's commander, von Vietinghoff, and 1st Parachute Division's commander, Heidrich, were on leave, thus confirming that the deception plan had succeeded. Yet again Alexander had gained surprise over Kesselring, for the third time in 1944. Furthermore, the latter believed that this offensive was only a continuation of the Polish advance, albeit with reinforcements from other formations.[1]

Canadian troops in the Metauro bridgehead were amazed to see Alexander drive into their area in a jeep but even more amazed when they recognized his passenger: Winston Churchill. Ten days earlier the premier had watched Allied troops land in southern France before returning to Italy where he visited his old regiment, 4th Queen's Own Hussars, of which he was Colonel, and flew on to Leese's HQ.[2]

The first two days of OLIVE saw Canadian, Polish and British troops make steady progress with the Canadians, despite considerable opposition, eight miles beyond the Metauro and approaching the hilltop town of Monteciccardo. An hour into the 28th the Edmontons entered Monteciccardo at much the same time as some Germans. They clashed and the Edmontons withdrew but returned later to take the town after a day of skirmishes in the heat; they also took the nearby monastery. To their right 1 Canadian Brigade had attacked under cover of darkness, their objective a ridge held by paras. The Germans fought with their usual determination, even setting fire to haystacks to illuminate the attackers. With daylight the Canadians were able to look down on the Foglia with its far bank cleared

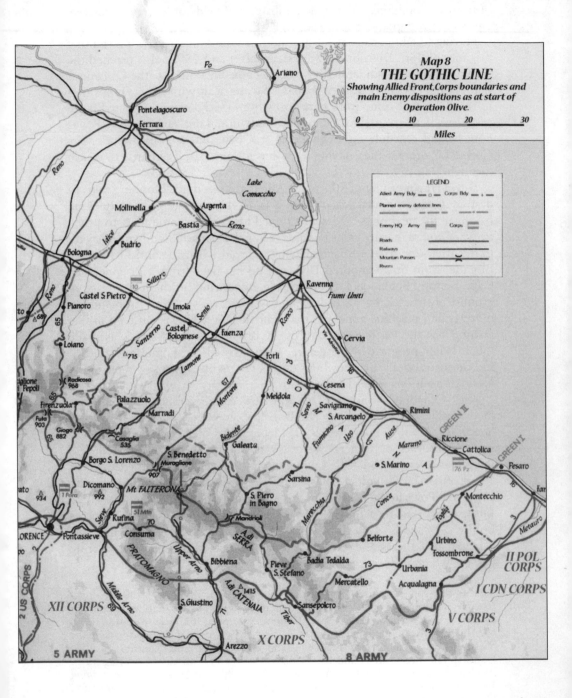

Map 8
THE GOTHIC LINE
Showing Allied Front, Corps boundaries and main Enemy dispositions as at start of Operation Olive.

0	10	20	30

Miles

LEGEND

Allied Army Bdy ——□—— Corps Bdy ——┴——

Planned enemy defence lines

Enemy HQ   Army ▓▓▓   Corps ▓▓▓

Roads ————
Railways ————
Mountain Passes ～
Rivers

Po

Ariano

Pontelagoscuro

Ferrara

Reno

Lake Comacchio

Mollinella   Argenta

Bastia   Reno

Bologna   Budrio

Reno   Idice   Sillaro   10

Castel S.Pietro   Imola   Ravenna

Pianoro   Santerno   Senio   Fiumi Uniti

65   689   Castel Bolognese   Faenza

Loiano   715   Lamone   Forli   Cervia

Radicosa 968   67   Montone   Cesena

Firenzuola   Palazzuolo   Meldola   Savignano   Rimini

Futa 903   Marradi   Bidente   S.Arcangelo   GREEN II

Giogo 882   Casaglia 535   Galeata   Uso   Riccione   GREEN I

Borgo S.Lorenzo   Muroglione   Sarsina   Marano   Cattolica

934   1 Para   Dicomano   907   S.Piero in Bagno   S.Marino   Pesaro

Mt FALTERONA   992   Marecchia   Conca   76 Pz   Far

51 Mtn   Mandrioli   Montecchio

FLORENCE   Rufina   70   Belforte   Urbino   Metauro

Pontassieve   Consuma   A.di SERRA   Fossombrone

PRATOMAGNO   Upper Arno   Bibbiena   Pieve S.Stefano   Badia Tedalda 73   Urbania   Acqualagna   **II POL CORPS**

XII CORPS   Middle Arno   68   S.Giustino   A.di CATENAIA 1415   Mercatello   **I CDN CORPS**

2 US CORPS   Sansepolcro   **V CORPS**

90   **X CORPS**

5 ARMY   Arezzo   **8 ARMY**

of trees and buildings to provide unobstructed fields of fire from concrete and steel strongpoints above the river.[3]

Having fought hard over the ground from the Metauro, both assaulting brigades of 46th Division – 128 (Hampshire) and 139 – also reached the Foglia during the 29th, and 5th Kresowa came up alongside the Canadians that evening. Pesaro had been by-passed to be dealt with later. Opposition to the Poles had come from paras on whom the Poles had inflicted more casualties than at Cassino. From the speedy initial movement, OLIVE was now behind schedule although Leese still believed he could bounce the Gothic Line rather than having to mount a large set-piece battle to smash through.[4]

During the morning of 30 August Allied aircraft made bombing raids to destroy German minefields, thereby easing the passage of the attacking troops in the next phase. Leese instructed his corps commanders to probe forward and make any gains possible. Thus the Canadians advanced again in the afternoon with 3 Brigade having relieved 1 Brigade and 11 Infantry Brigade, from 5th Armoured Division, taking over from 2 Brigade. The Cape Breton Highlanders of 11 Brigade, advancing on the left over open ground obstructed by barbed wire, sustained many losses from mines, mortars and machine guns. On the right the West Novas suffered in like fashion but the Perth Regiment, of 11 Brigade, and the Patricias made much better progress in the centre; both crossed the Foglia and pushed the Germans out of their positions during the night. Dawn saw most of the German positions in Canadian hands.[5]

Fifth Canadian Armoured Division now took over but their advance met considerable opposition. The British Columbia Dragoons lost thirty Shermans in half a mile; their CO, Lieutenant Colonel Frederick Vokes, younger brother of General Vokes, was among the dead. Nonetheless the advance continued with Canadians inflicting loss on the enemy. On 1 September 1st Canadian Division thrust northward to the coast, cutting across the Poles in the process. In this advance the Edmontons took Monte Luro, supported by Churchills of 12th Royal Tanks, and 4th Princess Louise's Dragoon Guards* captured Monte Peloso. Meanwhile the Carpathian Lancers and 1st Household Cavalry Regiment were clearing Pesaro, which task was complete by 3 September.[7]

---

* As its title suggests this was a cavalry regiment, which had been the divisional recce regiment before being converted to infantry as part of the reorganization that gave 5th Armoured Division a second infantry brigade. Its recce role was taken over by the Royal Canadian Dragoons. The other two units of 12 Brigade were the Westminsters, a motorized regiment, and the Lanark and Renfrew Scottish Regiment, formed from 89 and 109 LAA Batteries of 1st Canadian LAA Regiment. At first the latter was styled unofficially 89th/109th Battalion before becoming 1st Canadian LAA Battalion. It did not receive the Lanark and Renfrew title until October. Another proposed title had been Laircraft Scots of Canada.[6]

140

By then the Canadians were closing on Rimini, having pushed the paras out of that section of the Gothic Line and across the Conca river, while 46th Division, still with 128 and 139 Brigades leading, had made a similar advance from the Foglia. During this advance the Hampshires gained another Victoria Cross. On the night of 30 August the Hampshire Brigade, supported by the North Irish Horse and 46 Recce, attacked Montegridolfo, a key German bastion.[8] All went well and 1/4th Hampshires, with B Squadron North Irish Horse made the final assault, taking Montegridolfo a little before 6.00am on the 31st. In the course of this battle Lieutenant Gerard Ross Norton MM,* a South African attached to the Hampshires, found his platoon pinned down by heavy fire.

> On his own initiative and with complete disregard for his own safety, he advanced alone and attacked the first machine-gun emplacement, killing the crew of three. He then went on to the second position containing two machine guns and 15 riflemen, and wiped out both machine-gun nests, killing or taking prisoner the remainder of the enemy. Throughout these attacks he was continuously under fire from a self-propelled gun, nevertheless he calmly went on to lead his platoon against the remaining enemy positions.[9]

Other hillside or hilltop villages had fallen to 46th Division. Fifth Sherwood Foresters, of 139 Brigade, seized a village on Monte Vecchio from which 2/5th Leicesters attacked to take Mondaino at night. During this operation it was discovered that the German 71st Division had been reinforced by troops of 26th Panzer Division but even with that bolstering the enemy were turned out quickly from seemingly impregnable positions.[10]

Over to the left 4th Indian Division, with 5 and 7 Brigades up, had advanced over 20 miles of high ground, liberating Raphael's birthplace of Urbino on 28 August en route to hit the Gothic Line, which they did on the 30th. Monte Calvo was assaulted by 3/10th Baluchis who had already taken Monte della Croce without a shot being fired. Although their supporting tanks were disabled by mines, the Baluchis pressed on, supported by fighter-bombers, and took the height against strong resistance, while 1/9th Gurkhas swept round to take commanding positions behind Monte Calvo before making for Tavoleto.[11]

V Corps' commander, Lieutenant General Keightley, then committed 56th (London) Division to the struggle, placing them between 4th Indian and 46th Divisions. Thus the battle 'started a little unsatisfactorily' for 56th Division since it was 'insinuated at short notice between the two

* His Military Medal had been earned as a sergeant following his escape from Tobruk. Subsequently Norton had been commissioned into the Kaffrarian Rifles.

formations'. Known as the Black Cats from their divisional symbol of Dick Whittington's cat, the newcomers made steady progress, with 2/6th Queen's, supported by 2/5th Queen's and a squadron of 8th Royal Tanks, taking Monte Capello on 1 September in spite of heavy casualties from 'terrific spandau fire'. The opposing 98th Division, also the proud possessors of a black cat badge, though presumably not Dick Whittington's, had arrived but recently from the Russian front and put in some strong counter-attacks. Despite this, 169 (Queen's) Brigade had patrols beyond the Ventana river, two miles from Mondaino on the 3rd. That night 167 Brigade received the unwelcome and, by now, unusual attention of the Luftwaffe in a bombing raid that caused over a hundred casualties and killed or injured many German prisoners awaiting evacuation. However, 167 Brigade went on to attack Tavoleto with 7th Oxfordshire and Buckinghamshire LI capturing Cappucini and 8th Royal Fusiliers on Monte Foggetto by last light on 4 September. By then 168 Brigade was preparing to join 167 and secure a crossing of the Conca before striking towards the Marano river.[12]

The Canadians had already crossed the Conca and 46th Division, led by 6th York and Lancaster, crossed on the night of 2/3 September, to secure a crossing for 1st Armoured. At Morciano 2/4th King's Own Yorkshire LI seized the bridge after which 138 Brigade advanced to take San Clemente, a village on high ground two miles beyond the Conca. This brought 46th Division roughly level with the Canadians; 1 Brigade was also engaged two miles beyond the Conca. The Canadians had created a bridgehead that gave Leese the opportunity to loose his armour but the army commander had failed to have 1st Armoured Division close enough to the front to exploit this opportunity.[13] In fact, Leese had deliberately kept 1st Armoured well back, anxious to avoid blocking the roads forward; he was probably remembering the traffic chaos at El Alamein. And he had also been surprised by the speed with which the Canadians had jabbed into the German lines. Had he then committed 1st Armoured to the Canadian Corps, for which there was sufficient space, the armour might have been able to play a major exploitative role. But

> Leese's mind worked at infantry pace. At Alamein he had com-
> manded [XXX] Corps which had done most of the infantry work
> to crack the line, for the armour had at first refused to fight its way
> through the German positions, insisting that its task was to go through
> the 'gap' and 'pursue' the enemy. The 1st Armoured Division still
> held that outdated notion – shared, apparently, by Leese. It was
> looking for a gap.[14]

The Canadians now prepared to make for Rimini believing that the road was open. Two miles beyond the Conca they realized their mistake when

German resistance forced them to take to their feet to break through enemy positions. Forty-sixth Division had opened the way for the New Brunswick Hussars to attack Coriano but the Canadian tankmen were repulsed and heavy shellfire prevented 5th Hampshires from moving beyond their start line. With reinforcements arriving, German resistance was increasing and the opportunity for launching 1st Armoured Division had been lost.[15] The Gothic Line had been pierced but no easy road lay ahead to Rimini, or Bologna, and Venice was as far away as ever. As for Leese's pipe dream of Vienna, it would remain simply that, a dream.*

As ever the terrain was also an enemy with Eighth Army fighting across ridges and valleys that provided cover for the Germans. Coriano ridge, 10 miles from Rimini, was a major obstacle for 1st Armoured and 46th Divisions and a number of attacks were brought to a stop by its defenders. The ridge was the last such barrier before relatively open country but V Corps failed to bounce it and von Vietinghoff rushed reinforcements, including tanks and anti-tank guns, there. By 5 September six divisions, including one panzer and one panzer grenadier, faced Eighth Army from Coriano ridge. Thus breaking through the German defences on the ridge required more soldiers on the ground, more artillery and more armour. It also required more time but that commodity was in limited supply since every day brought closer the possibility of heavy rains – rain had already impeded 56th Division's crossing of the Foglia – that would end the fine summer weather and bring back the conditions of the previous autumn and winter.[17]

To move forward Eighth Army had to clear Coriano ridge of Germans. Efforts elsewhere could not bring the same results and, in any case, faced similar obstacles. V Corps devised a plan to clear the ridge, with D-Day set for 12 September. Fire support would come not only from the corps artillery but also from naval vessels offshore, while Allied aircraft would make their usual contribution. The operation was successful but cost V Corps many casualties. In preliminary operations, 4th Indian Division attacked and, after a lengthy and bloody struggle, captured Piandicastello and the neighbouring ridge. At much the same time 169 Brigade of 56th Division was tackling Gemmano but found that

the opposition was much stronger than had been anticipated and it was not long before the attackers found themselves being stubbornly resisted, in particular by determined Austrian troops trained in hill-fighting tactics. Every boulder hid a resolute defender, while the houses and buildings on the slopes had each to be dealt with

* James Lucas, then serving in 2/7th Queen's, told the author that he recalled Leese addressing his battalion and assuring them that they would be in Bologna in two days, Venice in four and Vienna in seven.[16]

separately. In addition to a heavy barrage put down by the Division's artillery, the Desert Air Force straddled the upper and more rugged parts of the massif. The light infantrymen pressed slowly upwards and were within sight of their objective when the enemy mounted a strong counter-attack and forced them to withdraw to the lower slopes.[18]

The Ox and Bucks rallied and advanced again to take the heights, but another counter-attack forced them back to the lower slopes and into a 36-hour battle 'fought with relentless courage and determination' before relief by elements of 169 Brigade. Thereafter 2/7th Queen's passed through to take Gemmano and the eastern slopes, thereby denying the Germans domination of the Conca valley and the approaches to Croce where the Black Cats would have another tough fight. Although Gemmano had been taken, the Conca valley's western slopes remained in German hands, affording them a view of the valley itself and of I Canadian and V Corps' support zones.[19]

On 10 September, before the launch of Eighth Army's renewed offensive, Alexander ordered Fifth Army to attack in the hope of knocking the enemy completely off-balance by striking with alternating attacks.[20] The confusion thus engendered should break the German lines and allow both Allied armies through the Gothic Line and on to the Lombardy plain. But rather than throwing his left fist at this stage, Alexander might have done better to reinforce Eighth Army's attempts to crumble German defences on his right flank. However, the sensitivities of the Americans, especially Clark, probably compelled Alexander to act as he did.

Leese had planned that Eighth Army would leap forward from Coriano ridge towards Ravenna, 35 miles away in the third phase of his attack. But Eighth Army was incapable of such a leap, or of any leap at all. Heaving against the ridge was probably its limit. German defences were well sited, camouflaged and manned with determined soldiery. As British tanks advanced they met anti-tank fire that took a terrible toll of the Shermans and Churchills, but especially the former. German tanks also played their part in hammering the British armour. Tigers and Panthers were better armed and armoured than their opponents and Shermans had gained the reputation of being liable to burst into flames when hit. The Sherman had thereby gained two soubriquets: to German tankmen and anti-tank gunners it was the 'Tommy cooker', while its own crewmen called it the 'Ronson' from the eponymous cigarette-lighter manufacturer's slogan 'lights first time'.

In the van of V Corps' attack on 12 September were 18 Infantry and 43 Gurkha Brigades of 1st Armoured Division. Although both 2/8th and 2/10th Gurkhas were making their first assaults the Germans offered little resistance, having been buffeted and dazed by heavy bombardment. The

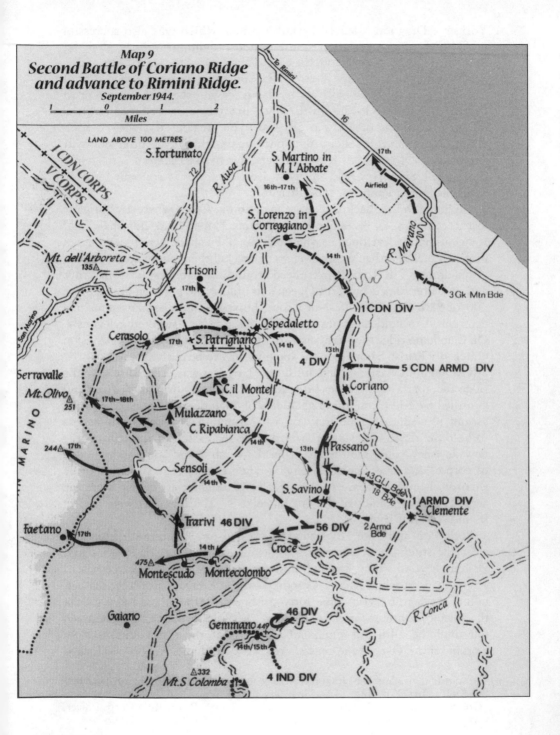

Map 9
**Second Battle of Coriano Ridge
and advance to Rimini Ridge.**
September 1944.

Miles

LAND ABOVE 100 METRES

I CDN CORPS
V CORPS

S. Fortunato

S. Martino in
M. L'Abbate

R. Ausa

16th–17th

S. Lorenzo in
Correggiano

Airfield

17th

R. Marano

Mt. dell'Arboreta
135

Frisoni

17th

14th

1 CDN DIV

3 Gk Mtn Bde

Cerasolo

17th
S. Patrignano

Ospedaletto

14th

4 DIV

13th

5 CDN ARMD DIV

Serravalle
Mt. Olivo
251

17th–18th

C. il Montei

Coriano

Mulazzano

C. Ripabianca

14th

13th

Passano

MARINO

244 17th

Sensoli

14th

S. Savino

43 Glı Bde

18 Bde

1 ARMD DIV
S. Clemente

Faetano

17th

Trarivi 46 DIV

14th

Croce

56 DIV

2 Armd
Bde

475

Montescudo

Montecolombo

Gaiano

46 DIV

Gemmano 449

R. Conca

14th/15th

332

Mt. S Colomba

4 IND DIV

145

Yorkshire Dragoons* led 18 Brigade's attack which was also successful with San Savino taken after house-to-house fighting. Shortly after 1st Armoured Division moved off, the Canadians entered the fray: 11 Brigade's Perth Regiment and Cape Breton Highlanders, attacking either side of Coriano, gained their objectives by dawn leaving the Irish Regiment of Canada to mop up in the town, which proved no easy task. In all the infantry battalions of 1st and 5th Canadian Armoured Divisions took about a thousand prisoners. But, once again, there had been no swift exploitation: 9th Queen's Royal Lancers, due to exploit from San Savino, found their Shermans held up by a deep ditch while concealed enemy tanks, including Panthers, took their toll.[22]

On the 13th the Black Cats were in action at Croce where 169 Brigade lost its commander, Brigadier Smith-Dorrien,† killed by enemy shellfire.[23] A vicious battle developed in which 9th Royal Fusiliers were pinned down in their attack. Further attacks were repulsed but then, under cover of mist, a squadron of 7th Royal Tanks raced around the Fabbri spur from Croce and was later joined by 2/7th Queen's to unlock the position and capture 300 of 98th Division. West of Croce, however, the Germans remained determined to hold their positions and the attackers suffered grievously. On Gemmano ridge the Germans also proved obstinate and a 46th Division attack saw British troops gain the summit, only to be pushed off quickly by 5th Mountain Division. Then 4th Indian Division was ordered to take the ridge and, on the night of the 14th, attacked under a storm of fire from 260 guns, led by 2nd Cameron Highlanders of 11 Indian Brigade. The Jocks' assault proved to be the limit of 5th Mountain Division's willingness to hold the ridge. The Cameron men were successful; in the light of the new day they could see the chaos on the summit and 'survey the tangle of corpses and tree trunks ... having taken twenty-four survivors of its garrison. Round the base of the great black crucifix at the top were the arms of a dead soldier of the 6th Lincolns.'[24] The Lincolns were in 138 Brigade of 46th Division.[25]

Both 46th and 56th Divisions had pressed on, trusting 4th Indian to clear the stubborn defenders from Gemmano ridge on their left flank. Pushing beyond Croce, through difficult countryside, 2/5th Leicesters of 139 Brigade reached Monte Colombo on the evening of 14 September, taking the feature with some forty prisoners. Rather than Leese's leap, the advance continued in fits and starts, a series of probes and pushes, and not until the 14th did Canadian troops clear the last Germans from Coriano ridge. Over in the coastal area, 1st Canadian Division was locked

---

* In spite of their name the Dragoons were an infantry unit with the rarely used title 9th King's Own Yorkshire LI and had served as a motor battalion.[21]
† Grenfell Horace Gerald Smith-Dorrien DSO, a King's Royal Rifle Corps officer, was the son of General Sir Lockwood Smith-Dorrien GCB GCMG DSO.

with Heidrich's paras and Leese chose to place 4th British Division under command of I Canadian Corps. On the 14th, 12 British Brigade passed through 11 Canadian Brigade en route to the Marano river while, later that day, 1st Royal West Kents forded the Marano and were in Ospedaletto by dawn of the following day. In the original plan 128 (Hampshire) Brigade should have been in Ospedaletto on 5 September.[26]

First Armoured Division's tanks met many problems, not least the presence of well-camouflaged anti-tank guns which inflicted grievous harm while deep, muddy ditches impeded progress. However, on the evening of the 15th, 43 Gurkha Brigade crossed the Marano in a successful assault that displayed disorder in the defences. And the rain had come back to help the Germans with heavy downpours making the going even more difficult for the tanks. While 28 Brigade from 4th Division attacked across the front of 1st Armoured Division to take Cerasolo ridge on the night of 16/17 September, the latter was ordered to reorganize in readiness for its next move.[27]

At 6 o'clock on the morning of 17 September Point 475 fell to the Hampshire Brigade in spite of spirited resistance from 5th Mountain Division. The Black Cats' 167 Brigade, having crossed the Marano, captured Mulazzano ridge, allowing 168 Brigade to pass through in an advance intended to conform with 4th Division. But 168 Brigade met strong opposition and suffered heavy enfilading fire from the left. Another river, the Áusa, lay before 4th Division's advance units, and beyond was the last range of hills before the plain. These hills sweep down from the tiny republic of San Marino to San Fortunato, guardian of the approach to Rimini. On 4th Division's right flank the Canadians and German paras were still battling it out along a ridge on which stood two villages, San Lorenzo and San Martino, one at either end of the ridge, with San Martino closer to Rimini. Although the Canadians had taken San Lorenzo from the paras, they had thus far been rebuffed in their efforts to capture San Martino. And Greek troops had returned to active service in Eighth Army's order of battle: 3 Greek Mountain Brigade was now engaged on the coastal plain.[28]

To throw the Germans out of their positions overlooking the Áusa, General Burns, I Canadian Corps' commander, prepared an attack across that river using 4th British and 1st Canadian Divisions. The latter were to maintain pressure on the Germans in San Martino. Burns hoped to evict the Germans from those positions over the Áusa before they could settle reserves into newly-created switchline positions. Following heavy aerial and artillery bombardment, Burns planned to attack on the night of 17/18 September. In the meantime aircraft flew 486 sorties a day against the enemy positions, while the artillery of 2nd New Zealand Division, still in army reserve, would strengthen the usual gunner support. The attacking troops would also have the benefit of artificial moonlight, created by searchlights aimed at the base of the clouds.[29]

All seemed well and 12 Brigade's West Kents led off, crossing the Áusa and reaching Sant'Antima* where, since they were under observation from the next ridge, they lay low throughout the following day. On the West Kents' right 2nd Beds and Herts of 10 Brigade bit out another small lodgement but were unable to bite any more.[30] The two British battalions were in uncomfortable enough situations but their plights were as nothing compared to their Canadian cousins who had

> met disaster and spent the 18th writhing amid ditches and vineyards on the flats below San Fortunato, with shells pelting upon them, together with bombs from Allied aircraft and with black smoke billowing from Churchills of the hard-fought 21 Tank Brigade.[31]

This situation was eventually resolved on the night of 18/19 September when 2nd Duke of Cornwall's LI penetrated beyond Sant'Aquilina allowing 10 Brigade to secure the right flank for fresh Canadian attacks on the ridge above San Fortunato the next night. These attacks were supported by Churchills of 21 and 25 Tank Brigades as well as Wolverine tank-destroyers from anti-tank units.[†] The presence of the slow Churchills instead of the speedier Shermans epitomized just how Leese's leap had become a tired heave. In a series of short sharp attacks, with well co-ordinated artillery support, the Royal 22e reached their objective while the Edmontons did likewise to their right. When day broke the Canadians at last held the ridge and had a mixed bag of prisoners that bore testimony to the haste, if not desperation, with which von Vietinghoff had reinforced his line. As well as paratroopers, panzer grenadiers and panzer troops, the Canadians' prisoners included personnel from a Luftwaffe ground division (20th) and a Turcoman division (162nd).[33]

With no strategic or tactical advantage to be gained from holding Rimini the Germans made another night-time departure, and on the morning of 22 September men of 3 Greek Mountain Brigade were the first Eighth Army soldiers to enter the ancient city. Although a series of explosions had been heard from Rimini the night before, the Greeks found the Ponte di Tiberio to be intact.[34]

Although the little republic of San Marino was neutral this proved irrelevant to the Germans who established defensive positions on every

* Blaxland calls this hamlet San Antimo.
† Wolverine was the name given to the American M10 tank-destroyer in British service. Based on the M4 Sherman tank chassis the M10 mounted a 3-inch gun in an open-topped turret and carried less armour than the M4 tank. Many British M10s were refitted with the 17-pounder gun and renamed Achilles.[32]

suitable piece of high ground. On its advance through the mountains 4th Indian Division was confronted with the German occupiers of San Marino. Leading 5 Brigade's advance on 19 September, 3/10th Baluchis gained a lodgement at Faetano, which had provided the Germans with a valuable observation point, and 1/9th Gurkhas passed through to continue the advance. Almost immediately, the Gurkhas were hit by a counter-attack aimed at regaining Faetano.[35] Taken by surprise the battalion was saved by the valour and quick thinking of one man, Rifleman Sherbahadur Thapa who,

> with his section commander, who was afterwards badly wounded, charged and silenced an enemy machine gun. The rifleman then went on alone to the exposed part of a ridge where, ignoring a hail of bullets, he silenced more machine guns, covered a withdrawal and rescued two wounded men before he was killed.[36]

Sherbahadur Thapa's gallantry saved the Faetano position and was rewarded with a posthumous Victoria Cross.

The Cameron Highlanders spent 20 September flushing men of 278th Division from their posts. By dusk, their task complete, the Camerons entered Borgo Maggiore, the state capital, which sits like something from an artist's imagination looking down on the slopes falling away to the coastal plain.[37]

Elsewhere the battalions of 168 Brigade had struggled to cross the Áusa against 356th Division. Celtic in its order of battle – with 1st Welch, 1st London Scottish and 1st London Irish – the brigade crossing was spearheaded by the London Scottish and, as they had appeared to be having more success, the brigade commander reinforced their effort with London Irish companies. The group thus formed not only crossed the river but took Point 140 and held it against the usual counter-attacks. These lasted throughout the night, the third night of intense activity for these men, and 'men made prisoners in one action were released in the other'.[38] Successful operations on either flank, and the liberation of San Marino, eased the pressure on 168 Brigade but by noon on the 19th the London Scottish had fewer than a hundred men and the London Irish were little better with only two weak companies.[39]

While the London Scots and Irish fought off counter-attacks during the night of 18/19 September, the Yorkshire Dragoons had taken Monte Arboreta but lost the most important part of the feature to an armour-supported counter-attack. When 8th Royal Tanks later attacked Ceriano ridge, to the left of Monte Arboreta, they met determined Germans and called for reinforcements, but 2nd Royal Tanks were also unable to make the ridgetop. Eventually, two weak companies of Ox and Bucks with some Queensmen reached the summit where they relieved two much-diminished squadrons of Royal Tanks. From this sector 1st Armoured Division was to break out, making for Point 153, a mile north-east of 7 Armoured Brigade's foremost position, but before the plan could be implemented it came unstuck. The Queen's Bays, in the van, could not advance due to the very difficult going on the approach. However, the Yorkshire Dragoons regained the lost part of Monte Arboreta that night while 2/6th Queen's attacked Ceriano but met heavy fire while ascending the ridge and were counter-attacked.[40]

Tragedy hit the Bays on 20 September. While forming up to renew their attack, the regiment came under fire and a troop of Shermans was despatched to deal with enemy machine guns. These ran into 88s and were knocked out. Although the brigade commander then tried to have the attack cancelled or postponed he was told that the Bays had to move forward at 10.15am to support the Canadians on their right. They did so but met opposition so fierce that, within an hour, all but three tanks from two squadrons had been disabled; six officers and fifteen men were dead.[41]

Leese had planned that the Canadians would advance on Ravenna while V Corps pushed north-westwards to Bologna to cut off and destroy retreating German forces but heavy rain, falling in torrents throughout the 21st, delayed the move. As the rain eased and stopped, the advance, codenamed Operation CAVALCADE, began on 22 September with 2nd New Zealand Division, under command of I Canadian Corps, leading. With 5th Canadian Armoured on its left the New Zealanders set off on the axis of the coast road to Ravenna but could move no faster than a marching infantryman.[42] The surrounding country was low lying and boggy, much of it drained marshland, criss-crossed with streams, ditches and minor rivers, all hindering tank movement. And vineyards abounded: in full leaf they were ideal for concealing ambush parties, as well as impeding the tanks whose crewmen waited in dread for the clunk of a *panzerfaust* round on the hull of their vehicle, or the glowing patch that told them that death was burning through the armour. These were problems and impediments enough but there were even more: the countryside was dotted with many farmhouses and outbuildings, all built solidly and each and all capable of being turned into an enemy strongpoint. As more rain fell from the skies the infantry plodded wearily forward through an area where many had expected the tanks to race.

To clear the start line for V Corps' advance to Bologna, 43 Brigade's Gurkhas were to cross the Marécchia river and cut Highway 9, the main road to the city. However, while they crossed the river they failed initially to penetrate far enough to cut the road and did not do so until 24 September. Now 1st Armoured Division was to lead the advance on Bologna but that plan evaporated when the news broke that the division was to be disbanded. Although 2 Armoured Brigade would survive as an independent support brigade, the Gurkhas were to be transferred to 56th (London) Division –

an unusual home for the Nepalese hillmen – whose recent losses had been such that 168 Brigade was to be amalgamated with 167. The former's battalions were either disbanded, in the case of 8th Royal Fusiliers and 7th Ox and Bucks, or reduced to cadre size in the case of 1st Welch Regiment (as a regular battalion it could not be disbanded). First Armoured's other infantry brigade, 18, was not to be retained and its soldiers were to be used as reinforcements for 46th Division, with 1st Buffs reducing to cadre while 14th Foresters and the Yorkshire Dragoons disbanded. So, instead of racing for Bologna, 1st Armoured Division was, in the manner of old soldiers, to fade away; its HQ was declared non-operational at the end of October and disbanded in January 1945.[43]

Perhaps most pain was felt in the ranks of 18 Brigade which had formerly been 7 Motor Brigade and had the greatest proportion of desert veterans of any Eighth Army formation, with more Africa Star ribbons with the distinctive '8' on its soldiers' uniforms than in any other. Its veterans were welcomed to the ranks of 46th Division by its GOC, Major General John Hawkesworth.

> Propped on his long ashplant stick, he told them that they should regard themselves as footballers transferred from one team to another and that in his division the infantry were regarded as the elite, always to be allotted the best billets when out of the line, always to be provided with every possible ounce of fire support when making an attack. Certainly, the men needed every possible ounce of encouragement to keep them going.[44]

The official history suggests that OLIVE may be said to have ended on 21 September as Eighth Army crossed the Marécchia in pouring rain.

> It had reached its 'promised land', but was to find mud rather than the milk of good tank 'going' and frustration rather than the honey of rapid exploitation. Leese could rightly claim in his report, written immediately after the offensive on 26 September that [Eighth] Army's achievement was 'a great one'. It had crossed the Apennines secretly and on time. It had gate-crashed 'the powerful Gothic Line defences at very small expense and before the enemy was ready'. Moreover it had defeated eleven German divisions in sustained battle and had broken into the plains of the Romagna.[45]

The infantry of Eighth Army would have been unlikely to have accepted his analysis of 'very small expense'. It was the infantry casualty toll that led to the breaking up of 1st Armoured Division, the disbandment of 18 Brigade, the reduction to cadre of two regular battalions and the

151

disbanding of four others. Nor was this the full picture: most infantry battalions in Italy were reduced to three rifle companies, and those few retaining four would also reduce through attrition to three during the winter. In the course of Operation OLIVE, Eighth Army had suffered over 14,000 casualties, the majority in the infantry. Of the infantry casualties half had been in British units, in which 1,700 men had been killed, while II Polish Corps had sustained over 3,500 casualties.[46] No further infantry reinforcements were available from the UK – the last had been posted to battalions in July – and Eighth Army now depended on anti-aircraft gunners who had received two months' infantry training to fill the gaps in its infantry battalions. Prior to OLIVE about 9,000 retrained AA gunners had joined infantry units and the disbandment of further AA regiments provided another 5,000 men for infantry training. These latter would not be available to front-line units until October at the earliest as they had only begun training in August.[47]

This manpower crisis was not unique to Eighth Army but afflicted the Army generally in the last eighteen months of the war. Never before had the British Army been stretched as it was now, with commitments in north-west Europe, Italy and the Far East, as well as garrisons elsewhere. Without the Dominion and Imperial formations, Britain could not have deployed field armies in several theatres, including Italy. It was the ultimate paradox of the Italian campaign that, in its concluding phase, Eighth Army was to rely heavily on Italian formations. Thus the army that had done most to force Italy out of the war found former foes included in its final order of battle.

On 1 October there was another major change in Eighth Army with the departure of Sir Oliver Leese to command 11 Army Group in the Far East. Although this was a promotion, many Eighth Army soldiers thought that Leese had been moved because of the collapse of Operation OLIVE and his failure to reach the Lombardy plain. That was not the view in Whitehall where Leese was considered a successful commander who had broken through the Gustav, Hitler and Gothic Lines. Perhaps history, and many of his soldiers, might have seen him in more favourable light had he not promised so much with his final offensive.[48]

A disciple of Montgomery to the last in one respect at least, Leese imitated his 'master' by taking with him to India many of Eighth Army's best staff. Among them was a man who, although out of the limelight, had played one of the most important roles in the Italian campaign, Brigadier Kenneth Ray, Eighth Army's Chief Engineer.[49]

Leese's successor was Lieutenant General Sir Richard McCreery who was to be Eighth Army's final commander. Of Irish stock, he adopted an entirely different style of command from that of Leese who had used the

Montgomery model of being seen as much as possible by his troops, and operated, as had Montgomery, from a forward HQ; he had, however, eschewed any idiosyncratic choice of headgear. Although McCreery would remain based with his staff at Eighth Army's Main HQ, he would also be a frequent visitor to the front – perhaps more than Montgomery had ever been – but his visits usually had a practical purpose rather than being exercises in public relations. McCreery had never been a friend of Montgomery and had no intention of imitating his style: at all times he wore regulation dress and headgear.[50]

In a message to the Army, Leese wrote that he was handing over to McCreery 'with complete confidence' and that the latter's 'long connection with [Eighth] Army is known to many of you'. For his part McCreery commented that 'It was the proudest day of my life when I was appointed to take over the Eighth Army from Lieutenant General Sir Oliver Leese.'[51] Richard McCreery was commissioned into 12th (The Prince of Wales's Royal) Lancers in 1915 as a seventeen year old. Before the First World War was over he had been decorated with the Military Cross and wounded, which left him with a permanent limp. In the Second World War he had proved himself an outstanding commander at all levels and seemed possessed of limitless energy. Since the beginning of the Italian campaign he had been in action as a corps commander and had impressed Alexander so much that he was the obvious choice to command Eighth Army; he had also been Alexander's chief of staff prior to commanding X Corps. During the final battle of El Alamein, McCreery, Alexander and Casey, the resident minister in Cairo, had visited Montgomery's HQ, where McCreery suggested that Operation SUPERCHARGE should be launched farther south than Montgomery planned, proposing that it be made against the junction of German and Italian forces. Montgomery's chief of staff, de Guingand, had persuaded his chief of the validity of this idea but Montgomery never gave McCreery any credit since to do so would have tarnished that image of military genius he had created for himself. Others, including Alexander, believed that this was the decision that won the battle and knew where the credit lay.[52] And so Richard McCreery assumed command of Eighth Army, the only cavalryman to do so.* He would bring a cavalryman's appreciation of the need for rapid movement to his new command.

On the face of it, this was not the best time to take command of Eighth Army. The offensive was bogged down in the mud of the Romagna and a sweeping manoeuvre to cut off the retreating enemy was impossible. Eighth Army seemed committed to a steady war of attrition, continuing operations at a reduced scale as part of a two-fisted pummelling of the

* With the exception of its first commander Alan Cunningham, who was a gunner, the others had all been infantrymen.

enemy in concert with Fifth Army. Just as a year before in southern Italy, Eighth Army was to contain the enemy while Fifth Army struck for Bologna in a fresh offensive along a more direct axis. As if to underline this new role the reinvigorated 78th Division, returned from Egypt and waiting at Fano to join V Corps, was ordered, at twenty-four hours' notice, to join XIII Corps in Fifth Army.[53]

Understandably, morale in Eighth Army was affected by the prevailing situation, but the Army continued to jab at the enemy throughout the winter. The steady push that had replaced Leese's leap was maintained so that by 1 October units were about ten miles beyond Rimini on Highway 16, the coast road, and a similar distance along Highway 9, the Via Emilia, in the direction of Bologna. But now small rivers that had been streams in September were in full flood and the Royal Engineers were on constant call. The demands on the sappers had been doubled at least, especially for bridge-building, and a great effort in men and equipment was necessary to maintain the lines of communication.[54]

With its leading units over the Uso, Eighth Army faced two further major river obstacles: the Fiumicino and the Pisciatello. One of these three rivers had, in ancient times, been the Rubicon over which Julius Caesar had crossed in open defiance of Pompey and the Senate, thereby prompting civil war; today one of the latter's tributaries is called the Rubicone which makes the Pisciatello the most likely to have been Caesar's river where the die was cast.* Some unit war diaries of 1944 note the crossing of the Rubicon but whether the soldier on the ground saw any significance in this is doubtful. He was certainly aware that there was no shortage of rivers to cross.

The Canadians were still on the coastal sector with the Greek brigade by the sea and Freyberg's and 5th Canadian Armoured Divisions continuing the corps front inland to the junction with Keightley's V Corps whose right flank was held by 56th Division. The latter was advancing along Highway 9 with 167 Brigade across the Uso on 25 September where 169 Queen's Brigade had taken over. Savignano ridge and village fell to the Queen's Brigade, but 168 Brigade's London Scottish had taken a hammering after crossing the Fiumicino on the last night of September. Forty-sixth Division was also stepped up along the Fiumicino, as was 4th Indian which had earlier suffered a repulse at Sogliano.[55]

Prior to his departure Leese had ordered II Polish Corps to move forward so that Eighth Army's advance might be refreshed using the same three corps that had opened Operation OLIVE. McCreery changed this order on his second day in command and instructed Anders to take his

---

* On crossing the Rubicon, Caesar is reputed to have said 'Iacta alea est' 'the die is cast' although Plutarch believed that he spoke in Greek, using the words of the poet Menander, 'Aneristho kubos', 'let the die be thrown'.

corps leftward through the mountains, where X Corps' line had been. From there Anders was to advance down the valleys and into the plain behind the German lines. Having commanded X Corps, McCreery had much experience of mountain fighting and his intention now was to use the grain of the country to his advantage rather than working against it. Since HQ X Corps had not been operational as its sole division, 10th Indian, had been transferred to V Corps to relieve 4th Indian, the corps' sector was taken over by an ad hoc force under command of HQ 1st Armoured Division, the last operational function of that HQ.[56] This force included the Lovat Scouts and Nabha Akal Infantry, the latter a State Forces' unit rather than Indian Army, raised in 1757.*

McCreery directed V Corps on the line of the Fiumicino to throw the Germans out of their defensive positions. Tenth Indian Division, skilled in outflanking tactics, took the lead and by dawn on 5 October 1/2nd Punjabis with 2/3rd Gurkhas held Sogliano al Rubicone which allowed 3/5th Mahrattas to cross the Fiumicino. With weather conditions worsening the Mahrattas advanced in gale-force winds and rain to assault Monte Farneto which fell on the night of 6/7 October. Once again there was the customary counter-attack; the ferocity of this indicated the importance the Germans assigned to Monte Farneto. The Hampshire Brigade of 46th Division then crossed the Fiumicino to conform with 10th Indian and extend the line. Prior to the Hampshire attack two officers had carried out a reconnaissance patrol but had been captured with, it had to be assumed, marked maps showing details of the planned operation. Very quickly, the plans were changed in what was a wise precaution since, as the brigade attacked on the night of 7 October, enemy artillery bombarded the original intended lines of approach. Conditions proved difficult enough for the advance since heavy rain began falling at midnight; this caused problems with bridging and some pack mules drowned in the prevailing flood conditions. Not until dawn on the 9th was the brigade able to consolidate on its objectives; 138 and 139 Brigades then passed through to continue the advance.[58]

Major General Denys Reid, GOC of 10th Indian Division, had been lent 43 Gurkha Brigade for his new move forward and was thus able to commit three brigades: from right to left these were 25, 10 and 43 Gurkha. Once again the skill of Indian soldiers was demonstrated as the attacking infantry moved stealthily and quickly. In some cases the Germans were taken completely by surprise. But of all the qualities shown by Reid's *jawans* perhaps the most important was fortitude as they assaulted their objectives, fought off counter-attacks and brought forward supplies. One remarkable example of their soldiering skills was provided by Naik Trilok

---

* In 1954 it was redesignated 14th (Nabha) Battalion, The Punjab Regiment of the Indian Army.[57]

Singh of the Royal Garhwal Rifles near San Carlo. Naik Singh 'stalked a German machine-gun crew, killed them and took their weapon and ammunition'. He then single-handedly beat off a counter-attack but was killed later that same day while covering his section's withdrawal. The Indians' supporting tankmen in the Churchills of 25 Tank Brigade were equally stoic as the rain brought much suffering and caused mud so deep and liquid that 'the muleteers, Indian and Italian, often sank in it up to their waists, and their wretched beasts collapsed, enforcing the abandonment of their loads'.[59]

A major crossing of the Fiumicino was made redundant as the advance through the mountains prompted a German withdrawal. On the night of 10/11 October I Canadian Corps, with elements of 56th Division under command, crossed the river to pursue the Germans to the Pisciatello. In the course of the pursuit the Black Cats were squeezed out by the Canadians; the division was then withdrawn to become non-operational for a time due to the shortage of infantry. In the pursuit the Indians proved the most effective harriers of the foe with 2/6th Gurkhas fighting a major engagement on Monte Chicco between dusk on 13 October and dawn of the 15th that saw the Germans forced off the height. Artillery and aircraft supported the Gurkhas' efforts and even the best efforts of 90th Panzer Grenadiers only delayed their departure time.[60]

Then, ten miles left of the Indians and to the Germans' complete surprise, 5th Kresowa Division descended from the mountains. As the Poles made for the Ronco valley they found the Germans off balance completely. Monte Grosso fell after four days of hard fighting and, supported by Italian troops, the Poles resumed their advance, capturing Predáppio, birthplace of Mussolini,* on 27 October. Elsewhere 138 Brigade had taken Carpinetta ridge, forcing the enemy back to the Savio river in a retreat during which the Germans suffered heavy casualties from artillery fire intended to support a Canadian attack. Then, on 20 October, 16th Durham LI, of 139 Brigade, entered Cesena, the first sizeable town to be liberated by 46th Division, at the end of two months of fighting for the division; there was considerable happiness when the news was received that 4th Division was relieving 46th which would then enjoy a brief spell out of the line. The Official History notes that 139 Brigade was under command of 4th Division when it entered Cesena.[62]

When 4th Division took over the impetus did not diminish. A ridge dominating the Savio was cleared of Germans allowing 2nd Royal Fusiliers

---

* Benito Mussolini was born at Dovia di Predáppio on 29 July 1883, the first son of a blacksmith who was also an ardent revolutionary, and who chose to name the boy after the Mexican revolutionary, Benito Juarez, who had led Mexico's rebellion against the rule of the French emperor Maximilian. Mussolini's mother was 'a long suffering schoolteacher'.[61]

to wade across, in spite of wide, fast-flowing waters, to surprise the enemy on the far bank and establish a bridgehead. The Germans were quick to recover and launched several counter-attacks. Although the Fusiliers' only anti-tank weapons were the unloved PIATs, they fought off tanks as well as infantry. Artillery observers on the ridge behind were also able to call down fire to support the Fusiliers whose fellow battalions of 12 Brigade, 1st Royal West Kents and 6th Black Watch, moved into the bridgehead to strengthen it. In spite of heavy shelling the sappers of 59 Field Company had bridged the Savio by the morning of the 24th.[63]

A Canadian bridgehead over the Savio had also been established following a crossing on the night of 20/21 October. The usual counter-attacks followed during one of which Private Ernest Alvia Smith, Seaforth Highlanders of Canada, showed outstanding courage as

> With a PIAT gun he put an enemy tank out of action at a range of 30 feet, and while protecting a wounded comrade, he destroyed another tank and two self-propelled guns, as well as routing a number of the enemy infantry.[64]

Those infantry were seen off with a Tommy gun and 'Smoky' Smith was subsequently awarded the Victoria Cross. Among the criteria for the VC is that the action should have a positive effect on the battle, and Vokes later wrote that 'Smith's valorous little personal war did just that. The rest of us were able to press on because of it.'[65] For three days the Germans continued counter-attacking until pressure from the flanks forced withdrawal and the Canadians could resume their onward march. Ravenna now beckoned. But it would not be taken until early December.

It was then that McCreery decided to relieve the commander of I Canadian Corps, General E.L.M. Burns, whom he considered 'not thrusting enough'. The relief was a surprise to Burns although not to his successor, Chris Vokes, who noted that 'Burns didn't come up to the front' but called his commanders back to his HQ. Hardly a recipe for confidence, this must have influenced McCreery's decision.[66]

In those opening days under McCreery's command Eighth Army had made some steady progress. It was not spectacular, there had been no dashes and no leaps, but the new army commander had used his experience of mountain warfare to show that success could be achieved by using the topography to advantage rather than working against it. He had brought Eighth Army out of the mountains and on to the plains but this new terrain was hardly better suited to mobile warfare than the Apennines. Although the land on to which the Army had advanced is flat it is also low lying, with much of it reclaimed from marshland. Nature seemed intent on its return to that state as October's heavy rains transformed the region into a nightmare of mud. Being reclaimed land it is also provided with an extensive drainage system with many ditches added to the small streams and canals criss-crossing the area. Many of those streams and canals have flood banks to protect the neighbouring land but those waterways, mostly running west to east to drain into the sea, also made fine tank obstacles. Once again the engineers would be kept busy as stream after stream and canal after canal would have to be bridged.

Eighth Army had pierced the Gothic Line but had not been able to penetrate all the German defences which were, as ever, constructed in great depth. There had been no great breakthrough to Bologna and beyond, and with the Gothic Line now in tatters it remained to be seen if Eighth Army could summon the strength to deliver a final blow to destroy the German armies in Italy. Or would their surrender depend on defeat in Germany itself?

As early as 2 October Alexander had suggested that his armies might not be strong enough to deliver the killer blow before winter began. Although no major offensive would be possible until spring, Alexander briefed McCreery and Clark on plans for limited operations that were conditional upon the weather and would be suspended by 15 December. Eighth Army was to take Ravenna and advance to the Santerno river, while Fifth would take Bologna before meeting up with Eighth in a pincer movement. However, the strategic imperative behind these proposals did not lie in Italy. Eisenhower wished to invade Germany in December and wanted the armies in Italy to maintain pressure on Kesselring's forces to prevent any withdrawal of formations to strengthen the German homeland.[67]

Alexander, however, still saw strategic possibilities in Italy. The fall of Bologna would compel the enemy to fall back beyond the Po to the Adige river thereby allowing Eighth Army to outflank the Germans through an amphibious operation on the other side of the Adriatic, following which the Army, with Tito's Yugoslav forces, could strike for Vienna. But this was never going to happen. The Americans indicated that landing craft would be made available but showed no interest in the proposal, being as ever suspicious of British intentions in the Mediterranean. The scheme's real death knell came from Tito who withdrew consent, perhaps thinking that Eighth Army on his side of the Adriatic would reduce his chances of acquiring new territory.[68]

Allied soldiers in Italy remained committed to a war of attrition. In such circumstances commanders find it difficult to ask for sacrifices from their men, including the possible loss of their lives. Soldiers knew that the Italian campaign had become subordinate to other theatres and wondered if clear-cut victory in Italy would be possible, or if they would have to continue fighting and dying in small numbers until the war was over in Germany. Some must have wondered if those who decided grand strategy in London,

158

Moscow and Washington had any interest in the armies in Italy. The withdrawal of formations for Operation MANNA suggested that those in high places did not really care if Fifth and Eighth Armies remained static or moved forward.

Operation MANNA was the response to the German evacuation of Greece, threats of civil war and a communist takeover. Churchill's government had agreed to deploy a force to Greece to prevent either possibility becoming reality and maintain order until elections could be held. This appeared a worthy ideal but the force could be drawn only from Eighth Army and thus began a drain on McCreery's resources which started in mid-October when 2 Parachute and 23 Armoured Brigades were sent to Greece. Fourth Indian Division followed, when it was relieved from the line by 10th Indian, as did 3 Greek Mountain Brigade. As the demands of Greece continued, both 4th and 46th British Divisions would also move there, as would X Corps Tactical HQ under Lieutenant General Hawkesworth. The latter corps had been in reserve in Italy and would act as the commanding HQ in Greece until III Corps was formed.[69]

Meanwhile McCreery, knowing that maintaining his army in static positions would breed defensive attitudes, planned to take Ravenna after first directing Eighth Army's attention to Forlí, to distract the Germans from his true objective. And opening Highway 67, the main road from Florence to Forlí, would also ease his supply situation. Eighth Army troops were closing on Forlí following the liberation of Cesena on 20 October. Three days later 3/5th Mahrattas and 2/3rd Gurkhas of 20 Indian Brigade captured Monte Cavallo and the Germans began withdrawing to the Ronco which, as it wends towards the Adriatic, flows within less than two miles of Forlí. Thus, on the night of the 25th, 1st King's Royal Rifle Corps (KRRC), of 2 Armoured Brigade but now under command of 4th Division, crossed the Ronco with 2nd Duke of Cornwall's LI. Two companies of each established a bridgehead using a ford that appeared suitable for tanks. The weather intervened, heavy rain raised the water level and, when the first tank was knocked out on the ford by an anti-tank round, it became impossible for others to cross.

Four companies were now stranded across the Ronco with no immediate support as infantry of 278th Division, with tanks alongside, made counter-attack after counter-attack. Casualties mounted amongst the Green Jackets and light infantrymen and, gradually, all four companies were ground down and overrun. This setback was balanced out by Indian and Polish operations as men of 43 Gurkha Brigade and the Nabha Akal Infantry, now attached to 20 Brigade of 10th Indian Division, crossed the Ronco, pushed into the hills beyond Méldola and attacked troops of 356th Division. Those Germans were already under attack from Poles and the intervention of the Indians was enough to loosen their grip, permitting 1st King's Own, of 25 Indian Brigade, to strike towards Grisignano which they reached on 2 November, to be almost within a sergeant major's shout of Forlí. Eighth Army's leading troops were only two miles from the town.[70]

Meanwhile 4th Division's sappers were clearing damage done by recent flooding and replacing bridges damaged or washed away as far back as the Savio. They also brought forward folding boats and spans of Bailey bridging to consolidate another bridgehead over the Ronco. As the weather brightened on the 4th, Allied aircraft could attack the defences of Forlí; these included planes firing rockets, deployed in Italy for the first time and to great effect. Over the following three days the aerial bombardment continued with particular attention given to defences around the airfield at Cárpena, south of the main road.[71]

V Corps attacked Forlí on the night of 7/8 November, its operation led by 1/6th East Surreys who assaulted across Cárpena airfield following a silent approach* that included crossing a 13-foot-deep, 6-foot-wide ditch before the moon rose. Once clear of that obstacle the Surreys charged across the runway to the surprise of the defenders around the control buildings; almost half the attackers had reached there before the Germans realized what was happening. Fighting continued throughout the night but with first light came Churchills of 51st Royal Tanks, and resistance soon ended. On the left flank, 46th Division had relieved 10th Indian and attacked from Grisignano led by 128 (Hampshire) Brigade. (Forty-sixth Division had a new GOC, Major General Charles Weir, a Gunner who had been Brigadier Royal Artillery (BRA) of 2nd New Zealand Division, which he had also commanded in Freyberg's absence.)[72]

Then 28 Brigade of 4th Division made a third attack, an early-morning assault in the gap between Grisignano and Cárpena. When the Germans finally decided that Forlí should be abandoned the withdrawal began with some Tiger tanks deployed in the subsequent rearguard actions. These massive tanks caused some damage but the retreating Germans suffered much harassment and loss from air attack, and from the Vickers MMGs of 2nd Royal Northumberland Fusiliers, 4th Division's machine-gun battalion. The aircraft were operating a cab-rank system, with planes circling the area awaiting a call for direct support to ground forces, while the Northumberlands' machine guns, effective to over 2,500 yards, took a heavy toll.[73]

With Forlí liberated, 4th Division pushed out in pursuit of the enemy, the Northumberlands again providing support from both MMGs and 4.2-inch mortars. In a five-day period two MG companies fired 461,250 rounds in harassing-fire tasks; Lieutenant J.H.G. Deighton was later

---

* That is, without artillery support.

awarded the Military Cross. The mortars also supported an attack by 6th Black Watch that earned Captain Gorst the MC. Gradually the division pushed the Germans back to the Montone river. A battalion of 46th Division, 2/4th KOYLI, had advanced to the Montone on the day the Germans evacuated Forlí and a platoon crossed the river only to suffer the same fate as that of the KRRC and DCLI companies over two weeks earlier. Once again a sudden downpour led to the river rising to such a level that the platoon was cut off and overrun. For a time the Montone was so swollen that it was impassable, but both 4th and 46th Divisions later crossed where the river loops around Forlí.[74]

While Germans remained close to Forlí the town was of no value to Eighth Army as a communications centre or supply base and thus it was important to push the enemy back as far as possible. The operations to do so were to be 4th Division's swansong in Italy before departing for Greece. Having crossed the Montone the division was faced with yet another river obstacle: the Cosina, which flows into the Montone and, although a narrow steam, was 'capable of being defended by determined troops'.[75] The divisional operation was part of Eighth Army's drive to the Lamone river and Faenza in which both II Polish and V Corps were to participate. Between the Poles, who were south of V Corps, and the bend in the Montone north of Highway 9, both 46th and 4th Divisions were to attack with the latter on the right. As the attack was being prepared 4th Division's front was held by two Reconnaissance Corps units: 4 Recce and 44 Recce. To divert German attention from the main assault 4 Recce made a feint attack on the right at 2.00am on 21 November. This 'drew a furious reply from the Germans; defensive fire came down, the German posts in front of the Montone fought off the approaching Troopers and machine guns fired continuously from the far bank of the river'.[76] Ten Brigade's attack was made simultaneously, directed towards the Cosina between the Montone and the railway line. In spite of considerable courage the leading Surrey companies were beaten back by mines, machine-gun fire and artillery. One company commander was among the many dead but one subaltern, Lieutenant Street of 13 Platoon, rallied some survivors and consolidated around a house about 200 yards short of the Cosina and only yards from the Montone floodbank. The DCLI on the left were delayed in moving off by a German spoiling attack and also suffered heavily. Only A Company crossed the Cosina where Major Rork, the company commander, realizing that he was cut off, brought down effective artillery fire in front of his positions to protect his foothold. Some time later, General Ward ordered the withdrawal of all forward companies which was achieved with fire support from 22nd Field Regiment. Preparations then began for a renewed attack.[77]

The second phase of 4th Division's assault fell to 28 Brigade, assisted by 139 Brigade, who established a bridgehead the next night. With the aid of tanks from 142nd Regiment RAC, a detachment from 1st Assault Regiment RAC/RE and sappers from 7 Field Company, the bridgehead was consolidated and expanded, and 28 Brigade renewed its attack at 3.30pm on 23 November.

The enemy's stubborn resistance on the division's left flank, however, had prevented 46th Division from advancing far enough to secure 28 Brigade's left flank. Brigadier Preston therefore proposed to send in B Squadron, 142nd RAC, on the left, to take a house half a mile beyond the river and in 46th Division's sector. The army commander, who was visiting Brigadier Preston's headquarters at the time, approved the plan, and the tanks moved off. They were soon in difficulties in the soft ground, but their appearance was enough for the German garrison, which surrendered shortly afterwards to the Somersets.[78]

At dusk on 23 November 28 Brigade held more than a thousand yards of Highway 9 beyond the Cosina. Shortly afterwards a loud explosion and brilliant flash marked the German demolition of the bridge carrying Highway 9 over the Lamone in Faenza's eastern suburbs. It was a sure sign that only rearguards, demolitions and mines would impede the division's advance to the Lamone where, on the night of 24/25 November, 4th Division ended its time in Italy.[79]

Forty-sixth Division had also crossed the Cosina to establish bridge-heads where infantry were soon joined by armour which helped repel the inevitable counter-attacks. Forward troops were probing into the eastern outskirts of Faenza before noon on 24 November and, with a further bridgehead across the Marzeno, just over a mile south of its junction with the Lamone, Major General Weir decided to continue to the latter across the higher ground between the two rivers. During the night of 25/26 November, 26th Panzer Division, reduced to a fighting strength of about 850, made a further withdrawal, this time across the Lamone, allowing Weir's command to close up to that river on the 26th. Plans to cross were underway when rain started again. With only an Ark bridge across the Marzeno, insufficient for the division's traffic in such conditions, and the road forward breaking up, a further pause was imposed.[80]

Anders' Poles had also made steady progress, although not as much as V Corps. The terrain had slowed their advance, although their efforts not only assisted V Corps but also allowed XIII Corps in Fifth Army to shorten its front. Fifth Army was preparing its offensive towards Bologna and Kesselring had identified Eighth Army's activities, which he had earlier believed to be a major offensive, as a prelude to this. By 26 November 305th Infantry, 26th Panzer and 278th Infantry Divisions were behind the Lamone ready to defend Faenza. A regiment of 278th Division was deployed in intermediate positions, known as the Ausberger Line,* while 356th Infantry and 114th Jäger Divisions held the line of the lower Montone from Casa Bettini to the Fiumi Uniti south of Ravenna and thence to the coast. Changes had taken place in the German high command with General Herr taking over Fourteenth Army following General Ziegler's injury when his car was attacked by partisans, but Herr commanded only until 8 December when he was admitted to hospital for surgery. He was succeeded by General Kurt von Tippelskirch, while General Hauck took over Herr's old command, LXXVI Panzer Corps, which lost 356th Division to the recently formed LXXIII Corps under General Dostler; this had been the Venetian Coast Command. Hauck was responsible for defending Faenza and Highway 9 while Dostler covered Ravenna and the coastal highway.[81]

The Poles had captured Montefortino before advancing on Monte Ricci, overlooking Santa Lucia, from where they swung westward across the Marzeno, brushing aside slight opposition from 305th Division. By 28 November II Polish Corps was along the Lamone from Brisighella to San Ruffillo.[82]

While V Corps and II Polish Corps had been in the fighting area, McCreery had been resting I Canadian Corps so that they could return to the battle early in December. In the interim the Canadian sector had been held by dismounted cavalry regiments. Some were critical of the use of cavalrymen in the infantry role, but the comment of one commanding officer – Val ffrench-Blake of 17th/21st Lancers – is worth noting: 'It is wasteful to use tank men as infantry, when there is tank work to be done, but it is even more wasteful *not* to use tank men as infantry when there is *no* tank work to be done.' Amongst the units relieving the Canadians was McCreery's own regiment, 12th Lancers, which formed the core of Porterforce with 27th Lancers, a wartime regiment built around a cadre from 12th Lancers. Lieutenant Colonel Horsburgh-Porter commanded 27th Lancers, and hence Porterforce, which also included a melange of British and Canadian units, as well as Popski's Private Army. The latter was one of those small units that seemed to proliferate during the Second World War. Having begun life as the Desert Raiding Squadron it was still a raiding unit, but became much better known by the soubriquet of its Russo-Belgian commander, Victor Peniakoff, or Popski. Never before had Popski's Private Army been assigned a defensive role but Peniakoff still contrived to carry out some raiding and maintained close contact with the communist partisans of the Garibaldi Brigade. The Italians, waiting to help liberate Ravenna, assisted Peniakoff's men in mounting several ambushes.[83]

* From Scaldino on the Lamone to Casa Bettini on the Montone. This line was intended to defend Ravenna.

While Porterforce stood watch in the Adriatic sector, 10th Indian Division passed through 12th Lancers to cross the Montone north of Highway 9 and widen V Corps' front on the advance to Faenza. Several days of tough fighting followed for 10 and 20 Indian Brigades as 356th Division, with tank support, tried to stop their advance. Floodbanks had been breached to inundate the countryside while farmhouses and outbuildings were converted into small fortresses. Nonetheless, the Indians cleared the German positions by 2 December to reach the Lamone alongside 4th Division's gains. There they were relieved by the New Zealanders.[84]

Ravenna now became Eighth Army's objective and its capture was to be coordinated with two other attacks. All three of the Army's corps – X Corps was non-operational – would participate with the Canadians advancing from 10th Indian Division's gains in two attacks, north-west to the Senio and Santerno rivers, and north-east to Ravenna; V Corps would make for Faenza and envelop the city, while II Polish Corps flanked through the hills to V Corps' left.[85]

Notes

1. Blaxland, op. cit., pp. 173–4.
2. Ibid., p. 173; Jackson, *The Mediterranean and Middle East,* vol. VI, pt II, p. 174; Nicholson, op. cit., pp. 506–7.
3. Nicholson, op. cit., pp. 508–9.
4. Jackson, op. cit., pp. 241–3; Anon, *The Story of 46th Division 1939–1945,* p. 74; Blaxland, op. cit., pp. 174–5; Nicholson, op. cit., pp. 508–10; Anders, op. cit., p. 215.
5. Nicholson, pp. 514–5.
6. Ibid., pp. 480–1.
7. Ibid., pp. 516–8; Vokes, *My Story,* p. 165.
8. Anon, *The Story of 46th Division,* op. cit., p. 75; Doherty, *The North Irish Horse,* pp. 174–5; NA, Kew, WO170/475, war diary, 46 Recce, Jul–Dec 1944.
9. *London Gazette,* 26 Oct 1944.
10. Blaxland, op. cit., pp. 176–7.
11. Ibid., p. 177.
12. Williams, *The Black Cats at War,* pp. 100–1.
13. Jackson, op. cit., pp. 250–1.
14. Bidwell and Graham, op. cit., p. 359.
15. Nicholson, op. cit., pp. 526–9.
16. Lucas to author.
17. Jackson, op. cit., pp. 258–9; Blaxland, op. cit., pp. 179–80.
18. Williams, op. cit., p. 101.
19. Ibid., pp. 101–2.
20. Jackson, op. cit., pp. 263–7.
21. Frederick, *Lineage Book of British Land Forces,* vol. I, p. 58.
22. NA, Kew, WO170/571, war diary, 18 Bde, 1944; WO170/1413, war diary, 9 KOYLI, 1944; Blaxland, op. cit., p. 193.
23. Williams, op. cit., pp. 102–3; www.cwgc.org

24. Blaxland, op. cit., p. 196.
25. Joslen, op. cit., pp. 75 & 324.
26. Jackson, op. cit., pp. 252–3; Williams, op. cit., pp. 101–3; Blaxland, op. cit., pp. 195–6; Nicholson, op. cit., pp. 526–30; Williamson, op. cit., pp. 223–5; NA, Kew, WO170/559, war diary, 12 Bde, Jul–Dec 1944.
27. Jackson, op. cit., pp. 277–8; Williamson, op. cit., pp. 226–7; WO170/597, war diary, 28 Bde, Sep–Oct 1944.
28. Blaxland, op. cit., pp. 196–7; Williams, op. cit., pp. 104–5.
29. Nicholson, op. cit., pp. 541–5; NA, Kew, CAB44/145, *Gothic Line 24 Aug–30 Sep*, p. 147.
30. NA, Kew, WO170/559, war diary, 12 Bde, op. cit.; WO170/551, war diary, 10 Bde, Sep–Oct 1944; Williamson, op. cit., pp. 228–9; Blaxland, op. cit., p. 197.
31. Blaxland, op. cit., p. 197.
32. Hogg and Weeks, *Illus Encyclopedia of Military Vehicles*, pp. 162–3.
33. NA, Kew, WO170/551, war diary, 10 Bde, op. cit.; Williamson, op. cit., pp. 230–1; Jackson, op. cit., pp. 290–4; Nicholson, op. cit., pp. 555–9.
34. Jackson, op. cit., p. 296; Blaxland, op. cit., pp. 200–1.
35. Jackson, op. cit., p. 293; Blaxland, op. cit., pp. 197–8; Doherty, *A Noble Crusade*, op. cit., p. 251.
36. *London Gazette*, 28 Dec 1944. No photograph exists of Sherbahadur Thapa.
37. WO170/1371, war diary, 2 Cam Hldrs, 1944.
38. NA, Kew, WO170/629, war diary, 168 Bde, 1944; Anon, *London Irish at War*, p. 180.
39. NA, Kew, WO170/629, war diary, 168 Bde, op. cit.
40. NA, Kew, WO170/629, war diary, 168 Bde, op. cit.; WO170/571, war diary, 18 Bde, 1944; Jackson, op. cit., p. 291; Doherty, op. cit., p. 252.
41. Jackson, op. cit., p. 292; Doherty, op. cit., p. 252; NA, Kew, WO170/820, war diary, Bays, 1944; Merewood, *To War with The Bays*, p. 137.
42. Kay, *From Cassino to Trieste*, p. 284.
43. Jackson, op. cit., pp. 288–93; Nicholson, op. cit., pp. 560–1; Williams, op. cit., pp. 105–6.
44. Blaxland, op. cit., p. 203.
45. Jackson, op. cit., pp. 299–300.
46. NA, Kew, CAB44/145, op. cit., p. 147.
47. Molony, *The Mediterranean and Middle East*, vol. VI, pt I, op. cit., pp. 447–50 discusses the problem of reinforcements for the Mediterranean theatre.
48. Jackson, op. cit., pp. 360–3; Blaxland, op. cit., p. 204; Ryder, *Oliver Leese*, op. cit., p. 191.
49. Orpen, op. cit., p. 49.
50. Doherty, *Ireland's Generals in the Second World War*, pp. 152–9; Smart, *Biographical Dictionary of British Generals of the Second World War*, p. 206.
51. NA, Kew, WO170/1386, war diary, 1/4 Essex, 1944 (Apps J-3 & 4).
52. Doherty, op. cit., pp. 155–6; Alexander, *Memoirs*, pp. 27–8.
53. Ray, *Algiers to Austria*, op. cit., p. 160.
54. Jackson, op. cit., pp. 365–9; Anon, *Engineers in the Italian Campaign*, op. cit., pp. 40–2; Blaxland, op. cit., p. 207.
55. Jackson, op. cit., pp. 352–3; Blaxland, op. cit., p. 208.
56. Blaxland, op. cit, p. 208.
57. Gaylor, *Sons of John Company*, p. 266.
58. Jackson, op. cit., pp. 399–401; Blaxland, op. cit., pp. 208–10; Doherty, *A Noble Crusade*, op. cit., pp. 257–8; NA, Kew, WO170/617, war diary, 128 (Hants) Bde, Jul–Dec 1944.

59. Jackson, op. cit., pp. 402–3; Anon, *The Tiger Triumphs*, op. cit., pp. 148–9; Blaxland, op. cit., pp. 209–10.
60. Jackson, op. cit., pp. 404–5; Nicholson, op. cit., pp. 576–8; Williams, op. cit., p. 106.
61. Barzini, *The Italians*, p. 156.
62. Jackson, op. cit., p. 409; Blaxland, op. cit., pp. 210–11; NA, Kew, WO170/460, war diary, 46 Div, Oct 1944; WO170/ 620, war diary, 138 Bde, Jul–Oct & Dec 1944; WO170/1385, war diary, 16 DLI, Jan–Mar & Jul–Dec 1944.
63. Jackson, op. cit., p. 410; Blaxland, op. cit., p. 211; NA, Kew, WO170/559, war diary, 12 Bde, op. cit.; Williamson, op. cit., pp. 240–2.
64. *London Gazette*, 30 Dec 1944.
65. Vokes, op. cit., p. 181.
66. Burns, *General Mud*, op. cit., p. 218; Vokes, op. cit., p. 182.
67. Jackson, op. cit., pp. 380–6.
68. Ibid., pp. 385–6.
69. Ibid., pp. 323 & 385.
70. Ibid., pp. 386 & 427–9; Williamson, op. cit., pp. 247–50; Blaxland, op. cit., p. 227; NA, Kew, WO170/1417, war diary 1 King's Own, Apr–Dec 1944.
71. Williamson, op. cit., pp. 251–3; Blaxland, op. cit., p. 227 who suggests that the rocket-firing aircraft were Typhoons although no record exists of these machines operating in Italy.
72. Jackson, *The Mediterranean and Middle East,* vol. VI, pt III, pp. 37n & 39–40; Blaxland, op. cit., pp. 227–8; Squire and Hill, *The Surreys in Italy*, op. cit., p. 51.
73. Williamson, op. cit., pp. 262–7; Barclay, *The History of The Royal Northumberland Fusiliers*, pp. 141–2; NA, Kew, WO170/409, war diary, 4 Div, Oct–Nov 1944; WO170/598, war diary, 28 Bde, Nov–Dec 1944.
74. Barclay, op. cit., pp. 141–2; Williamson, op. cit., pp. 268–70; NA, Kew, WO170/461, war diary, 46 Div, Nov 1944.
75. Williamson, op. cit., p. 277.
76. Jackson, op. cit., pp. 41–4; Williamson, op. cit., pp. 277–8.
77. Ibid., pp. 279–81.
78. Ibid., pp. 282–4.
79. Ibid., pp. 286–7.
80. Jackson, op. cit., p. 51.
81. Anders, op. cit., pp. 234–5; Jackson, op. cit., pp. 50–2.
82. Ibid., p. 50.
83. Nicholson, op. cit., pp. 606–11; Jackson, op. cit., p. 37n; ffrench-Blake, 'Italian War Diary', p. 15; Blaxland, op. cit., pp. 230–1.
84. Blaxland, op. cit., p. 230.
85. Jackson, op. cit., pp. 2–3; Blaxland, op. cit., pp. 230–1.

Chapter Eight

Another Winter:
More Mountains and Floods

That winter lion.

Operation CHUCKLE, the Canadian element of Eighth Army's final offensive of 1944, derived its title from a Canadian officer's sense of humour. In early November I Canadian Corps HQ had planned to take Ravenna by encirclement, including an amphibious landing using DUKWs north of the city. An unknown officer's comment gave the operation its name which was retained even when subsumed into a group plan.[1] McCreery defined Eighth Army's intention: to provide 'all assistance to Fifth Army in the capture of Bologna'; and take Ravenna. The overall offensive was intended to 'afford the greatest possible assistance to the Allied winter offensives on the Western and Eastern fronts by bringing the enemy to battle, thereby compelling him to employ in Italy manpower and resources which might otherwise be available for use on the other fronts'.[2]

With Eighth Army continuing its advance to the Santerno, whence it would develop its main thrust from Imola to Budrio, and a secondary one via Argenta to Ferrara, Fifth Army would support Eighth's left flank before launching its own attack towards Bologna 'at three days notice from 7 December when ordered to do so by AAI',[3] although the weather remained an uncertain factor. Weather-induced uncertainties were exacerbated by changes in command, with Alexander promoted to Supreme Allied Commander Mediterranean, succeeding Wilson who went to Washington following the death of Field Marshal Sir John Dill, head of Britain's Military Mission to the United States, while Clark was promoted to command AAI and Lucian Truscott to command Fifth Army. The latter appointment was on Alexander's personal recommendation through Churchill to President Roosevelt and thus gave an army command to probably the best American general to serve in Europe.[4] John Harding also departed with Alexander (although he would return to command XIII

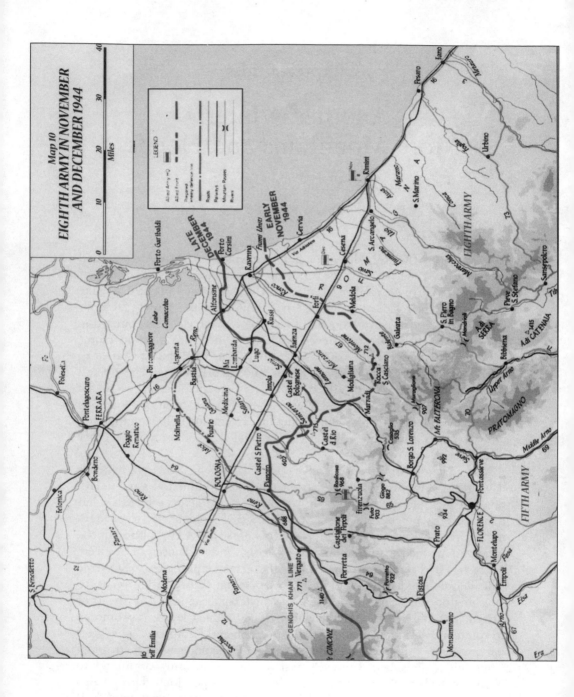

Map 10

EIGHTH ARMY IN NOVEMBER
AND DECEMBER 1944

Corps[5]) while Wilson's move allowed Alexander's promotion to field marshal, backdated to June to maintain his seniority to Montgomery who had received his baton in September. It would have been inappropriate to have elevated Alexander earlier since Wilson was a general and could not have had a field marshal reporting to him. Amidst all this change the only constant was Sir Richard McCreery, which made it fortunate that Eighth Army was to make the first move in the new offensive.

The Canadians had returned to the line on 25 November, relieving Porterforce, which remained in being, and prepared for CHUCKLE. They had another new corps commander, Lieutenant General Charles Foulkes, who had arrived on 16 November from the Netherlands where he had commanded 2nd Canadian Infantry Division. CHUCKLE began on 2 December on a two-brigade front with, on the right, 12 Brigade, the second infantry brigade of 5th Armoured Division, and, on the left, 3 Brigade. Success met the Canadian efforts; 3 Brigade took Russi during that night before, on the 3rd, wheeling left to push the Germans over the Lamone. By nightfall on day two, 12 Brigade was at Godo on the road to Ravenna. En route 12 Brigade had encountered several drainage ditches, complete with high floodbanks, but had overcome these obstacles. On 4 December the brigade pushed forward a battlegroup of Princess Louise's Dragoon Guards, now infantry, and British Columbia Dragoons towards Ravenna. The Dragoons' Shermans raced the four miles to the city. That afternoon the first Princess Louise's troops entered Garibaldi Square to be joined, successively, by elements of Porterforce, partisans of the Garibaldi Brigade and Popski's Private Army.[6]

Popski's men had raided audaciously en route to Ravenna while the Garibaldi Brigade had proved a particular nuisance to the Germans, disrupting their communications so much that they were probably happy to evacuate the city. The leader of the Garibaldi Brigade was Arrigo Boldrini, known as Bulow to protect his family from German reprisals; he and Peniakoff had become firm friends. Wounded before Ravenna fell, Boldrini recovered to receive the Italian Gold Medal for Valour from Sir Richard McCreery at a parade of partisan forces.[7] A former Italian army officer, Boldrini later took his Garibaldi Brigade into the Cremona Group, one of the Italian formations that joined Eighth Army in early 1945.*

That night 1 Brigade attacked across the Lamone, the Royal Canadians and Hastings leading, but suffered a repulse with heavy losses. In spite of this, liberating Ravenna, a historic and beautiful city of substance, boosted

---

* Peniakoff considered that it was Boldrini's military experience that brought him to the attention of the Italian partisan leader, Longo. When the latter asked him to command the Garibaldi Brigade the partisan group was not even in existence and Boldrini had to raise and train the formation. He became an outstanding partisan leader which surprised some Italians who believed that he did not possess leadership qualities as he was no great speaker.[8]

Eighth Army morale since it was a tangible sign that progress was being made, even though much behind schedule. It is worth remembering that signs such as the liberation of a city are understood and appreciated much more easily by soldiers than nebulous strategic objectives of 'maintaining pressure' in a bitter attritional campaign intended to assist progress on another front in another country.[9]

II Polish Corps had been continuing their advance and, following the capture of Brisighella by the partisan Banda Maiella on 29 November, the Carpathian Division crossed the Lamone to make for San Rinaldo, Cassette and Besdone, to the south-west of Faenza and south of the Senio. This was the third occasion on which the Carpathians had assaulted such an objective and the strain of hard campaigning was beginning to tell. Granted they were tough and dedicated soldiers imbued with a desire to see the defeat of Germany, but even such warriors are worn down by battle. During this phase they were opposed by soldiers from 305th and 715th Divisions who inflicted heavy casualties on the Poles. German resistance had benefited from a contracting front which allowed them to present a stronger defence. Stoically, the Carpathian Division continued the fight and their efforts assisted V Corps' advance which saw the New Zealanders enter Faenza, midway between Forlí and Imola on Highway 9, on 16 December, and Eighth Army reach the Senio.[10] Anders was later to write that his corps' operations

in the Emilian Apennines had needed strenuous effort by the men, who, battling in the hills or paddling in mud, fought, attacked and pushed back the enemy. There were no spectacular achievements; it was a case of steady, relentless fighting, and duty well done. The Army Corps losses in these battles amounted to 42 officers and 627 other ranks killed, 184 officers and 2,630 other ranks wounded and 1 officer and 32 other ranks missing.[11]

On the 17th, the day after the New Zealanders entered Faenza, McCreery sent a signal to Anders paying tribute to the Carpathians' recent efforts.

My best congratulations to you and 3rd Carpathian Division on your successful operations in difficult country, which have driven back the enemy to the Senio on a wide front with heavy losses. The mounting of this attack with the great lack of roads in your area was a fine achievement. Engineers and gunners deserve every credit.[12]

A visitor to the area might wonder at McCreery's comment on the 'great lack of roads' for there appears to have been no shortage of roads in the Faenza area. Move off Highway 9 north-west of Faenza, however, and

170

drive west and south-west into the mountains where the Poles were operating and there is a tale of a different hue where the demands on the engineers may be appreciated.

McCreery's third corps, V, had not attacked until the night of 3/4 December. This was not due to any tactical imperative, nor any clever scheme, but to the need for bridge repairs along the corps' supply routes. The Hampshire Brigade led once again, providing the van of 46th Division's assault crossing of the Lamone, some four miles from Faenza. As the Hampshires moved off they were assisted by New Zealanders making diversionary attacks on the other side of Faenza to confuse the enemy. As a reconstituted 1st KRRC gave flank protection to the brigade, 2nd Hampshires crossed the Lamone by wading and a ladder bridge before emerging to scale slippery banks and push on. On the brigade left 1/4th Hampshires also crossed to fight their way forward and upward by a series of ascending features. The 2nd Battalion took their objective with a bayonet charge on a two-company front, the sight and sound of which must have proved unnerving even for German soldiers. With the leading battalions on their objectives, 5th Hampshires passed through but made no significant progress. Then it began raining again and the Hampshire bridgehead was endangered. As on several previous occasions there was the risk of being cut off without resupply, but portering parties made frantic efforts to keep the brigade supplied and sappers again showed their mettle by putting an Ark bridge across.[13]

That bridge allowed 2 Armoured Brigade to cross after dark on the 4th with 138 Brigade following to expand the bridgehead where they were joined by 169 Queen's Brigade of 56th Division, now under command of 46th Division to maintain the latter at full three-brigade strength; 139 Brigade had been airlifted to Greece. But even expanding the bridgehead to divisional group strength was no guarantee that it would be maintained. Before long, 46th Division came under great pressure.[14] Von Vietinghoff, temporarily commanding all German forces in Italy in the absence of Kesselring, who was recovering from injuries sustained in a car crash on 23 October while visiting formations under his command,* was determined to eliminate the bridgehead and brought 90th Panzer Grenadier Division back to reinforce 305th Division. But 46th Division held its positions and, moreover, pushed forward steadily. Then, on 9 December, the bridgehead was hit by the full fury of a determined counter-attack by 90th Panzer Grenadiers under an umbrella of fire from artillery and tanks.

* He was travelling from Bologna to Forlí when his car collided with a long-barrelled gun emerging from a side road. In his *Memoirs* he comments that after this incident the story among German troops was that the Field Marshal was doing well but that the gun had had to be scrapped.[15]

But the panzer grenadiers were trying to push back British troops who had no intention of withdrawing and, in spite of their best efforts, the Germans were stopped. Their sole gain was a feature that had been held by Captain John H.C. Brunt's Carrier Platoon of 6th Lincolns from 138 Brigade.[16]

Three Mark IV tanks supported the infantry who attacked the Lincolns' position, destroying the house around which the platoon was dug in and knocking out two Shermans.

> Captain Brunt rallied his remaining men, moved to an alternative position and continued to hold the enemy infantry, although he was heavily outnumbered. Personally firing a Bren gun, Brunt killed about fourteen of the enemy. When his Bren ammunition was exhausted he fired a PIAT and 2-inch mortar, left by casualties. This aggressive defence caused the enemy to pause and enabled Captain Brunt to re-occupy his previous position and get away the wounded that had been left there.[17]

During another German attack later that day, Brunt demonstrated similar aggressive and inspiring leadership. Tragically, the 22-year-old was killed next morning, 10 December, by a chance enemy mortar bomb that landed beside him as he waited for his breakfast.[18] Not surprisingly, he was awarded the Victoria Cross posthumously. John Brunt had been commissioned in the Sherwood Foresters.

The Lincolns had fought hard to rebuff the Germans of 90th Panzer Grenadier Division, as had 6th York and Lancaster on their right. Both battalions were now exhausted, as was much of 46th Division which was in need of relief. This had been planned and began that afternoon when 25 Brigade of 10th Indian Division relieved the Hampshires, while both 138 and 169 Brigades were relieved by New Zealanders.[19] John Brunt was one of 46th Division's last casualties in Italy as the remainder of the Division would soon join 139 Brigade in Greece. Although returning to Italy before the fighting ceased in May 1945 the division saw no more active service in the peninsula.[20]

In counter-attacking 46th Division's bridgehead on 9 December, von Vietinghoff had demonstrated his determination to hold the Lamone line, but that was not the day's only attack. Near Ravenna a position held by 27th Lancers was also assaulted. During this battle Popski's Private Army rushed to support the Lancers with Peniakoff leading five jeep loads of his men into action.

> He took position on a flank and pumped bullets into wave after wave of heedless [Jägers]. When at last the latter withdrew they left eighty dead behind them. The loss incurred by Popski's Army consisted only of their commander's [left] hand. In exchange he won the DSO.[21]

172

Another attack across the Lamone was launched on the night of 10/11 December, this time by the Canadians. Two brigades, 3 Brigade from 1st Division and 11 Brigade from 5th Armoured, made successful assault crossings some 3 miles apart. However, their way ahead was cut by several small rivers, each with floodbanks and, as if that were not enough, the hard-pressed 114th Jäger and 356th Divisions had been reinforced by the fresh 98th Division. All three formed LXIII Corps and, although the former two divisions had seen much recent hard fighting, the reinforcement meant that the Canadians would have to fight for every yard of ground. On the night of 12/13 December attacks across the Naviglio canal were contested strongly. To the Canadian right 12 Brigade made a lodgement but was forced back by a series of determined counter-attacks. It was a different story on the left where 1 Brigade attacked. The Hastings led and stood firm to establish a bridgehead in face of all that the Germans threw at them. With the support of the Carleton and York Regiment the positions were consolidated and, with fighter-bombers harassing the Germans, armour and artillery came up to join 1 Brigade and expand the bridgehead.[22]

As we have seen, elements of the New Zealand and 10th Indian Divisions had relieved 46th Division whose bridgehead became the jumping-off point for the next attack. Seven battalions from three brigades – three from 5 New Zealand and two each from 10 and 25 Indian – made the attack, supported by tanks from 4 New Zealand and 7 Armoured Brigades.[23] Beforehand there had been a tremendous artillery bombardment, the outcome of careful husbanding of shells to provide support when most needed, while sappers had laid tracks and built bridges that allowed the attackers to deploy much force into the difficult, 'sharp-featured and rain-drenched country beyond the torrent-prone Lamone'.[24]

The Germans, aware of the difficulties of the country, had not expected an Allied force of such strength to burst into it. Even when taken by surprise, however, they did not cave in easily, putting up stout resistance, especially in the path of 10 Indian Brigade. But the attackers maintained their momentum to grind down the opposition and advance towards their objectives. On the night of 15/16 December German troops began evacuating Faenza and the first New Zealanders entered the town next day. Some 300 prisoners, mainly from 90th Panzer Grenadiers, were taken by the New Zealanders on the 16th. By the morning of the 17th Faenza was clear of enemy troops and the New Zealanders and Indians pushed forward to the Senio where, following an abortive attempt to create a bridgehead over the river, the advance was halted. To the left the Poles were also along the Senio. Further attacks were made from Faenza by 6 New Zealand and 43 Gurkha Brigades, both of which also reached the Senio while, on 21 December, the Canadians came up in an eight-battalion attack that gained Bagnacavallo.[25]

This was to be Eighth Army's forward line for what remained of the winter. The combined attack by Fifth and Eighth Armies was not to take place although Clark, now AAI commander, was still planning for this on 20 December, giving McCreery instructions that Eighth Army was 'to clean up the area between the Munio and the Senio and be prepared to assault across the latter river at the same time that Fifth Army struck northward at Bologna'.[26]

But events overtook Clark and the signal to attack was never given. On 26 December the German 148th Division with elements of two Italian fascist divisions, Monte Rosa and Italia, drove into Fifth Army's western flank, deflecting a light screen provided by 92nd Division and penetrating some five miles down the Serchio valley. Coming as this did so soon after the German Ardennes offensive, there was a fear that it was a more serious attack than in reality – one German source claimed that its purpose was to take prisoners and relieve pressure on LI Mountain Corps – and that exploitation could threaten Livorno. First US Armored Division and two brigades of 8th Indian Division were moved quickly to the threatened area and restored the situation. But this offensive completely upset Clark's plans and at the beginning of January 1945 Allied Armies in Italy were ordered to adopt a stance of offensive defence.[27]

McCreery chose to interpret this as permitting operations to improve his positions for the offensive that would come with springtime. Furthermore, there were still some Germans lodged south and east of the Senio and matters would be tidier all round if such lodgements could be squeezed out. McCreery was determined that should happen as part of a general tidying up of Eighth Army's front. For once the weather came to his help with a hard frost at the turn of the year making the ground solid enough for armour to operate. Taking advantage of the conditions, 5th Canadian Armoured Division advanced on the right flank of I Canadian Corps between 2 and 6 January. In a sweeping ten-mile move the Canadians gained the southern shore of Lake Comácchio and the base of the spit between the lake and the Adriatic. Not best pleased with this turn of events the Germans counter-attacked from Alfonsine to the south-east. However, that attack was subjected to heavy fire from the Perth Regiment, 12th Lancers and 1st King's Royal Rifle Corps, the latter pair forming part of yet another ad hoc force, under 9 Armoured Brigade, charged with holding the coastal sector. Such was the intensity of fire directed on them that the Germans lost almost a thousand men before abandoning their attack.[28]

The Canadians cleared another German lodgement south-east of Bagnacavallo and north of Faenza. In this operation Canadian troops worked in conjunction with a 56th Division assault in which the Canadian 2 Brigade, led by the Princess Pats, took the town of Granarolo, between Faenza and Bagnacavallo, on the night of 3 January. At dawn the Black Cats, now rebuilt, began a converging attack from the left, Operation

CYGNET, led by a battlegroup of 10th Royal Hussars, 2nd Royal Tanks and 2/6th Queen's. The Queensmen were in unusually close support as they were riding in fifty-three Kangaroos, basic armoured personnel carriers (APCs) created by removing turrets and ammunition stowage from Shermans,* which could move at the same pace as the armour and provide the foot soldiers with protection, as well as eliminating much tiring marching. Kangaroos, from the eponymous marsupial's method of conveying its young, had already been used by the Canadians in north-west Europe but this was their first operational outing in Italy.[29] They were manned by personnel from 4th Hussars and 'gave the infantry four invaluable advantages: protection while on the move; better communication, especially with the gun tanks; carrying capacity for ammunition and personal kit; and a feeling that, at last, something had been done to help them in their hard, tiring and dangerous work'.[30] Each Kangaroo carried an infantry section and stopped to allow its section to debus behind houses or on top of the more open defences. The speed of these attacks gave the Queensmen the great advantage of surprise and soon Kangaroos were being sent back full of prisoners, of whom over 200 were taken in quick time. If there was any disadvantage to deploying the Kangaroos it lay in revealing the beasts to the Germans; but this was more than compensated for by the advantages: Eighth Army had been able to execute an essential task quickly with minimum loss of life and much less use of scarce artillery ammunition than might otherwise have been the case.[31] The war diary of 11th (HAC) Regiment RHA notes that CYGNET was 'supported by a small fireplan due to limited ammunition'; 25-pounders were restricted to ten rounds per gun.[32]

It is worth noting that McCreery was a keen proponent of the Kangaroo whereas his counterpart in north-west Europe, Sir Miles Dempsey, Second Army's commander, was not, leaving it to the Canadians to make first use of the Kangaroo even though Sir Richard O'Connor, one of Dempsey's corps commanders, had advocated the use of APCs.[33]

With these operations complete, Eighth Army was poised to strike behind Bologna's defenders towards Ferrara, thereby severing the German line of retreat to the Po, while Fifth Army was still stuck in the Apennines before Bologna. But with the terrain offering greater chances for mobile warfare and the APCs giving the infantry more mobility and flexibility, enthusiasm built in Allied headquarters about the chances of destroying completely the German armies in Italy. Although totally unrelated to this increased enthusiasm the former title of the army group was reintroduced in January and Allied Armies in Italy once again became 15 Army Group. On the other side von Vietinghoff still commanded Army Group C –

* Others were created by removing the armament from Priest SPGs. Inevitably, these latter were known as defrocked Priests.

Kesselring would not return until February – with Lemelsen commanding Tenth Army and von Senger in charge of Fourteenth. In the first month of 1945 von Vietinghoff had twenty-one German divisions in the field with another two protecting the eastern approach to Italy. While these were not all full-strength formations, and manpower varied considerably, they still made a formidable fighting force, especially in defensive warfare. In most cases they would be restored to full strength by the time the Allied spring offensive began. That the German high command still attached importance to the Italian front was demonstrated during the month by the transfer from Norway of 710th Division, a move that occurred when Allied forces had already penetrated into Germany and the Germans were organizing the greatest seaborne evacuation in history, that of some two million Germans from Courland, Pomerania and Prussia across the Baltic and away from the advancing Red Army.[34]

Kesselring returned to duty at the beginning of February and, true to form, began visiting front-line units again. Considering such visits to be important boosts to morale he ignored the fact that he had not recovered fully. But he was not on the road constantly and spent much time at his headquarters reorganizing his forces in preparation for the Allied spring offensive.[35] He had some slightly encouraging news on air operations: the Luftwaffe's new Arado Ar234 Blitz twin-engined reconnaissance aircraft was available in limited numbers in Italy. Powered by two turbojet engines, the Blitz was faster than any Allied fighter and 'brought back useful information and *very slightly* lifted the curtain over the enemy's back areas and the sea area near the front'. Some Italian fascist air units, operating German fighter aircraft, also made a nuisance of themselves by attacking Allied raiders. But the Allies maintained air superiority. As with the Allies, German personnel from other services were retrained with large numbers of *Kriegsmarine* seamen being formed into army units and trained by the army; Admiral Löwisch 'gladly fell in with' Kesselring's suggestion that this should be done.[36]

Kesselring's command included four Italian divisions, of which three were in Marshal Graziani's Army of Liguria, deployed to guard the western flank, and the fourth in Fourteenth Army; it was not, however, in an area considered under threat. The Germans had a major security problem in occupied Italy although operations against partisans were not conducted by Kesselring's formations but fell to a separate command under SS General Karl Wolff. This command deployed the equivalent of ten divisions and personnel included Italian fascists, Cossacks, Slovaks and even some Spaniards as well as Germans. Wolff's men fought a bitter and vicious campaign against Italian partisans and committed many atrocities against civilians.[37] One of the forgotten stories of the Second World War is that of Italian resistance to the German occupation: Italians resisted to a

176

much greater level, and to more effect, than did the French whose story is much better known.

Reinforcements were still arriving in Italy for Kesselring's formations, although the numbers were much smaller, as was ammunition while industry in northern Italy was being harnessed to meet German war demands. Kesselring's greatest shortages were in aircraft with, as we have seen, the Luftwaffe almost non-existent, and petrol. The lack of the latter commodity had its greatest effect on his mobile divisions of which there were now five: 26th Panzer, 29th and 90th Panzer Grenadier and 1st and 4th Parachute, the last two being Luftwaffe formations which formed I Parachute Corps with an overall strength of 30,000. Kesselring left Italy in late March to take command of all German forces in the West in succession to Field Marshal Gert von Rundstedt. Once again command of Army Group C passed to von Vietinghoff, who had been posted to the Baltic but now returned to Italy, with Lemelsen commanding Fourteenth Army and Herr commanding Tenth.[38]

Alexander's forces in Italy suffered further reduction in early 1945. The Supreme Commander was summoned to Malta at the end of January to meet the Combined Chiefs who were en route to meet their Soviet counterparts at Yalta. There Alexander received the disturbing news that he was to lose I Canadian Corps to Crerar's First Canadian Army in north-west Europe. This was a major blow for Alexander and McCreery: the latter's plans for the offensive included a prominent role for the Canadians in whom he placed great trust. But the loss of the Canadians was not the end of the bad news as three further divisions, all British, were to follow to north-west Europe. In the event only one was transferred: 5th Division, known as the Cook's Tour Division,* had spent an almost unbelievable eight months in Palestine before returning to Italy in February 1945 to relieve 1st Division. Hardly had 5th Division carried out that relief than it moved to Naples to board ships for Marseilles and travel northwards from there, entering the war again in Germany in mid-April.[39]

From the many British, Commonwealth and Imperial divisions that had served in Italy only seven remained for the spring offensive; the chances of others returning from Greece were very slight. Alexander had seventeen

---

* The soubriquet referred to the travelling done by 5th Division during the war which was greater than that of any other British division. As part of the BEF in 1939–40, the Division was warned of possible moves to Norway or Finland, neither of which happened, although a brigade went to Norway. Following service in Northern Ireland, it went to India in 1942, taking part, en route, in operations against the Vichy French in Madagascar while shore leave was granted in South Africa and Kenya. The Division spent less than two months in India before being ordered to Persia via Iraq. It moved from there by road to Syria from where it travelled to Egypt, and thence to join Eighth Army for the invasion of Sicily.

divisions in total, including three armoured, against twenty-one German divisions, although the manpower of the latter was generally weaker. However, early 1945 saw the strengthening of the army group with the arrival of four Italian combat groups, equipped with British arms and wearing British uniforms. Three were assigned to Eighth Army and made a considerable contribution to its overall strength. Cremona Combat Group, with 21st and 22nd Regiments and the Garibaldi Brigade, was assigned to V Corps, while Friuli Combat Group, including 87th and 88th Regiments, went to X Corps. After its time with Fifth Army, XIII Corps returned to Eighth Army and took Folgore Combat Group, including the Nembo and San Marco Regiments, into its order of battle. The fourth Italian group, Legnano, with 68th and 69th Regiments, deployed with II US Corps. There was also an Italian SAS unit.[40]

Also joining Eighth Army in January 1945 was the Jewish Brigade of three Palestine Regiment battalions; the regiment had been raised during the British mandate in Palestine. The War Office had long been reluctant to accept a Jewish formation under British command since such might appear to indicate a lack of balance in British attitudes to Arab and Jew, especially with the prospect of the mandate ending. Thus it was that proposals to raise an identifiably Jewish formation to fight the Germans had met luke-warm enthusiasm from British officials. Persistence pays, however, and after four years of discussion the War Office finally allowed the formation of a Jewish Brigade. One man who was markedly enthusiastic about the proposal was Churchill who told Roosevelt that the Jewish people 'of all people have the right to strike at the Germans as a recognisable body'. He also supported their desire to fight under the Star of David.[41]

While the Palestine Regiment was the main source of recruits for the Jewish Brigade there were others, principally the Polish Army which included many men who, although Polish citizens, were not ethnic Poles; these included Ukrainians and Jews. Such was the Polish contribution to the Jewish Brigade that Moshe Dayan would later describe Anders as the 'father of the Israeli army'. Brigadier Ernest Frank Benjamin, a British regular officer, born in Canada in 1900, became brigade commander. Commissioned in the Royal Engineers, Frank Benjamin had 'a reputation for competence and complete dependability' and had commanded British forces in the campaign against the Vichy French in Madagascar during which his men repaired blown bridges and roads within twelve hours and kept unrelenting pressure on the enemy. Benjamin had not been the first choice: that had been Brigadier E. Myers DSO MC who had gone missing in Greece. Under his command, Brigadier Benjamin had Jews from Russia, Poland, Hungary, Italy, France and the Yemen, as well as Britain.[42]

Freyberg's New Zealand Division had been reorganized to include a third infantry brigade, giving much better balance, especially in sustained fighting. This brigade had been created in a manner similar to that adopted by the Canadians: the divisional cavalry regiment had been converted to infantry as had both the Motor and Machine-Gun Battalions. Reinforcements had also been received from New Zealand which allowed repatriation of soldiers with three years' active service. Many New Zealand reinforcements were men with combat experience, having served with 3rd New Zealand Division in the Pacific before that formation had returned home in February 1944.* Freyberg himself remained in command and would do so until the end of the war, establishing a record of commanding for five years in seven countries, under nine superior commanders.[43]

In February 2 Commando Brigade rejoined Eighth Army. Formerly 2 Special Service Brigade, it included four commando units – Nos 2 and 9 Army, 40 and 43 Royal Marine – as well as the Special Boat Service. They were followed in March by 2 Parachute Brigade – 4th, 5th and 6th Parachute Battalions – which had been in Greece.[44]

While Kesselring could write about German morale being far better than he had imagined on his return to duty with no talk even in private of 'throwing up the sponge',[45] the same was not true in the Allied ranks. Both Fifth and Eighth Armies had a persistent morale problem during the final winter of war, although the peak had probably been passed by February. Contributory factors included the perceived imminence of victory with the subsequent feeling that it would be even more tragic to die so close to the end. There was also the widespread feeling that the campaign was regarded in far-off London and Washington as a sideshow which made it even more difficult to contemplate making sacrifices, especially the ultimate one. To many the thought of desertion became very attractive and certainly much more so than suffering the rigours of warfare – and for what? Not surprisingly, desertions increased.

Desertion had created a headache for the Allies for some time and had peaked twice in 1944: in March as a result of the strain of service at Anzio, and in June during the advance to Rome. But its worst manifestation came in late 1944 when 1,200 British soldiers – not all in Eighth Army as XIII Corps was with Fifth Army and there were also troops in rear areas and on lines of communication – were posted as absent without leave (AWOL) or as deserters in both November and December. The problem may be seen in perspective when it is realized that, at its peak, the deserter numbers equalled the infantry strength of a division that had been in the line for some time,† and that an equivalent number was needed to guard captured deserters. At its worst the number of deserters in prison was 5,150.[46]

---

* First New Zealand Division remained at home as a defence force throughout the war.
† With nine battalions each deploying about 600 men, this would be 5,400.

179

There were three main categories of deserter. The two principal types were the straightforward cowards, defined by one senior officer as 'those who will not take it', who could have been deterred only by the death penalty, abolished for desertion in 1939, and 'those that cannot take it'.[47] This latter group was made up of men who had used up their personal quota of courage but who could, in many cases, be rehabilitated by careful handling within their own units, although that might have an adverse effect on others.* Finally, there were those who felt no sense of identity within a unit, a particular problem in the latter phase of the campaign when AA gunners, RAF personnel and some sailors were remustered as infantry. Where members of an AA battery stayed together as an infantry company, however, a good sub-unit might result. In some cases the problem was lessened by the fact that several LAA units had been converted from infantry battalions and were allowed to maintain regimental distinctions which made the process of re-converting to infantry much easier. Some also felt a lack of identity on returning from convalescence when the reinforcement system sent them to a unit other than their own. Of course, even returning to a soldier's original unit might leave him in the midst of strangers if his company had taken heavy casualties, or he had been away for a long spell.

Nonetheless, the majority remained at their posts. Their spirits were

> now immune to whatever the fates might do – like Wellington's men in the Peninsula, or Lee's or Napoleon's, or any others long together. I think it was Stonewall Jackson who said in Virginia, 'It is fortunate that war is so horrible ... otherwise we might grow to like it.' Like it? Never – but our soldiers had grown accustomed to it, and some of us had forgotten what any other life was like.[48]

It was actually the US General William Tecumseh Sherman who opined that it was as well that war was so horrible, but otherwise this is an accurate comment on the mental attitude of many Eighth Army soldiers in early 1945. Good leadership at all levels was critical and helped maintain morale, especially when soldiers heard about some of the shortages. Most

---

* In 1993 the author was asked to visit an old soldier who had been a neighbour in the 1950s and 1960s and who had heard one of the author's radio programmes. In the course of conversation the author was surprised when the veteran told him that he had lost his nerve early in the Italian campaign but had later been accepted back to his own battalion. Since he was also in contact with a number of senior retired officers, one his former CO and another the battalion's Adjutant, it seemed that he had been rehabilitated successfully. A measure of the man's quota of courage was that he had been recommended for the Military Medal in Tunisia, although no award was made.

may not have been aware that 25-pounder ammunition was rationed to five rounds per gun per day, but many did know that Vickers MMGs were restricted to 100 rounds per gun per day and mortar crews to four bombs per day, except for defensive tasks and emergencies.[49]

The last direction from which Eighth Army's soldiers would have expected an attack on their morale was from home, and especially from the House of Commons, but they learned that a Member of Parliament, Nancy Lady Astor, had called them 'D-Day Dodgers'. This was an affront of the worst type and suggested that Eighth Army had been sitting out the war in relative comfort while Second Army in north-west Europe was fighting, suffering and dying. Eighth Army's cartoonist, Jon, was quick to produce a cartoon for the Army's newspaper in which he showed his famous characters, the 'Two Types', sitting in a jeep emblazoned with names such as Salerno and Anzio and wondering just which D-Day they had dodged. One CO, Bala Bredin, now commanding 2nd London Irish, used the Jon cartoon as a pattern for decorating his own jeep, much to the chagrin of some in higher quarters. Soldiers composed songs or wrote poems on the same theme, the best known being a ballad called 'D-Day Dodgers' sung to the tune of 'Lili Marlene', itself purloined from the Germans in North Africa to become Eighth Army's anthem.[50]

It seems that Lady Astor did refer to Eighth Army as D-Day Dodgers, but did so in the honest belief that this was a soubriquet the troops had adopted for themselves. Receiving a letter from soldiers in Italy which had been signed 'D-Day Dodgers', the Plymouth MP had assumed that this was a nickname in common use in Italy and so repeated it publicly. Little harm was done and, in a sense, the misunderstanding boosted morale. Following the example of the BEF in 1914 in adopting the title 'Old Contemptibles', Eighth Army adopted 'D-Day Dodgers' as a badge of honour. In a serendipitous fashion, therefore, Lady Astor did Eighth Army a favour.[51]

But the greatest boost to morale in Eighth Army came from its commander, Richard McCreery. His handling of the Army was superb and did much to build confidence for the offensive. In dismounting cavalry regiments to allow his infantry to rest and recuperate he showed that he cared about the welfare of his soldiers. When 56th Division had used Kangaroos to return to battle they were the beneficiaries of McCreery's willingness to innovate and his eye for battle. His preparation for the spring offensive had all the hallmarks of great generalship and imbued Eighth Army with a level of confidence that was probably the equal of that achieved at any time in its existence. All this was done without the showmanship of a Montgomery for McCreery was determined to see Eighth Army advance to success and victory in 1945 while giving his soldiers the best possible chances of surviving. It is worth recording the comment of Major General John Strawson, himself an Eighth Army veteran, when he wrote that McCreery was 'the greatest cavalry soldier of his generation and at the same time that rare coalition of a brilliant staff officer and higher commander'.[52]

Although three months separated the ending of major operations and the spring offensive, which opened in April, there were many engagements during that time. The Germans were determined not to wait for the Allies to attack but to take the fight to them whenever possible. In late December 1945 Canadian soldiers found an order from Richard Heidrich, now Parachute Corps commander, which emphasized to his soldiers that fighting should never cease and that 'The "leave me alone and I will leave you alone" attitude must be entirely absent.' Not that his soldiers needed much exhortation as they proved to be skilled practitioners of small-scale operations.[53] Nor were the paras alone in this: German minor operations allowed their opponents little opportunity to relax with raids intended to disrupt communications, some of which were carried out by parties of about twenty men landed from E-boats, or groups of two to five Italian fascist paratroopers.[54]

The soldiers of Eighth Army were not to be intimidated and were also active in small-scale operations that took the fight to the enemy. Daily press communiqués – this was before the days of 'press releases' – noted how

'patrols were active on the Italian front' and few but the front-line soldier knew what those words meant in danger, in toil and in the hardships of rain, mud, snow and cold. The patrols supplied a steady stream of prisoners – and of information.[55]

The front-line infantryman, on either side, was experiencing conditions usually associated with those of the First World War. There were patrols, raids into opposing lines, mortar fire and harassing fire from rifles and machine guns. Such activity would have been familiar to a veteran of the earlier conflict as would have been the proximity of the opposing front lines, separated only by the width of the Senio. Sometimes they were even closer since the Germans still held some outposts on Eighth Army's side of the river, usually on the reverse of the British-held floodbank. Those floodbanks were impressive and could be up to 30 feet high and about 10 feet across at the top. The Senio itself was less than 20 feet wide.

It was along that river that the Canadians performed their last duties as part of Eighth Army. The historian of Princess Patricia's Canadian Light Infantry noted that

until the end of their war in Italy, the Patricias engaged in static warfare along the Senio, patrolling and raiding. As one remarked,

'If it had not been for the weather, we'd have enjoyed it.' There were many successes and one notable disaster. Two platoons of C Company raided a group of buildings on the Fosso Vecchio after a heavy artillery concentration. The enemy fled and as the Patricias entered the first of the buildings, a delayed charge brought it down on their heads. When others ran to dig them out, the enemy brought down a devastating mortar concentration. The action cost thirty-seven casualties.[56]

The Patricias later spent some weeks in reserve as a counter-attack force before returning for a final two-week stint along the Senio. Relieved by 5th Royal West Kents on 25 February they joined the Canadian migration to north-west Europe. A memory of their time in Italy remains to this day: the regimental slow march, chosen after the war, is 'Lili Marlene', to which veterans of Italy would doubtless have their own words.[57]

As it flows from the Apennines to the sea the Senio meanders considerably. The many loops thus created often gave one side or the other the local tactical advantage of being able to look behind the opposition's front line. In places where the Germans held positions on the reverse side of a British floodbank they built bridges or rafts to allow them either to man or reinforce their positions. Since those bridges were so close to British troops it was frequently impossible to call artillery fire down on them and so the infantry improvised, using PIATs as mortars to bombard the German bridges.[58]

Trench warfare, which this certainly was, was fraught with many dangers and soldiers quickly learned, among other lessons, to keep their heads below the parapet during daylight hours. A head peering over the parapet was an invitation to a sniper. With the fall of darkness, however, activity intensified 'when we kept up a continuous fusillade of small arms, grenades, 2 in mortars and a new use for the PIAT – fired as a mortar. The bomb made quite a noise falling and must have proved unnerving to the opposition.'[59]

A warrant officer of the same battalion detailed how both the 2-inch mortar and PIAT were used:

> Amongst platoon weapons in constant use ... was the 2″ mortar. ... In order to reduce the range ... and bring targets 40–75 yards away into effective range, half the propellant charge from the cartridge ... was removed. Mortar crews became very proficient at hitting close-range targets on the opposite bank. ... On the Senio [the PIAT] was used as a mortar and fired at high angle. PIAT bombs exploding on the roof of a dugout could cause damage and severe shock waves underneath and its blast effect was quite considerable.[60]

183

A high state of alert had to be maintained as the Germans made frequent attacks. On occasions they echoed another First World War tactic by tunnelling through the floodbank to raid a British position, a tactic frequently reciprocated by Eighth Army's soldiers. In such circumstances it is always the case that newly-arrived units are most at risk, a truth brought home to 56th Reconnaissance Regiment when they entered the line to relieve 44 Recce. Less than an hour later a German raiding party appeared while mortars bombarded the centre troop's position. German infantry attacked with machine guns and grenades and the raid left three 56 Recce men dead, four wounded and five taken prisoner in a flurry of activity that seemed to be over almost as soon as it began.[61]

The Germans hoped that such raids would damage British morale and adopted another tactic to achieve this: propaganda. Eighth Army units would find themselves bombarded by paper. Leaflets fired over warned British soldiers of the dangers before them along the Po, a river, according to the propagandists, that was worse than the sum of all the previous river crossings. And there were other leaflets that tried to cause friction between Allies: British soldiers were told that American servicemen in Britain were making free with their wives and girlfriends while they faced the dangers of the Senio line. Loudspeakers were also used to broadcast propaganda, some of it directed at specific units. Recforce, 44 Recce and 12th Lancers, was subjected to such propaganda at the beginning of April when the broadcaster claimed that 'someone out of uniform at home is taking your job; they are not longing for your return so die quicker pal.' A quick burst of artillery fire brought that broadcast to an end. In general, the propaganda was quite crude and tended to provide entertainment rather than erode morale in Eighth Army.[62]

All the while the weather was improving and signs of spring were evident. Preparations continued behind the lines for Operation GRAPESHOT, the spring offensive, with ammunition, fuel and other necessities being stockpiled ready for D-Day. It had been Clark's intention to give Fifth Army the major role in the offensive since he believed that Eighth Army was worn out and incapable of anything more than subsidiary operations in support of Fifth. Another factor in Clark's plan to sideline Eighth Army was his dislike of McCreery. However, both army commanders had discussed the renewed offensive and agreed that Fifth and Eighth Armies should have as their primary objective the destruction of the German armies in the field. Clark, not surprisingly, had his eyes on yet another territorial objective: Bologna. The city was to be liberated by US divisions of Fifth Army. McCreery and Truscott argued for a different plan and, to his credit, Clark accepted.[63] A new army group plan was devised but 'The final plan was not a compromise, a course invariably fatal, but contained the inputs of two highly professional army commanders.'[64]

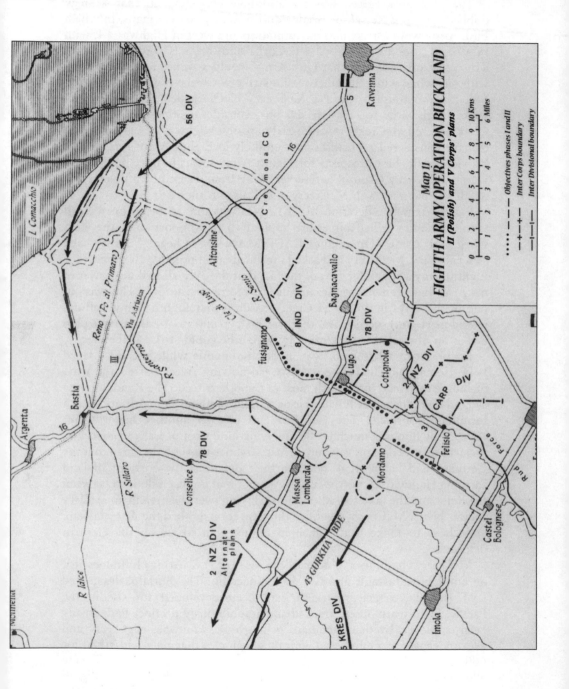

Map II

EIGHT ARMY OPERATION BUCKLAND
II (Polish) and V Corps' plans

| 0 1 2 3 4 5 6 7 8 9 10 Kms |
| 0 1 2 3 4 5 6 Miles |

⋯⋯⋯⋯ Objectives phases I and II
+·+·+·+· Inter Corps boundary
———————— Inter Divisional boundary

The plan now agreed was for a double encirclement, that strategy dubbed *Keil und Kessel*, or 'wedge and trap', by the Germans, in which Fifth Army would strike into the Emilian plain, west of Highway 64, with IV Corps, prior to sidestepping II Corps onto an axis west of Bologna. Truscott's intention was that Fifth Army would advance towards Verona with one wing, while the other would strike north then swing east behind Bologna and south of the Po. McCreery had intended Eighth Army to strike northwards to cross the Po but, considering this too ambitious, Clark ordered McCreery to strike eastwards on Highway 9. Clark appears to have considered a breakthrough unlikely in Eighth Army's sector and his view of the best prospects for Eighth Army seems to have been that it would pull Army Group C's reserves away from Truscott. In this he was much mistaken as both McCreery and Truscott knew.[65]

Eighth Army's Operation BUCKLAND was due to begin on 9 April with the entire Allied air effort applied to its support until the 12th when Fifth Army's Operation CRAFTSMAN would begin.[66] As far back as 6 February, McCreery had asked for the greatest possible air support for Eighth Army's attack 'in view of the fact that the over-all striking power of my Army has been materially curtailed by recent decisions'.[67] This was but one of the ways in which McCreery ensured that Eighth Army's efforts would meet with success. Another was his perception of Lake Comácchio not as an obstacle but as a route by which he could strike at the enemy.

Eighth Army's left flank was in the mountains while the right faced Lake Comácchio. In between, eastward-flowing rivers barred the way, including the Reno into which most of the others feed. The Reno, looping around Bologna before flowing east and then south into the Adriatic, was a formidable obstacle. The Germans had created another major water obstacle by flooding much of the low-lying land west of Lake Comácchio; this was intended to prevent any British advance through that area. But the Germans had left a weak point in their defences: the corridor of land carrying Highway 16 north-west to Argenta had not been flooded between the Reno and the lake's southern shore. Flying over the area in an artillery spotter plane, McCreery identified this gap, soon dubbed the Argenta Gap, and chose to make it the linchpin of his plan to smash the German defences.

McCreery had also obtained the use of US Army Buffaloes for an amphibious assault across Lake Comácchio. The Buffalo, designated LVT (landing vehicle, tracked), had been developed for use in the Pacific. Lightly armoured, tracked and amphibious, Buffaloes had already been employed by the Canadians in north-west Europe. McCreery and Alexander were so impressed with these vehicles that they had asked for 600 to carry three assault brigades in the Po valley. Only 400 LVsT were allocated to Italy for both armies but Army Group HQ had offered Eighth Army the loan of the American allocation as well as its own. The codename 'Fantail' was applied to the Buffaloes so as to hide their true nature for as long as possible. With the Buffaloes Eighth Army would be able to throw a right hook at the Germans by deploying a brigade across Lake Comácchio. The Buffaloes were added to Eighth Army's Kangaroos which were also joined by Duplex-Drive amphibious Shermans, known as DD tanks, which had been used with great success in north-west Europe. Second Army, and 21 Army Group generally, had the use of the specialist tanks, or 'Funnies', of 79th Armoured Division which had no equivalent in Italy. That did not deter McCreery from creating his own specialized armour.[68]

Armoured regiments were re-equipped with flame-thrower tanks, upgunned Sherman and Churchill tanks, and with tank-dozers. Some ... tanks were fitted with widened 'Platypus' tracks to enable them to move over the soft fields of the Romagna. New armoured engineer equipment was also produced within the theatre for rapidly bridging ditches, canals and rivers. All these new equipments and devices needed specially trained crews to man them and new tactical techniques. In the rear areas, particularly around Lake Trasimene, intensive experimental work and training went on throughout the winter.[69]

As early as September 1944, armoured regiments had received some 105mm-gunned Shermans for close-support work,[70] which had been used in the September/October battles. These had been followed by 76mm Shermans and some 17-pounder Shermans, the redoubtable Fireflies. In the final campaign the 76mm Sherman was the standard tank deployed in Eighth Army's armoured regiments. Typically, an armoured regiment had thirty-seven 76mm Shermans, nine 17-pounder Shermans, six 105mm Shermans and eleven Stuarts for reconnaissance work.[71] John Skellorn noted that 16th/5th Lancers were first shown 76mm and 105mm Shermans on 20 September 1944, with the regiment eventually receiving six of the 105mm-equipped tanks and forty-six of the 76mm tanks (a figure that actually includes the Fireflies). Although welcome as providing a heavier punch, there was a downside: the new tanks had petrol engines 'which did not have the slogging power of the diesels';[72] the redundant Shermans had all been diesel-powered. He also noted that his squadron had two Fireflies but that only one crew had been able to practise using the 17-pounder gun as the other tank had a faulty firing pin – its crew later went into action 'without ... having experienced a round being fired'.[73]

Infantry divisions were taken out of the line to undertake concentrated training programmes and divisional battle schools were established. With McCreery's plan calling for a rapid thrust on a narrow front through the Argenta Gap with Kangaroo-borne infantry, the units selected for the operation underwent specialist training. Seventy-eighth Division, now returned to Eighth Army with XIII Corps but reallocated to V Corps, commanded by Charles Keightley, their old divisional commander, was selected for the Argenta operation. For this the Battleaxe Division would be reinforced heavily with 2 Armoured Brigade under command while 4th Hussars, already converted to Kangaroos, would train the chosen infantry battalion in APC operations. The unit selected to be carried into battle in Kangaroos was 2nd London Irish Rifles. Their alliance with 4th Hussars produced what became known in 78th Division as the 'Kangaroo Army'.[74] Infantry and armour trained together with each infantry division assigned an armoured brigade, thus creating balanced divisional groups. In 6th Armoured Division the armoured regiments of 26 Armoured Brigade were to form the core of battlegroups, each with an allied infantry motor battalion, a battery of 12th Regiment RHA, a self-propelled troop of 72nd Anti-Tank Regiment, a troop of 8 Field Squadron RE, a reinforced section of 165 Light Field Ambulance RAMC, a squadron of 1st Derbyshire Yeomanry and a half-squadron from 25 Armoured Engineer Brigade.[75] (However, the armoured units trained with the battalions of 1 Guards Brigade only to be switched at almost the last minute to going into battle with those of 61 Brigade. In the case of 17th/21st Lancers there was no opportunity at all to rehearse with 7th Rifle Brigade as the battlegroup was formed only on the morning of 20 April. It says much for the quality of their training that the units of the group worked so well together.[76])

Knowing that many water obstacles faced Eighth Army, and mindful of the difficulties created by such obstacles in the past, McCreery's new Chief Engineer, Brigadier B.T. Godfrey-Faussett, proposed that the existing assault engineer regiment be upgraded to a brigade. McCreery agreed and 25 Tank Brigade was reformed as 25 Armoured Assault Brigade, Royal Engineers, achieving a marriage of tanks and sappers. Within the new brigade were flame-throwing Churchills, known as Crocodiles, mine-destroying Flail tanks, bridging, or Ark, tanks and tank-dozers. Problems in obtaining equipment from the UK led to REME workshops in the Mediterranean theatre being called on to produce almost 200 specialized armoured vehicles to equip 25 Brigade, which included 51st Royal Tanks, operating Flail and Crocodile tanks, and 1st and 2nd Armoured Engineer Regiments, previously 1st Assault Regiment RAC/RE and 1st Armoured Divisional Engineers.[77] McCreery had his answer to Hobart's 'Funnies'.

The Gunners had also been busy working on their plan for BUCKLAND and 1,020 guns had been made available with 2,000,000 rounds of ammunition stockpiled. The Royal Artillery had also produced a further aid for the assaulting infantry with searchlight regiments, now redundant in their intended role, deploying to provide artificial moonlight to assist the troops at night-time. First used in 1944, this tactic had a further benefit: the searchlights' glare diminished the vision of opposing troops.[78] And

McCreery had his massive air support, including fighter-bombers and medium bombers to which were added heavy bombers of the USAAF based in Italy whose targets in Germany had been overrun by the Soviets.[79] On the other side, General Traugott Herr, commanding Tenth Army, unwittingly assisted McCreery and the bombers by drawing his main body into positions along the Santerno river while maintaining a forward line on the Senio. Herr intended this to place his main force out of range of Eighth Army's artillery but it meant that the Allied strategic bombers were able to pound the Santerno line unremittingly while the artillery bombarded the Senio line.[80] Herr's soldiers must have felt that he had done them no favours.

Cooperation with tactical aircraft was much improved through an increase in the number of Rover Control teams on the ground. These, the joint army/air teams providing direct links with the fighter-bombers of the aerial cab-ranks, were also given greater mobility with scout cars or tanks. Closer contact with brigade commanders and battalion COs permitted strikes on targets to be made almost as soon as these were requested. Each battlegroup would be able to call on a 'Rover' team while light aircraft, Taylorcraft Austers, which had been used by artillery observers (AOPs, or aerial observation posts) for some time, were yet another valuable asset.[81]

The German preoccupation with possible seaborne assaults was used to advantage to create an impression that Eighth Army was planning such an attack north of Venice. However, that area of Italy, both offshore and on land, was unsuitable for amphibious operations while most Allied landing craft had been withdrawn from the Mediterranean. But the Germans were not aware of these facts and, believing a landing to be a possibility, von Vietinghoff deployed 29th Panzer Division to meet it. Never having practised amphibious warfare the German army had no relevant doctrine and no knowledge of what was involved or required for such operations. Once again, this played to British advantage: not only did the deception plan remove 29th Panzer Division, placing it about 80 miles from where it would be needed, but it also disguised preparations for crossing Lake Comácchio.[82]

The Comácchio operation was to be executed by 56th Division with both 2 Commando and 9 Armoured Brigades under command; it will be remembered that, as well as four commandos, the former brigade included the Special Boat Service and the partisan Garibaldi Brigade. All were part of V Corps which was carrying out the main attack: while the Black Cats crossed Lake Comácchio, 8th Indian and 2nd New Zealand Divisions would cross the Senio and Santerno rivers and, from a bridgehead over the latter, 78th Division would cross to thrust rapidly to its right for Bastia and the bridge over the Reno, link with 56th Division and clear the Argenta corridor. With this achieved 6th Armoured Division would begin its advance, part of which would swing west to join up with Fifth Army. The point at which V Corps split in two would signal the time for HQ XIII Corps, now under John Harding, to assume command of the left wing. Eighth Army's direct push to Bologna on Highway 9 was to be undertaken by II Polish Corps, now under General Bohusz-Szyszko since Anders had been promoted to Commander-in-Chief of the Polish forces, and XIII Corps.[83] However, before Operation BUCKLAND began, McCreery had a major problem to resolve with the Poles.

This problem was not of McCreery's making and was one that would have taxed the persuasive skills of any Allied commander. Its roots lay in the Yalta Conference during which the intransigence of Stalin and the Soviets over Poland's future eastern frontier had held sway over the Western leaders. As a result Polish troops in Italy were feeling bitter. Sharing that bitterness and sense of having been betrayed, Anders threatened to withdraw the Polish Corps from Eighth Army. He even suggested to McCreery that his soldiers be made prisoners, but relented when McCreery asked how he might fill the gap left in Eighth Army's ranks by their departure. Then, to demonstrate his confidence in the Poles, McCreery placed 7 Armoured and 43 Gurkha Brigades under Polish command. When added to reinforcements already received, which had allowed the formation of a third brigade in both Carpathian and Kresowa Divisions, this brought the size of II Polish Corps to almost twice that at Cassino.[84]

As April began Eighth Army's deployment included V Corps on the right flank, with II Polish Corps astride Highway 9. Holding the line from left of the Poles to south of Imola was X Corps, while XIII Corps was positioned from south of Imola to Monte Grande. In Army Reserve were 6th Armoured Division and 2 Parachute Brigade, for both of which roles in the forthcoming offensive had been planned. However, although 6th Armoured Division would perform its intended tasks, 2 Parachute Brigade would not: the plan had been for the brigade to drop behind German lines but this operation was cancelled due to the strength of German anti-aircraft defences; thirty different plans had been drawn up for the brigade's deployment but all were cancelled.[85]

V Corps was composed of 56th (London) Division, now including 24 Guards Brigade in place of the disbanded 168 Brigade, 8th Indian Division, 78th Division, 2nd New Zealand Division and Cremona Group. Three brigades of armour, 2 and 9 Armoured (the latter with 755th (US) Tank Battalion under command) and 21 Tank, were also included in the corps' order of battle, as well as 2 Commando Brigade, each usually under command of one of the divisions. As we have seen II Polish Corps was strengthened by 7 Armoured and 43 Gurkha Brigades, as well as 2 Polish Armoured. X Corps included only two formations, the Jewish Brigade and Friuili Group, while XIII Corps included 10th Indian Division and Folgore

Group. Facing Eighth Army were the German Tenth Army's LXXVI Panzer and I Parachute Corps, each with four divisions on McCreery's front; I Parachute Corps also deployed 305th Division against II US Corps.[86]

Such was the situation on the front on Easter Day, 1 April 1945, as the first element of Eighth Army's plan got underway.

Notes

1. Nicholson, op. cit., p. 612.
2. Jackson, *The Mediterranean and Middle East,* vol. VI, pt III, p. 113.
3. Ibid.
4. Ibid., pp. 69–70; Clarke, *With Alex at War,* op. cit., pp. 182–3.
5. Carver, *Harding of Petherton,* op. cit., pp. 146–7.
6. Nicholson, op. cit., pp. 606–7 & 614–7; Jackson, op. cit., p. 116; Blaxland, op. cit., p. 231.
7. Doherty, *A Noble Crusade,* op. cit., p. 266.
8. Ibid.
9. Nicholson, op. cit., pp. 619–21; Jackson, op. cit., pp. 116–7; Blaxland, op. cit., p. 231.
10. Jackson, op. cit., pp. 119–24; Blaxland, op. cit., pp. 231–6.
11. Anders, op. cit., p. 235.
12. Ibid.
13. Jackson, op. cit., pp. 117–18; NA, Kew, WO170/617, war diary, 128 (Hants) Bde, Jul–Dec 1944.
14. Jackson, op. cit., pp. 117–18; Blaxland, op. cit., pp. 232–3; NA, Kew, WO170/525, war diary, 2 Armd Bde, 1944; WO170/620, war diary, 138 Bde, Dec 1944; WO170/634, war diary, 169 (Queen's) Bde, Dec 1944.
15. Kesselring, op. cit., p. 218.
16. Blaxland, op. cit., pp. 232–3.
17. Smyth, *The Story of the Victoria Cross,* op. cit., pp. 412–13; *London Gazette,* 8 Feb 1945.
18. Smyth, op. cit., p. 413; www.cwgc.org
19. Blaxland, op. cit., p. 233.
20. Ibid.
21. Ibid.
22. Nicholson, op. cit., pp. 622–33; Jackson, op. cit., pp. 121–2.
23. Blaxland, op. cit., p. 235; NA, Kew, WO170/536, war diary, 7 Armd Bde, 1944.
24. Blaxland, op. cit., p. 235.
25. Ibid., pp. 235–6; Nicholson, op. cit., pp. 635–40.
26. Nicholson, op. cit., p. 641.
27. Jackson, op. cit., pp. 126–30 & 144; Blaxland, op. cit., pp. 238–9; Nicholson, op. cit., p. 641; Kesselring, op. cit., p. 220.
28. Blaxland, op. cit., pp. 239–41; Nicholson, op. cit., pp. 645–51; NA, Kew, WO170/4422, war diary 9 Armd Bde, 1945; WO170/4626, war diary 12 L, 1945.
29. Nicholson, op. cit., pp. 646–51; Blaxland, op. cit., p. 241; Williams, op. cit., pp. 108–9; NA, Kew, WO170/4367, war diary HQ 56 Div G, Jan–Feb 1945; WO170/5060, war diary 2/6 Queen's, 1945.
30. Jackson, op. cit., p. 58.
31. Blaxland, op. cit., p. 241.

32. NA, Kew, WO170/4831, war diary 11 (HAC) RHA, 1945.
33. Doherty, *Ireland's Generals*, op. cit., pp. 86 & 158; Baynes, *The Forgotten Victor*, pp. 204–5.
34. Blaxland, op. cit., pp. 242–3; Jackson, op. cit., pp. 143–56; Hastings, *Armageddon*, pp. 328–32.
35. Kesselring, op. cit., pp. 219–21.
36. Ibid., p. 220.
37. Blaxland, op. cit., pp. 242–3.
38. Kesselring, op. cit., pp. 220–1; Blaxland, op. cit., pp. 245–6 & 251.
39. Blaxland, op. cit., p. 242; Nicholson, op. cit., pp. 659–60; Aris, op. cit., p. 250.
40. Jackson, op. cit., pp. 195–210; Blaxland, op. cit., pp. 247–8 & 274.
41. Beckman, *The Jewish Brigade*, pp. 13–14 & 43; Blaxland, op. cit., p. 248; Doherty, *A Noble Crusade*, op. cit., p. 274.
42. Beckman, op. cit., p. 46.
43. Kay, op. cit., pp. 190, 385–7 & 406; Blaxland, op. cit., pp. 246–7.
44. Jackson, op. cit., pp. 208 & 222; Joslen, op. cit., p. 409.
45. Kesselring, op. cit., p. 221.
46. Blaxland, op. cit., pp. 221–3.
47. NA, Kew, WO170/4466, war diary 38 (Ir) Bde, Aug–Dec 1945 – 'Morale' notes by Brig T.P.D. Scott.
48. Horsfall, op. cit., pp. 212–13.
49. Jackson, op. cit., pp. 29–31; Doherty, op. cit., p. 276; Blaxland, op. cit., p. 226.
50. Blaxland, op. cit., p. 222; Doherty, op. cit., p. 276; Bredin, interview with author, Feb 1989.
51. Blaxland, op. cit., p. 222; Doherty, op. cit., p. 276.
52. Strawson, *The Italian Campaign*, op. cit., pp. 183–4.
53. Nicholson, op. cit., p. 652.
54. NA, Kew, WO170/4456, war diary 26 Armd Bde, 1945.
55. Anon, *Finito*, p. 5.
56. Williams, op. cit., p. 63.
57. Ibid., pp. 63 & 120.
58. Doherty, *CTW*, op. cit., pp. 220–2; Harpur, *The Impossible Victory*, pp. 143–4.
59. Colonel J. Trousdell, notes to author.
60. R.J. Robinson DCM, notes to author.
61. NA, Kew, WO170/4395, war diary 56 Recce, Jan–Apr 1945; Doherty, *OTE*, op. cit., p. 227.
62. NA, Kew, WO170/4372, war diary 44 Recce, 1945; Doherty, op. cit., p. 233.
63. Jackson, op. cit., pp. 202–6; Bidwell and Graham, op. cit., pp. 388–91; Harpur, op. cit., pp. 144–6.
64. Bidwell and Graham, op. cit., p. 390.
65. Ibid.
66. NA, Kew, CAB106/441, 'The campaign in Lombardy 1945'.
67. Ibid.
68. Jackson, op. cit., pp. 199–200 & 402–7.
69. Jackson, *The Battle for Italy*, op. cit., pp. 293–4.
70. ffrench-Blake, 'Italian War Diary', p. 11.
71. NA, Kew, WO170/4456, war diary, 26 Armd Bde, op. cit.
72. Skellorn, 'What Did You Do in the War, Grandpa?', p. 19.
73. Ibid.
74. Ray, op. cit., pp. 191–2; Doherty, *CTW*, op. cit., pp. 232–6; Scott, *Account of the Service of the Irish Brigade*, op. cit.; Bredin, interview with author, Feb 1989.

75. NA, Kew, WO170/4456, war diary, 26 Armd Bde, op. cit.
76. ffrench-Blake, op. cit., p. 48.
77. Jackson, op. cit., p. 402; NA, Kew, WO170/4456, war diary, op. cit.
78. Doherty, *A Noble Crusade*, op. cit., p. 284; Routledge, *Anti-Aircraft Artillery*, p. 317.
79. Jackson, op. cit., pp. 262–3; Blaxland, op. cit., pp. 255–6.
80. Jackson, op. cit., p. 260.
81. ffrench-Blake, op. cit., p. 48.
82. Jackson, op. cit., p. 235; Blaxland, op. cit., p. 251.
83. Jackson, op. cit., p. 226n.
84. Blaxland, op. cit., pp. 247–8.
85. Jackson, op. cit., pp. 221–4; NA Kew, WO170/4410 war diary 2 Ind Para Bde.
86. Jackson, op. cit., pp. 221–4; Blaxland, op. cit., pp. 242–5.

Chapter Nine

Final Days

Once more unto the breach!

On the evening of Easter Day soldiers of 2 and 9 Commandos boarded Buffaloes to begin Operation ROAST. As they set off their Royal Marine comrades of 40 and 43 Commandos were about to launch a co-ordinated attack across the Reno, which flows close to the lake's south shore. Operation ROAST was intended to eliminate German positions on the spit separating Lake Comácchio from the Adriatic, thus denying the enemy observation of Eighth Army's right flank. There was also a subsidiary operation, FRY, to seize the lake islands.[1]

Moltke may have said that no plan survives the first contact but 2 and 9 Commandos found their plans going awry even sooner with more than a hint of farce, and considerable frustration, as the Buffaloes wallowed and floundered in slime but could not get underway. A change of plan was implemented with stormboats, plywood, flat-bottomed and 20-foot-long, quickly substituted. Following navigation lights laid out by M Squadron SBS, under Major Anders Lassen, the stormboats, each carrying twenty men, raced across the lake. Overhead, RAF aircraft circled to drown the noise of the boats' engines – someone seemed to have learned something from Keightley's plan to use DUKWs on Trasimene ten months earlier – and tanks drove up and down the lateral road behind the front line for the same reason. Not content with the decibel level, 43 Commando, at the base of the spit, played Wagner over loudspeakers. And, to crown it all, the gunners bombarded the German positions.[2]

In spite of that bombardment, the Germans were taken by surprise when the stormboats reached the shore at 3.00am on the 2nd and the commandos assaulted their objectives. It took two days of fighting to clear the spit but 'despite rifle, machine gun, mortar and artillery fire, and many mines, the whole spit was in our hands, along with nearly 1000 prisoners. Small enemy outposts in the lake were also wiped out.'[3]

That success was hard won and achieved through an operation that was a classic of its type and a credit to the planners as well as to the courage of the men of 2 Commando Brigade. The fighting included many small but vicious actions such as that in which Nos 1 and 2 Troops of 9 Commando took the German strongpoint codenamed 'Leviticus'. To reach this strongly-defended post the commandos had to cross 150 yards of open ground against heavy machine-gun fire. Not only did they achieve this, but did so to the strains of a piper playing, appropriately, *The Road to the Isles*. 'Leviticus' was captured as were almost a hundred Germans.[4]

The Royal Marines had secured the spit's east side with 43 Commando making good use of 4th Hussars' Kangaroos to tackle resistance in this strongly-fortified area. On Easter Tuesday both 2 and 43 Commandos resumed the advance, moving off at 2.00pm with armour support. After a thousand yards heavy artillery and mortar fire forced 2 Commando to go to ground but 43 Commando pressed on to take Scaglioca before advancing towards the Valetta canal. As C Troop, which was leading, approached the canal, they encountered heavy fire.[5] Among the casualties of the ensuing action was Corporal Thomas Peck Hunter whose reactions saved many of his comrades' lives and eliminated a German strongpoint. Tom Hunter, who was in charge of a Bren-gun section,

> offered himself as a target to save his Troop. Seizing the Bren gun he charged alone across 200 yards of open ground under most intense fire towards a group of houses where three Spandau machine guns were lodged. So determined was his charge that the enemy were demoralized and six of the gunners surrendered, the remainder fled. He cleared the house, changing magazines as he ran and continued to draw the enemy fire until most of the Troop had reached cover and he was killed, firing accurately to the last.[6]

Corporal Hunter was awarded a posthumous Victoria Cross. The commandos were later relieved by 24 Guards Brigade who secured their gains and made some offensive moves towards Porto Garibaldi. These latter would heighten the German anticipation of an amphibious operation in the Porto Garibaldi area as McCreery had secured the assistance of the Royal Navy with some LCTs and LCAs, as well as minesweepers, to simulate preparations for landings at Porto Corsini and Ancona. One effect of these feints was that a regiment of 29th Panzer Division was moved from the Venice area to be ready to meet a landing near Porto Garibaldi.[7]

While the commandos had been clearing the spit, M Squadron SBS and partisans had launched Operation FRY to take the islands in Lake Comácchio. This was achieved in two days. Led by Major Anders Lassen MC (and two Bars), a Dane, M Squadron had made a series of raids on the German-held shore. On the night of 8/9 April Lassen led a 'fighting reconnaissance' on Comácchio town. The raiders were held up by a German strongpoint which was engaged until the garrison surrendered.[8] When Lassen went forward to secure the prisoners a machine gun opened fire from across the causeway. Several men were wounded, including Lassen, and a battle developed in which M Squadron suffered further casualties. The situation was difficult and Lassen decided to withdraw but heavy enemy fire prevented recovery of the wounded. He ordered those who were fit enough to withdraw to do so but refused to allow his soldiers to evacuate him as 'he said it would impede the withdrawal and endanger their lives. But he had certainly achieved his object; three enemy positions were wiped out, six machine guns destroyed, eight of the enemy were killed, several more wounded and two prisoners were taken.'[9]

Lassen continued to provide covering fire for his men until he was killed but two of M Squadron's wounded escaped. A merchant seaman at the outbreak of war, Anders Lassen was awarded a posthumous Victoria Cross. According to the official history this award was as much for 'consistently brave leadership' as for his actions at Comácchio.[10]

With a brigade of 56th Division due to cross Lake Comácchio in Buffaloes, the lesson from 2 and 9 Commandos' experience was taken to heart and action was taken to ensure that this was not repeated. On the night of 5/6 April, 167 Brigade, led by 1st London Irish, crossed the Reno westwards from San Alberto to create a wedge between the Reno floodbank and the flooded area west of the lake, thereby securing a slime-free launching point for the Buffaloes. No opposition met the first troops to cross and two troops of Shermans from 10th Hussars were rafted across to support them, but the Germans later reacted with *Jägers* of 42nd Division firing on the intruders from pillboxes. Many casualties occurred amongst 167 Brigade's men with their accompanying sappers suffering most losses. But the Brigade made good their new positions, the wedge was in place and V Corps' right flank was secure with 167 Brigade along the Navigazione Canal.[11]

Montgomery might have described Eighth Army as now being 'tee'ed up' for Operation BUCKLAND but Richard McCreery was not given to such language and his order of the day declared simply that the enemy 'must not be allowed to use his Armies in Italy to form a garrison for a Southern German stronghold. ... We will destroy or capture the enemy south of the Po.'[12]

As he drafted that order McCreery knew that morale in Eighth Army was high. Its soldiers had a sense of purpose which was reflected in the number posted as deserters: the lowest since landing in Italy nineteen months earlier. His order of the day was also short and pithy with none of the rhetoric of Montgomery. McCreery knew his soldiers well, probably better than Montgomery had ever done, and had earlier compared his Army to 'an old steeplechaser, full of running, but rather careful'.[13] Knowing his

Army's strengths he intended using those to best advantage. In his order of the day, Field Marshal Alexander noted that the time had come for the armies in Italy to play their part in the final defeat of Germany but that there would be no walkover as a wounded beast could still be dangerous.[14]

Twenty years later, McCreery told Eighth Army veteran Brian Harpur that he considered four conditions essential to success in battle:

> One, you must have good intelligence ... in every sense of the word ... Two, you must have good organization – your troops must be well trained, well supplied, and well motivated. Three, you must always have up your sleeve an enormous element of surprise because this can fox the enemy, give you the initiative, save lives, and provide an unforeseen bonus which [it] is up to you to identify and exploit before it disappears. Four – you must never give the enemy any rest. Never let him rest. Always be doing something to which he has to re-act. If you don't then he'll be doing something to which you have to re-act and you have lost the initiative. No, never let him rest. And I mean that literally as well.[15]

Eighth Army's performance in the days that followed show just how sound was McCreery's handling of it through meeting all four conditions.

On 9 April, at 1.50pm, 825 B-17 Flying Fortresses and B-24 Liberators of the American Fifteenth Air Force began a ninety-minute bombardment during which they dropped 125,000 fragmentation bombs on the German artillery and reserve lines facing Eighth Army's assaulting formations. The bombing was aided by carefully devised navigational aids, including one of the last tasks performed by Eighth Army's 3.7-inch heavy AA guns which fired smoke shells to produce a bomb, or marker, line for the aircraft. Targets on the ground were 'completely drenched' while, at the same time, over 600 medium bombers attacked defensive positions and troop concentrations back towards the Santerno. On the morrow the heavy bombers would also strike along that river while the tactical air forces, the British Desert Air Force and the US XXII Air Support Command, some 720 machines in all, would attack command posts, gun and mortar positions and strongpoints right on the forward edge of the German line. Some idea of the ferocity of the attacks to which the Germans were being subjected can be gleaned from the fact that one tank might find as many as fifteen planes swooping on it. There was no aerial protection for the German troops, save for their anti-aircraft guns; the Luftwaffe had vanished from Italian skies.[16]

> The blows that knocked out the Germans in Italy began as slow, deliberate punches with heavy fists. Within two weeks the enemy

was staggering; the fists became wide-stretched hands, with fingers probing, then grasping vast numbers of Germans and all of Italy's north. After a campaign lasting only 23 days, the remnants of the foe surrendered; he had been destroyed south of the Po River.[17]

The punches of the airmen were followed by those of the artillery. As the last aircraft departed, 1,500 guns and mortars began a 42-minute bombardment. Previous experience led the Germans to expect that the end of this bombardment would mark the arrival of the first attackers. But the pattern had changed. As the roar of the guns died away, the fighter-bombers – *jabos** to the Germans – returned to strafe the riverbanks before moving on to the area behind the river. Then the guns and mortars opened fire again and when they finished back came the planes. This storm of bombs, rockets, shells and mortars persisted for five-and-a-half hours, during which the Germans suffered four 'false alarm' bombardments. Then, at 7.20pm, came false alarm number five. This time the *jabos* swooped on the riverbanks but climbed away without firing. Instead, Crocodile and Wasp† flame-throwers opened their jets to pour a flood of flame across the river. Although producing a spectacular display, this probably had little physical effect on the Germans, but was certainly a morale sapper. On the other hand, the attackers' morale was raised by the flame-throwers and after ten minutes of their work the leading soldiers of Eighth Army stepped forward to do battle in their last major operation.[18]

V Corps was assaulting with 8th Indian and 2nd New Zealand Divisions, separated by five miles of the Senio as it wraps itself around Lugo. Each division had four assaulting battalions. On the right, 8th Indian was led by 1st Argylls and 6/13th Frontier Force Rifles of 19 Brigade, with 1/5th Mahrattas and 3/15th Punjabis of 21 Brigade on the left. For the leading companies in the assault there was little difficulty in seizing their first objective, the forward floodbank, wreathed now in smoke, but the defenders, men of 362nd Division, began recovering their poise as the following companies came through. German soldiers left their dugouts to man weapons and fire on the attackers. In the divisional centre, near Fusignano, the Frontier Force and Mahrattas came up against very determined opposition, but from each battalion came forth a heroic soldier whose deeds enabled the advance to continue.[19]

The Frontier Force *jawans* had dropped their assault boats and waded into the Senio, which was but 15 feet wide and 4 deep at their crossing point, when they were met by intense machine-gun fire. Only three men from the left platoon reached the far bank in a state fit enough to continue

* From the German word for a fighter-bomber *jagdbomber*.
† The Wasp was based on the universal carrier, better known as the Bren-gun carrier, and was a recent innovation.

the battle, but one of them was Sepoy Ali Haidar, who was about to change the course of the battle. Covered by fire from his two comrades, Ali Haidar attacked a machine-gun post.

> Having hurled a grenade, he was immediately hit in the back by a shell splinter from a German grenade. He lurched onwards, captured the machine-gun and four wounded Germans, and at once assailed another post, from which multiple automatic fire was coming. He was felled by two further hits, on an arm and a leg, and yet managed to crawl forward, hurl grenade with his left hand and flop upon the post in a state of collapse, to receive the surrender of two unharmed and two badly wounded Germans.[20]

Another twenty-six Germans also surrendered. Ali Haidar's courage had permitted his battalion to continue the attack and, as darkness crept over the land, they cleared the Germans from the far floodbank. Against all the odds Sepoy Ali Haidar survived and was later able to receive the Victoria Cross that, so clearly, he had earned.[21]

The Mahrattas had also waded the Senio with Sepoy Namdeo Jadhao the only man of his group to reach the enemy bank unscathed. Once over, Namdeo Jadhao, a company runner, lifted one of the wounded and carried him back across the river and over the east floodbank. Occasionally soldiers perform such an act in order to get out of the firing line – which is one reason they are supposed to leave the wounded to the stretcher-bearers. But this was certainly not the case, and was always unlikely anyway with Indian soldiers whose code of honour and respect for comrades demanded that the wounded be helped and the bodies of the dead recovered. Namdeo Jadhao returned to the enemy bank and lifted another wounded man whom he carried back to safety. Surely this was valour enough? Not for this *jawan* who, once again, made the crossing to return single-handedly to the attack. Determined to wreak vengeance for his dead comrades he

> made a lone assault with a Tommy-gun, wiped out one post on the first bank, was wounded in the hand, and wiped out two more posts by hurling grenades. He then galvanized the remains of the company (whose commander had been wounded next to him in the initial crossing) by cheering them on [with the Mahratta war cry 'Shivaji Maharaj Ki Jai!'] from the top of the bank with mortar bombs falling fast around him.[22]

Not only did Namdeo Jadhao's actions save many lives but they also enabled 1/5th Mahrattas to secure the bridgehead. The battalion overcame all resistance in its area. Namdeo Jadhao was also recommended for the Victoria Cross which he survived to receive.*

Eighth Indian Division had pushed out a mile and a half beyond the Senio by dawn although fighting lasted all night at some points. Their sappers had also bridged the river at three places and Churchills of 21 Tank Brigade were able to join the infantry. With support from the Churchills, and from the tactical air forces, both 19 and 21 Brigades had reached the Santerno, almost 4 miles from the Senio, by daylight on the 11th. On that day, also, Lugo was liberated by 1st Jaipur Infantry, who were greeted by the town's mayor, complete with white flag and a bottle of wine. In readiness for crossing the Santerno, 17 Brigade now joined the leading brigades. And the Italian soldiers of Cremona Group had also been in action, crossing the Senio to advance through Fusignano towards Alfonsine.[23]

The New Zealanders had reached the Santerno after dark on the 10th, crossing the river next morning with 6 Brigade's 24th and 25th Battalions leading. Their bridgehead secured, 28th (Maori) Battalion, of 5 Brigade, then extended it on the right flank. The fourth of the attacking New Zealand battalions was 5 Brigade's 21st Battalion; all four had taken part in the five-mile advance from the Senio. En route they had eliminated three of 98th Division's battalions and pummelled severely the remaining three. Freyberg's men had also taken over 700 prisoners while sustaining fewer than 200 casualties, some of them from Allied bombs falling short at the Santerno.[24]

Crucial to the speed with which the New Zealanders had been able to move had been the work of the divisional engineers. Freyberg's CRE, Colonel Hanson, knowing that bridging was critical, had brought equipment as far forward as possible so that bridges might be built on site and rafted across. Another technique had been to assemble girders, launch them on a raft and continue building the bridge while pushing the raft across the river. With 40- to 50-foot-long bridges being assembled in times between thirty-five minutes and an hour, the New Zealand sappers had five tank bridges over the Senio by 6.30am on 10 April.[25] As a comparison, the Poles had no bridges while 8th Indian had but one.† There was one price to pay for the speed of the New Zealand advance: both flanks were exposed

* The awards illustrate vividly the character of the Indian Army and its religious composition with one VC to a Hindu and another to a Muslim. In Fifth Army two posthumous Medals of Honor were awarded in this final campaign to Pfc Sadao S. Munemori, a Nisei or Japanese-American, of 442nd (Nisei) Infantry on 5 April and Pfc J.D. Magrath, an Irish-American, of 85th Mountain Infantry on 14 April. The Allied armies in Italy were nothing if not multi-racial.
† Although Hanson had organized demonstrations of the New Zealanders' methods for Engineer officers of other formations, none adopted the techniques.

as 8th Indian had yet to come up on the right while the Poles were farther back on the left.[26]

On the Polish Corps' front the Senio crossing had been executed by 3rd Carpathian Division with three brigades – its own original pair plus 6 Lwow Brigade attached from Kresowa; the two recently formed brigades were assigned to a holding position astride Highway 9. Even before they moved off the Carpathians suffered casualties when an American heavy bomber dropped its bombs in their forming-up positions; one battalion suffered 160 casualties. Anders was watching the bombing with the Army Group commander and, when Clark apologized for the bombing of the Carpathians, commented wryly that soldiers do not like becoming casualties before battle is joined. The tragedy did not delay the Carpathians in moving off but they then ran into mines on their half-mile approach to the Senio, through an area from which they had not previously cleared the Germans.[27]

In spite of this, the Poles forced a crossing of the Senio with two brigades over by the following morning, the 10th. Their attack was aimed at an inter-corps boundary, between 98th Division of LXXVI Corps and 26th Panzer of I Parachute Corps. While General Graf von Schwerin, commanding LXXVI Corps, tried cobbling together a cohesive force from the remains of 98th and 362nd Divisions, the Parachute Corps commander adjusted his front to accept the brunt of the Polish attack. The stiff resistance offered by 26th Panzer meant that the Poles, having to fight for every yard, did not reach the Santerno until the night of the 11th, a day behind Freyberg's soldiers.[28]

On the morning of 11 April, as the New Zealanders crossed the Santerno, eighty Buffaloes carried two battalions of 169 Queen's Brigade across Lake Comácchio. The Buffaloes, crewed by men of 27th Lancers and the US 755th Tank Battalion, were transporting 2/5th and 2/6th Queen's towards the villages of Menata and Longastrino at the edge of the inundated area west of the lake. There had been delays launching the Buffaloes but they were able to lay down a smokescreen, fired from guns mounted in the vehicles, which hid them completely as they approached firm ground in full daylight. As the massive amphibians hit the rising ground below the water and seemed to mount higher as they emerged from the mud and floodwater, very few shots were fired at them. From each leading Buffalo emerged a platoon of Queensmen while Browning machine guns gave covering fire from the turrets of the ponderous vehicles. (The historian of 2/7th Queen's described the Buffaloes as 'large, tracked and very lightly armoured with a high performance in deep water and over normal country though deep mud brought them to a standstill' and armed only with a Browning machine gun.)[29]

The Buffaloes had given 169 Brigade that most coveted of military advantages – surprise. So confident had been the soldiers of 42nd Jäger Division that the flooded area was impassable, they were taken completely unawares by the arrival of British troops in such a manner, and from an unexpected direction. This was not something that they had thought likely with the British but they had reckoned without McCreery's ingenuity. Taken off balance, the *Jägers* made little resistance and about 300 were taken prisoner while 169 Brigade suffered very few casualties. The task of exploiting their gains was given to 40 Commando who advanced towards a bridge north of Menata by wading along a ditch; there was no shortage of water in this area. But the Germans were beginning to recover and although they took the bridge the Marines did so with considerable losses.[30]

Similar stiff opposition met 17 Brigade of 8th Indian Division attacking across the Santerno late on 11 April. It was with much difficulty, and many losses, that 1/5th Gurkhas and 1/12th Frontier Force established footholds. The brigade's other battalion, 1st Royal Fusiliers, crossed to link both lodgements and it was on the Fusiliers that the Germans fell in full fury next morning. Tanks and infantry pressed hard against the Fusiliers' positions and the situation looked very dangerous until, at 11.30am, Churchills of 21 Tank Brigade arrived to add their punch. The Churchills, which had crossed by an Ark bridge, swung the battle for the Fusiliers who were able to move on to take Mondaniga; it would be inaccurate to say that they liberated the village since all that was left was a pile of rubble, Allied bombers having flattened it.[31]

By dusk on the 12th the New Zealanders were in the outskirts of Massa Lombarda. They had fought hard throughout the day and were now only 14 miles south of Argenta. Their advance, on an axis parallel to Highway 9, also threatened Bologna. Freyberg's soldiers had succeeded in gaining ground from which an outflanking attack might be made on Argenta while, at the same time, drawing attention away from that possibility through the apparent threat to Bologna. And that threat might be converted into reality should the advance on Argenta fail. Harding, commanding XIII Corps, had already been told that 2nd New Zealand Division might be transferred to his command, to operate in concert with 10th Indian. But now it was time for 78th Division to pass through the bridgeheads created by the assaulting divisions.[32]

Keightley intended 78th Division's attack to be coordinated with a further attack by 56th Division thereby producing a pincer movement. The former would attack northwards towards Bastia to take the bridge over the Reno, while the latter would attack westwards. In their advance 78th Division's units were to use the 'line of fewest water obstacles' while trying to seize important canal crossings: a captured bridge might save a day at least.

202

Eleven Brigade was to hold a firm line while 36 and the Irish Brigades linked up with their supporting armour and other arms in 'wedding' areas before striking out. To the Irish Brigade fell the critical task of breaking out and exploiting for which role the Brigade was reinforced almost to the size of an armoured division. Brigadier Pat Scott's command deployed three elements: 'breakout force' included two battlegroups, each based on a battalion of either Inniskilling or Irish Fusiliers with a squadron of Bays, a machine-gun platoon of 1st Kensingtons, a sapper recce party and either a scissors bridge, for the Irish Fusiliers' group, or a Crocodile squadron of 51st Royal Tanks for the Inniskillings; 'mobile force', the Kangaroo Army, under command of HQ 2 Armoured Brigade, with 9th Lancers, 4th Hussars, who 'owned' the Kangaroos, an SPG troop, a sapper assault troop and 2nd London Irish; and 'reserve force' which could be called on for special roles and which included another squadron of Bays, an anti-tank battery, a troop of SP anti-tank guns, an armoured sapper troop, a Kensingtons' mortar platoon, a sapper field company and a field ambulance. Immediate artillery support for the breakout force was provided by 17th Field Regiment, the self-styled Royal Hibernian Artillery,* and 11th (HAC) Regiment RHA. It was an impressive command for a brigadier.[33]

The Kangaroo Army deployed over 100 main tracked vehicles from 9th Lancers and 4th Hussars. Each London Irish company travelled in eight Priest Kangaroos,† while Battalion HQ had a further eight, two for reserve ammunition and two for medical purposes. Each company had ammunition and food for forty-eight hours of independent operations. Experience had taught the division the need for speed with 'no halts at night-fall, for instance, for we had learnt in 1944 that the enemy was often able to re-establish a line or a rearguard position during the night because of our failure to follow up with tanks or infantry during the dark hours'.[34] Thus would the Kangaroo Army ensure that McCreery's condition that the enemy be allowed no rest was met.

Congested tracks and bridges delayed the Irish Brigade's H-Hour until 6.30am on 13 April, although 36 Brigade had already struck out on the left towards San Patrizio and Conselice to create manoeuvre room and disturb the enemy's equilibrium. Such disturbance had been created but, as the advance progressed, enemy resistance stiffened with 'slow and stubborn fighting' between the Santerno and the canal: the axis of advance ran through a triangle whose apex was formed by the meeting of canal and river, just before Bastia. German strong points were many and, as the front contracted, became more difficult to overcome. Fighting was especially hard for both Inniskilling and Irish Fusiliers in the villages of San

---

* So called because the regiment normally formed part of the Irish Brigade group.
† Converted from Priest SPGs.

Bernadino and Giovecca before the battalions were ordered to consolidate short of Cavamento.

The left flank of this main advance was now exposed, for there was a gap between them and the Royal West Kents, in front of Conselice, but this was not the only reason for halting the [Irish] Fusiliers and the Inniskillings; the thrust for Bastia was to be made by the composite Kangaroo Force.[35]

The fusilier battalions had cleared the way, allowing the Kangaroo Army to move off at noon against opposition that was, initially, light and ill organized. Some *Panzerfausten* parties did make nuisances of themselves and one tank was knocked out by an AA gun, but the Germans seemed to have been shaken. Their normal cohesive defence was missing but, after all, they were seeing the British doing something out of the ordinary and lacked an immediate answer.

The objective of the mobile force was to take the crossings on the Conselice canal and then, if possible, exploit to the Reno. As the leading elements neared the canal the flanking rivers opened out and H Company with C Squadron 9th Lancers was able to come up on the left of G Company. Some resistance ... in ... la Frascata ... was by-passed. However, just as the leading tanks arrived at the Conselice canal the bridge was destroyed. H Company had also by-passed la Frascata and, quickly de-bussing on the canal banks, forced a crossing over what was left of the road and rail bridge. For this they had the support of their tanks and got into the houses on the far bank so rapidly that they rounded up most of the defenders.[36]

As G Company cleared the area up to the canal bank, E advanced to clear la Frascata and assist H Company to hold and expand the bridgehead. By 6.30pm eighty prisoners had been taken and some ten Germans killed by these three companies. The bridgehead was secured quickly and sappers began building a new bridge that would be ready by morning. Meanwhile the two fusilier battalions were positioned at Giovecca and west of the Fossatone protecting the divisional flank.[37]

As the other arm of Keightley's pincer, 56th Division had also been in action. Their plan had involved 24 Guards Brigade seizing Argenta, their right flank being protected by 2 Parachute Brigade, which would be dropped around Bando. The morning of Friday, 13 April saw 1st Buffs, who had replaced 5th Grenadiers in 24 Guards Brigade, ready to move off in their Buffaloes, their padre, the Reverend G. Tyson accompanying them. The Buffs were to seize the banks of the Fossa Marina, two miles in front of 169 Queen's Brigade's foremost positions, while 9 Commando, also waterborne, came in from their left and the paras landed about a mile away. This plan came unstuck, at least partially, the night before as the paras arrived to board their aircraft. Reports that elements of 26th Panzer Division had been moved to the Fossa Marina had been confirmed by air reconnaissance which also indicated increased local AA defences. With Fifth Army's operation beginning, the tactical air forces could not divert enough aircraft to deal with these problems and McCreery cancelled the airborne assault. This was bad enough but it was then discovered that 9 Commando's route was blocked by a high bank with no suitable diversion available. Only the Buffs would attack.[38]

The artillery support provided proved insufficient, a rare occurrence in Eighth Army, and the Buffs were hit hard with all four of C Company's Buffaloes being struck by enemy tanks.

No opposition was met until the leading LVT was less than 100 yds from the landing point, when it became evident that the enemy was prepared, and determined, to contest the landing. What had appeared to be a house revealed itself as a MkIV [tank], opening up on the leading LVT at point-blank range, and at the same time the remaining [vehicles] were engaged by at least two more [tanks] on the flank. All LVTs were hit, and, with one exception, all ramps jammed, men coming down under [heavy] enfilade fire from MGs sited on the Left and Right as they tried to leave the damaged vehicles.[39]

Thirty-five of those who got ashore were hit as they crossed the crest of the bank at the water's edge. The company had to reorganize as a platoon although its OC, Major W.S. Riley, continued with the planned attack before being told to abandon his efforts and consolidate. Later the Germans offered medical assistance to some of the badly wounded and Riley, with no more than twenty men left, decided to withdraw after dark. Another thirteen soldiers, with two American crewmen and a prisoner, reached their own lines that night.[40]

The Buffs' other attacking company also met enemy fire although this was less effective than that directed at C Company and Sergeant Whitbread's No. 3 Platoon captured a canal bridge, while No. 2 Platoon, under Lieutenant Aylett, cleared houses to the flank and made nine Germans prisoners. Since the American crewmen of the Buffaloes had been given permission to decide where to land, the third company debarked in safer territory, although it still met opposition, and was unable to assist the others. This company, however, went on to capture a farm and take prisoner about 100 Germans and Turcoman SS. A junction was made with the surviving forward company after dawn on the 14th but Whitbread's men at the bridge had to wait until that evening when 2nd Coldstream, with 10th Hussar tanks, relieved them. Whitbread's platoon had also taken thirty-four prisoners. Sergeant Whitbread had been one of the many AA gunners converted to infantry and was obviously a very competent soldier who had taken to his new discipline with enthusiasm.[41]

With resistance hardening and reconnaissance reports showing that 29th Panzer Grenadier Division was coming down from north of the Po, an attempt to cross the Fossa Marina was made by 9 Commando on the night of 14/15 April. The attack was beaten off and it seemed that no approach to Argenta from the north was possible. Two brigades of 56th Division, 167 and 169, were converging on Bastia, some five miles south-east of Argenta and, on the 14th, 2/5th Queen's were at Filo while, to their left, 9th Royal Fusiliers passed through a large minefield.[42]

Thus far in this offensive, Richard McCreery had demonstrated a handling of Eighth Army that was much superior to that shown by his immediate predecessor or Montgomery. Practical application of his four conditions for success had been demonstrated throughout the planning and execution of the offensive. Intelligence, in every sense as he so aptly put it, had been shown at the planning stage; organization was excellent while morale was at a new high (Brian Harpur considered that McCreery's revitalization of the Army, and of the Italian campaign, 'was the most unlikely miracle in military history since David slew Goliath'[43]); surprise had been achieved through the deception plan and by knocking the enemy off-balance through the use of the Buffaloes on Lake Comácchio and the floodlands. Now the enemy was being allowed no rest.

The Kangaroo Army's advance towards the Reno resumed on the 14th. One of the two columns had to swing right near Lavezzola to avoid minefields, but the Germans had been thoughtful enough to leave mine-warning signs in place. They had not had time to remove these, such was the haste of their departure, and those signs drew the sting from the heavy crop of mines in the area and booby traps in houses. Destroying the minefields kept the Sherman Crabs busy with their heavy flails.[44]

As the flail tanks continued their task the Kangaroos drove on with the first elements reaching the Reno at 9.40am to find road and rail bridges demolished. However, the riflemen crossed dryshod by using the rubble. Two platoons established a bridgehead but were counter-attacked sharply and overrun with most being captured after a fierce fight. The Reno's high floodbanks and the absence of a bridge meant that the tanks could give no help. A reconnaissance was made for an assault crossing but it was decided to maintain positions on the near bank for the night. Subsequently the battalion was told to hold those positions for the next two days.

This was a setback but Keightley was resolved to keep V Corps' operation moving. Irish Fusilier patrols cleared the marshland up to the Sillaro river on the 15th, a task from which they were relieved by 36 Brigade that evening. Bridging the Reno began as 56th Division moved across the front of the Irish Brigade towards Bastia and Argenta and the Brigade was put on four hours' notice to resume its advance next morning.[45]

The New Zealanders had already crossed the Sillaro, seven miles beyond the Santerno, on the night of 13/14 April with 24th Battalion in the lead. Their speedy advance continued while the Poles had taken Imola and drawn level with the New Zealanders who were making for Budrio, about ten miles from Bologna, on an axis diverging from that of the advance to Argenta. As a result, McCreery passed 2nd New Zealand Division to XIII Corps which was now between II Polish Corps and V Corps; this transfer took effect from 6.00pm on 14 April. Harding then moved 10th Indian Division into reserve behind the New Zealanders while the mountain sector passed to X Corps. This was also the day on which Fifth Army began its attack, Operation CRAFTSMAN, and already it was making good progress with 1st Armored Division, 10th Mountain Division and the Brazilian Expeditionary Force leading the way. Clark's 15th Army Group was punching with both fists and the Germans had now lost three important river lines in five days.[46]

With his original plan to close the Argenta Gap with a north–south pincer move foiled, Charles Keightley decided to send 11 Brigade, of 78th Division, across the Reno on a Bailey bridge some three miles east of Bastia where Cremona Group was established firmly. The Brigade began advancing before dawn on 15 April as 56th Division continued advancing on Bastia with 167 and 169 Brigades leading. Having all but wiped out 42nd Jäger Division, the most serious obstacles facing them were natural rather than the work of their foes. Thus when X Company 9th Royal Fusiliers attacked the remains of a factory they found themselves in a 'sticky situation'. Usually this is typically British understatement for 'we're in serious trouble' but on this occasion it was literally a sticky situation: the factory had produced treacle and much of its product was flowing from the building thanks to the work of the bombers. There was no opposition but the attack slowed down of itself. Troops were wading through a black, sticky substance which, on closer inspection, proved to be treacle and one warrant officer almost drowned when he fell into a treacle-filled shellhole. A Sherman crew were enjoying the WO's plight until they realized that their tank had become mired in treacle: 'it disappeared into a 1,000-lb bomb crater filled to the brim.' Fortunately the Germans had abandoned Bastia or this situation might have become doubly sticky.[47]

The GOCs of 56th and 78th Divisions had agreed that the main breach of the enemy line should be made across the Fossa Marina north-east of Argenta. This had to be done at speed if the line of retreat of the main German body was to be cut; already a regiment from 29th Panzer Grenadier Division was deployed in the fortified line of the Fossa. Both generals, Whitfield of 56th and Arbuthnott of 78th, accepted that there

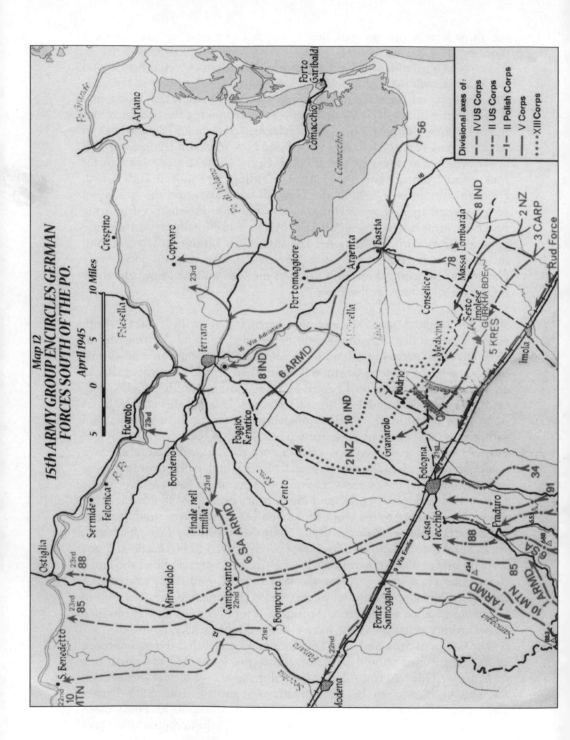

Map 12
**15th ARMY GROUP ENCIRCLES GERMAN
FORCES SOUTH OF THE PO.**
April 1945

Divisional axes of:
IV US Corps
II US Corps
-I- II Polish Corps
V Corps
XIII Corps

was no time to wait for a heavy bomber attack and so 11 Brigade passed through 169 Brigade before daylight on 16 April. The leading battalions, 1st East Surreys and 5th Northamptons, advanced over five miles of flat, but wet and mined, ground. Flails from 51st Royal Tanks beat paths for Shermans of the Bays to support the attacking infantry who also met resistance from pockets of German soldiers. These received the attention of fighter-bombers, called down from the cab rank, before being assaulted by infantry. It was a slow advance but nightfall saw the Northamptons holding the cemetery on the outskirts of Argenta with the Surreys still short of the Fossa. However, the latter moved forward again after dark to gain a covering position through which passed 2nd Lancashire Fusiliers.[48]

In spite of having their CO wounded and losing contact with their Flails, the Lancashires moved on under cover of a hastily-arranged bombardment of the Fossa which they then scaled 'in haste and disorder' before crossing the chest-deep barrier to attack the defenders with bayonets and grenades. The battle for mastery of the Fossa lasted two hours before the Lancashire Fusiliers had evicted the enemy. Heavy shellfire was then unleashed on them and they faced three counter-attacks. Not only did the Fusiliers beat off those counter-attacks and withstand the shelling but they also managed to advance as far as a farm, some 200 yards from the Fossa. Three Shermans from the Bays had crossed by an Ark bridge, launched under shell-fire, and arrived to support them. As the Lancashire Fusiliers consolidated they held nearly forty enemy prisoners but many more Germans lay dead on and between the banks of the Fossa Marina; the British bombardment had hit them during a handover.[49]

The Ark bridge was destroyed by enemy shelling which also knocked out two Shermans but Arbuthnott was determined that the Lancashire Fusiliers' bridgehead, won with such élan, would not be lost and assigned the Irish Brigade the task of enlarging it. On the 17th Brigadier Scott sent his two fusilier battalions out to extend the flanks which they did against stiff resistance. The Inniskillings captured objectives beyond Argenta and across the railway, while the Irish Fusiliers pushed almost as far as the Scolo Cantenacci. Meanwhile 2 Commando Brigade advanced along floodbanks through inundated ground north-west of Argenta which was cleared by that evening. The Northamptons had joined in the final battle with the support of both gun and flame-thrower Churchills.[50]

Needless to say, the Germans launched counter-attacks and fighting lasted throughout the night. One counter-attack, of about company strength with the support of tanks, was beaten back by the new defenders of Argenta into the arms of 2nd Inniskillings.[51] But Argenta had been destroyed, its buildings reduced to rubble and its people to terror. Many citizens lay dead on the streets, their bodies a horrible testimony to what war had cost the ordinary people of Italy. Was one British soldier thinking of this grim sight when he made an announcement over the loudspeakers at

Argenta's railway station, scene of much hard fighting? In words typical of the black humour of front-line soldiers he proclaimed that 'The next train will be calling at Oxshott, Bagshot, Bloodshot and all the other bloody stations down the line.'[52]

Satisfied that the enlarged bridgehead was secure, Arbuthnott ordered 36 Brigade to push out northwards that night and Boccaleone, less than three miles away, was taken by 6th Royal West Kents as day broke while 8th Argylls, supported by tanks, artillery and aircraft, advanced another two miles to capture Consándolo.[53] Aircraft also supported the Kangaroo Army, now moving ahead to the right of 36 Brigade.

> This was an unforgettable move. Through the orchards north of Argenta, in the narrow gap between the Lake and Canal, moved a mass of armour, all passing over one bridge that had been constructed over the main water obstacle. Wrecked vehicles, equipment and enemy dead strewed the route, while machine-gun fire ... crackled away on the left flank.[54]

As the Kangaroo Army surged ahead they took a haul including two bridges over the Fossa Benvignante, four tanks, twenty artillery pieces from 88mm to 150mm and 455 prisoners. Theirs was a

> great achievement, far from lightly won, gained under the command of two officers who had fought the Germans in 1940 and had suffered wound and won decoration at regular intervals ever since, Price of the 9th Lancers and 'Bala' Bredin of the London Irish Rifles.[55]

This was the same Bala Bredin who had commanded 6th Inniskillings at Cassino and who had tried to carry on even when wounded in both legs. When finally he was again fit to rejoin a battalion he had taken command of 2nd London Irish.

Good progress was also being made by 56th Division to the right with 2/5th Queen's and Churchills of 12th Royal Tanks capturing intact a bridge over the Fossa Benvignante. That Crocodiles were spewing flame across the Fossa may have persuaded the Germans to depart without demolishing the bridge. Elsewhere, 1st Scots Guards had crossed the Fossa Marina with 2nd Coldstream exploiting from their bridgehead. However, a minefield put paid to a plan to rush and capture another bridge over the Fossa Benvignante.[56]

The night that followed was like a bonfire night with flames lighting the sky as houses, vehicles and store dumps blazed around the Fossa Benvignante. Pockets of resistance were still being dealt with but there was forward movement too, with 5th Buffs of 36 Brigade passing through the Argylls at Consándolo to advance to San Nicolo, ten miles beyond Argenta and a similar distance from Ferrara. McCreery was preparing to unleash his reserve, 6th Armoured Division, on the following morning, the 19th. To secure that division's jumping-off area, Pat Scott of the Irish Brigade was to coordinate an operation involving 2nd Inniskillings, 6th West Kents and 2 Commando Brigade. That operation was successful with a German position that had threatened 78th Division's rear areas as well as 6th Armoured's advance, being eliminated by dawn. The road was clear for 6th Armoured Division; the Argenta Gap had been cracked open.[57]

Such was the pace of the overall advance that congestion was building up on the main supply routes. Bringing forward the bridging equipment so necessary to maintain the advance in a land cut across by canals, rivers and streams was becoming more difficult. If the speed of the advance was to be maintained then armour and infantry had to be able to cross the wider canals as quickly as possible.

No one realised this more than did the Royal Engineers, and they worked heroically to bring the equipment up despite the over-crowded and dust-laden roads. Dust, was there ever such! In many respects it was worse than sand. Nothing was safe against it – the troops ate dust-covered food and drank water that was heavily laced with the stuff.[58]

East of Bologna, Freyberg's New Zealanders were still advancing, crossing one water obstacle after another, and drawing numbers of enemy troops, from parachute battalions and 278th Division, against them. After the Poles liberated Imola and crossed the Sillaro on the night of 15/16 April, 43 Gurkha Brigade was transferred from Polish to New Zealand command and it was the Nepalese soldiers, carried in Kangaroos manned by 14th/20th King's Hussars and supported by 2nd Royal Tanks, who took Medicina on the night of the 16th/17th. Two nights later crossings of the Gaiana river were made by XIII and II Polish Corps after the Germans had beaten off an earlier effort. In the successful crossing 10th Indian Division formed XIII Corps' right flank.[59] 'Great slaughter was inflicted on the men of 4th [Parachute], and there were signs that even their morale was beginning to wither, most of all under the flame cast upon them by Crocodiles and Wasps.'[60]

Early on 20 April the New Zealanders were in Búdrio whence they crossed the Idice river, dubbed the Genghis Khan Line by the Germans. The Idice was formidable, with high banks, and troops had been rushed to man the line which they did with fervour, although some were caught resting, with their boots off – a great relief for an infantryman – when called to action. When 1/2nd Punjabis of 20 Indian Brigade attacked on the New Zealanders' right they found the Germans ready for them. Two platoons were ambushed beyond the river near Mezzolara and a night of furious fighting began. The Indians won but the men of those leading platoons had almost all perished and were found 'interlocked with staunch opponents of the 278th Division'.[61]

On the evening of 20 April, von Vietinghoff had sought Hitler's permission to abandon the now untenable Bologna. Although the Führer refused permission, von Vietinghoff began evacuation anyway and the following morning the first Allied soldiers, men of 3rd Carpathian Division, entered the city, followed two hours later by 34th (US) Division and the Friuli Group, of X Corps.[62] As they advanced on Bologna the Poles had met stiff resistance from paras, especially on the Gaiana river where

> for the third time in the Italian campaign they encountered the 1st Parachute Rifle Division, the same one that had defended Cassino. An unrelenting and merciless night followed, but the enemy was at length defeated and forced to withdraw during the night of April 20, pursued by our infantry and tanks.[63]

'With great kindness,' Anders subsequently wrote, Clark indicated that he would be very glad if II Polish Corps were to take Bologna later. This was a 'thank you' from the American for the efforts and sacrifice of the Poles as an army in exile and some little consolation for the fact that Poland would have no V-Day. Clark took the salute at a parade of American, British and Polish soldiers in Bologna on 21 April while, two days later, McCreery issued a special order of the day to II Polish Corps in which he outlined their recent achievements, concluding:

> You have shown a splendid fighting spirit, endurance and skill in this great battle. I send my warmest congratulations and admiration to all ranks, and I wish you all the best of luck as you continue the march with Eighth Army until the enemy's final collapse in Italy is achieved.[64]

McCreery had transferred 6th Armoured Division from Army Reserve to Keightley's V Corps at noon on 18 April, placing it once again under the man who had first taken it to war in 1942. The present GOC, Major General Nap Murray, had orders which were clear and simple: to pass through 78th Division's left flank, swinging north-eastwards, advance to Bondeno, with the divisional left flank along the Reno, and link up with Fifth Army. With that junction made, the destruction of the remains of Tenth and Fourteenth Armies, 'caught in the noose of Bologna's defences', would be complete.[65]

On the afternoon of the 19th, the bulk of Murray's armour and infantry moved off, passing through the Battleaxe Division and with 8th

Indian Division providing left-flank protection. Meanwhile 78th and 56th Divisions were to continue attacking towards Ferrara and the Po crossings north of the city. Sixth Armoured Division deployed its armoured reconnaissance regiment, 1st Derbyshire Yeomanry, 26 Armoured Brigade of three regiments – 16th/5th Lancers, 17th/21st Lancers and 2nd Lothians and Border Horse – as well as two infantry brigades, 24 Guards and 61 Green Jackets.[66] The breakout from the Argenta Gap – the 'gap', in the ruins of Argenta, was 'literally only a few yards wide'[67] – provided a rare opportunity for an armoured division to perform its role and the regiments rode to battle with enthusiasm.

Along the first water obstacle, the Po morto di Primaro, elements of 26th Panzer Division were determined to curb that enthusiasm. At San Nicolo the Lothians/2nd Rifle Brigade group met stout opposition as did the 16th/5th Lancers/1st KRRC group at Traghetto. The setback was but temporary: the King's Royal Rifles crossed the river that night, established a bridgehead and were joined by 16th/5th Lancers in the morning, the Shermans using a Bailey bridge. While the riflemen remained to secure the bridgehead the lancers pushed out to the right, over ideal land for anti-tank operations, and, with 17th/21st Lancers on the left, advanced some four miles beyond Traghetto. As the two regiments pushed ahead, 17th/21st had the advantage of better going, closer to the Reno and, at the end of the day, had drawn well ahead of 16th/5th who had encountered many obstacles with ditches and thickets imposing caution on the tanks as they hid many *Panzerfausten* parties and even anti-tank guns.[68] Five tanks were knocked out by enemy action. Val ffrench-Blake, commanding the 17th/21st Group, noted that the 'Air OP plane was ahead of us, and spotted a tank which was destroyed by the "cab-rank" of Rover David – a specially trained Mustang squadron'.[69]

The enemy action that delayed 16th/5th Lancers was not to be allowed to slow the advance. Richard McCreery would ensure that there would be no repeat of the Gothic Line battles when the armour had been bogged down. Keightley observed admiringly that the army commander was usually closer to the battle than he was himself; and from McCreery 'pungent and pertinent criticism descended, based on his assessments of the grouping demanded by the terrain'.[70] The Guards were ordered through 16th/5th while, at 4.00am on 21 April, 17th/21st resumed their advance with 7th Rifle Brigade completing the battlegroup. Lancers and Green Jackets had advanced another four miles by daylight to enter Segni where some stiff opposition was encountered. German troops were dug in along the Fossa Cembalina where it meets the Reno but were not allowed to slow the advance. Air support was called for and fighter-bombers dived on enemy tanks, putting them to flight and allowing the battlegroup to make an attack that permitted sappers to bridge the Fossa with an Ark.[71]

With the position at Segni consolidated by 4.00pm, and mindful of McCreery's axiom that the enemy should be allowed no rest, 17th/21st Lancers moved off again. As they advanced they fired into buildings prompting the surrender of many Germans.[72] Ninety minutes after moving off they had seized the bridge near Gallo; Highway 64, the main Bologna–Ferrara road was cut.

> Push on with two squadrons and your infantry to Póggio Renatico (M0178). This is the chance of a lifetime. Leave one squadron on the bridge at Gallo and hold it at all costs until relieved.[73]

That was the message from 26 Armoured Brigade HQ and it was, indeed, a cavalryman's idea of heaven. For almost the first time in the campaign they could display cavalry élan. The Brigade war diary notes that the Regiment 'tore into Póggio Renatico down the main road with C Squadron leading and firing liberally as they went'.*[74] Many enemy guns and vehicles were knocked out en route. Although for the last 2,000 yards the Shermans were under fire from 88s there were no hits (these were flak gunners unused to firing at ground targets[75]) and by nightfall the battlegroup was four miles from Gallo at Póggio Renatico from where they blocked every exit, cutting the only alternative road from Bologna to Ferrara. Since moving off the 17th/21st Lancers battlegroup had advanced a spectacular 11 miles.[76]

Haystacks blazing 'particularly well' added a surreal air to a situation in which disparate groups of Germans, some AA gunners, some service and support personnel, either tried to surrender or fought with little coordination. The most determined were given the attentions of the Rifle Brigade. Lieutenant Colonel Val ffrench-Blake, CO of 17th/21st Lancers, and later their historian, wrote that

> At Corps and Army headquarters, the victory was now assured, but in the dark, under the walls of Póggio Renatico the Regiment felt very insecure. There had been heavy expenditure of ammunition on a large number of targets and possible enemy positions during the advance, petrol was down to below twenty-five miles, and there was no prospect of replenishment until the route was cleared of the enemy.[77]

Nap Murray's HQ was concerned about the situation of ffrench-Blake's regiment, a concern heightened when a company of 1st Welch Regiment, having crossed the Fossa Cembalina, was forced to withdraw by enemy

---

* The normal practice was to advance parallel to the road but not on it since the Germans would probably have mined it.

infantry and armour, the latter apparently including Tiger tanks. But Murray's concerns were later eased when the Welch made a further, successful, assault across the Fossa Cembalina at dusk. This time the attack was aided by an entire German platoon deserting their posts. The Welch bridgehead was then enlarged by 3rd Grenadier Guards and, at dawn, the Lothians moved forward in a reckless advance to Bondeno, during which they lost eleven tanks. However, they reached Bondeno in the afternoon where two of their Shermans crossed the bridge over the Panaro. The Shermans were followed by two German tanks and were almost immediately cut off when a huge explosion toppled the bridge into the river.[78]

While ffrench-Blake's battlegroup mopped up at Póggio Renatico, where they captured an 88mm flak battery – the gunners who had engaged them unsuccessfully on their run in – and took 200 prisoners, their fellow lancers of 16th/5th with their Green Jackets passed on the flank en route to the second key objective along the Panaro, Finale Emilia, which they reached early on St George's Day. Having taken Bondeno, the Lothians battlegroup then struck northward towards the Po and, while 17th/21st Lancers and 7th Rifle Brigade were taking San Agostino, the 16th/5th battlegroup was making contact with II US Corps at Finale.[79]

That contact with the Americans almost became a disaster. The British battlegroup had intercepted a German convoy and had called down an air strike when they learned that II Corps was about to attack Finale. Fortunately, the air strike was cancelled as was a planned major bombardment intended to cover 12 South African Brigade's attack on Finale. Peaceful contact was then made between 6th British and 6th South African Armoured Divisions.[80] Sixth Armoured Division had lived up to the promise inherent in its divisional sign of a mailed fist: it had struck the Germans a killer blow.

As always there were mopping-up operations to be carried out as some Germans remained in the area and were still aggressive. During these operations Lieutenant Colonel John Hope DSO MC and Bar, CO of 1st King's Royal Rifle Corps, was shot as he conferred with Denis Smyly, CO of 16th/5th Lancers, beside a 'sawn-off' Stuart tank.* Hope died on 24 April; Corporal Stanley Waring, the tank commander, who went to give him first aid, was also shot dead.[81] John Hope had served with 1st King's Royal Rifles since joining the battalion as a subaltern in late 1940 and took over command on 1 March 1945.[82] Highly regarded by his riflemen, he was one of the very few veterans of the original Eighth Army to have

---

* An American light tank used by the Reconnaissance Troops of armoured regiments and also known as the Honey in British service. After Cassino most of these had their turrets removed to become 'sawn-off'.

215

survived to this point and there was a particular edge to the sadness felt at his death, especially so close to the end of hostilities.[83]

And the end did seem to be coming ever closer with German troops falling back to the Po, fighting rearguard actions along the way. Many had no way of escape: Hitler had refused to sanction a withdrawal while five divisions around Bologna had no transport and thus no means of evading the encircling Allies. Although 6th Armoured Division's rapid advance had threatened the German paras' withdrawal, the destruction of the bridge at Bondeno had given them the time they needed to escape Murray's armour. The paras' withdrawal was aided by 278th Volksgrenadier Division, although neither that formation nor 362nd was able to pull back to the Po. Much of Schwerin's LXXVI Corps had been destroyed in Eighth Army's operations.[84]

Tragically,

> On the last day after the main fighting was over, our two Honey light tanks, carrying ammunition and fuel, were attacked by American fighters, and two men were killed, while coming back up to us. Both other armoured regiments were attacked by the same party of aircraft, which had mistaken the Po for the Adige, and were sixty miles south of their bomb line.[85]

The war diary of 17th/21st Lancers recorded that the Honeys had been attacked by RAF Spitfires that mistook the vehicles for enemy tanks. In contrast 1st KRRC's diary identified the attacking aircraft as USAAF Mustangs and the Lancers later noted that the planes were American.[86]

The American 10th Mountain Division* was the first Allied formation to reach the Po, at San Benedetto on the evening of 22 April. Next day, Major General Russell's 8th Indian Division also came up to the river, having been inserted by Keightley into the widening gap between 6th Armoured and 78th Divisions. Led by 21 Brigade, Russell's men struck for Ferrara where resistance proved strong and 19 Brigade became locked with the defenders, while 21 worked its way around the city to the left. As 1/5th Mahrattas attacked the airport, also held tenaciously, the Jaipur Infantry advanced but it was 5th Royal West Kents who found a gap well to the left of the city and swept through, supported by North Irish Horse tanks, to race for the Po which they reached on the morning of the 23rd. The West Kents bagged more than 150 prisoners with no loss to the battalion. The Derbyshire Yeomanry were also heading for the Po as the spearhead of 6th Armoured Division.[87]

---

* Many years later one of its officers, wounded in Italy, was to run for the Presidency of the USA, but Senator Bob Dole lost that race.

Although the Germans at Ferrara continued fighting, resistance south of the Po was crumbling. Eighth Army's pressure was unremitting as the Army's war diary narrative for 24 April shows:

CREMONA GP advanced in coastal sector and captured ARIANA ... Between them and FERRARA 56 DIV and 78 DIV continued to reduce the enemy's bridgehead South of the Po against stiff resistance from enemy infantry supported by quite a large number of tanks. By last light the enemy's line was beginning to weaken and our advances had brought us to within two miles of the river PO at several different points. Ferrara was occupied in the morning without opposition with the assistance of partisans who had taken over the city as the enemy withdrew. Resistance continued on the Northern outskirts. There was no change on the 6 Brit Armd Div sector, 2 NZ Div closed up to the PO on the left of 6 Brit Armd Div and patrolled across the river. Many prisoners have been taken in mopping up operations during the day.[88]

At Pontelagoscuro that evening the Jaipurs ran into a panzer group but found help in the form of 9th Lancers, from the Kangaroo Army of 78th Division, who set upon the Germans from the right flank in what developed into a 'tremendous battle' on open marshland. For the North African veterans of the Lancers memories of desert days were stirred as they sought cover from folds in the ground from which to return fire at the German tanks. But the British tanks had superior firepower as the German heavies, the Tigers, and mediums, the Panthers, had all been lost in isolated actions to support infantry, and all that remained were Mark IVs to confront Shermans, most with high-velocity 76mm guns, or 17-pounders.* Mark IV after Mark IV was hit, the fires that continued after darkness testimony to the destruction wrought by the Shermans, only one of which was knocked out.[90]

Following this battle the Jaipurs took Pontelagoscuro the next morning. There was no opposition and later that day the German front in V Corps' sector collapsed, save for an area in a bend of the Po 'where an enemy group continued to fight fiercely'.[91] That was the only notable resistance on the day that 27th Lancers captured Lieutenant General Graf von Schwerin, LXXVI Panzer Corps' commander. Asked about the dispositions of his corps, von Schwerin replied succinctly: 'You will find them south of the Po.' Schwerin issued an order to his soldiers to be printed on Eighth Army leaflets and dropped on what remained of his command. He advised them

* The Firefly had one major disadvantage in northern Italy as it was 'very clumsy travelling across country. If a tank dipped into a ditch, the gun-barrel was likely to catch on the opposite bank and the elevating gear would be smashed.'[89]

to surrender noting that 'It is the duty of every officer, of every NCO and of every soldier bravely to look facts in the face and to realize that it is criminal to throw away more human lives.'[92]

LXXVI Corps had been routed thoroughly and the devastation promised to the Allies in German propaganda leaflets had instead been inflicted upon the Germans. The Allied advance had been so swift that the Po, rather than being a defensive barrier, became the Dunkirk, *sans* evacuation, of von Vietinghoff's command. Among those British battalions that had experienced France in 1940 a feeling of satisfaction could be excused.

Since German resistance along the Po had been anticipated, Eighth Army had planned an assault crossing with Hawkesworth's X Corps taking the lead but, when Hawkesworth became ill,* McCreery changed his plan and kept V Corps in action, but with Harding's XIII Corps swinging to face north on its left and taking over 6th Armoured and 8th Indian Divisions from Keightley; 2nd New Zealand Division was already under Harding's command. The corps commanders were told to cross the Po wherever an opportunity presented itself. Harding obtained bridging 'by hook or by crook' to get 6th Armoured across, while the New Zealanders are reputed to have used an American bridge to cross by paying a 'toll' of three bottles of whiskey for the right to pass; other New Zealanders crossed by assault boats.[93] Nap Murray's Grenadier Guards crossed in Buffaloes with 7th Hussars following in DD Shermans. This, noted the Grenadiers' war diarist, 'was the first amphibious crossing in Italy [made by] DD Shermans' although the squadron's tanks had their tracks on the bottom all the way over. Some light opposition on the far bank was brushed aside.[94]

Fifty-sixth Division had no bridges and had to use DUKWs and Buffaloes to get 169 Brigade across and resupply the brigade. 'As this method rather limited the number of men that could be employed forward, General Whitfield decided that the advance should be continued by 169 Brigade and 167 and the Guards Brigades were temporarily grounded.'[95]

From the Po, Eighth Army advanced the 10 to 15 miles to the Adige river, another formidable barrier behind which was the Venetian Line. Had this been manned as intended it might have caused many headaches but now there were few German troops left and certainly nowhere near enough to man the Venetian Line. General Murray, of 6th Armoured, created Nicforce 'to exploit infantry gains over the Po'. Commanded by Colonel W.R. Nicholson DSO, Nicforce included C Squadron 7th Hussars with DD Shermans, D Squadron 12th Lancers with armoured cars and A Squadron 1st Derbyshire Yeomanry with Stuarts and Shermans in an

* He died at Gibraltar on 3 June while being evacuated home.

armoured recce role. Nicforce was disbanded on 27 April having taken about 100 prisoners, killed between forty and fifty Germans, destroyed sixteen vehicles and an armoured car, captured three 105mm howitzers and two other guns as well as forty 'machine rifles and *faustpatronen*'. This was described as 'a very conservative estimate'.[96]

Freyberg's New Zealand Division, still with 43 Gurkha Brigade under command, crossed the Adige at Badia Polesine on the night of 26/27 April. They met no opposition but Freyberg chose to mark time and build up his divisional strength before probing towards the Venetian Line with 12th Lancers reconnoitring. At dawn on the 28th the New Zealanders' advance began but the Lancers met no real opposition as they drove forward throughout that day. Gregory Blaxland described the essence of those days:

> The troops surged onwards like hounds in full cry, jostling each other, blasting aside spasmodic opposition, and often speeding across bridges proudly preserved for them by partisans. Entering Rovigo late on 26 April, the Queen's found that the German garrison had already been incarcerated in the gaol. But next day the 2/7th Queen's were strongly counterattacked after crossing the Adige and had a grim fight to retain a bridgehead.[97]

Blaxland's comments are supported by Eighth Army's war diary, which notes, for 28 April: 'During the day rapid advances were made by our troops from the two bridgeheads across the Adige and by last light leading elements were reported at MONSÉLICE 2330 and ESTE 1529.'[98]

Barriers forced the Lancers to stop briefly as they made for Este but they were there by 3.00pm and were told to make for Padua which they entered at midnight. Once again there was no German garrison, or rather there was but all 5,000 members had been imprisoned by partisans who, in spite of all the suffering of the Italian people, had taken no major reprisals against German soldiers.[99]

Following the success of operations carried out by F Squadron SAS (the Italian squadron), the Partisans' Committee of Liberation called for a general uprising against the Germans on 25 April. Reinforced by volunteers from Folgore Group*, the Italian SAS men had parachuted into German-held territory in groups of three or four on the night of 20/21 April in an operation undertaken on McCreery's orders.[101] However, while the SAS were successful, the men of 2 Parachute Brigade remained on the ground; as they studied plans for their thirty-second proposed operation, scheduled

* The original Folgore Division had been an airborne formation. Today's Italian army includes a parachute brigade called the Folgore Brigade with HQ in Livorno.[100]

for 25 April, they were told to stand down: their services would not be needed.[102]

The speed of Eighth Army's advance and the way in which advancing formations and units had fanned out placed great demands on the sappers who were working hard to ensure that the leading elements could be maintained by building bridges across the Po. A Bailey pontoon, 1,100 feet long, was in use at Ficarolo, in XIII Corps' sector, early on the 27th and, by midnight, a similar bridge was carrying traffic in V Corps' sector at Pontelagoscuro.[103]

Having dealt with a rearguard party at Mestre, west of Venice, 2/5th Queen's of 169 Brigade, 56th Division, entered Venice on 29 April, pipping 44th Reconnaissance Regiment to the distinction. The Recce unit had raced for the city to be first there, but missing out on that claim added to the frustration felt by a regiment that had seen little action in this final phase of the war. 'For us the break-through was disappointing, as the great number of blown bridges slowed us down so much that infantry often did the job faster, and consequently we were not employed as much as we should have liked.'[104]

The race for Venice had also included elements of 2nd New Zealand Division and Popski's Private Army, the latter having travelled up the coast by jeep and Army-manned landing craft, taking Chióggia along the way. Eighth Army's soldiers were welcomed enthusiastically by the people of Venice and were also handed about 3,000 German prisoners by the partisans; once again there had been no vengeance killings. A New Zealand officer travelled by boat to the Lido and the islands of Murano and Burano next day to take the surrender of local German garrisons and Peniakoff, in spite of the loss of his left hand, achieved what he described as his war's ambition: driving a jeep around St Mark's Square. More accurately he led a procession of jeeps that travelled seven times around the square. Another thousand Germans, including the local commander, were taken by 43 Gurkha Brigade which cleared Padua that same day; the outskirts of the city had been reduced to rubble.[105]

Udine had also been liberated, with 6th Armoured Division first into the city. Fifty-sixth Division remained in Venice while, on 1 May, 2nd New Zealand Division, reinforced by 12th Lancers and 1st Scots Guards, set out to race the 75 miles to Trieste. Their task was not simply that of liberating the city but to ensure that it did not fall into the hands of Tito's Yugoslav forces. Since Tito was hoping to claim Trieste as part of Yugoslavia in the post-war drawing of borders, possession of the city would have strengthened his claim although most of Trieste's people wished to remain Italian. The city had been part of the Austro-Hungarian Empire until it had been ceded to Italy in 1915.[106]

220

There was now no resistance worth describing. While soldiers on the ground could sense that the war was all but over what they could not know was that negotiations to end it had been underway for some time between the SS commander in Italy, Karl Wolff, and the Allies. Those negotiations led to an agreed date and time for a German surrender which was pre-empted by an hour when von Vietinghoff, learning of Hitler's death, issued immediate surrender orders. On 29 April an agreement was reached for the unconditional surrender of all Axis forces in Italy and in certain Austrian provinces; 230,000 men were involved. This agreement was signed at Field Marshal Alexander's HQ at Caserta in the presence of Lieutenant General Morgan, Alexander's chief of staff, and all fighting was to end by noon on 2 May.[107]

Just before that final surrender the New Zealand Division reached Trieste to find that Yugoslav partisans had arrived the day before and that the citizens were in terror of their so-called liberators. That afternoon Freyberg accepted the surrender of the German garrison which had withdrawn into the harbour area. Meanwhile the politicians discussed the future of Trieste and Tito's ambitions were nullified when Stalin made it clear that he would not support the claim on Trieste. A strong Allied force, including a US division, the only American formation to serve under Eighth Army command, moved into the area.[108] (In 1947 Trieste became part of a free territory under United Nations protection and remained so until an Italo-Yugoslav agreement on frontiers was reached in 1954 when Trieste became part of Italy, and British and US troops left the area.)

Although there were celebrations in Eighth Army that night of 2 May, these were muted. While it was a blessed relief to know that the morrow would not bring more fighting, it took time for the truth to sink in that the war was over at last. Every Eighth Army soldier had his own memories of war and the comrades he had lost. Some were still suffering from wounds, others were dying and bodies were still being recovered from the recent battlefields, and from some not so recent. It was a strange time which was probably best summed up by the commander of the Irish Brigade, Brigadier Pat Scott, who wrote:

Poor old 'D-Day Dodgers'; they had a long fight for their money.
What a long time ago it seemed since those early days in North Africa with the appalling discomforts of that campaign. It seemed a long time, too, since the epic battles of Sicily and Southern Italy.
How very few had seen them all.
How few in the Rifle Companies who had landed in North Africa were still with us to see the culmination of their efforts.
One's mind turned that evening to a lot of faces of old friends whom one would not see again. One hopes that they, too, were able

221

to join in the feeling of satisfaction and thankfulness that the last shot had been fired.[109]

Notes

1. Blaxland, op. cit., p. 251; Doherty, *A Noble Crusade*, op. cit., pp. 286–7; Messenger, *The Commandos*, pp. 369–70.
2. Blaxland, op. cit., pp. 251–2; Doherty, op. cit., p. 287; Messenger, op. cit., pp. 370–1.
3. Anon, *Finito*, op. cit., p. 12.
4. Messenger, op. cit., pp. 372–3.
5. Ibid., pp. 373–4.
6. *London Gazette*, 12 Jun 1945.
7. Doherty, op. cit., p. 285.
8. Messenger, op. cit., pp. 374–5.
9. Smyth, op. cit., p. 427.
10. Jackson, *The Mediterranean and Middle East*, vol. VI, pt III, p. 259.
11. Williams, op. cit., pp. 115–7; NA, Kew, WO170/4483, war diary 167 Bde, 1945; Anon, *The London Irish at War*, op. cit., pp. 193–8.
12. NA, Kew, WO170/4468, war diary 61 Bde, 1945.
13. ffrench-Blake, op. cit., p. 209.
14. NA, Kew, WO170/4979, war diary 3 Gren Gds, 1945; Doherty, op. cit., p. 289.
15. Harpur, op. cit., pp. 122–3.
16. Jackson, op. cit., p. 262; Blaxland, op. cit., pp. 255–6; Doherty, op. cit., p. 289; Routledge, op. cit., p. 284.
17. Anon, *Finito*, op. cit., p. 13.
18. Doherty, op. cit., p. 289.
19. Blaxland, op. cit., p. 256; Doherty, op. cit., pp. 289–90; Kay, op. cit., pp. 413–21.
20. Blaxland, op. cit., p. 257; Pal, op. cit., p. 622.
21. *London Gazette*, 3 Jul 1945.
22. Blaxland, op. cit., p. 257; Pal, op. cit., p. 626.
23. Pal, op. cit., pp. 625–8; Jackson, op. cit., p. 265; Blaxland, op. cit., pp. 257–8; Doherty, op. cit., pp. 290–1.
24. Ray, op. cit., p. 421; Blaxland, op. cit., p. 258.
25. Ray, op. cit., pp. 383–4.; Jackson, op. cit., p. 264; Doherty, op. cit., p. 291.
26. Doherty, op. cit., p. 291.
27. Anders, op. cit., pp. 266–7; Jackson, op. cit., pp. 262 & 266.
28. Blaxland, op. cit., p. 259; Doherty, op. cit., p. 292.
29. Jackson, op. cit., pp. 267–8; Blaxland, op. cit., pp. 259–60; Doherty, op. cit., pp. 292–3; Bullen, *History of the 2/7th Battalion The Queen's Royal Regiment*, p. 137; NA, Kew, WO170/4485, war diary 169 (Queen's) Bde, Jan–Aug 1945.
30. Jackson, op. cit., p. 267; Blaxland, op. cit., p. 260; NA, Kew, WO150/4485, war diary 169 (Queen's) Bde, op. cit.
31. Blaxland, op. cit., p. 260; Doherty, op. cit., p. 293.
32. Jackson, op. cit., pp. 266–8 & 271; Blaxland, op. cit., p. 259; Doherty, op. cit., p. 293.
33. Ray, op. cit., pp. 200–3; Ford, *Battleaxe Division*, op. cit., pp. 202–3; Doherty, *CTW*, op. cit., pp. 233–4.
34. Ray, op. cit., p. 201.

35. Ibid., p. 205.
36. Doherty, op. cit., p. 239.
37. Ibid.; Scott, *Account of the Service of the Irish Brigade*, op. cit.
38. Jackson, op. cit., p. 271; Williams, op. cit., pp. 116–17; Blaxland, op. cit., pp. 260–1; Doherty, *A Noble Crusade*, op. cit., pp. 293–4; NA, Kew, WO170/4448, war diary, 24 Gds Bde, Jan–May 1945; WO170/4992, war diary 1 Buffs, 1945.
39. NA, Kew, WO170/4992, op. cit.
40. Blaxland, op. cit., p. 261; Doherty, op. cit., p. 294; NA, Kew, WO170/4992, op. cit.
41. Blaxland, op. cit., p. 261; Doherty, op. cit., p. 294; NA, Kew, WO170/4992, op. cit.
42. Blaxland, op. cit., p. 262; Doherty, op. cit., pp. 294–5; NA, Kew, WO170/4483, war diary 167 Bde, 1945; WO170/4485, war diary 169 (Queen's) Bde, op. cit.
43. Harpur, op. cit., p. 101.
44. Scott, op. cit.; Doherty, *CTW*, op. cit., p. 240.
45. Scott, op. cit.; Doherty, op. cit., p. 240; Anon, *The London Irish at War*, p. 204.
46. Jackson, op. cit., p. 270; Blaxland, op. cit., p. 263.
47. Parkinson, op. cit., p. 243.
48. Jackson, op. cit., pp. 281–2; Blaxland, op. cit., pp. 264–5; Ray, op. cit., pp. 207–8.
49. Ray, op. cit., pp. 208–9.
50. Scott, op. cit.; Ray, op. cit., pp. 209–10; Doherty, op. cit., pp. 242–3.
51. Scott, op. cit.
52. Harpur, op. cit., p. 162.
53. Ray, op. cit., pp. 210–11.
54. Bredin, notes to author.
55. Blaxland, op. cit., p. 267.
56. Ibid.; Williams, op. cit., pp. 117–18; NA, Kew, WO170/4485, war diary 169 (Queen's) Bde, op. cit.
57. Blaxland, op. cit., p. 267; Scott, op. cit.; Doherty, op. cit., p. 245; Ford, *Mailed Fist*, op. cit., p. 185.
58. Williams, op. cit., p. 118.
59. Jackson, op. cit., pp. 278–81; Blaxland, op. cit., p. 271; NA, Kew, WO170/4627, war diary 14/20 H, 1945; WO170/4634, war diary 2 RTR, Jan–May 1945.
60. Blaxland, op. cit., p. 271.
61. Ibid.
62. Jackson, op. cit., pp. 284–8; Blaxland, op. cit., pp. 271–2; Doherty, *A Noble Crusade*, op. cit., pp. 305–6.
63. Anders, op. cit, p. 267.
64. Ibid., p. 268.
65. Blaxland, op. cit., p. 268.
66. Ford, op. cit., p. 185; Ray, op. cit., pp. 214–5; Blaxland, op. cit., pp. 267–8; Doherty, op. cit., pp. 306–7.
67. ffrench-Blake, 'Italian War Diary', op. cit., p. 48.
68. Blaxland, op. cit., p. 268.
69. ffrench-Blake, op. cit., p. 48.
70. Blaxland, op. cit., p. 268.
71. Ibid., pp. 268–9.

72. Ibid., p. 269; ffrench-Blake, op. cit., p. 50.
73. NA, Kew, WO170/4456, war diary 26 Armd Bde, 1945.
74. Ibid.
75. ffrench-Blake, op. cit., p. 51.
76. NA, Kew, WO170/4629, war diary 17/21 L, 1945.
77. ffrench-Blake, *A History of the 17th/21st Lancers*, op. cit., p. 222.
78. Ibid.
79. NA, Kew, WO170/4456, war diary 26 Armd Bde, op. cit.; WO170/4628, war diary 16/5 L, 1945; WO170/4629, war diary 17/21 L, op. cit.
80. Jackson, op. cit., pp. 291–2; NA, Kew, WO170/4456, war diary 26 Armd Bde, op. cit.
81. NA, Kew, WO170/5026, war diary 1 KRRC, 1945; Blaxland, op. cit., p. 270; Wallace, *The King's Royal Rifle Corps ... the 60th Rifles*, p. 178; www.cwgc.org
82. NA, Kew, WO170/5026, war diary 1 KRRC, op. cit.
83. Blaxland, op. cit., p. 270.
84. Jackson, op. cit., pp. 291–4; Doherty, op. cit., p. 309.
85. ffrench-Blake, *Italian War Diary*, p. 52.
86. NA, Kew, WO170/4629, war diary 17/21 L, op. cit., & WO170/5026, war diary 1 KRRC, op. cit.
87. Jackson, op. cit., pp. 288–94; Blaxland, op. cit., p. 273.
88. NA, Kew, WO170/4180, war diary Main HQ Eighth Army, April 1945.
89. ffrench-Blake, *A History of the 17th/21st Lancers*, op. cit., p. 209.
90. Blaxland, op. cit., p. 275; NA, Kew, WO170/4624, war diary 9 L, 1945.
91. NA, Kew, WO170/4180, war diary Main HQ Eighth Army, April 1945, op. cit.
92. Scott, op. cit.
93. Jackson, op. cit., pp. 315–20; Blaxland, op. cit., pp. 273–5.
94. NA, Kew, WO170/4979, war diary, 3 Gren Gds, op. cit.
95. Williams, op. cit., p. 119.
96. NA, Kew, WO170/4456, war diary, 26 Armd Bde, 1945, op. cit.
97. Blaxland, op. cit., p. 276.
98. NA, Kew, WO170/4180, war diary, Main HQ Eighth Army, April 1945, op. cit.
99. NA, Kew, WO170/4626, war diary 12 L, 1945; Blaxland, op. cit., p. 277.
100. Bennett, *Fighting Forces*, p. 71.
101. Jackson, op. cit., pp. 294–5.
102. NA, Kew, WO170/4410, war diary 2 Ind Para Bde, 1945.
103. Jackson, op. cit., pp. 317–9.
104. NA, Kew, WO170/ 5059, war diary 2/5th Queen's, 1945 & WO170/4372, war diary 44 Recce, 1945.
105. Jackson, op. cit., pp. 324–6; Doherty, op. cit., p. 313.
106. Jackson, op. cit., p. 326; Ford, op. cit., p. 190; Doherty, op. cit., pp. 317–18.
107. Doherty, op. cit., p. 318; Jackson, op. cit., pp. 332–3.
108. Jackson, op. cit., pp. 336–9; Doherty, op. cit., p. 318.
109. Scott, op. cit.

Chapter Ten

Peace at Last

We few, we happy few, we band of brothers.

The long, hard slog was over, the war in Italy at an end. Eighth Army sent many of its soldiers, and Army HQ, into Austria where, at the end of July, its name vanished from the order of battle and HQ Eighth Army became HQ British Troops Austria.[1] In the early days in Austria there were many unpleasant tasks to perform, not least the repatriation of Cossacks to the Soviet Union. Those tasks are, however, outside the scope of this book although they will remain a subject for intense and heated debate for years to come.

For those who remained in Italy life was much more pleasant, except around Trieste. For all, however, there was the opportunity to look back on the Italian campaign and reflect on Eighth Army's achievements. How had this army, born in the deserts of North Africa, performed in a campaign in a European country? And how well had it been handled by its three commanders in that time?

Eighth Army had come into Italy from Sicily, a brief campaign that depended on the infantry formations rather than the armour. And it had been two divisions from the army of Sicily, 1st Canadian and 5th British, forming XIII Corps, which first set foot in Calabria.[2] Although XIII Corps was the old Western Desert Force in a new guise, neither of its divisions had desert fighting experience; 5th Division joined Eighth Army for the invasion of Sicily and 1st Canadian arrived from Britain to land in Sicily.[3] Of the other divisions in Sicily, 50th (Northumbrian) and 51st (Highland) were desert veterans of Eighth Army while 78th Division, which had fought in Tunisia, had come from First Army.[4] The two British armoured brigades deployed in Sicily were desert veterans, both 4 and 23 Armoured having been at El Alamein (the Canadians deployed 1 Canadian Tank Brigade which, since it was equipped with Shermans, was really an armoured brigade and was soon reclassified as such).[5] On balance, however, the force that fought in Sicily was a much-changed Eighth Army. Indeed it had been intended to be a new field army – Twelfth Army – in

225

keeping with the practice of forming discrete armies for new theatres, but Montgomery had argued, successfully, to retain the former name.[6]

Thus it was that the Eighth Army that first set foot on mainland Italy was far from being the Eighth Army of desert fame; neither division had desert experience and nor had the next major formation to arrive, 1st Airborne Division.[7] But desert formations joined later, as we have seen, and the spirit of the desert army continued in Italy. However, it was a very different form of warfare. The wide flanking movements possible in the desert were impossible in Italy unless by sea; but there were insufficient landing craft available to allow that, although the Germans never lost their fear of British seaborne operations. The many who had expected a land of permanent sunshine were shocked to find that it rained – and heavily – in Italy and that snow fell during the winter months. Mud and cold in two Italian winters were to provide some of the most painful memories of the campaign for veterans.

Those weather conditions, and the topography of Italy, influenced the way in which the war would be fought. Italy has a mountainous spine from which flow numerous rivers and streams that have formed valleys cutting across the path of anyone trying to travel up or down the peninsula. Napoleon commented that since Italy is shaped like a boot any invader should enter it from the top. This advice Bonaparte himself heeded while a British force that landed in Calabria in 1805 fought only briefly before withdrawing.[8] But the Allied armies of 1943 entered from the toe and instep, in the case of Eighth Army, and just above the ankle, in the case of Fifth Army. Belisarius, who liberated Rome from its Ostrogoth, or German, conquerors in AD 537, had landed from Sicily and went on to seize the Ostrogoth capital, Ravenna. He had been the only general in history to take Rome from the south. Even Giuseppe Garibaldi had failed twice in this endeavour. Of course, in 1943 Napoleon's preferred option was not open to the Allies. Paradoxically, had it been there would have been no necessity for an Italian campaign.

In Eighth Army's first operation in Italy the scale of troops committed was small and movement was slow due to the difficulties imposed by the terrain and German demolitions. With the capture of Taranto an additional division was added and others followed, but not until late September did the Army have significant strength. Building up a support base and ensuring a sound logistical tail also took time and reinforced Montgomery's usual reluctance. There were opportunities for swift movement as Force A proved, but Montgomery seemed to see only risks. Not for him the opportunistic dashes of a Rommel or a Patton. Montgomery's trademark was the set-piece battle, for which he had to 'tee up' in his usual plodding way. Much more might have been achieved in the first months of the Italian campaign had Eighth Army been led by a commander with a more imaginative approach to battle and who was prepared to take more risks. With the port of Taranto available to him, Montgomery had an excellent administrative base from where his logistical tail would not have been too long. One wonders, for example, what McCreery could have done at this stage, especially when the latter showed himself the most skilful corps commander in Fifth Army.

Montgomery's failure to bring one of the Indian divisions to Italy earlier must also be questioned. Fourth Indian Division was battle proven, had a first-rate GOC in Tuker and might have made a real difference in September and early October, especially with its mountain-fighting skills. But Montgomery had a problem with the Indian Army. He had sidelined 4th Indian in the opening phase of Operation LIGHTFOOT when it should have been used as an assault division, and seems to have suffered from that superior attitude of so many British officers to the Indian Army and its officers – also overwhelmingly British, of course, at this stage. Since Montgomery had failed to be selected for the Indian Army at Sandhurst, was he carrying a chip on his shoulder?

Montgomery handed over to Leese, his disciple in many ways. Leese gave Eighth Army its victory in Operation HONKER at Cassino, a battle fought almost on a Montgomery template. That it did not end with the destruction of the German armies was not Leese's fault but that of his American counterpart, Clark. However, it could be argued that had Leese fought a tidier battle, without the congestion that occurred in the Liri valley with three corps operating, then Eighth Army might have made better progress. Even had that been the case it is doubtful if it would have led to the end of the German armies since the advance of VI Corps from Anzio was the critical factor in this. As for the congestion in the Liri valley, Leese was commanding a coalition army and, as has been made clear in Chapter Five, had to be aware of national sensitivities; thus the need to involve Canadians and Poles as well as XIII Corps, which also included Indian troops. However, it is interesting to note that Vokes, commanding 1st Canadian Division, was critical of Leese's failure either to place 78th Division under Canadian command or place the two Canadian divisions under command of XIII Corps. In Vokes's view, Leese 'screwed up the battle arrangements. He made a great mistake.'[9] Vokes's criticism was based on his lack of confidence in Burns, the Canadian Corps commander. One of McCreery's first acts as army commander was to relieve Burns.

Where even more criticism may be made of Leese is in Operation OLIVE. What was planned as a leap by Eighth Army to take it onto the Lombardy plain and thence to Venice, and even Vienna, proved everything but. Although Eighth Army made significant progress Leese had promised much more. He might have delivered much more had he relied less on his armour. Convinced by Kirkman's argument that Eighth Army's superiority in armour should be taken advantage of, and that the coastal sector was the best place to use that armour, Leese put this argument to Alexander

227

who eventually accepted it, allowing the transfer of Eighth Army to the Adriatic sector. Alexander's original concept, of moving through the mountains where enemy defences were at their weakest, would have been a better option and would have made best use of the mountain-fighting skills of 4th and 10th Indian Divisions; the latter had trained for such warfare in Cyprus, Syria and Palestine.[10] Eighth Army's armour suffered heavily in the following operations with many casualties in the Coriano ridge fighting which contributed to the subsequent disbandment of 1st Armoured Division. The contrast with McCreery's handling of Eighth Army in the final offensive could not be greater.

This is not to suggest that Leese was other than a competent general. 'A thorough and capable commander, always careful of the lives of his men',[11] he had been an excellent corps commander, with both armour and infantry under his command, in North Africa and Sicily – and the first GOC of Guards Armoured Division – and delivered success at Cassino. On the plus side, Leese had done much to enhance the training of Eighth Army, improving cooperation between armour and infantry. This had involved taking formations out of the line so that infantry and armour could train together down to troop and platoon levels. This policy paid dividends at Cassino in May 1944 and makes all the more surprising the misuse of armour on Coriano ridge. Leese would go on to deliver more success as an army group commander in Burma with the capture of Rangoon in early May 1945, a success overshadowed by the German surrender in Europe. But while Leese was a good general he was not a candidate for that upper tier of great generals, whereas his successor was.

When Sir Richard McCreery assumed command of Eighth Army it was a tired formation that seemed to have little stamina left. The fighting of the OLIVE offensive had drained both infantry and armour, and McCreery knew well the problems facing his army, not least the diminished morale which had led to so many desertions in late 1944. Much has been written, and most of it inaccurate, about low morale in Eighth Army when Montgomery became its commander in August 1942, but the real problem at that time was confusion rather than lack of morale. McCreery took charge of an army in which morale truly was low and it was he who was largely responsible for its restoration. We have noted that Clark, who disliked McCreery, wanted to assign a subsidiary role to Eighth Army in the final offensive, regarding it as being of limited value, but had been persuaded otherwise by both Truscott and McCreery. In the event, Eighth Army fought a 23-day battle in which it achieved its greatest ever success and at the end of which the German armies in Italy had been destroyed south of the Po, while the few enemy forces that managed to cross that river were pursued so relentlessly that they could make no further stand.

McCreery had nurtured Eighth Army to the point that it fought with 'most impressive [determination] in the last major battle in Italy ... when it was clear to all that the end of the war with Germany was in sight and when the offensive spirit was less easy to sustain'.[12] That point is worth bearing in mind by any who would argue that the war was almost over anyway and that the Germans were beaten. They had not been beaten on 9 April when the battle opened and their determined opposition in the following days shows that there was no easy victory. John Strawson, a veteran of Italy and a military historian of note, wrote that among the requirements for high command are 'clarity, courage, sheer mastery of the profession of arms, the essential *feel* for a battle, [and] a robustness which can counter the shocks of war'.[13] All of these requirements were met by Richard McCreery who also met Napoleon's criteria for a great commander: accuracy, simplicity and character.

> If this is true, how fitting a commander was McCreery, for these three almost sum the man up. He was always absolutely insistent on accuracy and there is an interesting story which illustrates the point. As a Corps Commander he would often discuss the military situation at the dinner table, and on one occasion before the Rapido battles, he is said to have asked his Intelligence Officer how he interpreted the movement of German supply vehicles across on the other side. The Intelligence Officer was unwise enough to make a casual and ill-considered reply, whereupon, stage by stage, with arithmetical meticulousness but needless to say, no malice, General Dick showed his calculations to be utterly without foundation. These dinners, at which staff were closely questioned about the day's fighting, were not often comfortable affairs. It was this same insistence on facts and accuracy and proper preparation which characterized his command of an Army. As for simplicity, not only was his whole nature made up of simple elements, but his clarity of thought, the way in which he put over his ideas so that all instantly grasped his meaning, and his uncanny tactical and strategic instinct for hitting on the right solution speak eloquently for this indispensable quality. And his character . . . was the key to the man, and the key to what made others follow and obey him. Honest, loyal, true to himself and others, with an integrity so absolute that it could never compromise either with the truth or what needed to be said or done. If character is the immortal part of oneself, McCreery is immortal indeed. For his character lives on. Small wonder therefore that it burned so fiercely and inspiringly when he was a commander in war.[14]

It was this inspiring commander who planned and executed Eighth Army's final offensive and who led that army to victory on the Lombardy plain in the spring of 1945. He has been described as 'an original and highly intelligent commander', while Alexander admired him as 'a scientific soldier with a gift for the offensive'. In planning Operation BUCKLAND, McCreery applied his clear and unorthodox thinking to the problems facing his army.[15]

Four days before the offensive began he had gathered all the senior officers of Eighth Army, down to lieutenant colonel, in the cinema at Cesena where, as the CO of 17th/21st Lancers recalled:

> In his quiet, almost apologetic voice, he said that the theatre had been stripped of troops for France; that the army was like an old steeple-chaser, full of running, but rather careful; that it was his intention to destroy the Germans south of the Po, rather than to allow them to withdraw to further defence lines to the north, on the Adige, and finally within the 'fortress' of the Austrian Alps. The plan was then outlined.[16]

That plan showed McCreery's ability to analyze problems and develop solutions, his awareness of innovation, his appreciation of the need for speedy manoeuvre and maintaining pressure on the enemy, and, above all, the need to keep casualties in his command to the minimum. Training played an important part in that preparation and, while McCreery's soldiers may have groaned about the amount of training they undertook while out of the line, this paid off handsomely in their final battles. McCreery's unorthodox thinking comes through in the deployment of the Buffaloes on Lake Comácchio, exploiting that mass of water as a tool for manoeuvre rather than seeing it as a barrier; the Kangaroos in which so many of his infantry rode speedily to battle and were thus able often to obtain local surprise; the creation of Eighth Army's own specialist armour and the use of recent scientific developments: infra-red equipment, code-named Tabby, had been produced for tank driving at night and was used by sappers of 25 Armoured Engineer Brigade in bridging operations, and by 9 Armoured Brigade for LVT navigation.[17]

All these elements combined to produce a plan that resulted in Eighth Army's greatest victory. The army that went into battle for the last time in April 1945 did so with great confidence, knowing that its commander had done all in his power to ensure success and preserve the lives of his soldiers. McCreery kept his eye constantly on the battle, offering advice and criticism to his subordinates and ensuring that the impetus was never lost. He did so much more effectively than Montgomery ever had, preferring to come forward to his subordinates rather than to exhort from his Tactical HQ.

Not only did the army break through the enemy defences, as it had done on other occasions, but it pursued the enemy to the bitter end, gaining the fruits of victory that are harvested in the pursuit. BUCKLAND became probably the best example of manoeuvre warfare on the part of the

Western Allies in the Second World War. Its success allows Richard McCreery to be described as Eighth Army's greatest commander, as the man who led Britain's most famous field army to final victory and to peace.

Notes

1. Doherty, *A Noble Crusade*, op. cit., pp. 329–30; NA, Kew, WO170/4187, war diary Main HQ Eighth Army, Jul 1945.
2. See Ch One, p.1; WO169/8496, war diary Eighth Army HQ GS, Sep 1943.
3. Aris, op. cit., p. 106; Nicholson, op. cit., p. 20.
4. Doherty, op. cit., pp. 141 & 146.
5. Ibid., p. 141; Nicholson, op. cit., pp. 166–8.
6. NA, Kew, WO201/1812, Twelfth Army Op Order No. 1.
7. See Ch One, p. 00.
8. This force defeated a French force at the Battle of Maida on 4 July 1806. London's Maida Vale commemorates the action.
9. Vokes, op. cit., p. 159.
10. Anon, *The Tiger Triumphs*, op. cit., pp. 87–8.
11. Orgill, op. cit., p. 15.
12. Blaxland, op. cit., p. 246.
13. Strawson, *General Sir Richard McCreery*, op. cit., p. 55.
14. Ibid., pp. 54–5.
15. Orgill, op. cit., p. 192.
16. ffrench-Blake, *A History of the 17th/21st Lancers*, op. cit., p. 209.
17. Jackson, *The Mediterranean and Middle East*, vol. VI, pt III, p. 407.

Chapter Eleven

Reflections

Warriors for the working day.

They had come from across the globe, these soldiers of Eighth Army, to fight in Italy. Thousands of them found their last resting place in the soil of Italy. The dead who rest in neatly tended cemeteries, or are commemorated on sad memorials, the length of the peninsula include men from Europe, North America, South America, Africa, Asia and Australasia. Eighth Army was a truly multi-national force even though it is remembered as a British army; its Britishness lay in the fact that most of its soldiers came from countries that were part of the British Empire or Commonwealth and who regarded King George VI as their head of state. There were others including Poland, Italy, Greece and Nepal that made significant contributions, while many volunteers from neutral Éire (the only Commonwealth country not to declare war) were to be found in British uniform.

All these men were united in their aim to free Europe of the tyranny of Nazism and few were as dedicated to that aim as the Poles whose memorial on Point 593 at Cassino must rank as one of the most poignant of war memorials. While its simplicity, and that of the inscription, is a major element of that poignancy there is the added factor that when the memorial was built, in the immediate aftermath of war, the men of II Polish Corps knew that freedom had not been achieved for Poland and that their nation, which had already suffered so much, faced a new form of tyranny. Not until the early 1980s did Poland at last achieve the freedom those men fought for and there is a sense of historical appropriateness that a Polish pope, John Paul II, Karol Józef Wojtyla, who had experienced the German occupation of his country and the Soviet 'liberation', played a major role in the downfall of the communist empire.

Italy had suffered horrendously as war raged on its soil. Civilians lost their homes and many died at the hands of their former German allies, some in brutal acts of reprisal, while the infrastructure of the country was all but destroyed. Allied air operations that did so much to disrupt German communications and logistics achieved that aim through wrecking

232

railways, bridges, roads and homes. And what Allied aircraft missed, the retreating Germans destroyed in their efforts to delay the Allied advance. It took many years for Italy to recover from the war and travellers in the country in the 1950s often found themselves crossing rivers and streams over Bailey bridges left by Allied engineers at the end of the war. Many towns and cities continued to bear the scars of war while one of the more obvious after effects of the war was the decision to remove the Italian royal family and declare the country a republic.

For the average British soldier there were many happy memories of Italy and its people. In spite of the horror of war, many of those soldiers found themselves falling in love with the country. Some fell in love with Italian girls whom they married and brought home, although a few remained in Italy to make their homes there. The author has known many veterans of the Italian campaign, hardly any of whom did not have positive memories of the country and its people. One gunner commented on how he felt desperately sorry for an Italian family as his troop of guns established a position on their farm. To do so the family's crop of tomato plants had to be destroyed and the soldier found it heartrending to watch the farmer, his wife and children as their livelihood was bulldozed. In recompense the gunners provided British rations – some of which were inevitably 'liberated' – to feed the family; some gave them money even though soldiers were themselves poorly paid. But it is a mark of the impression that incident made that the veteran should talk to the author about it more than four decades after it had occurred. In spite of the negative aspect of the memory it still reflects a positive attitude towards the people of Italy.

Some soldiers made friends with Italian families whenever their units were static for any length of time and were invited to family events, enjoying the hospitality of people who had been an enemy nation only months earlier. In his possession the author has a souvenir prayer card of the First Holy Communion and Confirmation of two Italian children in June 1944. The card belonged to his father, a veteran of the Italian campaign, who had been given it by the children's family. Not only was the author's father a veteran of Italy, but so also were his two immediate childhood neighbours. One of them, Joseph Radcliffe, to whose memory this book is dedicated, served in the Royal Corps of Signals in North Africa and Italy where he met Lucia Bederchi; the couple married in St Patrick's Church, on the Via Boncompagni, in Rome on 6 October 1946. When he eventually retired from the Ministry of Defence in the 1980s, Joe Radcliffe decided to move to Rome where he died in February 2005.

Of course, there were unpleasant memories. Soldiers were too often witnesses to death in the many obscene forms that the violence of war brings. Friends were lost to gunshot, mines, mortar bombs and artillery shells while others lost their minds. But such memories were not ones to dwell upon. Individuals did their best to push these as deep into their minds as they could but they could never be eliminated. Some men could draw down a veil for many years but the memories returned to haunt them, often in their sleeping hours when the brutality of war became every bit as real as it had been so many years before. Others found their waking hours stalked by the ghosts of the war years, including the memory of having killed fellow human beings.

Most of the men who fought in Italy were either conscripts or wartime volunteers, although there was a small proportion of veteran professional soldiers; the Indian Army was entirely volunteer and remains the largest volunteer army in history. The majority were, therefore, in Shakespeare's words, 'warriors for the working day', men who hoped to return to a normal civilian life when the war was over. For some the war ended with death in Italy, or with wounding, while for others the war never ended in their minds. Nonetheless, those men achieved the freedom of Italy, played a major part in the destruction of Nazism and did so stoically and purposefully. As Pope Pius XII declared, they fought for 'peace with justice' and, in large measure, they succeeded.

To Joe Radcliffe, and his many comrades who served in Italy, a peaceful Europe owes a debt that only those who lived through the Second World War can appreciate fully.

Tante grazie!

Bibliography

Alexander, Field Marshal Sir Harold, *Memoirs*, John North (ed.) (Cassell, London, 1962).
———, (Supreme Allied Commander, Mediterranean), *Report on the Italian Campaign, Pts I–III* (HMSO, London, 1946–1948).
Anders, Lieutenant General W., CB, *An Army in Exile. The Story of the Second Polish Corps* (Macmillan, London, 1949).
Anon, *Finito! The Po Valley Campaign 1945* (Headquarters 15th Army Group, 1945).
Anon, *The Story of 46th Division 1939–1945* (np, Graz, 1945).
Anon, *The History of 61 Infantry Brigade* (np, Klagenfurt, 1945).
Anon, *The Tiger Triumphs* (HMSO, London, 1946).
Anon, *The London Irish at War* (Old Comrades' Assn, London, 1948).
Aris, George, *The Fifth British Division 1939 to 1945* (The Fifth Division Benevolent Fund, London, 1959).
Arthur, Max, *Symbol of Courage: A History of the Victoria Cross* (Sidgwick and Jackson, London 2004).
Ascoli, David, *A Companion to the British Army 1660–1983* (Harrap, London, 1983).
Badoglio, Pietro, *Italy in the Second World War* (Oxford University Press, London, 1948).
Bailey, Lieutenant Colonel D.E., *Engineers in the Italian Campaign 1943–1945* (Central Mediterranean Force, 1945).
Barclay, C.N., *The History of The Royal Northumberland Fusiliers in the Second World War* (William Clowes and Son, London, 1952).
Barclay, C.N., *History of the 16th/5th Queen's Royal Lancers 1925–1961* (Gale and Polden, Aldershot, 1963).
Barzini, Luigi, *The Italians* (Hamish Hamilton, London, 1964).
Bateson, Henry, *First Into Italy* (Jarrolds, London, 1944).
Baynes, John, *The Forgotten Victor: General Sir Richard O'Connor* (Brassey's, London, 1989).
Beckman, Morris, *The Jewish Brigade. An army with Two Masters 1944–45* (Spellmount, Staplehurst, 1998).
Bennett, Richard, *Fighting Forces, An Illustrated Anatomy of the World's Great Armies* (Quarto, London, 2001).
Bidwell, Shelford and Graham, Dominick, *Tug of War. The Battle for Italy: 1943–45* (Hodder & Stoughton, London, 1986).
Blaxland, Gregory, *Alexander's Generals. The Italian Campaign 1944–45* (William Kimber, London, 1979).
Blumenson, Martin, *Mark Clark* (Jonathan Cape, London, 1984).

Bowlby, Alex, *Countdown to Cassino. The Battle of Mignano Gap, 1943* (Pen & Sword, Barnsley, 1995).

Brooks, Stephen (ed.), *Montgomery and The Eighth Army*, (The Bodley Head, London, 1991).

Bryant, Sir Arthur, *The Turn of the Tide, 1939–1943. A history of the war years based on the diaries of Field Marshal Lord Alanbrooke* (Doubleday, New York, NY, 1957).

————, *Triumph in the West. Completing the War Diaries of Field Marshal Viscount Alanbrooke* (Collins, London, 1959).

Bullen, Roy E., *History of the 2/7th Battalion The Queen's Royal Regiment 1939–1946* (np, 1958).

Burns, E.L.M., *General Mud* (Clark and Irwin, Toronto, 1984).

Carver, Field Marshal Lord, *Harding of Petherton: Field Marshal* (Weidenfeld and Nicolson, London, 1978).

————, *The Imperial War Museum Book of the War in Italy 1943–1945* (Sidgwick & Jackson, London, 2001).

Churchill, Winston S., *The Second World War*, vols VII & VIII, *The Hinge of Fate*; vol. IX, *Closing the Ring*; vol. XI, *Triumph and Tragedy* (Cassell, London, 1951, 1952, 1954).

Clarke, Rupert, *With Alex at War from the Irrawaddy to the Po 1941–1945* (Leo Cooper, Barnsley, 2000).

Cloake, John, *Templer. Tiger of Malaya* (Harrap, London, 1985).

Cole, David, *Rough Road to Rome, A Foot-soldier in Sicily and Italy 1943–44* (William Kimber, London, 1983).

Cooper, Matthew, *The German Army 1933–1945. Its Political and Military Failure* (Macdonald and Jane's, London, 1978).

Danchev, Alex and Todman, Daniel, *War Diaries 1939–1945 Field Marshal Lord Alanbrooke* (Weidenfeld & Nicolson, London, 2001).

Daniell, D.S., *History of the East Surrey Regiment* (Ernest Benn, London, 1957).

Delaforce, Patrick, *Monty's Marauders. Black Rat and Red Fox* (Tom Donovan, Brighton, 1997).

Doherty, Richard, *Wall of Steel: The History of the 9th (Londonderry) Heavy Anti-Aircraft Regiment, Royal Artillery (SR)* (North-West Books, Limavady, 1988).

————, *Clear the Way! A History of the 38th (Irish) Brigade, 1941–47* (Irish Academic Press, Dublin, 1993).

————, *Only The Enemy in Front: The Recce Corps at War 1940–1946* (Tom Donovan, London, 1994).

————, *A Noble Crusade. The History of Eighth Army 1941–45* (Spellmount, Staplehurst, 1999).

————, *The North Irish Horse. A Hundred Years of Service* (Spellmount, Staplehurst, 2002).

————, *Ireland's Generals in the Second World War* (Four Courts Press, Dublin, 2004).

Durnford-Slater, John, *Commando* (William Kimber, London, 1953).

Ellis, John, *Cassino. The Hollow Victory: The Battle for Rome January–June 1944* (Andre Deutsch, London, 1984).

ffrench Blake, R.L.V., *A History of the 17th/21st Lancers 1922–1959* (Macmillan, London, 1962).

————, *The 17th/21st Lancers 1759–1993* (Leo Cooper, London, 1993).

Ford, Ken, *Battleaxe Division. From Africa to Austria with the 78th Division 1952–45* (Sutton, Stroud, 1999).

————, *Cassino. Breaking the Gustav Line* (Osprey, Botley, 2004).

————, *Mailed Fist. 6th Armoured Division at War 1940–1945* (Sutton, Stroud, 2005).

Forman, Sir Denis, *To Reason Why* (Andre Deutsch, London, 1991).

Forty, George, *Battle for Monte Cassino* (Ian Allan, Hersham, 2004).

Fox, Sir Frank, *The Royal Inniskilling Fusiliers in the Second World War, 1939–45* (Gale & Polden, Aldershot, 1951).

Fraser, David, *Alanbrooke* (Collins, London, 1982).

————, *And We Shall Shock Them: The British Army in the Second World War* (Hodder & Stoughton, London, 1983).

————, *Knight's Cross. A Life of Field Marshal Erwin Rommel* (HarperCollins, London, 1993).

Frederick, J.B.M., *Lineage Book of British Land Forces 1660–1978* (Microform Academic Publishers, Wakefield, 1984).

French, David, *Raising Churchill's Army. The British Army and the War against Germany 1919–1945* (Oxford University Press, Oxford, 2000).

Gaylor, John, *Sons of John Company, The Indian & Pakistan Armies 1903–1991* (Spellmount, Staplehurst, 1992).

Gore, Enid A., *This Was The Way It Was. Adrian Clements Gore* (privately produced, 1977).

Graham, Andrew, *Sharpshooters At War: The 3rd, the 4th and the 3rd/4th County of London Yeomanry 1939 to 1945* (The Sharpshooters Regimental Association, London, 1964).

Gunner, Colin, *Front of the Line: Adventures with The Irish Brigade* (Greystone Books, Antrim 1991).

Hallam, John, *The History of The Lancashire Fusiliers 1939–45* (Sutton, Stroud, 1993).

Hamilton, Nigel, *Monty: Master of the Battlefield, 1942–1944* (Hamish Hamilton, London, 1983).

Hapgood, David and Richardson, David, *Monte Cassino* (Angus & Robertson, London, 1984).

Harpur, Brian, *The Impossible Victory. A Personal Account of the Battle for the River Po* (William Kimber, London, 1980).

Hastings, Max, *Armageddon: The Battle for Germany 1944–45* (Macmillan, London, 2004).

Hinsley, F.H., *British Intelligence in the Second World War (Official History of the Second World War)* (Abridged Edition) (HM Stationery Office, London, 1993).

Hogg, Ian V. and Weeks, John, *The Illus Encyclopedia of Military Vehicles* (Quarto, London, 1980).

Horsfall, John, *Fling Our Banner to the Wind* (Kineton Press, Kineton, 1978).

Howard, Michael, *Grand Strategy*, vol. IV (Official History of the Second World War) (HM Stationery Office, London, 1972).

————, *Grand Strategy*, vol. V, *Strategic Deception* (Official History of the Second World War) (HM Stationery Office, London, 1990).

Howarth, Patrick, *My God, Soldiers. From Alamein to Vienna* (Hutchinson, London, 1989).

Jackson, W.G.F., *The Battle for Italy* (Batsford, London, 1967).

————, *The Battle for Rome* (Batsford, London, 1969).

————, *The Mediterranean and Middle East*, vol. VI, *Victory in the Mediterranean, Part II – June to October 1944* (Official History of the Second World War) (HM Stationery Office, London, 1973).

————, *The Mediterranean and Middle East,* vol. VII, *Victory in the Mediterranean, Part III – November 1944 to May 1945* (Official History of the Second World War) (HM Stationery Office, London, 1984).

Joslen, Lieutenant Colonel H.F., *Orders of Battle Second World War 1939–1945* (HM Stationery Office, London, 1960).

Kay, Robin, *From Cassino to Trieste,* vol. II, *Italy: History of New Zealand in the Second World War* (Department of Internal Affairs, Wellington, 1967).

Keegan, John (ed.), *Churchill's Generals* (Weidenfeld & Nicolson, London, 1991).

Kesselring, Field Marshal Albert, *Memoirs* (William Kimber, London, 1953).

Kippenberger, Major General Sir Howard, *Infantry Brigadier* (OUP, London, 1949).

Lamb, Richard, *War in Italy 1943–1945. A Brutal Story* (John Murray, London, 1993).

Lewin, Ronald, *Rommel as Military Commander* (Batsford, London, 1968).

————, *Montgomery as Military Commander* (Batsford, London, 1971).

Liddell Hart, B.H. (ed.), *The Rommel Papers* (Harcourt, Brace, New York, NY, 1953).

Linklater, Eric, *The Campaign in Italy* (HMSO, London, 1959).

Lord, Cliff and Watson, Graham, *The Royal Corps of Signals: Unit Histories of the Corps (1920–2001) and its Antecedents* (Helion, Solihull, 2003).

Lunt, James, *The Scarlet Lancers. The Story of 16th/5th The Queen's Royal Lancers 1689–1992* (Leo Cooper, London, 1993).

McLaughlin, Redmond, *The Royal Army Medical Corps* (Leo Cooper, London, 1972).

Macksey, Kenneth, *Rommel: Battles and Campaigns* (Arms and Armour, London, 1979).

————, *Kesselring. German Master Strategist of the Second World War* (Greenhill Books, London, 1996).

Majdalany, Fred, *The Monastery* (John Lane, The Bodley Head, London, 1945).

————, *Cassino. Portrait of a Battle* (Longmans, Green & Co, London, 1957).

Mead, Peter, *Gunners at War 1939–1945* (Ian Allan, London, 1982).

Merewood, Jack, *To War with The Bays. A Tank Gunner Remembers 1939–1945* (1st The Queen's Dragoon Guards, Cardiff, 1996).

Messenger, *The Commandos 1940–1946* (William Kimber, London, 1985).

Mitcham, Samuel W., Jr, *Hitler's Field Marshals and their Battles* (William Heinemann, London, 1988).

Molony, C.J.C., *The Mediterranean and Middle East,* vol. V, *The Campaign in Sicily 1943 and the Campaign in Italy 3rd September 1943 to 31st March 1944* (Official History of the Second World War) (HM Stationery Office, London, 1973).

————, *The Mediterranean and Middle East,* vol. VI, *Victory in the Mediterranean, Part I – 1st April to 4th June 1944* (Official History of the Second World War) (HM Stationery Office, 1974).

Montgomery of Alamein, Field Marshal the Viscount, *El Alamein to the River Sangro* (Hutchinson, London, 1948).

Montgomery of Alamein, Field Marshal the Viscount, *The Memoirs of Field Marshal Montgomery* (Collins, London, 1958).

Nicholson, Lieutenant Colonel G.W.L., *Official History of the Canadian Army in the Second World War, vol. II, The Canadians in Italy 1943–1945* (Queen's Printer, Ottawa, 1956).

Nicolson, Nigel, *Alex: the Life of Field Marshal The Earl Alexander of Tunis* (Weidenfeld & Nicolson, London, 1973).

Orgill, Douglas, *The Gothic Line: The Autumn Campaign in Italy, 1944* (Heinemann, London, 1967).

Orpen, Neil, *Victory in Italy* (Official History of South Africa in the Second World War) (Purnell, Cape Town, 1975).

Pal, Dharm, *The Campaign in Italy: Official History of the Indian Armed Forces in the Second World War* (Orient Longmans, 1960).

Parker, Matthew, *Monte Cassino. The Story of the Hardest-Fought Battle of World War Two* (Headline, London, 2003).

Parkinson, C. Northcote, *Always A Fusilier* (Sampson Low, London, 1949).

Piekalkiewicz, Janusz, *Cassino. Anatomy of the Battle* (Orbis, London, 1980).

Phillips, N.C., *The Sangro to Cassino*, vol. I, *Italy: The History of New Zealand in the Second World War* (Department of Internal Affairs, Wellington, 1957).

Place, Timothy Harrison, *Military Training in the British Army, 1940–1944. From Dunkirk to D-Day* (Frank Cass, London, 2000).

Platt, Brigadier J.R.I., *The Royal Wiltshire Yeomanry 1907–1967: Britain's Oldest Yeomanry Regiment* (Garnstone Press, London, 1972).

Prince, A.R., *Wheeled Odyssey: The Story of the Fifth Reconnaissance Regt., Royal Armoured Corps* (np, nd).

Ray, Cyril, *Algiers to Austria. The History of 78 Division 1942–1946* (Eyre & Spottiswoode, London, 1952).

Richardson, General Sir Charles, *Flashback. A Soldier's Story* (William Kimber, London, 1985).

Richardson, General Sir Charles, *Send for Freddie. The Story of Montgomery's Chief of Staff, Major General Sir Francis de Guingand KBE CB DSO* (William Kimber, London, 1987).

Rosignoli, Guido, *The Allied Forces in Italy 1943–45* (David & Charles, Newton Abbot, 1989).

Ross, Alexander M., *Slow March to a Regiment* (Vanwell, Ontario, 1993).

Routledge, Brigadier N.W., *Anti-Aircraft Artillery, 1914–55* (Brassey's, London, 1994).

Ryder, Rowland, *Oliver Leese* (Hamish Hamilton, London, 1987).

Saunders, Hilary St G., *The Green Beret: The Story of the Commandos 1940–1945* (Michael Joseph, London, 1949).

Senger und Etterlin, Frido von, *Neither Fear Nor Hope: the wartime career of General Frido von Senger und Etterlin, defender of Cassino* (Macdonald, London, 1963).

Shepperd, G.A *The Italian Campaign 1943–45. A political and military re-assessment* (Arthur Barker, London, 1968).

Short, Neil, *German Defences in Italy in World War II* (Osprey, Botley, 2006).

Smart, Nick, *Biographical Dictionary of British Generals of the Second World War* (Pen & Sword, Barnsley, 2005).

Smith, E.D., *The Battles for Cassino* (Ian Allan, London, 1975).

Smith, Kenneth B., *Duffy's Regiment: A History of the Hastings and Prince Edward Regiment* (Dundurn Press, Toronto and Oxford, 1987).

Smyth, Sir John, *The Story of the Victoria Cross 1856–1963* (Frederick Muller, London, 1963).

Squire, Lieutenant Colonel G.L.A. and Hill, Maj P.G.E., *The Surreys in Italy* (Queen's Royal Surrey Regiment Museum, Guildford, 1992).

Steer, Frank, *To The Warrior his Arms* (Pen & Sword, Barnsley, 2005).

Stevens, Lieutenant Colonel G.R., OBE, *Fourth Indian Division* (McLaren & Son, Ontario, 1948).

Strawson, John, *General Sir Richard McCreery* (Published privately by Lady McCreery, 1973).

————, *The Italian Campaign* (Secker & Warburg, London, 1987).

Trevelyan, Raleigh, *Rome '44. The Battle for the Eternal City* (Secker & Warburg, London, 1981).

Tuker, Francis, *The Pattern of War* (Cassell, London, 1948).

Vokes, Major General Chris, CB CBE DSO CD, *My Story* (Gallery Books, Ottawa, 1985).

Wake, Sir Hereward and Deedes, W.F., *Swift and Bold: The Story of the King's Royal Rifle Corps in the Second World War 1939-1945* (Gale & Polden, Aldershot, 1949).

Wallace, Sir Christopher, *The King's Royal Rifle Corps ... the 60th Rifles. A Brief History: 1755 to 1965* (The Royal Green Jackets Museum Trust, Winchester, 2005).

Ward, Robin (ed.), *The Mirror of Monte Cavallara: An Eighth Army Story by Ray Ward* (Birlinn, Edinburgh, 2006).

Whiting, Charles, *The Long March on Rome. The Forgotten War* (Century Hutchinson, London, 1987).

Williams, David, *The Black Cats at War. The Story of the 56th (London) Division TA, 1939-1945* (Imperial War Museum, London, 1995).

Williams, Jeffery, *Princess Patricia's Canadian Light Infantry 1914-1984: Seventy Years' Service* (Leo Cooper with Secker & Warburg, London, 1985).

Williamson, Hugh, *The Fourth Division 1939 to 1945* (Newman Neame, London, 1951).

Wilson, Lieutenant General Sir James, *Unusual Undertakings. A Military Memoir* (Pen and Sword, Barnsley, 2002).

Unpublished

Bredin, Major General H.E.N. (Bala), CB DSO** MC* 'An Account of the Kangaroo Army'.

Chavasse, DSO* Colonel Kendal George Fleming, 'Some Memories of My Life'.

————, 'Some Memories of 56 Reconnaissance Regiment'.

Clark, Lieutenant Colonel B.D.H., MC GM, notes on a lecture on the final Battle of Cassino given to the Military History Society of Ireland.

Davies, Major Sir Mervyn, MC, 'An Account of E Company 2nd London Irish Rifles in Italy'.

ffrench-Blake, DSO, Colonel R.L. Valentine, 'Italian War Diary 1944–45'.

Ledwidge, John, Notes on his service with 2nd London Irish Rifles.

Parsons, Captain Alan, MC, extracts from letters to his parents during the war.

Russell, Brigadier Nelson, DSO MC, 'Account of the Service of the Irish Brigade' (to Feb 1944).

Scott, Brigadier T.P.D., DSO, 'Account of the Service of the Irish Brigade' (Feb 1944–May 1945).

Skellorn, John, 'What Did You Do In the War Grandpa?' (An account of his service with 16th/5th Lancers).

Woods, MC?, Colonel A.D., A personal account of his service with 2nd London Irish Rifles in Italy.

National Archives, Kew

Official history narratives:

From the Committee of Imperial Defence, Historical Branch and Cabinet Office, Historical Section: War Histories: Draft Chapters and Narratives, Military.

CAB44/128–149: Section IV, Chapters H–Q, by Major F. Jones: from the prelude to and plan for the invasion of Italy to the final operations in Lombardy. CAB44/131 and 132 were not consulted as these deal with Fifth Army operations at Salerno and the number 142 was not used.
From the War Cabinet and Cabinet Office: Historical Section: Archivist and Librarian Files: (AL Series).
Sub-series within CAB106: War of 1939–1945: Mediterranean and Middle East.
CAB106/409–441 covering the operations in Italy of British, Indian and Dominion forces with material also included on the operations of II Polish Corps.

Formation and Unit war diaries:
WO169/8495, war diary HQ Eighth Army, G Plans, Jul–Aug 1943.
WO169/8496, war diary HQ Eighth Army, G Main, Sep 1943.
WO169/8497, war diary HQ Eighth Army, G Main, Oct 1943.
WO169/8498, war diary HQ Eighth Army, G Main, Nov 1943.
WO169/8499, war diary HQ Eighth Army, G Main, Dec 1943.
WO169/8520, war diary HQ Eighth Army GS, Sep–Dec 1943.
WO170/140, war diary HQ Eighth Army, G Main, Jan 1944.
WO170/146, war diary HQ Eighth Army, G Main, Feb 1944.
WO170/151, war diary HQ Eighth Army, G Main, Mar 1944.
WO170/156, war diary HQ Eighth Army, G Main, Apr 1944.
WO170/160, war diary HQ Eighth Army, G Main, May 1944.
WO170/167, war diary HQ Eighth Army, G Main, Jun 1944.
WO170/174, war diary HQ Eighth Army, G Main, Jul 1944.
WO170/177, war diary HQ Eighth Army, G Main, Aug 1944.
WO170/181, war diary HQ Eighth Army, G Main, Sep 1944.
WO170/185, war diary HQ Eighth Army, G Main, Oct 1944.
WO170/190, war diary HQ Eighth Army, G Main, Nov 1944.
WO170/194, war diary HQ Eighth Army, G Main, Dec 1944.
WO170/4174, war diary HQ Eighth Army, G Main, Jan 1945.
WO170/4176, war diary HQ Eighth Army, G Main, Feb 1945.
WO170/4178, war diary HQ Eighth Army, G Main, Mar 1945.
WO170/4180, war diary HQ Eighth Army, G Main, Apr 1945.

In addition war diaries of corps, divisions, brigades and individual units (including AOP squadrons of the RAF) were also consulted. A complete listing would take too much space but those from which information was extracted are referred to in the appropriate chapter notes.

Index

242

243

Part 2

General

Burma, 228
Burns, Lt Gen E. L. M., 80, 101–2, 104, 157, 227
Butler, Lt Col Beauchamp, 29

C Line, 82, 100, 108
Caesar, Julius, 154
Cáira, 72, 75, 79
Cairo, 153
Calabria, 2, 5, 7, 8, 225–6
Campobasso, 24, 27
Campriano, 131
Cantalupo, 32, 34
Capua, 15, 74
Cappucini, 142
Carovilli, 42
Cárpena, 160
Carpinetta, 156
Capracotta, 42
Capri, 79
Casa Berardi, 51–2
Casablanca conference, 2
Casamaggiore, 126
Casa Bettini, 163
Casa Montemara, 125
Casa Petracone, 92
Casa Sinagoga, 98
Caserta, 15, 221
Cassette, 170
Cassino, 27, 67–72, 74, 76–8, 81, 83, 87, 90, 92, 94, 97, 99, 101, 105, 134, 140, 212, 227–8
Castèl di Sangro, 36, 42
Castèl Frentano, 45, 47
Castellanata, 8
Castelpetroso, 34
Castiglione, 30
Castiglione Alberti, 128
Castle Hill, 67–8, 76
Castropignano, 32
Castrovillari, 10
Catanzaro, 9
Catola river, 26
Catola valley, 26
Cavamento, 204
Celenza, 30–1
Ceprano, 106–7
Ceriano ridge, 150
Cesena, 156, 159, 230
Chavasse, Lt Col Kendal, 18–20, 57, 120
Chiana canal, 122, 128

Chiana valley, 127
Chianciano, 126
Chianti hills, 129, 131
Chiefs of Staff, Br, 36, 114
Chieti, 46
Chióggia, 220
Chiusi, 122, 126
Churchill, Winston, 2, 4, 114, 138, 159, 167, 178
Civitello di Chiana, 127
'Cider Cross-Roads', 49, 50–2
'Cigarette', 74, 77
Città di Castello, 130
Città della Pieve, 121–2, 126
Civitavecchia, 15, 70–1
Clark, Capt Brian, 98–9, 121
Clark, Lt Gen Mark, 27, 66–7, 108–9, 118, 133–4, 144, 158, 167, 174, 184, 201, 207, 212, 227–8
Clive, Brig A.F.L., 80
Colle Belvedere, 72
Colle Chiamato, 47, 49
Colle d'Anchise, 31–2
Colle Monache, 98
Colle Sant'Angelo, 99–100
Collingwood, Gen, 131
Comácchio, 195–6
Comácchio, Lake, 186–7, 189, 194, 196, 201, 206, 230
Combined Chiefs of Staff, 2–5, 177
Conca river, 141–4
Congo bridge, 91–2
Consándolo, 210
Conselice, 203–4
Cope, Lt D.G., 9
Coriano, 144
Coriano ridge, 143, 146, 228
Corsica, 4
Cortona, 127
Cosenza, 9
Cosina river, 161–2
Court, Lt Roderick, 16
Coventry, 34
Crecchio, 53
Crerar, Lt Gen Harry, 62, 102, 177
Croatia, 109
Croce, 144, 146
Crotone, 8
Cunningham, Lt Gen Alan, 153n
Cunningham, Adm Sir Andrew, 4
Currie, Brig John, 44–5
Cyprus, 228

251

Graham, Brig H.D., 24, 26, 33
Granarolo, 174
Graziani, Marshal, 176
Greece, 3, 159, 172, 177–9, 232
Grisignano, 160
Grottaglie, 7
Guardiagrele, 45, 47, 63
Gubbio, 117
Guglionesi, 17, 23
Gully, The, 50–1
Gunner, Lt Colin, 60, 74
Gurbiel, Lt, 99
Gustav Line, 28, 66, 69–70, 72, 81–2, 96, 101–2, 151

Haidar, Sepoy Ali VC, 198
Hamburg, 34
Hangman's Hill, 68
Hanson, Col, 200
Harding, Lt Gen A.F. (Sir John), 70–1, 131, 167, 190, 202
Harpur, Brian, 197, 206
Harris, Maj, 9
Hartland-Mahon, Maj Marcus, 12–13
Hauck, Maj Gen Friedrich-Wilhelm, 82, 163
Hawkesworth, Maj Gen John, 151, 159, 218
Heber-Percy, Brig, 91
Heidrich, Maj Gen Richard, 24, 68, 99–100, 102, 103, 105, 121, 135, 138, 182
Hermon, Brig R.A., 80
Herr, Gen Traugott, 7, 12, 23, 45, 55, 163, 177, 189
Highway 5, 39
Highway 6, 66–7, 69, 78, 80–1, 93–4, 96, 99, 102, 104, 107–9
Highway 9, 150, 154, 162–4, 170, 186, 190, 202
Highway 16, 12, 15, 49–50, 154, 186
Highway 17, 15, 24–6, 32, 42
Highway 18, 2
Highway 60, 128
Highway 64, 214
Highway, 67, 159
Highway 71, 121–2, 127
Highway 73, 127, 130
Highway 82, 107
Highway 87, 18, 23
Highway, 97, 12
Hill, Maj, 23

Hill 569, 95
Hillian, Lt, 97
Hitler, Adolf, 3, 6, 13, 57, 82, 102, 104, 109, 212, 215, 221
Hitler Line, 81–2, 88, 99–101, 104–5, 107, 151
Hoffmeister, Brig (later Maj Gen) H. M., 24, 54, 80
Holworthy, Maj Gen A.W.W., 80
Hope, Lt Col John DSO MC & Bar, 215
Hopkinson, Maj Gen G.F., 7, 8
Horsfall, Maj (later Lt Col) John, 97, 121, 123, 125–6
Hotel des Roses, 78
Howlett, Brig 'Swifty', 19, 45
Hube, Lt Gen Hans-Valentin, 7
Hungary, 109, 178
Hunter, Tpr Thomas Peck VC, 195

Idice river, 211
Imola, 167, 170, 190, 207, 211
'Impossible Bridge', The, 50
Iraq, 62
Isernia, 15, 17, 30–5
Ives, Tpr Alfred, 19, 22

Jackson, Stonewall, 180
'Jacob's Ladder', 130–1
Jadhao, Sepoy Namdeo VC, 199–200
James, Brig John Gwynne DSO, 125
Jarrett, Lt Hugh, 9
Jefferson, Fus Francis VC, 97–8
Jodl, Gen, 131
John Paul II, Pope, 232
Jon, 181
Juin, Gen, 67, 106, 113–14

Karauli, 90
Keightley, Maj Gen Charles F., 80, 97, 122–3, 135, 141, 154, 188, 194, 202, 204, 206–7, 212–13, 216
Kelleher, The Revd Dan MC, 79
Kemp, L/Cpl S.C., 23
Kesselring, FM Albrecht, 6, 7, 13, 17, 22–3, 27, 39, 53, 57, 70–1, 82, 99, 102, 108–9, 114, 116–17, 131–2, 138, 158, 162, 171, 176–7, 179
Kippenberger, Brig Howard, 48
Kirkman, Lt Gen Sidney, 80, 81, 127–9, 133, 227
Kurek, Col, 105

Ray, Brig Kenneth, 152
Reggio di Calabria, 1, 5–6, 40
Reid, Maj Gen Denys, 80, 155
Reno river, 186, 194, 202, 204, 206, 212–13
Rhine crossing (on Rapido), 85
Rhône valley, 135
Riley, Maj W.S., 205
Rimini, 6, 70, 113, 134, 141–3, 147, 154
Rionero, 35
Ripa ridge, 119–20
Ripi, 107
Rocca, 45
Rocca d'Arce, 107
Roccamondolfi, 34
Roccaspromonte, 32–3
Romagna, 134, 151, 187
Romanian oilfields, 4
Rome, 5, 7, 15, 36, 39, 53, 55–6, 61, 63, 66, 69–70, 82, 99, 108–9, 113–14, 116–17, 120, 179, 233
Rommel, FM Erwin, 6, 113, 226
'Romulus' bridge, 118
Ronco river, 156, 159–60
Roosevelt, President, 2, 167, 178
Rork, Maj, 161
Rossano, 8
Rubicon, 154
Rubicone river, 154
Rundstedt, FM Gert von, 177
Russell, Brig Nelson, 20–1, 28–9, 44–5
Russell, Maj Gen D., 53, 80, 91n, 119, 216
Russi, 169

Sacco river, 107n
Sacco valley, 39, 107
Salerno, 8, 12, 17, 70, 181
Sambuco ridge, 25
Sanfatúcchio, 122–3
San Agostino, 215
San Angelo, 42
San Apollinare, 49, 82
San Benedetto, 216
San Bernadino, 203–4
San Carlo, 156
San Carlo Opera House, 79–80
San Casciano, 131
San Felice, 123
San Fortunato, 147
San Giacomo, 17, 19, 21, 28

San Leonardo, 49–51
San Leolino, 128
San Marco, 26
San Marino, 147–8
San Martino, 18, 46, 63
San Massimo, 34
San Nicolo, 210, 213
San Patrizio, 203
San Pietro, 42
San Rinaldo, 170
San Ruffillo, 163
San Salvo, 29–30, 39
San Stefano, 47
San Vito, 45, 49, 55
Sangro Line, 39–4
Sangro river, 30, 35, 39–40, 42–3, 45–6, 49, 55, 59
Sant'Agata, 61
Sant'Angelo, 87–9, 91–2, 105
Sant'Antima, 147
Sant'Aquilina, 147
Sant'Elia, 72
Santa Lucia, 163
Santa Maria, 44–5
Santa Nicola, 55
Santa Oliva, 82
Santa Tomassa, 55
San Savino, 146
Santerno river, 158, 164, 167, 189, 197, 200–1, 203, 207
Sapri, 9
Sardinia, 2–4
Sarteano, 126
Savignano, 154
Savio river, 156–7, 160
Scaldino, 163n
Scerni, 42
Scilla, 2
Schlemm, Gen, 131–2
Schwerin, Gen Graf von, 216–17
Scolo Cantenacci, 209
Scott, Brig Montagu-Douglas, 85
Scott, Brig Pat, 75, 97, 123, 209, 211, 221
Scott-Elliott, Lt Col, 18–19
Secco valley, 72
Segni, 214
Senger Line, see Hitler Line
Senger und Etterlin, Lt Gen Frido von, 82–3, 176
Senio river, 164, 170, 173–4, 182–4, 189, 198, 200–1

Serchio valley, 174
Serracapriola, 15–16, 18
Sfasciata ridge, 46, 48
Sherman, Gen William Tecumseh, 180
Shoosmith, Brig, 85
Sicily, 2–3, 8, 21, 221, 225, 228
Sieckenius, Maj Gen Rudolf, 7, 23
Sikorski, Gen, 62
Sillaro river, 206–7, 211
Simarca river, 19, 22, 28
Simonds, Gen Guy, 1, 24, 49n, 62
Sinalunga, 122
Singh, Naik Trilok, 155–6
Skellorn, John, 128, 187
Smith, Pte Ernest Alvia VC, 157
Smith, Lt Col H.B.L. MC, 23
Smith, Brig Ivan, 72
Smith-Dorrien, Brig Horace G. DSO, 146
Smyly, Lt Col Denis, 215
Snake's Head ridge, 99
Soara river, 130
Sogliano, 154
Sogliano al Rubicone, 155
Sora, 107–8
Sosnkowski, Gen, 133
Soviet Union, 62, 225
Spezzano, 8, 10
Spinete, 32–3
Spry, Lt Col D.C., 25–6, 50
St Patrick's Church, 233
Stalin, 62, 190, 221
'Stalingrad of the Abruzzi', 49
Stazione di Chiusi, 126n
Straorina, 1
Strawson, Gen John, 181, 229
Street, Lt, 161
Stroud, Maj M.A.G., 24
Sulik, Maj Gen, 80
Syria, 228

Taranto, 7–8, 10, 12, 226–7
Tavoleto, 141–2
Taylor, Lt Col J.M.C, 101
Tedder, Air Marshal, 4
Terelle, 72
Termoli, 15–18, 20–5, 28, 39, 55–6, 75
Terni, 15, 69, 107, 118
Terracina, 82
Tesoro river, 53
Tetley, Brig J.N., 80

Thapa, Rfn Sherbahadur VC, 149
Tiber river, 116–18, 127, 130, 134
Tippelskirch, Gen Kurt von, 163
Tito, Marshal, 158, 220–1
Tollo, 63
Torella, 31–3
Torrebruna, 30
Torre Mucchia, 53, 55
Traghetto, 213
Trasimene, Lake, 117–23, 126–7, 187, 194
Trident conference, 3
Trieste, 220–1, 225
Triflisco, 105
Trigh el Rahman, 105
Trigno river, 28–30
Triquet, Captain Paul VC, 51–2
Truscott, Lt Gen Lucian, 103, 108, 114, 134, 167, 184, 186, 228
Tufillo, 30–1
Tuker, Maj Gen 'Gertie', 68, 227
Tunisia, 2, 19, 47n, 72, 73, 225
Turkey, 2
'Twazabuga' bridge, 129
'Two Types', The, 181
Tyrrhenian coast, 10
Tyson, The Revd G., 204

ULTRA, 56
United States, 2, 6
Urbino, 141
Uso river, 154
Utili, Gen Umberto, 129

Vaiano, 122, 125
Vallemaio, 82
Vallerotonda, 72
Valetta canal, 195
Vallo, 10
Valmontone, 81–2, 108–9
Valvori, 72
Vandra river, 35
Vasto, 16, 30, 43, 55, 62, 69
Velletri, 82
Venafro, 28, 69
Venetian Line, 218–19
Venice, 136, 143, 189, 195, 220, 227
Verdun, 52
Verona, 136
Vesuvius, 79
Via Casilina, 66
Via Emilia, 154